THE
CAMBRIDGE EDITION OF
THE LETTERS AND WORKS OF
D. H. LAWRENCE

THE WORKS OF D. H. LAWRENCE

EDITORIAL BOARD

MR NOON

D. H. LAWRENCE

EDITED BY
LINDETH VASEY

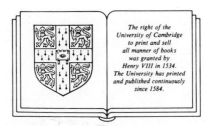

The right of the
University of Cambridge
to print and sell
all manner of books
was granted by
Henry VIII in 1534.
The University has printed
and published continuously
since 1584.

CAMBRIDGE UNIVERSITY PRESS

CAMBRIDGE
LONDON   NEW YORK   NEW ROCHELLE
MELBOURNE   SYDNEY

Published by the Press Syndicate of the University of Cambridge
The Pitt Building, Trumpington Street, Cambridge CB2 1RP
32 East 57th Street, New York, NY 10022, USA
296 Beaconsfield Parade, Middle Park, Melbourne 3206, Australia

This, the Cambridge Edition of the text of *Mr Noon* now correctly established from the original sources and first published in 1984, © the Estate of Frieda Lawrence Ravagli 1984. Introduction and notes © Cambridge University Press 1984. Permission to reproduce this text entire or in part, or to quote from it, can be granted only by the Literary Executor of the Estate, Laurence Pollinger Ltd, 18 Maddox Street, Mayfair, London W1R OEU. Permission to reproduce the introduction and notes entire or in part should be requested from Cambridge University Press. Acknowledgement is made to William Heinemann Ltd in the UK and the Viking Press in the USA, who hold the exclusive book publication rights for the work as published (copyright 1934) in their respective territories, for the authorisation granted to Cambridge University Press through the Frieda Lawrence Ravagli Estate for use of the work as published in preparing the new scholarly text.

Reprinted 1984

Printed in the United States of America

Library of Congress catalogue card number: 83–24082

British Library Cataloguing in publication data
Lawrence, D. H.
Mr Noon. – (The Cambridge edition of the the letters
and works of D. H. Lawrence)
I. Title   II. Vasey, Lindeth
823'.912[F]   PR6023.A93
ISBN 0 521 25251 2

CONTENTS

GENERAL EDITORS' PREFACE

D. H. Lawrence is one of the great writers of the twentieth century – yet the texts of his writings, whether published during his lifetime or since, are, for the most part, textually corrupt. The extent of the corruption is remarkable; it can derive from every stage of composition and publication. We know from study of his MSS that Lawrence was a careful writer, though not rigidly consistent in matters of minor convention. We know also that he revised at every possible stage. Yet he rarely if ever compared one stage with the previous one, and overlooked the errors of typists or copyists. He was forced to accept, as most authors are, the often stringent house-styling of his printers, which overrode his punctuation and even his sentence-structure and paragraphing. He sometimes overlooked plausible printing errors. More important, as a professional author living by his pen, he had to accept, with more or less good will, stringent editing by a publisher's reader in his early days, and at all times the results of his publishers' timidity. So the fear of Grundyish disapproval, or actual legal action, led to bowdlerisation or censorship from the very beginning of his career. Threats of libel suits produced other changes. Sometimes a publisher made more changes than he admitted to Lawrence. On a number of occasions in dealing with American and British publishers Lawrence produced texts for both which were not identical. Then there were extraordinary lapses like the occasion when a compositor turned over two pages of MS at once, and the result happened to make sense. This whole story can be reconstructed from the introductions to the volumes in this edition; cumulatively they will form a history of Lawrence's writing career.

The Cambridge edition aims to provide texts which are as close as can now be determined to those he would have wished to see printed. They have been established by a rigorous collation of extant manuscripts and typescripts, proofs and early printed versions; they restore the words, sentences, even whole pages omitted or falsified by editors or compositors; they are freed from printing-house conventions which were imposed on Lawrence's style; and interference on the part of frightened publishers has been eliminated. Far from doing violence to the texts Lawrence would have wished to see published, editorial intervention is essential to recover them. Though we have to accept that some cannot now be recovered in their entirety because early states have not survived, we must be glad that so much evidence remains. Paradoxical as it may seem, the outcome of this recension will be texts which differ, often radically and certainly frequently, from those seen by the author himself.

Editors have adopted the principle that the most authoritative form of the text is to be followed, even if this leads sometimes to a 'spoken' or a 'manuscript' rather than a 'printed' style. We have not wanted to strip off one house-styling in order to impose another. Editorial discretion has been allowed in order to regularise Lawrence's sometimes wayward spelling and punctuation in accordance with his most frequent practice in a particular text. A detailed record of these and other decisions on textual matters, together with the evidence on which they are based, will be found in the textual apparatus or an occasional explanatory note. These give significant deleted readings in manuscripts, typescripts and proofs; and printed variants in forms of the text published in Lawrence's lifetime. We do not record posthumous corruptions, except where first publication was posthumous.

In each volume, the editor's introduction relates the contents to Lawrence's life and to his other writings; it gives the history of composition of the text in some detail, for its intrinsic interest, and because this history is essential to the statement of editorial principles followed. It provides an account of publication and reception which will be found to contain a good deal of hitherto unknown information. Where appropriate, appendixes make available extended draft manuscript readings of significance, or important material, sometimes unpublished, associated with a particular work.

Though Lawrence is a twentieth-century writer and in many respects remains our contemporary, the idiom of his day is not invariably intelligible now, especially to the many readers who are not native speakers of British English. His use of dialect is another difficulty, and further barriers to full understanding are created by now obscure literary, historical, political or other references and allusions. On these occasions explanatory notes are supplied by the editor; it is assumed that the reader has access to a good general dictionary and that the editor need not gloss words or expressions that may be found in it. Where Lawrence's letters are quoted in editorial matter, the reader should assume that his manuscript is alone the source of eccentricities of phrase or spelling. An edition of the letters is still in course of publication: for this reason only the date and recipient of a letter will be given if it has not so far been printed in the Cambridge edition.

ACKNOWLEDGEMENTS

I would like to thank Dr Warren Roberts and the Humanities Research Center for giving me the opportunity to edit this volume. Special thanks must go to Mr Michael Black of Cambridge University Press for his encouragement and guidance, Professor James T. Boulton of the Editorial Board, Mrs Lois Garcia and Mr Carlton Lake of the Humanities Research Center, Professor William B. Todd, who supervised the original thesis at the University of Texas at Austin, and Dr John Worthen for his practical help and enthusiasm.

I am grateful to the following for access to manuscript materials: the manuscript, typescripts of Part I and typescript of Part II of *Mr Noon*, Humanities Research Center, University of Texas at Austin; and carbon copy typescripts of Part I, Bancroft Library, University of California at Berkeley and Viking Press. Grateful acknowledgement is made to the Martin Secker estate for permission to quote from unpublished letters and to the University of Illinois Library at Urbana-Champaign for access to them.

I am indebted to many individuals who have given freely of their time and knowledge: Dr Carl Baron, Dr Helen Baron, Dr Simonetta de Filippis, Ms Ellen Dunlap, Dr Paul Eggert, Dr David Farmer, Ms Nadine Lane Gallagher, Professor Henry Gifford, Mrs Enid Hilton, Miss Jane Hodgart, Mrs Margaret Huttleston, Mr Frederick Jeffrey, Dr Mara Kalnins, Ms Carolyn Law, Mr Richard Law, Mr George Lazarus, Miss Maureen Leach, Ms Gay Marie Logsdon, Mrs Ann Mason, Dr Dieter Mehl, Dr Gareth Morgan, Mr D. B. Nash, Mrs Iona Opie, Miss Ann Parr, Ms Melissa Partridge, Dr Jim Peterson, Ms Conni Rumpf, Mr Roy Spencer, Dr Bruce Steele, Mr Erik Stocker, Mr John Titford, Mrs Vicki Tullius, Mrs Heidi Überla and Mr Iain White; also Dr Warner Barnes, Dr Brian Levack and Dr Walter Reed. I also wish to thank all the staff of the Humanities Research Center and Cambridge University Press for their patience and assistance. My very special thanks must go to Ronald Vasey for his generous, long-standing encouragement and his assistance – and persistence – in field research and proof reading.

May 1984   L.V.

CHRONOLOGY

11 September 1885	Born in Eastwood, Nottinghamshire
September 1898–July 1901	Pupil at Nottingham High School
1902–1908	Pupil teacher; student at University College, Nottingham
7 December 1907	First publication: 'A Prelude', in *Nottinghamshire Guardian*
October 1908	Appointed as teacher at Davidson Road School, Croydon
November 1909	Publishes five poems in *English Review*
3 December 1910	Engagement to Louie Burrows; broken off on 4 February 1912
9 December 1910	Death of his mother, Lydia Lawrence
19 January 1911	*The White Peacock* published in New York (20 January in London)
19 November 1911	Ill with pneumonia; resigns his teaching post on 28 February 1912
17? March 1912	Meets Frieda Weekley
3 May 1912	Leaves England with Frieda
4 May 1912	In Metz
6 May 1912	Baron von Richthofen's celebration day. To May fair and walks to Scy-Chazelles (or on 5th)
7 May 1912	Letter to Weekley; 'spy' incident
8 May 1912	To Trier (Wednesday)
9 May 1912	Writes 'German Impressions: I. French Sons of Germany'
11 May 1912	Frieda to Trier (or on 10 May); cables Weekley; returns to Metz. To Waldbröl by train, more than nine hours (Saturday)
12 May 1912	To Kermasse with Krenkows
15 May 1912	To Nümbrecht with Hannah Krenkow; writes 'German Impressions: II. Hail in the Rhineland'
c. 18 May 1912	Frieda to Munich
19 May 1912	To Bonn and Drachenfels with Krenkows (Sunday)
23 May 1912	*The Trespasser*

24 May 1912	To Munich to meet Frieda
25 May 1912	To Beuerberg with Frieda (Whitsunday weekend)
between 26–31 May 1912	To Kochelsee
1 June 1912	To Icking
6 June 1912	To Wolfratshausen; see Corpus Christi procession
8 June 1912	To Munich to shop
15–17 June 1912	DHL in Munich; stays in Jaffe's flat
3 July 1912	Frieda in Wolfratshausen with Else Jaffe's children for four nights
4 July 1912	DHL to Wolfratshausen
18 July 1912	Writing *The Fight for Barbara*
c. 23 July 1912	Starts fourth revision of 'Paul Morel' (*Sons and Lovers*)
24 July 1912	David Garnett to Icking; probably also on 28 July and 1 August
2 August 1912	'Schimpfed' by Baroness von Richthofen
4 August 1912	Has 'thought of a new novel' (possibly 'Scargill Street')
5 August 1912	Leave Icking for Tyrol and Italy; stay at Bad Tölz
6 August 1912	Crossing pass; see Röhrlmoos chapel and spend night in hay hut
7 August 1912	To Glashütte; spend night at Achensee
8 August 1912	To Kufstein; begins 'A Chapel Among the Mountains' and soon after 'A Hay-Hut Among the Mountains'
9 August 1912	To Mayrhofen
18 August 1912	David Garnett arrives; Harold Hobson joins them after 22nd
27 August 1912	The four start to cross Alps; spend night in hay hut
28 August 1912	Spend night at Dominicus Hütte
29 August 1912	Cross Pfitscher Joch; spend night in inn and Garnett and Hobson leave to catch train from Sterzing
30 August 1912	To Sterzing
1 September 1912	Start to Meran; spend night in resthouse on Jaufenpass
2 September 1912	Circle back to Sterzing; to Bozen
3 September 1912	To Trento
4–17 September 1912	Riva; writes 'Christs in the Tirol' ('The Crucifix Across the Mountains')
18 September 1912–30 March 1913	At Gargnano, Lago di Garda, Italy

by 21 January 1921	Begins *Sea and Sardinia*
before 25 January 1921	Decides to divide *Mr Noon* into parts so Part I can be published separately; sends MS to Ruth Wheelock to type Part I
5 February 1921	May be working on *Mr Noon* Part II
22 February 1921	Finishes revising *Mr Noon* Part I typescripts; sends carbon copy (TCCI) to Robert Mountsier; completes *Sea and Sardinia*
1 March 1921	Thomas Seltzer agrees to publish *Mr Noon* Part I
11–14 March 1921	To Palermo to see Frieda off for Baden-Baden
22 March 1921	Hears TCCI has arrived; sends ribbon copy (TSI) to Barbara Low
4 April 1921	Asks Curtis Brown to be his agent in England; Curtis Brown to get TSI and serialise
9–25 April 1921	To Capri, Rome and Florence
25 April–10 July 1921	Baden-Baden
29 April 1921	Martin Secker agrees to publish *Mr Noon* Part I
2 May 1921	Working on *Aaron's Rod*
10 May 1921	*Psychoanalysis and the Unconscious* (New York)
31 May 1921	Completes *Aaron's Rod*
1 June 1921	Secker to publish *Aaron's Rod* instead of *Mr Noon* Part I
5 July–16 August 1921	Mountsier with the Lawrences
11 July–25 August 1921	Zell-am-See
16 July 1921	Seltzer decides to publish *Aaron's Rod* instead of *Mr Noon* Part I
14 August 1921	Receives TSI back from Curtis Brown
26 August–21 September 1921	Capri
28 September 1921	Taormina
c. 5 November 1921	Asks Ruth Wheelock to type *Mr Noon* Part II; subsequently manuscript (MS) and typescript sent to Seltzer
12 December 1921	*Sea and Sardinia* (New York)
20–26 February 1922	Sail for Ceylon via Palermo and Naples
March–August 1922	In Ceylon and Australia
14 April 1922	*Aaron's Rod* (New York)
9 June 1922	Asks Seltzer to give *Mr Noon* materials to Mountsier
September 1922–March 1923	In New Mexico

CUE-TITLES

(The place of publication is London unless otherwise stated.)

Frieda Lawrence   Frieda Lawrence. "*Not I, But the Wind ...*". Santa Fe: Rydal Press, 1934.

Letters, i.   James T. Boulton, ed. *The Letters of D. H. Lawrence*. Volume I. Cambridge: Cambridge University Press, 1979.

Letters, ii.   George J. Zytaruk and James T. Boulton, eds. *The Letters of D. H. Lawrence*. Volume II. Cambridge: Cambridge University Press, 1982.

Letters, iii.   James T. Boulton and Andrew Robertson, eds. *The Letters of D. H. Lawrence*. Volume III. Cambridge: Cambridge University Press, 1984.

OED   Sir James A. H. Murray and others, eds. *A New English Dictionary on Historical Principles*. 10 volumes. Oxford: Oxford University Press, 1884–1928.

Phoenix   Edward D. McDonald, ed. *Phoenix: The Posthumous Papers of D. H. Lawrence*. Heinemann, 1936.

Phoenix II   Warren Roberts and Harry T. Moore, eds. *Phoenix II: Uncollected, Unpublished and Other Prose Works by D. H. Lawrence*. Heinemann, 1968.

Tedlock   E. W. Tedlock, ed. *Frieda Lawrence: The Memoirs and Correspondence*. Heinemann, 1961.

INTRODUCTION

INTRODUCTION

This volume of the Cambridge edition of D. H. Lawrence is of unique
interest; it presents for the first time a substantially new, largely unpublished
text. Part I of *Mr Noon* will be familiar to readers who have consulted the
volume *A Modern Lover*, published in 1934, and to those who have read it as
collected in *Phoenix II*, published in 1968; but, Part II, which is more than two
times as long, has never before been published. The Gilbert Noon of Part I,
based as he is on George Henry Neville,[1] is reminiscent of other heroes and
stories from Lawrence's youth and early manhood in the Midlands. In him
Lawrence mockingly celebrates the adolescent rite of 'spooning', the Sunday
evening walk after church in which passionate young men go as far as
cautious girls will let them (in Gilbert and Emmie's case, too far) but as part
of a socially regulated process, usually leading to marriage. He also satirises
the moral and social pressures applied by authorities: school managers on
their employees and families on their adult children. In Part II Gilbert
suddenly becomes another person in another place, in fact, Lawrence in
Germany in 1912, and the reader finds he is reading a kind of sequel to *Sons
and Lovers*, in which the Lawrence-figure has finally left his youth behind him
and has found compelling and fulfilling love, as Lawrence had with Frieda
Weekley.[2] Many of the events are familiar from Lawrence's own contemporary writings – the letters; 'The Crucifix Across the Mountains' in *Twilight in
Italy*; the travel sketches of 1912, the two 'German Impressions', 'A Chapel
Among the Mountains' and 'A Hay-Hut Among the Mountains', collected in
Phoenix and *Phoenix II*; poems in *Look! We Have Come Through!*; the play *The
Fight For Barbara* – and from biographies of Lawrence. But in this novel these
events have the special interest of being told sequentially in thinly fictionalised form, and of being told with an apparently exact recall of great
immediacy and vividness (despite being written eight years after the events
and without the earlier writings to hand). Though the manner appears light
the author penetrates deeply into certain crucial experiences of conflict with
the loved woman.

The story is unfinished. Lawrence put it aside in 1921, just as he had for a

---

[1] See explanatory note on 7:18.   [2] See explanatory note on 119:1.

time laid down *Aaron's Rod*; but whereas he worked intermittently for three and a half years (1917–21) on the latter, he never returned to *Mr Noon*. It was not unusual at this period for Lawrence to be anxious about experiencing difficulty in completing his novels: it occurred in the case of *The Lost Girl* in 1920 and *Kangaroo* in 1922. (It might be observed here that the long autobiographical chapter 'The Nightmare' in *Kangaroo* may have been originally intended for the third part of *Mr Noon*.) How to end the story of a life which was still in process, and a relationship which was continuing to evolve, was obviously one problem. Another was that living relatives – particularly Frieda's – would have objected to their portrayal in *Mr Noon*; by 1921 Lawrence had more than enough experience of such objections.

For whatever reason, he abandoned the novel, and it dropped completely out of sight. The five notebooks which contain all of Parts I and II in Lawrence's own hand, and one copy of the typescripts of both parts which had been made from four of these notebooks, were left for safekeeping in the possession of his American publisher Thomas Seltzer, and were never returned; they effectively disappeared for fifty years. (The carbon copy of the typescript of Part I was eventually returned to Lawrence's English agent Curtis Brown and was the source for the 1934 posthumous publication.) The manuscript and typescripts were offered for sale by auction in 1972 by Sotheby Parke Bernet, and were bought subsequently by the Humanities Research Center of the University of Texas at Austin to add to their already rich Lawrence collections; the Center has generously made these materials available for this edition. This Introduction recounts the history of the composition of *Mr Noon*, and the early unsuccessful attempts to publish Part I.

The composition of *Mr Noon*

May 1920–February 1921: 'Began Mr Noon'

Lawrence wrote in his diary for 7 May 1920: 'Began Mr Noon'.[3] How much, if anything, he wrote at this time is not known; no manuscript of this stage survives, and the references in his correspondence are ambiguous. He had finished *The Lost Girl* two days earlier, and on 6 May he wrote to Francis Brett Young, a fellow writer whom the Lawrences had met on Capri not long before: 'I don't know what I shall do, my novel finished, myself out of work.

---

3 *The Frieda Lawrence Collection of D. H. Lawrence Manuscripts: A Descriptive Bibliography*, ed. E. W. Tedlock (Albuquerque, 1948), p. 90.

Suppose I shall run hopelessly to seed one way or another.'[4] On the 7th he wrote to Rosalind Baynes: 'I'm a free man, from work', and on the 10th to Compton Mackenzie: 'But after my novel I am holidaying for one month. Then I should like to start again, with another I have in mind.'[5]

But it is significant that the date of the diary entry (7 May) suggests that the idea for the new book might have grown out of the just completed novel: most of *The Lost Girl* is set in a fictional Eastwood, where Lawrence was born and grew up. So is the first part of *Mr Noon*; Lawrence uses in both the same fictional name 'Woodhouse'. It is possible that some incident or character not used in *The Lost Girl*, either left over from the 1913 manuscript from which Lawrence rewrote it in 1920[6] or called to mind by thinking about Eastwood, led him to plan for another novel set in Eastwood around 1912. Indeed, Alvina Houghton, the title character in *The Lost Girl* makes a brief appearance.[7] When Lawrence resumed work on *Mr Noon* in November 1920, *Lost Girl* was once again on his mind: in late October he had had to alter a page in proof for his English publisher Martin Secker, and he wrote about this to Seltzer in early November; publication in England was, too, scheduled for late November.[8]

But in May Lawrence was soon distracted from any new work. He and Frieda left Fontana Vecchia, Taormina on 17 May with Mary Cannan for a trip to Malta which was meant only to last two days, but they were stranded there for ten days by a steamer strike. Then from early June to the 24th Lawrence revised *Studies in Classic American Literature* and the typescript of *The Lost Girl*, and reworked his essays on 'Education of the People'.[9] By the 28th he had heard that Mackenzie had bought a ketch in which Lawrence hoped they might both sail to the South Seas, and he read some books sent by Robert Mountsier, his American agent, about their possible destination.[10] This plan soon dissolved, and in mid-July Lawrence was considering various plans to go north to escape the Taormina heat; he left in early August partly

4 *Letters*, iii. 515.

5 *Letters*, iii. 520, 522. On 31 May DHL told Secker he had 'begun another novel': this was probably intended as a pacifier rather than as a statement of work in progress (ibid. 537).

6 The first version of *The Lost Girl* was begun in late 1912, and a second draft ('The Insurrection of Miss Houghton') was written January–March 1913; the novel was completely re-written from that manuscript early March–5 May 1920; see 'Introduction', *The Lost Girl*, ed. John Worthen (Cambridge, 1981), pp. xix–xxxii.

7 See explanatory note on 45:2.   8 *Letters*, iii. 619, 628.

9 *Letters*, iii. 556; ibid. 549 and entry for 23 June 1920, *Lawrence MSS*, ed. Tedlock, p. 91; and entry for 15 June 1920, *Lawrence MSS*, ed. Tedlock, p. 90 and *Letters*, iii. 554. *Studies in Classic American Literature* was first written in 1917, and 'Education of the People' in 1918 (published in *Phoenix* 587–665).

10 *Letters*, iii. 560, 563, 566. Robert Mountsier (1888–1972) was a journalist; see also footnote 66.

to travel and partly to stay with various friends, while Frieda went to Germany to see her family.

On 10 July Lawrence told Seltzer, who would have been interested in hearing about a new Lawrence work, especially a novel, that he had 'begun another novel', but this reference is definitely to *Aaron's Rod*.[11] He did not write much more of it, for on 13 July he wrote to Brett Young's wife Jessica: 'I'm working with ever-diminishing spasms of fitfulness at a novel which I know won't go forward many more steps', and five days later he reported to Secker that 'it stands still just now, awaiting events'.[12] Although Lawrence said that he had 'begun' *Aaron's Rod*, he had actually started it in November 1917; he now began to alternate working on it and *Mr Noon*.

While the Lawrences were travelling from mid-July (Frieda rejoined him in early October) and even for a month after their return to Taormina on 18 October, Lawrence was unsettled in his work. He corrected proofs of *Women in Love* for Secker and Seltzer and *The Lost Girl* for Seltzer; corrected proofs and wrote another chapter of his history textbook *Movements in European History* for Oxford University Press; wrote some poems; and worked fitfully on *Aaron's Rod*.[13] So he was unable to start a major new work; on 10 November he wrote to Secker: 'Am not working – too unsettled yet: and this autumn-winter is my uneasy time. Let the year turn', and on the 22nd to Mary Cannan: 'Am doing no serious work, but painting a picture.'[14]

But between 22 and 29 November Lawrence started to write *Mr Noon*; he told Brett Young in a letter conjecturally dated 29 November: 'I did more than half of *Aaron's Rod*, but can't end it . . . so I began a comedy, which I hope will end. Who knows.'[15] Since Lawrence had not worked on *Mr Noon* for almost six months, most likely he made a new beginning; his references to the novel do not sound as if he were returning to a work already seriously started. If he had something in manuscript from May, he probably discarded it. Although there were last-minute changes required by Secker to the *Women in Love* proofs and a flurry of cables and letters over copies of the English edition of *The Lost Girl* that Secker sent to America,[16] Lawrence continued writing *Mr Noon* until it came to a 'stop' about 9 December. As he informed Mountsier: 'I began *Mr. Noon* – ⅓ done – sudden stop – may go on soon.'[17]

And indeed he resumed writing: in his letter of 12 December to Secker he

---

[11] *Letters*, iii. 565; ibid. 572. (*Aaron's Rod* was published in April 1922 by Seltzer.)

[12] *Letters*, iii. 567, 572. DHL's comment in his 23 July letter to Mountsier ('I am doing another novel') again was probably intended as a pacifier (ibid. 576).

[13] *Letters*, iii. 586, 613 and 590; ibid. 622; entry for 4 November 1920, *Lawrence MSS*, ed. Tedlock, p. 91; and *Letters*, iii. 594, 602, 613.

[14] *Letters*, iii. 622, 624.   [15] *Letters*, iii. 626; cf. p. 629.

[16] *Letters*, iii. 628, 627, 633.   [17] *Letters*, iii. 634.

mentions having seen several reviews of *The Lost Girl*, and these reviews are commented on by name at the start of chapter xiv of *Mr Noon*, so work on the novel probably recommenced by about the 12th.[18] Lawrence also added – he knew his publisher would be glad to plan for a new novel – that Secker could count on the publication of *Aaron's Rod* ('which I have left again') or *Mr Noon* ('which I am doing'), both 'incensorable', after *Women in Love*. Lawrence wrote with some enthusiasm to a Taormina friend Marie Hubrecht on 16 December: 'I am writing a sort of comic novel – rather amusing, but rather scandalous.'[19] And on 31 December 1920 Lawrence confidently reported to Mountsier that '[I] now have done ⅔ of "Lucky Noon".[20] I hope to finish it in January: see no reason why I shouldn't. Probably you'll dislike it: it is peppery. I like it myself better than *Lost Girl* – much', and he recorded in his diary that he had completed up to p. 374 (the beginning of chapter xx) on 1 January 1921.[21] The next day he also wrote to Seltzer: 'I left off *Aaron's Rod* and began "Lucky Noon". Have done two-thirds, and if the infernal gods don't prevent, I shall finish it this month. I get much wicked joy out of it. Probably you and the world will detest it. But it is unique. Which, from a publisher's point of view, is I know a misfortune.'[22] Lawrence's view of how his publishers and agent would react to *Mr Noon* had changed in three weeks: what would become Part I was 'incensorable', but Part II was 'peppery' and 'unique'.

When Lawrence began *Mr Noon* cannot be precisely determined: the only specific reference prior to 29 November is the May diary entry. Since the question of his rate of writing has relevance at several points in the history of the composition of the manuscript, this should be examined in some detail. The five manuscript notebooks are a continuous narrative of 447 pages – numbered [1]–450 with a few errors – which ends in mid-sentence. The chapters are numbered in a single sequence (the manuscript is not divided into parts). Although the notebooks are almost the same size, 1 and 2 (pp. [1]–48, 49–161) have an average of just over 200 words per page, and 3–5 (pp. 162–275, 276–388, 389–450) of about 330 words.[23] Lawrence had

---

[18] *Letters*, iii. 638, and see also explanatory notes on 118:13 and 118:31.

[19] *Letters*, iii. 639.

[20] On the title 'Lucky Noon', see 'June 1921–October 1922: "finishing *Mr Noon* II"' below.

[21] *Letters*, iii. 645; *Lawrence MSS*, ed. Tedlock, p. 91. When DHL revised the typescripts of Part I (see below), he added three new chapter divisions, so that starting with chap. viii (p. 61; see also explanatory note) the numbering of the chapters in the manuscript is inaccurate. In addition DHL numbered two chapters in the manuscript 'xiv' (see textual apparatus for 206:1 and 238:1). In this Introduction and all editorial material, the chapter numbers have been corrected.

[22] *Letters*, iii. 646.

[23] The pages of notebook 1 (shiny dark-blue and black marbled soft cover with green tape spine) measure 8¼ × 5⅞ inches; notebooks 2–5 (dull olive grey-green soft covers with different

probably written most of what became Part I (pp. [1]–172) by 9 December 1920 when he mentioned his 'sudden stop'. While it is not possible to determine definitely where this occurred, there is a break in the writing in the manuscript at 92:16, 'Emmie now gave way . . .', after which Lawrence as narrator sounds impatient with the scene and abruptly brings it to an end. This shift is emphasised in the next chapter when the narrator tells the reader directly that he will not hear another word about Emmie (97:22–98:16), that he had better be prepared for a change, *and* re-introduces Gilbert Noon. Again, if Lawrence thought that the 373 pages which he had written by 1 January represented two-thirds of the novel as he envisaged it, then the end of Part I (p. 172) would be approximately the one-third he said he had written before the 'stop'. Lawrence had written *The Lost Girl* in just over eight weeks, with an average of about 3260 words per day for the whole: if he had worked at the same pace for *Mr Noon* he could have begun on 28 November or slightly earlier.[24] Between (at the latest) 12 December and the 31st Lawrence wrote 200 pages: he had started again on p. 171 and completed p. 373, and this would mean a rate of about 3300 words per day.[25] Lawrence was a rapid writer: he wrote 373 pages in just over five weeks: in less than a fortnight (c. 28 November–9 December) he wrote 170 pages of this total, and in just over three weeks (11 December–1 January) the other 200 pages. What survives in

borders; notebook 2 is more orangish red and 3–5 purplish red) measure 7¹⁵⁄₁₆ × 6 inches. All have lined exercise-type paper, but notebooks 1 and 2 have evenly spaced lines which DHL used in his writing (23 lines of writing per page) while notebooks 3–5 have unevenly spaced lines which he did not follow – he squeezed extra lines on pages, often filling them from top to bottom (33–40 lines per page, with an average of 35–6). The two groups of notebooks average nine and ten words per line respectively. (There is no significant break in the writing in the first notebook, and thus no indication that this notebook, despite its difference in physical appearance from the others, contains any of the May 1920 writing.)

On the lower cover of the third notebook DHL sketched a man experiencing moral 'uplift': he is floating above houses and a tiny figure with a cart and an animal drawing it; see 156:39ff. The notebooks are located at the University of Texas at Austin (hereafter UT).

24 See 'Introduction', *The Lost Girl*, ed. Worthen, pp. xxvii–xxviii. If DHL had started on the earliest possible date, 22 November, he would have had to write only 9 pages per day to complete the 171 pages, and if he began on the latest, the 29th, 16 pages per day (3200 words).

The next most likely place for the 'stop' is the end of chap. xiii (p. 203) just before DHL refers to the reviews of *Lost Girl*. This would mean an average of 11–18 pages per day with the last 40 pages being the more densely written sheets. If DHL started on 29 November, this would have meant writing 4000 words per day; if he had started on the 22nd, 2445 words. Thus he probably began writing closer to the earlier date; see next note.

25 This would mean an average of 10 of the more densely written pages per day; but if he began on the 11th and if p. 373 was completed on 1 January 1921 as seems possible from the diary entry for that day, this would give a rate of 3000 words (9 pages per day).

If DHL had stopped with p. 203 (see note above), then he would have written an additional 170 pages by 31 December: 8 pages per day (2640 words).

the five notebooks is a quickly written first draft, of which only the first part was subsequently revised: this accounts for the freshness of the writing in Part II.

An interruption followed in January 1921 in the form of a trip to Sardinia. The Lawrences toured Sardinia from 5–13 January to see if they would want to live there, and the day after their return Lawrence told Secker that he planned to write 'a sketch book' about Sardinia in the summer.[26] But a week later Lawrence had started his 'Diary' of the trip, later published as *Sea and Sardinia*, because he could not work on his novel: '*Mr Noon* holds me', and 'Novel having a little rest, it being a bit of a strain' he told Mountsier and Secker.[27] But Lawrence believed this constraint was only temporary: 'I think I may finish "Lucky Noon" – the new novel – next month. But you'll simply hate it', and '*Mr Noon* will be, I think, *most* dangerous: but humorously so. It will take me about a month still to finish – this month was lost moving about.'[28]

In early February Lawrence was restless and started making plans to move to a dilapidated farm in Connecticut which he could lease cheaply,[29] and he continued to work on the Sardinia diary. It is possible that he wrote some more of Part II of *Mr Noon* at this time: although he had told Secker on 4 February that the novel was 'having a little rest', in a postcard probably written the next day Lawrence said to Seltzer 'Am busy with *Mr Noon*.'[30] We know Lawrence was working energetically on *Sea and Sardinia* on 5 February and had 'nearly finished' it by the 12th;[31] thus it seems unlikely that he would have set it aside for *Mr Noon*. However on 7 February he wrote to Mackenzie: 'I am fighting my way through various pieces of work: and through life. It works out to a long fight, in which one doesn't emerge as much of a winner so far' – all of which *may* indicate that he was working on more than one book.[32]

The manuscript itself helps to settle the question of when Lawrence stopped writing *Mr Noon*. At first the most reasonable supposition seems to be that he put the novel aside for the trip to Sardinia and never returned to it, but the length of the manuscript requires a further explanation. The decision to go to Sardinia had not been made on 1 January 1921; so Lawrence and Frieda must have spent some time on the 2nd and 3rd making preparations,

[26] *Letters*, iii. 648. [27] *Letters*, iii. 650; ibid. 653, 660.
[28] *Letters*, iii. 648, 653; see also p. 651. [29] See *Letters*, iii. 659–78.
[30] *Letters*, iii. 662. It is dated in DHL's hand '5 Jan. 1921', but postmarked '8 FEB 1921'. It seems most likely that DHL's date is wrong; see *Letters*, iii. 622 n. 1.
[31] *Letters*, iii. 662; ibid. 664–5. [32] *Letters*, iii. 663.

e.g. booking a passage by ship, arranging to stay with Ruth Wheelock[33] overnight in Palermo, shopping and packing; and they left Taormina early on the 4th.[34] It is unlikely that Lawrence took the manuscript of *Mr Noon* with him to Sardinia since he would expect to do a great deal of walking and would not have time to write or want the extra bulk in his pack. We know that Lawrence had completed up to p. 374 by 1 January, and the manuscript ends on p. 450; this leaves 75 pages to be accounted for. It is possible that Lawrence – if he wrote at the pace which he seems to have set in December of 9–10 pages a day[35] – completed chapter xx (pp. 374–97), 25 pages, before he left for Palermo, but highly unlikely that he would be able to write 75 pages in two or three days (1/2–3 January). Thus the last fifty or more pages must have been written after the trip. This may have been in February 1921; perhaps when Lawrence wrote that he was doing 'various pieces of work', or later in the month when he had completed *Sea and Sardinia* and finished correcting the typescripts of *Mr Noon* Part I (see below).[36]

January–July 1921: Part I 'a little book all to itself'

Lawrence's intention to continue *Mr Noon* may have been deflected by a plan to publish the first part separately. Robert Mountsier occasionally sent questionnaires to Lawrence to enquire about details of past publications and with proposals for future works, and it must have been in reply to one of these that he conceived the idea of dividing *Mr Noon* into parts and publishing the first part on its own.[37] In the letter of 25 January in which he had predicted to Mountsier that he would finish the novel in 'about a month' he continued: 'I think the first 200 pages of *Mr Noon* might make a rather funny serial. It is an episode all by itself: a little book all to itself. And the girl in the American consulate who is typing it says: *so* like an American small town.'[38] Whether

---

33 Ruth Wheelock (1891–1958), an American; she worked in the American consulate in Palermo, 1919–22 and in Cologne before 1930; she married John Holbrook Chapman, who had been a consul in Cologne, in 1931. DHL must have heard of – or met – her in late October 1920 because he sent her the manuscript of *Birds, Beasts and Flowers* to be typed in early November (*Lawrence MSS*, ed. Tedlock, p. 91); she also typed *Mr Noon* Parts I and II and *Sea and Sardinia*.

34 See DHL's diary entries for 1 and 3 January: 'meditate trip to Sardinia' and 'Going to Palermo [to catch the boat] for Sardinia . . . in the morning' (*Lawrence MSS*, ed. Tedlock, pp. 91–2).

35 See footnote 25.

36 It is possible, but less likely, that DHL wrote some of the last fifty pages in November–December 1921; see p. xxxii below.

37 One questionnaire survives: see *Letters*, iii. 673–4.

38 *Letters*, iii. 653. This and the comment on finishing *Mr Noon* within a month are separate numbered points in the letter.

Mountsier had asked if Lawrence had any works suitable for magazines or specifically enquired about *Mr Noon* for this purpose is unknown. Lawrence was not doing any major writing from which he could expect to make much money: the prospect of a serialisation, of a kind he had wanted for *The Lost Girl*, would have been attractive.[39]

Lawrence had sent the manuscript for Part I[40] to Ruth Wheelock, 'the girl in the American consulate' in Palermo, to type before he wrote the letter of 25 January to Mountsier; he finished revising the typescripts on 22 February.[41] He worked on the ribbon copy first and then the carbon, making different alterations in each, and he added three paragraphs at the end of the typescripts which served to make Part I complete in itself and also to indicate that it was only the first volume of a longer work.[42] When the carbon copy was sent to Mountsier on 22 February (he received word of its arrival a month later) Lawrence commented: 'This first vol. is very small. You do as you like with it. I think it should serialise. For a serial, cut it and arrange it as you like. But keep an *intact* MS. for printing the *book* from, finally.'[43]

Most of the rest of this letter to Mountsier is concerned with arrangements about the Connecticut farm for which Lawrence showed a continuing enthusiasm; he wrote to Mary Cannan about his disenchantment with the cold Taormina winter.[44] On 25 February Lawrence wrote to Beatrice Bland, an artist he had met in Taormina: 'I've finished two bits of work and I am having a bit of a holiday.'[45] This might mean that he had corrected the *Mr Noon* typescripts and completed the *Sea and Sardinia* manuscript which he had sent to Ruth Wheelock to type. Lawrence offered to send the typescript of *Mr Noon* Part I to J. C. Squire, editor of the *London Mercury*, but Squire apparently did not express interest; eventually the ribbon copy typescript was posted to a friend in England, Barbara Low, who Lawrence hoped might act as his agent.[46]

But on 3 March Frieda received a telegram that her mother was very ill, and she quickly made preparations to leave for Baden-Baden to see her;[47] this scotched the plan for the Connecticut farm.[48] Lawrence corrected the typescript of *Sea and Sardinia*, sat for a portrait, and on 22 March announced

[39] See 'Introduction', *The Lost Girl*, ed. Worthen, pp. xxxi–xxxv. DHL also hoped to serialise *Sea and Sardinia*; see *Letters*, iii. 681, 700.

[40] Part I (pp. [1]–172) was contained in notebooks 1–3.   [41] *Letters*, iii. 667.

[42] See 'Selection of base-texts' below. The typescripts are at UT.

[43] *Letters*, iii. 689; 667; see also p. 678.   [44] *Letters*, iii. 670; see also p. 671.

[45] *Letters*, iii. 671 and entry for 22 February 1921, *Lawrence MSS*, ed. Tedlock. p. 92.

[46] *Letters*, iii. 681, 688.

[47] *Letters*, iii. 678 and entry for 3 March 1921, *Lawrence MSS*, ed. Tedlock, p. 92.

[48] *Letters*, iii. 684.

his new writing plans: 'I intend to try to finish *Aaron's Rod*. But am not in a good work-mood.'[49] He was restless: he considered going to Florence to be measured for a coat; or taking a walking tour of Sardinia with Jan Juta, a South African painter, who could draw illustrations for the Sardinia book; or meeting Frieda in Germany; or buying a boat with Mountsier.[50]

By 4 April Lawrence had decided that Curtis Brown, managing director of the literary agency, should act as his agent in England and told him to retrieve the typescript of *Mr Noon* Part I from Barbara Low; he asked Curtis Brown to try to get it serialised and repeated that it might be cut for this purpose.[51] Lawrence also wrote to Secker about the '*tiny* first vol.', hoping Secker would agree to consider it one of the five novels to be written by Lawrence to which Secker had a contractual right.[52] Lawrence left Taormina on 9 April, visited friends in Capri and Rome, and went on to Baden-Baden where he and Frieda planned to stay all summer. Curtis Brown 'seemed quite pleased with *Mr Noon*', and so did Secker: 'If Secker wishes to publish the first part of *Mr Noon* as a separate little book, let him: because the second part may be a bit startling.'[53] Secker decided to publish *Mr Noon* Part I on its own as he wrote to Curtis Brown on 29 April: 'It is certainly excellent, and I fully share your enthusiasm for it. It is quite clear from the last page that it is complete as it stands, and that the author intends it to be published in a book by itself, with one sequel, possibly more, to follow later', but he also commented that its brevity 'presents certain difficulties'.[54]

Lawrence had started working on *Aaron's Rod* again in early May and finished it on the 31st, and both he and Secker came to the conclusion that it would be better to publish this 'normal-length' novel and 'any decision regarding the little *Mr Noon* can be postponed'.[55] Lawrence's change of mind was partly the result of Secker's wanting 'to count this little *Mr Noon* novel as not a novel, but a bit thrown in with his legal five'.[56] As Secker wrote to Lawrence: 'I am very glad to hear that "Aaron's Rod" is practically finished ... I now think, in the circumstances that far the best plan to adopt with regard to "Mr. Noon" ... would be to make it an immediate successor to "Aaron's Rod", if you feel like turning to and writing the second half before you do anything else.'[57] Lawrence responded with his outline for the complete book (see below).

49 *Letters*, iii. 685–7; ibid. 688.   50 *Letters*, iii. 692. (Juta made the trip alone later.)
51 *Letters*, iii. 700.   52 *Letters*, iii. 700–2.   53 *Letters*, iii. 710, 717.
54 *Letters*, iii. 717n. DHL was very insistent about receiving proofs (ibid. 717, 722).
55 *Letters*, iii. 711, 729–30.   56 *Letters*, iii. 731.
57 Letter from Secker to DHL, 8 June 1921, University of Illinois at Urbana-Champaign. Secker had written to Curtis Brown on 1 June 1921: 'My feeling now about "Mr. Noon" is that it would be better for Lawrence to write the remaining half next and let it succeed

Seltzer had signed an agreement on 1 March 1921 for autumn publication of *Mr Noon* without having seen it.[58] On 17 June when he had read it but had not seen *Aaron's Rod*, he had another proposal for Mountsier: he hoped *Aaron's Rod* had the 'possibility of a popular success ... and if it is really unobjectionable, then AARON'S ROD ought to be the next novel for us', while *Mr Noon* 'may arouse a storm of protest which we could stand very well after a second success like THE LOST GIRL but not so well before'.[59] Like Secker Seltzer was thinking of the effect of the furore over *Women in Love* and what it had done for Lawrence's reputation. Although Secker still had not read *Aaron's Rod* a month later, he decided to publish it and postpone *Mr Noon* Part I: 'I prefer to bring out MR. NOON in one volume.'[60]

Lawrence's (and Mountsier's) plan to serialise *Mr Noon* or publish it separately had failed. Both his English and American publishers preferred to print the newly completed, full-length novel and postpone 'the little *Mr Noon*' until it was finished. In addition Seltzer had expressed reservations about the subject matter which Mountsier doubtless passed on to the author.

June 1921–October 1922: 'finishing Mr Noon II'

As early as 4 April 1921 Lawrence had attempted to reassure Secker that he would finish *Mr Noon*, but *after Aaron's Rod*: 'I shall try and finish *Aarons Rod* this summer, before finishing *Mr Noon II* – which is funny, but a hair-raiser. First part innocent'.[61] But on 6 May he had conceded to Mountsier that he would leave work on *Mr Noon* Part II for the winter; he confirmed this to Curtis Brown from Baden-Baden a week later: 'I have only half done it [the second part] – and I shan't be able to finish it till I go back to Taormina. Cant write it here.'[62] When Lawrence wrote to Secker a few days later about the delay he mentioned again that the second part might be a problem: 'I have postponed finishing Part II – it will give you a fit – of laughter also, I hope. But I intend to finish it in Taormina.'[63] After Secker's plan to publish Part I by itself collapsed, Lawrence sent him an outline on 12 June for the continuation of *Mr Noon*:

"Aaron's Rod" as the next novel under my contract. This seems to me the most straightforward course and, in the circumstances, much preferable to issuing it in two separate parts' (*Letters*, iii. 730n.).

58 A copy of the contract is in the Charles Smith collection.
59 Letter from Seltzer to Mountsier; UT (*D. H. Lawrence: Letters to Thomas and Adele Seltzer*, ed. Gerald M. Lacy, Santa Barbara, 1976, p. 207).
60 Letter from Seltzer to Mountsier, 16 July 1921; UT (*Letters to Thomas and Adele Seltzer*, ed. Lacy, p. 210).
61 *Letters*, iii. 702.   62 *Letters*, iii. 714, 717.
63 *Letters*, iii. 722.

I will finish 'Lucky Noon' before Christmas, God being with me. But it will be rather impossible, only funny – It is 3-parts done, nearly the first two vols – up to 1913. Sec. part ends 1914. Third part ends 1919. But third part not yet begun. Part I you have seen. Part II, which is 3 times as long – or more – is about ½ done. MS in Palermo. Will get it here.

Lawrence may have expanded his design for *Mr Noon*, perhaps after he revised the typescripts of Part I in February 1921. In late December 1920 and early January 1921 he referred to the novel as being two-thirds finished, but after he decided to divide it into parts and revised the typescripts of Part I separately, he said it would be in three volumes: 'The novel will have three vols, I think. I have nearly done the second'.[64] This may indicate that he planned to extend the material included in *Mr Noon*, or it may mean only that he now thought of the novel in parts. In February he also wrote that Part II was 'nearly done', but in May it was 'half done'. His outline suggested that the second volume would include two more years (perhaps not in the same detail as that which he had already written, which spans a little more than four months) and the third would cover five years.

Robert Mountsier joined the Lawrences at Baden-Baden on 5 July and went with them to Zell-am-See, the home of Frieda's sister Nusch von Schreibershofen.[65] He and Lawrence undoubtedly discussed publishing plans; Mountsier's questionnaire and Lawrence's detailed letters to him would indicate that Mountsier was intensely interested in Lawrence's writing.[66] He would have listened to Mountsier as a friend of long standing, and as his agent, especially about placing his work in magazines and promoting the sale of his books. Plans for *Mr Noon* were probably discussed during their several weeks together. In any event, Lawrence received the ribbon copy typescript of Part I back from Curtis Brown on 14 August:[67] whether he (or Mountsier) asked for it to be returned, or Curtis Brown just sent it is not recorded in the surviving correspondence, but the first is more likely, since Curtis Brown did not usually send back typescripts when he could not place the work. Mountsier may have suggested revision of the first part, bearing in mind Seltzer's concern about the 'storm of protest', as well as his own criticisms.

---

[64] *Letters*, iii. 667. [65] See explanatory note on 154:35.

[66] Mountsier had first met DHL in 1916 when he and a friend stayed with him in Cornwall; after this visit Mountsier was apparently interrogated as a possible spy (DHL and Frieda were being watched because of her German birth and their unusual, and therefore suspicious activities) which had strengthened their bond of friendship. See *Letters*, iii. 65, and the experiences of Monsell in *Kangaroo*, chap. xii.

[67] Letter to Curtis Brown, 14 August 1921.

Neither the New York nor the London office had any better luck than Curtis Brown or Mountsier in 1921;[90] as Nancy Pearn, head of the London serials department, wrote in a memorandum to Pollinger dated 20 April 1934: 'For one reason and another, I think we'd better not offer this very long story, "MR. NOON." I am having the copy returned to you in case you can make use of it.'[91]

The next step was to publish *Mr Noon* Part I in book form with other unpublished and uncollected fiction. Pollinger wrote to Frieda on 9 July 1934: 'Nancy Pearn has tried out all the unpublished fiction in all of the most likely places. The remainder is unsaleable serially and there is no point in not letting Secker bring it out under the title of "A MODERN LOVER" simultaneously with Viking Press this Autumn.'[92] There had been some frustration on Pollinger's side because Frieda had attempted to make independent arrangements with Viking Press, but it was eventually agreed that Secker and Viking would publish simultaneously in autumn 1934.[93] P. P. Howe, for Secker, listed the contents of the volume and noted that these 'are all early stories and would be stated to be such, with the exception of "Mr Noon", which would also be dated, with an explanation of its non-continuance'.[94] Secker's edition of *A Modern Lover* (hereafter E1) had the following statement in the preliminary pages (p. 5): 'NOTE The six shorter stories in this volume belong to Lawrence's earliest phase of authorship, and were written in 1910–11. The unfinished novel, "Mr Noon," was written in 1921.' The Viking Press edition (A1), however, merely noted on the dust-jacket: 'Containing six short stories and twelve chapters of an unfinished novel not previously published in book form ...'; and the blurb unhelpfully stated 'Most of them are from his earlier productive period ...'

The Secker edition was set from a copy of TCCII: E1 follows the errors of TCCII, most notably the change of Lewie Goddard's name to 'Lewis'.[95] A1 must have been set from a copy of the proofs of E1.[96] A1 was published on 11 October 1934, and E1 on 18 October; Pollinger sent copies of E1 to Frieda

---

90 See letter from Helen Everitt to Marshall Best, Viking Press, 20 June 1934; Viking Press.
91 Located at UT.   92 Located at UT.
93 The contract with Secker was not sent to Frieda until 7 November 1934; she signed it on the 28th; letter from Pollinger to Frieda Lawrence (UT), and Heinemann.
94 Memo from Howe to Pollinger, n. d. [*c.* 10 June 1934]; UT. Howe listed the contents as 'A Modern Lover', 'The Old Adam', 'Strike Pay', 'Her Turn', 'The Witch à la Mode', 'New Eve and Old Adam' and 'Mr Noon'. (The order of 'Strike Pay' and 'Her Turn' was reversed.) For publication details see *A Bibliography of D. H. Lawrence*, by Warren Roberts (2nd edn, Cambridge, 1982), pp. 173–4.
95 See 'Note on the text', point 6.
96 See letter from Pollinger to Howe, 18 July 1934; UT; see also textual apparatus entries for 27:40; 45:12; 62:35–63:7; and 83:2.

and to Lawrence's sisters and brother on 19 October.[97] *Mr Noon* Part I was reprinted from E1 in 1968 in *Phoenix II*.

Reception

Mr Noon Part I evoked a mixed response in 1934. Most reviewers had strong – and contradictory – views on it: several thought it very good, others that it should have remained unpublished. Those reviewers who were using the American edition (A1) concluded that the fragment dated from the pre-war period.

While L. A. G. Strong in the *Nineteenth Century* and the reviewer in *Newsweek* both briefly dismissed *A Modern Lover* without specific reference to any piece in it, and the *New Statesman and Nation* merely listed it,[98] Lorine Pruette in the *New York Herald Tribune Books* classed the six stories as 'good' (and *Mr Noon* as 'bad'). The reviewer in the London *Times* considered nothing beyond the title story was even in the second rank of Lawrence's work.[99]

Most reviewers mentioned the style and tone. The reviewer in *The Times* suggested that *Mr Noon* 'must really be read rather as a curiosity' and quoted the last few paragraphs as an example of 'its odd button-holing, interjectory style'. Pruette commented on Lawrence's 'providing his own Greek chorus of what is meant for sardonic comment, but is actually nothing but rather vulgar and unamusing carping'. Dilys Powell in the *London Mercury* noted that Part I 'has none of the signs of Lawrence's maturity except a certain truculence in mood and patches of a cynical devil-may-care manner'.[100]

But the lighter tone appealed to other reviewers as realistic.[101] 'The scene and the talk is as exactly reproduced as in a Bennett novel, and produces an

---

[97] Raymond Everitt of the New York office of Curtis Brown copyrighted *A Modern Lover* on 11 October 1934 (Pollinger); Secker advertised *A Modern Lover* as published on 18 October, and see letters from Pollinger to Frieda Lawrence, Ada Clarke and Emily King, 19 October 1934 (UT). (The 19 October letter to Frieda also mentioned George Lawrence.)

[98] 'Autumn Novels' in the 'Literary Supplement', cxvi (December 1934), p. vi; iv (13 October 1934), p. 43; 20 October 1934.

[99] 21 October 1934, p. 15; 'D. H. Lawrence's Short Stories' (22 October 1934), p. 20.

[100] Vol. xxxi (February 1935), p. 397.

[101] The blurb on the Viking jacket emphasised this point: 'Widely differing in subject matter, these stories again exemplify the broad range of the author's experience and understanding. They are particularly interesting in that they reveal the lighter side of Lawrence's character. As always, he is concerned with the psychological bases underlying modern life, but here his approach is predominantly one of good-natured satire. The agile wit he employs in "Mr. Noon" to dissect the modern technique of love-making provides some of the most entertaining reading in all his work.'

effect of realism' said H. J. Davis.[102] Currie Cabot in the *Saturday Review of Literature* was complimentary about its 'deft satire' and noted that *Mr Noon* 'reveals a Lawrence who might have been, if he had so chosen, a dryly humorous, inimitable observer of surfaces of those flaws and trivialities of human nature which are the stuff of which "characters" are composed'.[103] Peter Monro Jack in the *New York Times Book Review* came to the opposite conclusion: 'This is the familiar complex of an obdurate realism with an impossible idealism that marks Lawrence's work, reduced almost to an absurdity. The irony is gay on the surface and bitter below.'[104] Most of the short review in *Everyman* was devoted to *Mr Noon*, and the 'flippant' tone was its 'merit' according to the reviewer: 'it has gusto, exuberance, a continual good humour that borders on satire. In fact, although the gusto is sometimes overdone (as in the virtuoso chapter on spooning), on the whole the fragment contains that very quality which was too often lacking in Lawrence's work . . .'[105]

The 'spooning' chapter received particular notice. Ferner Nuhn in the *Nation* praised 'a brilliant scene, veritably a treatise with running illustration, on spooning', but the reviewer in *The Times Literary Supplement* was critical ('It's chapter on "the spoon" . . . must be read to be believed') and condemned the rest as a 'grotesque exposition of lower-middle-class vulgarity'.[106] Pruette mentioned the erotic scenes, and Jack noted that 'this unfinished moonlight sonata does for "spooning" what "Lady Chatterley's Lover" did for adult love'.

Several reviewers commented on the unfinished state of *Mr Noon*. Powell wondered if it had actually been written earlier than 1921, and although she said that as an early version it was 'brilliantly done', she wished Lawrence had had the chance to 'recast' it as he habitually did his novels. The *Everyman* reviewer concluded 'It was a pity that Lawrence never finished "Mr. Noon."' However the *Times Literary Supplement* reviewer decided that Lawrence 'would seem to have recognised, in the act of stopping short, that it had missed fire' and wondered who he had thought the audience would be. But the reviewers using the American edition believed *Mr Noon* to be early writing and were less exacting in their criticism.

The reviewer in *The Times Literary Supplement* did note *Mr Noon*'s relationship with *The Lost Girl* in date and one character; he felt it belonged to

102 'More about Lawrence', *Canadian Forum*, xv (January 1935), p. 159.
103 Vol. xi (10 November 1934), p. 273.
104 'Stories by Lawrence', xxxix (4 November 1934), p. 7.
105 'Lawrence Again' (2 November 1934), p. 82.
106 Vol. cxxxix (24 October 1934), p. 484; 'Stories by D. H. Lawrence' (25 October 1934), p. 731.

a time when Lawrence 'seemed deliberately striving for a wider popularity'. If *Mr Noon* had been published immediately after *Lost Girl*, reviewers could have been expected to notice the similarities in tone and setting, and they would probably have reacted to the later novel as they had done to the earlier: *The Lost Girl* received mediocre reviews in England, with some reviewers criticising it as a throwback to early writing, while those who liked it did not think it was the author at his best. Only a few had been extremely enthusiastic, mostly in the USA.[107]

Base-texts and sources

Selection of base-texts

The surviving manuscript and printed materials for *Mr Noon* are Lawrence's autograph manuscript of Parts I and II (hereafter MS), written *c.* 28 November 1920 – ? February 1921; the ribbon copy and carbon copy typescripts of Part I (TSI and TCCI), both revised by Lawrence by 22 February 1921; the posthumous carbon copy typescripts of Part I made from TCCI (TCCII and the Viking Press copy);[108] the English and American first editions of Part I (E1 and A1); and the incomplete carbon copy typescript of Part II, not corrected (or probably even seen) by Lawrence.

Lawrence's MS for Part I was superseded by the typescripts which he revised himself. TSI and TCCI both have 142 pages, numbered [1]–141 with a few errors.[109] Comparison of TCCI with TSI shows that where the changes are extensive enough to allow such an evaluation to be made TSI was usually revised first. For example, at the end of chapter ii (p. 37): Lawrence added a new paragraph in TSI with several deletions and continued writing around the typed chapter number and title, while in TCCI (with a few variant readings) the new paragraph is written carefully in the available space between the end of the chapter and the next chapter number with no deletions.[110]

Pages 30–1 in TSI and p. [141A] in TCCI (20:3–21:19; 93:6–15) have been retyped. The revision in TCCI (through 21:5) in the first instance is extensive (Lawrence crossed through each line and completely rewrote the

[107] See 'Introduction', *The Lost Girl*, ed. Worthen, pp. xliv–li.

[108] The Viking Press copy is identical with TCCII; no symbol has been assigned to it.

[109] TSI has a printed Curtis Brown label pasted in the lower right corner of the title sheet; TCCI has Mountsier's name and address in the lower right corner of the title sheet in DHL's hand.

[110] See textual apparatus entry for this passage and explanatory note on 24:39. For another example see explanatory note on 24:10.

passage between the typed lines), and TSI was also revised extensively from MS (perhaps with deletions) and was probably retyped for clarity by an unidentified person. In the second instance the page is in autograph in TSI and probably was originally so in TCCI, since Lawrence added it after the typescripts were prepared, so again the page was presumably typed out for clarity by an unidentified person. In both instances the originals are unlocated.

TCCII (and the Viking Press copy) has no textual authority and adds a layer of errors and typist's standardisations. E1 was produced from TCCII and adds a further layer of house-styling: it and its derivative A1 have no authority. However, although published after Lawrence's death, they have interest as the first printed editions of Part I.

TCCI and TSI are the only sources of the text of Part I with the authority of the author's revisions. Lawrence sent out both typescripts, and it was pure chance which one might have appeared in print, but TCCI contains his latest revisions and must be the base-text for this edition. Ruth Wheelock followed Lawrence's MS quite faithfully; where she made errors in transcription, the MS readings have been reinstated in this edition unless subsequent and extensive revision by Lawrence negates the error. Because TSI has nearly equal authority, all its variants are recorded in the textual apparatus. Some interesting deletions from MS and the two typescripts are included in the explanatory notes.

For Part II the only text with authority is MS. Although the incomplete carbon copy typescript was prepared at Lawrence's request, he did not correct it, so it has no textual authority. Editorial emendations in this edition have been made to correct minor errors, particularly in foreign languages, and standardise accidentals in accordance with Lawrence's normal practice in this MS. Since Part II is hitherto unpublished, and is an unrevised, uncompleted text, in keeping with the usual practice of the Cambridge edition in reproducing such texts, all deletions of complete words and phrases have been recorded in the textual apparatus.

Lawrence did not himself divide either the MS or TSI and TCCI into parts, but after he decided to try to publish the first part separately, he always referred to 'Part I' and 'Part II'. His letters from February 1921 onwards show that he also referred to the parts as 'volumes', further emphasising the division. In this edition his division of the novel into two parts has been retained.

Sources

The correspondences between *Mr Noon* and persons and events in Lawrence's life are numerous. Some have been touched on above, and many others are commented on in the explanatory notes. It is an obvious trap for the commentator to make over-simple correspondences between Lawrence's art and his life, but in this novel the resemblances are many and strong, especially in Part II; there they are significant enough to become a source for the biographer.

Gilbert Noon's adventures in Part I are loosely based on those of George Henry Neville, Lawrence's boyhood friend. But, for example, the Goddards are closely modelled on Willie and Sallie Hopkin;[111] their daughter Enid Hilton has confirmed the truth of some of Lawrence's observations, and her comments are recorded in the notes.

In Part II there is a shift in tone, and in scene (to Germany), but there is another, much more important change in Noon himself. He effectively becomes Lawrence, and his experiences are those of Lawrence (and Frieda) from May to September 1912. The connection for Lawrence between Neville–Noon of Part I and Lawrence–Noon of Part II was their real life 'marriages'. He had learned in early March 1912 of Neville's wedding, and just over a week later he met Frieda: on 8 March Lawrence wrote a humorous account for Edward Garnett, his literary advisor at that time, about Neville's relationships with women before marriage, and a play, *The Married Man*, about his relationships with women after marriage, following a visit to Neville, 25–31 March; Lawrence probably met Frieda on 17 March, and they eloped on 3 May. Lawrence may have compared the fates of two schoolboy friends at the time: one marriage the enforced result of the aftermath of 'spooning', and the other a true mating – and when he decided to use Neville's experiences in 1920 the same link recurred to him and was carried into his novel. An outline of the events of 1912 in Lawrence's life is included in the Chronology, and correspondences (and some differences) are included in the notes. Part II as it stands, i.e. in first draft form, is virtually autobiographical.

Lawrence and Frieda's elopement and their first few months together remained understandably fresh and vivid in their memories. Invariably the record of the events of that period and their feelings about them had already been included in Lawrence's contemporary writings, but these works were not available to him when he was writing *Mr Noon*, yet the parallels between them and this novel are often extraordinarily close. Lawrence's detailed memory, for example, supplied the quotation from the *ex voto* picture which is remarkably similar to that in 'A Chapel Among the Mountains'.[112] For Frieda too it was a memorable period which she described in her memoir of

---

[111] See explanatory notes on 3:4 and 3:26.   [112] See text and explanatory note on 243:32.

Lawrence, "*Not I, But the Wind . . .*", written twenty years after the events; it is instructive, for instance, to compare her recollection of her father's concern about her liaison with Lawrence's 'fictional' account.[113]

When in August 1913 Lawrence could not find the chapel and hay hut sketches which the *Westminster Gazette* claimed had been returned to Garnett,[114] Lawrence expressed his own and Frieda's concern: 'I should be sorry to lose them: they were so jolly' and 'Frieda is frightfully keen on them, and desolated for fear they are lost.'[115] Frieda later expressed her disappointment over the missing Part II: 'I wish we could find the second half to Mr Noon – '.[116] The sketches reappeared and were published posthumously. Now that the second part of *Mr Noon* has also been recovered, we have a chance to read a piece of fiction which is in addition a biographical document of the first importance. Since it was written rapidly as a draft, it has not been subjected to Lawrence's usual process of reworking – yet its vitality and essential veracity as a record of how and what he remembered of his experiences are what now strike us. But its lightness of touch is also remarkable: the humour, the capacity to see himself as a character in a comic novel are commendable because Lawrence was retelling some of the most crucial passages in his life: passages from which he drew much of his subsequent thought about love, and about the struggle between men and women:

> And yet all the while you are you, you are not me.
> And I am I, I am never you.
> How awfully distinct and far off from each other's being we are!
>
> Yet I am glad.
> I am so glad there is always you beyond my scope,
> Something that stands over,
> Something I shall never be,
> That I shall always wonder over, and wait for . . .
>
> And you will always be with me . . .[117]

---

[113] See text and explanatory note on 180:35.   [114] See explanatory note on 255:5.

[115] *Letters*, ii. 56, 60.

[116] Letter from Frieda Lawrence to Pollinger, [2 July 1934]; UT.

[117] 'Wedlock', vi. from *Look! We Have Come Through!* (*The Complete Poems of D. H. Lawrence*, ed. Vivian de Sola Pinto and Warren Roberts, 1964, i. 248).

MR NOON

Note on the text

The base-texts for this edition are the corrected carbon typescript (TCCI) of Part I which DHL revised in February 1921 and the manuscript (MS) of Part II which DHL stopped writing in ?February 1921; both are in the possession of the Humanities Research Center, University of Texas at Austin.

The apparatus records all textual variants, except the following silent emendations:

1 Clearly inadvertent spelling and typesetting errors have been corrected.
2 Inadvertent omissions, i.e. incomplete quotation marks, commas in a series and full stops omitted at the end of sentences where no other punctuation exists, have been supplied.
3 DHL's titles, e.g. 'Mr' and 'Mr.', have been emended to his most usual form, 'Mr'. The base-text (TCCI), Berkeley typescript (TCCII) and the American first edition (A1) consistently put the full stop after the title; these have not been recorded.
4 Omitted or misplaced apostrophes in possessive cases, colloquial contractions and the apostrophe in 'o'clock' have been supplied or corrected.
5 DHL often presented colloquial contractions without joining them up, e.g. 'does n't', and these have been normalised, 'doesn't'.
6 TCCII and all printed texts have 'Lewis' for 'Lewie'. DHL wrote 'Patty' as 'Pattie' from 8:1 through 8:38.
7 The English first edition (E1) consistently printed 'to-night', 'to-day' and 'to-morrow' whereas DHL wrote these as one unhyphenated word; A1 consistently printed 'Aye' and 'coo-ey' for DHL's 'Ay' and 'coo-ee' and 'realized', 'spiritualized', 'sympathizing', 'womanizer', 'theorizing', 'apologized', 'patronizing' and 'vaporize' whereas DHL spelled these words and their derivatives with '-is-'; his spellings have been preserved in this edition.
8 When a single punctuation mark at the end of a sentence may be read as a full stop, a dash or something in between, i.e. an elongated full stop, this has been interpreted as a full stop.

Contents

PART I.*

Chapter I.

Attack on Mr Noon.

Her very stillness, as she sat bent upon her book, gradually made him uncomfortable. He* twisted over, sprawling in his arm-chair, and pretended to go on with his perusal of the *New Age*. But neither Mr Orage nor Miss Tina* could carry him on the wings of the spirit this afternoon. He kept glancing at his wife, whose intensified stillness would have told a 'cuter man that she knew he was fidgetting, and then glancing at the window, and round the room. It was a rainy, dark Sunday afternoon. He ought to be very cosy, in the quiet by the roasting fire. But he was bored, and he wanted to be amused.

He perched his pince-nez on his nose and looked with an intellectual eye on his paper once more. Perhaps the light was fading. He twisted to look at the window. The aspidistras and ferns were not inspiring: it was still far from nightfall. He twisted the other way, to look at the little round clock on the mantel-piece. No use suggesting a meal, yet. He gave a heavy sigh, and rattled the leaves of the *New Age*.

But no response: no response. The little red metal devils frisked as ever on the mantel-piece, his own pet devils.* Having gone back on the Lord, he signified his revolt by establishing a little company of scarlet, tail-flourishing gentry on his sitting-room mantel-piece. But it was only half-past three, and there was nothing to be done. He would not insult himself by nodding off to sleep. So again he perched his pince-nez on his nose, and began to have a grudge against his wife. After all, what was she so absorbed in!

She* was a woman of about forty, stoutish, with very dark, glossy brown hair coiled on her head. She sat sunk deep in a chair, with her feet on a little footstool, and her spectacles right away on the tip of her nose. He, of course, did not observe that she never turned the page of her absorbing book.

His blue eye strayed petulantly to the fire. Ah-ha! Here he was in demand. In the well of the grate a mass of fire glowed scarlet like his devils, with a dark, half-burnt coal resting above. He crouched before the curb and took the poker with satisfaction. Biff! A well-aimed blow,

3

he could congratulate himself on it. The excellent coal burst like magic into a bunch of flames.

"That's better!" he said heartily.

And he remained crouching before the fire, in his loose homespun clothes.* He was handsome, with a high forehead and a small beard, a socialist, something like Shakspeare's bust to look at, but more refined. He had an attractive, boyish nape of the neck, for a man of forty-five, no longer thin.

So he crouched gazing into the hot, spurting, glowing fire. He was a pure idealist, something of a Christ, but with an intruding touch of the goat. His eyelids dropped oddly, goat-like, as he remained abstracted before the fire.

His wife roused, and cleared her throat.

"Were you sleeping, Missis?" he asked her in a jocular manner of accusation, screwing round to look at her. She had a full, soft, ivory-pale face, and dark eyes with heavy shadows under them. She took her spectacles off her nose-tip.

"No," she said, in the same sparring humour. "I was *not*."

"May I ask you what was the last sentence you read?"

"You may ask. But you mayn't expect me to answer."

"I'll bet not," he laughed. "It would be the tail-end of a dream, if you did."

"No, it would *not*," she said. "Not even a day-dream."

"What, were you as sound* as all that?" he said.

But she began rustling her book, rather ostentatiously. He crouched watching her. The coil of hair was rust-brown, on her dark, glossy head. Her hair became reddish towards the ends. It piqued him still, after twenty years of marriage. But since the top of her head was all she showed him, he went back to his big chair, and screwed himself in with his legs underneath him, though he was a biggish man, and once again settled his pince-nez. In a man who doesn't smoke or drink, an eyeglass or a pair of pince-nez can become a vice.

"Ay-y-y!" he sighed to himself, as he tried to find excitement in the well-filled pages of the *New Statesman*.* He kept his quick ears attentive to the outside. The church clock sounded four. Some people passed, voices chattering. He got up to look. Girls going by. He would have liked a chat, a bit of fun with them. With a longing, half-leering eye he looked down from the window.

"It's about lighting-up time Mrs Goddard, isn't it?" he said to his wife.

"Yes, I suppose it is," she said abstractedly.

He bustled round with the matches, lit three gas-jets, drew the curtains, and rocked on his heels with his hands in his pockets and his back to the fire. This was the precious Sunday afternoon. Every week-day he was at the office. Sunday was a treasure-day to the two of them. 5 They were socialists and vegetarians. So, in fine weather they tramped off into the country. In bad weather they got up late, had a substantial meal towards the end of the morning, and another in the early evening. None of the horrors of Sunday joints.

Lewie rocked on his heels on the hearth, with his back to the fire and 10 his hands in his pockets, whistling faintly.

"You might chop some wood," said Patty.

"I was just thinking so," he said, with rather a resentful cheerfulness in his acquiescence.

However, off he went to the back yard, and Patty could hear him 15 letting off some of his steam on the wood, whilst he kept up all the time a brilliant whistling. It wouldn't be Lewie if he didn't make himself heard wherever he was.

She mused on, in the brilliantly-lighted, hot room. She seemed very still, like a cat. Yet the dark lines under her eyes were marked. Her skin 20 was of that peculiar transparency often noticed in vegetarians and idealists. Her husband's was the same: as if the blood were lighter, more limpid, nearer to acid in the veins. All the time, she heard her husband so plainly.* He always sounded in her universe: always. And she was tired: just tired. They were an ideal married couple, she 25 and he. But something was getting on her nerves.

He appeared after a time.

"Can't see any more," he said. "Beastly rain still. The Unco Guid will want their just umbrellas* tonight. I'm afraid there'll be a fair amount of pew-timber showing beneath the reverend eyes, moreover. 30 There's nothing parsons hate more than the sight of bare pew-timber. They don't mind a bare bread-board half as much.—That reminds me, Mrs Goddard, what about tea?"

"What about it?" she answered, screwing up her face at him slightly, in a sort of smile. He looked down at her from under his eyelids. 35

"Is that intended as a piece of cheek?" he asked.

"Yes, it might be," she said.

"I won't stand it."

"I wouldn't. I wouldn't. No man ever does," she quizzed.

"When a woman begins to give her husband cheek—" 40

"Go and put the kettle on."

"*I've* got to go and get the tea, have I?" he asked.

"Yes, if you want it so early, you have. It's only five o'clock."

"The wiles and circumventions of a woman's heart, not to mention
5 her tongue, would cheat ten Esaus out of ten birth-rights* a day."

"All right, then put the kettle on."

"You have any more of your impudence, Patty Goddard, and *I won't*,
so I tell you straight."

"I'm dumb," she said.

10 "My word, then I'll make haste and clear out, while the victory is yet
mine."

So he retreated to the kitchen, and his brilliant whistling kept her
fully informed of his existence down the long length of the passage.
Nay, even if he went out of actual earshot, he seemed to be ringing her
15 up all the time on some viewless telephone. The man was marvellous.
His voice could speak to her across a hundred miles of space; if he went
to America, verily, she would hear him invisibly as if he was in the back
kitchen. The connection between a mother and her infant was as
nothing compared to the organic or telepathic connection between her
20 and Lewie. It was a connection which simply was never broken. And
not a peaceful, quiet unison. But unquiet, as if he was always talking,
always slightly forcing her attention, as now by his whistling in the
kitchen. When he was right away from her, he still could make some
sort of soundless noise which she was forced to hear and attend to.
25 Lewie, Lewie, her soul sounded with the noise of him as a shell with
the sea. It excited her, it pleased her, it saved her from ever feeling
lonely. She loved it, she felt immensely pleased and flattered. But the
dark lines came under her eyes, and she felt sometimes as if she would
go mad with irritation.

30 He was fumbling at the door, and she knew he was balancing the full
tray on his knee whilst he turned the door-handle. She listened. He
was very clever at these tricks, but she must listen, for fear.

"Well of all the idle scawd-rags!"* he said as he entered with the
tray.

35 "I'm the idlest, I know it," she said laughing. She had in fact known
that she ought to spread the cloth in readiness for his coming. But
today a kind of inertia held her.

"How much does that admission cost you?" bantered Lewie, as he
flapped the white cloth on to the round table.

40 "Less than the effort of getting up and laying the cloth," she laughed.

"Ay, such a lot," he said. He liked doing the things, really, on these days when the work-woman was absent.

There were buttered eggs in little casseroles; there was a stilton cheese, a salad, a pudding of chestnuts and cream, celery, cakes, pastry, jam, and preserved ginger: there were delicate blue Nankin cups,* 5 and berries and leaves in a jar. It had never ceased to be a delightful picnic *à deux*. It was so this evening still. But there was an underneath strain, unaccountable, that made them both listen for some relief.

They had passed the eggs and cheese and pudding stage, and reached the little cakes and tarts, when they heard the front gate bang. 10

"Who's this!" said Lewie, rising quickly and going to light the hall lamp. The bell pinged.

Patty listened with her ears buttoned back.

"I wondered if you'd be at home—"—a man's bass voice.

"Ay, we're at home. Come in,"—Lewie's voice, heartily. He was 15 nothing if not hospitable. Patty could tell he did not know who his visitor was.

"Oh Mr Noon,* is it you? Glad to see you. Take your coat off. Ay? Are you wet? Have you walked?—You've just come right for a cup of tea. Ay, come in." 20

Mr Noon! Patty had risen hastily, hearing the name. She stood in the sitting-room doorway in her soft dress of dark-brown poplin trimmed with silk brocade in orange and brown. She was waiting. The visitor came forward.

"How nice of you to come," she said. "Where have you been for so 25 long? We haven't seen you for ages.—You're sure your feet aren't wet? Let Lewie give you a pair of slippers."

"Ay, come on," said Lewie heartily.

Mr Noon, in a bass voice, said he had come on the motor-bicycle, and that he had left his overalls at The Sun. He was a young man of 30 twenty-five or twenty-six,* with broad, rather stiff shoulders and a dark head somewhat too small for these shoulders. His face was fresh, his mouth full and pursed, his eye also rather full, dark-blue, and abstracted. His appearance was correct enough, black coat and a dark blue tie tied in a bow. He did not look like a socialist. 35

The whole character of the room was now changed. It was evident the Goddards were pleased, rather flattered to entertain their visitor. Yet his hands were red, and his voice rather uncouth. But there was a considerable force in him.. He ate the food they gave him as if he liked it. 40

"Now tell us," said Patty, "what brings you to Woodhouse* on a night like this."

"Not any desire to sit at the feet of one of our famous administers of the gospel, I'll warrant," said Lewie.

5   "No," said Noon. "I'd got an appointment and was here a bit too soon, so I wondered if you'd mind if I called."

"Ah—!" exclaimed Patty. His answer was hardly flattering. "Of course! Of course! You may just as well wait here as at a street corner, or in a public-house."

10 "The public-houses, my dear Patty, don't open till half-past six, so that they shan't get an unfair start of the House of the Lord," said Lewie.

"No, of course," said Patty. "But you won't have to hurry away at once I hope," she added, to Gilbert Noon.

15 "I can stop till about half-past seven," said that gentleman.

"Till chapel comes out," said Lewie drily.

"Ha-a-a!" laughed Patty, half-scornfully, half-bitterly, as if she had found him out.

"That's it," said Mr Noon, going rather red.

20 "Which of the tabernacles is it then?" asked Lewie. "We'd better know, to start you off in good time. Pentecost is half an hour earlier than the others, and Church is about ten minutes before the Congregational. Wesleyan is the last, because the Reverend Mr Flewitt is newly arrived on the circuit, and wants to sweep the chapel very clean of sin,

25 being a new broom."

"Congregational," said Mr Noon.

"Ha-ha! Ha-ha!" said Patty teasingly. She was really rather chagrined. "You're quite sure the fair flame will have come out on such a night?"

30 "No, I'm not sure," said Mr Noon, rather awkwardly.

"Many waters cannot quench love,* Patty Goddard," said Lewie.

"They can put a considerable damper on it," replied Patty.

Gilbert Noon laughed.

"They can that," he replied.

35 "You speak as if you knew," laughed Patty, knitting her brow.

But Gilbert only shook his head.

"Ah well," said Patty, looking at the clock. "We can just clear away and settle down for an hour's talk, anyhow. I've lots of things to ask you. Do smoke if you'd care to."

40 Lewie, a non-smoker, hurried up with a box of cigarettes. But the

young man preferred a pipe. They were soon all seated round the
fire.

The reason the Goddards made so much of Gilbert Noon was
because he was so clever. His father owned a woodyard* in
Whetstone, six miles away, and was comfortably well off, but stingy. 5
Gilbert, the only son, had started his career as an elementary school-
teacher, but had proved so sharp at mathematics, music, and science
that he had won several scholarships, had gone up to Cambridge, and
might have had a Fellowship if only he had stayed and worked. But he
would neither work nor stay at the university, although he was 10
accounted one of the most brilliant of the young mathematicians. He
came back to Whetstone with his degree, and started the old round of
Whetstone life, carousing in common public-houses, playing his violin
for vulgar dances, "hops" as they were called, and altogether demean-
ing himself. He had a post as Science Master in Haysfall Technical 15
School,* another five miles from Whetstone, and so far, Haysfall
shut its ears to Whetstone misdemeanours. Gilbert's native town, a raw
industrial place, was notorious for its roughs.

Occasionally Mr Noon, being somewhat of a celebrity in the
countryside, would give popular lectures on scientific subjects. Lewie 20
Goddard was secretary for the Woodhouse Literary Society,* and
as such had had much pride in securing Gilbert on several occasions.
Gilbert's lectures to the people were really excellent: so simple, and so
entertaining.* His account of Mars, with lantern slides, thrilled
Woodhouse to the marrow. And particularly it thrilled Patty. Mars, its 25
canals and its inhabitants and its what-not: ah, how wonderful it was!
And how wonderful was Mr Noon, with his rough bass voice, roughly
and laconically and yet with such magic and power landing her on
another planet. Mephistopheles himself, in a good-natured mood,
could not have been more fascinating than the rough young man who 30
stood on the rostrum and pointed at the lantern sheet with a long wand,
or whose ruddy face was lit up at his dark-lantern, as he glanced at his
notes.

So had started the Noon–Goddard acquaintance, which had not as
yet ripened into a friendship. The Goddards warmly invited Gilbert, 35
but he rarely came. And his social uncouthness, though acceptable in
the Midlands as a sign of manliness, was rather annoying sometimes to
a woman.

He sat now with a big pipe in his fist, smoking clouds of smoke and
staring abstractedly into the fire. He wore a ring with a big red stone on 40

one finger. Patty wondered at him, really. He made no effort to be
pleasant, so his hostess fluttered her two neat little feet on her footstool,
settled herself deep in her chair, and lifted her sewing from under a
cushion. She perched her spectacles away on the slope of her nose,
then looked up at Gilbert from under her dark eyebrows.

"You won't be shocked if I stitch on the Sabbath, and sew clothes for
the devil?" she asked.

"Me?" said Gilbert. "Better the day, better the deed."*

"So they say," retorted Patty sarcastically. But it was lost on him.

"I'd rather clothe the devil than those up-aloft," said Lewie. "He
stands more need. Why he's never a rag to his back. Not even a pair of
bathing drawers, much less an immortal mantle. Funny thing that."

"Beauty is best unadorned," said Patty.

"Then the angels and the Lord must be pretty unbeautiful, under all
their robes and spangles," said Lewie.

But Mr Noon was not attentive. Patty called a sort of hush. From the
midst of it, she inquired in a small, searching voice:

"And what are you doing with yourself these days, Mr Noon?"

"Me? Making stinks* at Haysfall."

"Chemical, I hope, not moral," said Lewie.

"And what are you doing at Whetstone?" asked Patty.

Gilbert took his pipe from his mouth and looked at her.

"Pretty much as usual," he said.

She laughed quickly.

"And what is that?" she said. "Are you working at anything?"

He reached forward and knocked his pipe on the fire-bar.

"I'm doing a bit," he said.

"Of what?" she asked.

"Oh—thesis for my M.A.—maths.—And composing a bit as well."

"Composing music? But how splendid! What is it?"

"A violin concerto."

"Mayn't we hear it?"

"It wouldn't mean anything to you—too abstract."

"But mayn't we hear it?"

"Ay—you might some time—when I can arrange it."

"Do arrange it. Do!"

"Yes, do," put in Lewie.

"It's not finished," said Gilbert.

"But when it is," said Patty. "You *will* finish it, won't you?"

"I hope so, some day."

She stuck her needle in her sewing, and looked up, and mused.

"I think of all the wonderful things to create," she said, "music is the most difficult. I can never understand how you begin. And do you prefer music to your mathematics?"

"They run into one another—they're nearly the same thing," he said. "Besides it isn't any good. It's too abstract and dry for anybody but me, what I write." 5

"Can't you make it less abstract?" she said.

He looked at her.

"Somehow I can't," he said; and she saw a flutter of trouble in him. 10

"Why?" she asked.

"I don't know, I'm sure. I know it hasn't got the right touch. It's more a musical exercise than a new piece of work.—I only do it for a bit of pastime. It'll never amount to anything."

"Oh, surely not. You who have such talents—" 15

"*Who?*" said Gilbert scoffingly.

"You. You have wonderful talents."

"I'm glad to hear it. Where are they?" asked Gilbert.

"In your head, I suppose."

"Ay, and there they can stop, for all they're worth—" 20

"Nay now—" began Lewie.

"But why? But why?" rushed in Patty. "Don't you *want* to make anything of your life? Don't you want to produce something that will help us poor mortals out of the slough?"

"Slough?" said Gilbert. "What I should do would only make the slough deeper." 25

"Oh come! Come! Think of the joy I got out of your lecture."

He looked at her, smiling faintly.

"A pack of lies," he said.

"What?" she cried. "*Didn't* I get joy out of it?" 30

He had got his pipe between his pouting lips again, and had closed his brow.

"What is lies?" she persisted.

"Mars," he said. "A nice little fairy-tale. You only like it better than Arabian Nights." 35

"Oh *come*—!" she cried in distress.

"Ay, we like it better than Arabian Nights," said Lewie.

"I know you do," said Gilbert. "I'll tell you another some time."

"Oh but *come*!—come!" said Patty. "Is nothing real? Or nothing true?" 40

"Not that I know of," said Gilbert. "In that line."

"Why, dear me, how surprising," said Patty, puzzled. "Surely you believe in your own work?"

"Yes, I believe in mathematics."

5   "Well then—" she said.

He took his pipe from his mouth, and looked at her.

"There isn't any *well then*," he said.

"Why not?"

"Mathematics is mathematics, the plane of abstraction and perfec-
10   tion. Life is life, and is neither abstraction nor perfection."

"But it has to do with both," she protested.

"*Art* has. Life hasn't."

"Life doesn't matter to you, then?"

"No, why should it?"

15   The answer staggered her.

"How can anything matter, if life doesn't matter?" she said.

"How could anything matter, if life mattered?" he replied. "Life is incompatible with perfection, or with infinity, or with eternity. You've got to turn to mathematics, or to art."

20   She was completely bewildered.

"I don't believe it," she cried.

"Ay well," he retorted, knocking out his pipe.

"You're young yet. You'll find that life matters before you've done," she said.

25   "I'm quite willing," he said.

"No," she said, "you're not." Suddenly her ivory face flushed red. "Indeed you're not willing. When do you ever give life a chance?"

"Me?" he said. "Always."

"No, you don't. Excuse my contradicting you. You *never* give life a
30   chance. Look how you treat women!"

He looked round at her in wonder.

"How do I?" he said. "What women?"

"Yes, how do you—!" She stumbled, and hesitated. "Confess it's a girl you're going to meet tonight," she continued, plunging. "I'm old
35   enough to be able to speak. You've never really had a mother. You don't know how you treat women. Confess you're going to meet a girl."

"Yes—what by that?"

"And confess she's not your equal."

"Nay, I don't see it."

40   "Yes you do. Yes you do. How do you look on her? Do you look on

her as you do on your mathematics? Ha—you know what a difference there is."

"Bound to be," he said. "Bound to be a difference."

"Yes, bound to be. And the girl bound to be an inferior—a mere plaything—not as serious as your chemical apparatus, even."

"Different," protested Gilbert. "All the difference in the world."

"Of course," said Patty. "And who sinks down in the scale of the difference. Who does? The girl.—I won't ask you who the girl is—I know nothing about her. But what is she to you? A trivial Sunday-night bit of fun: isn't she?—isn't she now?"

"Ay, she's good fun, if I must say it."

"She is! Exactly! She's good fun," cried Patty bitterly. "Good fun, and nothing else. What a humiliation for her, poor thing!"

"I don't think she finds it so," said Gilbert.

"No I'll bet she doesn't," laughed Lewie, with his goat's laugh.

"She doesn't. She doesn't," cried Patty. "But how cruel, that she doesn't! How cruel for her!"

"I don't see it at all. She's on the look-out for me as much as I am for her," said Gilbert.

"Yes probably. Probably. And perhaps even more. And what is her life going to be afterwards? And you, what is your life going to be? What are you going to find in it, when you get tired of your bit of fun, and all women are trivial or dirty amusements to you? What then?"

"Nay, I'll tell you when I know," he answered.

"You won't. You won't. By that time you'll be as stale as they are, and you'll have lost everything but your mathematics and science—even if you've not lost them. I pity you. I pity you. You may well despise life. But I pity you. Life will despise *you*, and you'll know it."

"Why, where am I wrong?" asked Gilbert awkwardly.

"Where? For shame! Isn't a woman a human being? And isn't a human being more than your science and stuff?"

"Not to me, you know," he said. "Except in one way."

"Ay," laughed Lewie. "There's always the exception, my boy."

There was a moment's pause.

"Well," said Patty, resuming her sewing. "For your mother's sake, I'm glad she can never hear you, never know. If she was a woman, it would break her heart."

But Gilbert could not see it. He smoked obstinately until Lewie reminded him that he must depart for his rendez-vous.

Patty smiled at him as she shook hands, but rather constrainedly.

"Come in whenever you are near, and you feel like it," she said.

"Thank you."

Lewie sped his parting guest, and had full sympathy with him, saying:

5   "I'm all for a bit of fun, you know."

Chapter II.

Spoon.*

Patty stitched on in silence, angry and bitter. Lewie fidgetted and whistled.

"He's got his human side to him right enough," he said, to make a 5
breach in Patty's silence, which buzzed inaudibly and angrily on the atmosphere.

"*Human!*" she repeated. "Yes, call it *human*! A yellow dog* on the streets has more humanity."

"Nay—nay," said Lewie testily. "Don't get your hair off, Mrs 10
Goddard. We aren't angels yet, thank heaven. Besides, there's no harm in it. A young chap goes out on Sunday night for a bit of a spoon. What is it but natural?"

He rocked easily and fussily on the hearth-rug, his legs apart. She looked up, quite greenish in her waxen pallor, with anger. 15

"You think it natural, do you?" she retorted. "Then I'm sorry for you. *Spoon*! A bit of a *spoon*—" she uttered the word as if it was full of castor-oil.

Her husband looked down on her with a touch of the old goat's leer.

"Don't forget you've been spoony enough in your day, Patty 20
Goddard," he said.

She became suddenly still, musing.

"I suppose I have. I suppose I have," she mused, with disgust. "And I can't bear myself when I think of it."

"Oh really!" said her husband sarcastically. "It's hard lines* on 25
you all of a sudden, my dear." He knew that if she had been spoony with anybody, it was with him.

But yellow-waxy with distaste, she put aside her sewing and went out. He listened, and followed her in a few minutes down to the kitchen, hearing dishes clink. 30

"What are you doing?" he asked her.

"Washing-up."

"Won't Mrs Prince do it tomorrow?"

And to show his anger, he went away without drying the pots for her.

Spoon! "You've been spoony enough in your day, Patty Goddard." 35

—Spoony! Spooning! The very mental sound of the word turned her
stomach acid. In her anger she felt she could throw all her past, with
the dishwater, down the sink. But after all, if Gilbert Noon had been
spooning with *her* instead of with some girl, some bit of fluff, she might
5 not have felt such gall in her veins.

She knew all about it, as Lewie had said. She knew exactly what
Sunday night meant, in the dark, wintry, rainy Midlands. It meant all
the young damsels coming out of chapel or of church, brazen young
things from fifteen upwards, and being accompanied or met by young
10 louts who would touch their exaggerated caps awkwardly: it meant
strolling off to some dark and sheltered corner, passage, entry, porch,
shop-door, shed, anywhere where two creatures might stand and
squeeze together and *spoon*. Yes, spoon. Not even kiss and cuddle,
merely: *spoon*. Spooning was a fine art, whereas kissing and cuddling
15 are calf-processes.

Mr Gilbert had gone off for his Sunday-night's spoon, and her veins,
the veins of a woman of forty, tingled with rage against him. She knew
so much more.

But Sunday night, oh Sunday night: how she loathed it. There was a
20 sort of Last Day* suspense about it. Monday, and Monday
morning's work-day grip, was very near. The iron hand was open to
seize its subjects. And the emotional luxury and repletion of Sunday
deepened into a sort of desperation as the hour of sleep and Monday
approached. There must be a climax—there must be a consummation.
25 Chapel did not finish it off sufficiently. The elder men dashed off for a
drink, the women went to each other's houses for an intense
gossip* and a bit of supper, the young people went off for a spoon.
It was the recognised thing to do—only very stiff-necked parents found
any fault. The iron grip of Monday was closing. Meanwhile, dear young
30 things, while the *frisson* of approaching captivity goes through you to
add an intenser sting to your bliss, spoon, dears, spoon.

Mr Noon waited on the edge of the kerb, on the side of the road
opposite the chapel. They were late coming out. The big but rather
flimsy stained-glass window shed its colours on the muddy road, and
35 Gilbert impassively contemplated the paucity of the geometric design
of the tracery. He had contemplated it before. He contemplated it again
as he stood in the rain with his coat-collar turned up and listened
to the emotional moan of the vesper-verse which closed the last
prayer. He objected to the raspberry-juice aerated-water melody and
40 harmony, but had heard it before. Other louts were lurking in the

It is unlikely that Lawrence had the manuscript sent to him from Taormina, and even less likely that he would have worked on it. He again worked fitfully – correcting the typescript of *Aaron's Rod* – and even after his return to Taormina, he only pursued small projects, revising and 'pottering with short stories'.[68] He now spoke of *Aaron's Rod* as the 'last of my serious English novels' and said he had begun 'a proper *story* novel – in the Venetian lagoons'.[69] But also at this time he became furious with Secker's cautious handling of Philip Heseltine's threatened libel suit over his portrayal in *Women in Love*.[70] Lawrence's diary entry for 26 October expressed his frustrations:

> Hear from Wheelock who is just back from America that Tortoises & Sardinia are both ready for this month – wanted to see them ... Have had a month of loathing everybody, particularly the canaglia of England. Canaille! ... Sent [two cheques] to Haskard, but have not heard if they arrived. Post erratic ... Had impudent letters from CB & RM. about Aaron's Rod ... Lost the blank cheques R.M. gave me ... Want to know how many dollars I have, but M. does not tell me. Have only fifty pounds in England ... Have felt seedy & hateful all this month.[71]

His health was bad from November to mid-January 1922. He was still 'pottering' on shorter pieces, and he received a request from Seltzer in late November for alterations to *Aaron's Rod*.[72] Circumstances, then, were not propitious for his making progress with *Mr Noon*.

Lawrence also received in early October a letter from Mabel Dodge Sterne urging him to come to Taos, New Mexico; she had read excerpts of *Sea and Sardinia* and believed he was the only person who could write truly about the New Mexico landscapes. He toyed with the idea, and also with following Earl and Achsah Brewster to Ceylon; but in January 1922 he very suddenly decided to go to Ceylon first and to approach the USA from the west.[73]

Lawrence's irritability in the autumn is evident in his references to *Mr Noon*. In late October he snapped at Mountsier: 'I don't know whether I shall finish *Mr Noon*. I get so annoyed with everybody that I don't want to tackle

---

[68] Letter to Catherine Carswell, 25 October 1921; see letter to Seltzer, 8 October 1921 and entry for 26 October 1921, *Lawrence MSS*, ed. Tedlock, p. 93.

[69] Letter to Seltzer, 8 October 1921; see also letter to Seltzer, 26 November 1921. No manuscript survives for the Venice novel.

[70] DHL (and Secker) altered the descriptions of Halliday and Pussum, who was based on Heseltine's wife Minnie ('Puma') Channing (letter to Secker, 8 October 1921).

[71] *Lawrence MSS*, ed. Tedlock, p. 93.

[72] Letter to Seltzer, 26 November 1921; see entry for 13 November 1921, *Lawrence MSS*, ed. Tedlock. p. 93.

[73] See letter to Mountsier, 17 January 1922.

any really serious work. To hell with them all. Miserable world of canaille.'[74] And in his next mention of the novel on 21 December to Mountsier: 'If I am to finish *Mr Noon* it shall be in the States.'

Given such remarks it is surprising to discover that late in 1921 he arranged for Ruth Wheelock to type the second part. She had returned from New York at the end of October, and Lawrence expected her to visit him the weekend of 5–6 November.[75] There is no record in the correspondence of why he wanted an incomplete section typed, or when she actually typed it. It is certain that Ruth Wheelock was the typist: she used the same typewriter as for Part I, and one page of the paper matched some used in Part I.[76] She did not, however, type all of Part II: she stopped at the end of the fourth notebook, and Lawrence may have had the fifth notebook in case he wanted to go on writing.[77] Since her typing for Lawrence was in addition to her consulate work, she may not have finished his typing before he left in late February 1922 for Ceylon.[78] So Lawrence may have asked her to post the lot to Seltzer for safekeeping while he was on his travels, since he did not expect to work on the novel until he had settled.[79]

Seltzer certainly had the manuscript and typescript including the ribbon copy typescript of Part I, which had been returned earlier to Lawrence by Curtis Brown. (Mountsier still had the carbon copy typescript of Part I). Mountsier had encouraged Lawrence to recall several manuscripts from Seltzer; hence Lawrence's letter from Australia to the publisher, on 9 June 1922: 'Will you please hand back to Mountsier the MSS. of *Mr Noon* – till I see what I'll do further with it – and of *Birds Beasts and Flowers*. Please let him have them at once.' But Seltzer ignored this request and a further letter from Mountsier on 18 January 1923.[80] The material remained unlocated (and indeed unknown) for fifty years.[81]

74 31 October 1921.   75 Ibid.
76 Ruth Wheelock also used a second typewriter for Part II; p. 302 is on the same watermarked paper used for pp. 1–28 of Part I. The surviving carbon copy typescript is 267 pages, numbered 142–407 with one error (located at UT); the ribbon copy is unlocated.
77 The typescript stops with '. . . with snow.' (248:38).
78 Ruth Wheelock was no longer DHL's regular typist: from late October 1921 he sent his manuscripts to a Mrs Carmichael to be typed (*Lawrence MSS*, ed. Tedlock, pp. 93–5).
79 See quotation from letter of 21 December 1921 to Mountsier above. (Or DHL may have posted the manuscript, including the fifth notebook, and the typescript to Seltzer himself.)
80 A carbon copy draft survives at UT.
81 The manuscript and typescript were passed to Seltzer's nephew Albert Boni in settlement of a debt and were sold to Urling (Mrs O'Donnell) Iselin in 1936 (letter from Louis Henry Cohn, House of Books, to Eugene Delafield, Jr, 20 April 1936; UT). This letter states that the manuscripts were delivered to Curtis Brown who gave them to Seltzer. They remained in her family's possession until they were sent to be auctioned. Frieda remembered in 1951 that there had been a Part II, 'the second part disappeared', but apparently did not recall who had it (letter to Harry T. Moore, 18 February 1951; Tedlock 302).

Even though Lawrence no longer had the manuscript, he did not forget the novel. He was discouraged about the long 'stop's he had experienced on several novels: he had started *Kangaroo* in May 1922, and hoped to 'be able to finish it: not like *Aaron*, who stuck for two years, and *Mr Noon*, who has been now nearly two years at a full stop'.[82] His last reference to *Mr Noon*, on 6 October 1922 when he was settled in Taos, was in answer to a questionnaire from Mountsier: 'I doubt if I want to finish *Mr Noon*. One day I might.' Lawrence had dangled the prospect of the completed novel before his publishers from summer 1921 to autumn 1922, but his last comment showed no desire to complete it or even to retrieve the missing manuscript.

Lawrence consistently called the novel *Mr Noon* until late December 1920 and early January 1921 when he referred to it as 'Lucky Noon'. He may have been indicating a change in his attitude to his character: the Noon of Part I who had been locked in the 'spoony' phase of love had found his Johanna and experienced mature, lasting love in Part II. In short, his experiences paralleled Lawrence's own when he met Frieda (the 'Johanna' of the novel). Noon had escaped from 'Britten-women, Goddard-women, Emmie-women' to a new birth: 'Gilbert might have had a thousand Emmies, and even a thousand really nice women, and yet never have cracked the womb. It needed the incalculable fight such as he fought' with Johanna.[83] So Noon was 'lucky' in his choice of mate. This new title was soon dropped (although it occurs as an alternative title for Part I in a letter to Secker[84]), perhaps because publishers and agents called it by the original title.

Lawrence gave no reason for his inability to complete the novel. Although *Mr Noon* contained a great deal of very personal material in its second part, this cannot have been the only reason for his hesitation: *Aaron's Rod* and *Kangaroo* both drew on Lawrence's life with Frieda. However, the publication of *Kangaroo* in 1923 precluded Lawrence's re-using the war material, especially in a closely autobiographical form; and *Aaron's Rod*, finished in May 1921, had been set in the immediate post-war period. Rawdon Lilly (the character based on Lawrence) and Aaron Sisson leave England, as Lawrence himself had done, in autumn 1919: the year he had stated *Mr Noon* would end. In *Aaron's Rod*, furthermore, marriage is presented as unsatisfactory because women are too concerned with pleasing themselves sexually, and subsequently turn their attention to their children; the male is always subservient to the female, and the individual therefore looks for (though he does not find) alleviation for his loneliness in love or society. The ways forward proposed are the proper submission of the woman to the man, and of

[82] Letter to Seltzer, 21 June 1922.   [83] See 57:8–9 and 291:39–292:1 below.
[84] *Letters*, iii. 722.

the individual to the superior individual. In *Kangaroo*, the first of Lawrence's 'leadership' novels, the political world of men takes the major role; in *The Plumed Serpent* (finished in the summer of 1925) Lawrence concentrated primarily upon the recreation of a religious society, in which women worship men as gods. Part II of *Mr Noon* thus appears as an elegiac backward glance to Lawrence's old belief in the primacy of the loving relationship between man and woman: it is hard to imagine his wanting to return to a novel based on such a view. He must also have realised that his publishers would object to a novel which he himself had described to them as 'a hair-raiser' and 'a bit startling'; he had regarded the first part as 'innocent', but Seltzer had not even agreed about that. Lawrence did not in fact mention *Mr Noon* in any letter after June 1921 except in response to Mountsier's queries; and not at all after October 1922.

Publication

The revised carbon copy typescript of Part I (hereafter TCCI) prepared by Ruth Wheelock was probably still in Mountsier's possession in February 1923 when Lawrence broke off their business arrangement. Along with a number of other manuscripts it must have been returned to Curtis Brown's New York office as Lawrence requested in September 1924;[85] it was among the manuscripts held by that office when an inventory of Lawrence materials was prepared in 1932, after his death.[86] Thus this copy was available when Frieda and the Curtis Brown agency were considering posthumous publications.

TCCI was among the Lawrence manuscripts in the large London exhibition arranged by John & Edward Bumpus Ltd in 1933,[87] and Laurence Pollinger, of Curtis Brown's London office, made arrangements to have typed copies made of all the unpublished material in the exhibition.[88] At this time a further ribbon copy and at least two carbons were made from TCCI: the carbons survive at University of California at Berkeley (hereafter TCCII) and Viking Press. Pollinger then attempted to get *Mr Noon* Part I, along with other unpublished material, serialised in accordance with Frieda's wishes.[89]

---

[85] Letter to Mountsier, 18 September 1924.
[86] Memorandum from Laurence Pollinger to Raymond Everitt 17 March 1932 and a list of 18 May 1931; UT.
[87] See their catalogue *David Herbert Lawrence: An Exhibition of Original Manuscripts, Corrected Typescripts, Sketches, Needlework Pictures, Photographs, Relics and First Editions* (1933).
[88] Letter from Pollinger to Edward Garnett, 6 April 1933 and memorandum of 23 September 1933; UT.
[89] Letters from Pollinger to P. P. Howe, 14 December 1933 and from Frieda Lawrence to Pollinger, [2 July 1934] and 27 July 1934; UT.

shelter like spiders down the road, ready to pounce on the emerging female flies.

Yes, the congregation was beginning to filter out: the spider-youths who scorned to go to chapel emerged from their lairs. Their cigarette-ends, before only smellable, now became visible. The young 5 dogs waited to snap up their fluffy rabbits.

People oozed through the chapel gateway, expanded into umbrellas, and said, of the rain: "Well I never, it's as hard as ever!"—and called "Goodnight then. So long! See you soon! Too-ra-loo! Keep smiling!—" and so on. Brave young dogs of fellows sniffed across the 10 road. Sanctioned young hussies seized the arm of the "boy," who had his cap *over* his nose and his cigarette *under* his nose, his coat-collar turned up, and they* set off down the road. Trickling dark streams of worshippers ebbed in opposite directions down the rainy night.

Mr Noon was a stranger, and really too old for this business of 15 waiting at the chapel gate. But since he had never got fixed up with a permanent girl, what was he to do? And he had the appointment. So, feeling rather self-conscious, he loitered like a pale ghost* on the edge of the chapel stream.

She did not appear. It suddenly occurred to him that young people 20 were emerging from the darkness of the tiny gateway at the other end of the chapel shrubbery, where there was no light. Sure enough, through that needle's eye* the choir were being threaded out; and he remembered she was in the choir. He strolled along on the pavement opposite. 25

Of course he heard her voice.

"It's fair sickening. You'd think the Lord *liked* rain, for it pours every blessed Sunday. There comes Freddy! Oh Agatha,* you *are* short-sighted, can't see your own boy. Hello Fred."

A tall youth in a bowler hat had stalked up to the two girls, who were 30 dim under the trees on the wet pavement.

"Hello you two! How's things?"

"Oh swimming," came Emmie's voice.*

"You don't mean to say you're on the shelf tonight, Emmie?" sounded the young man's resonant voice. 35

"'Pears as if I am: though it's not the oven shelf* this time, my lad. What?"

"But aren't you expecting anybody?"

"Shut up.—Well, Goodnight Agatha—see you Wednesday. Goodnight Freddy. Lovely night for ducks." 40

"Ay, an' tad-poles,"* came Freddy's guffaw. "So long."

She had caught sight of Gilbert on the opposite pavement, and came prancing across the muddy road to him, saying in a guarded voice:

5 "Hello! Thought you hadn't come."

"Yes, I'm here."

"Hold on a minute."

She darted from him and went to speak to another girl. In a moment she was back at his side.

10 "Come on," she said. "I don't want our Dad to see me. I just said to our Sis I was going to Hackett's* for a book. Come on."

She tripped swiftly along the pavement. She was a little thing, in a mackintosh and a black velvet cap. A lamp's light showed her escaping fair hair, which curled more in the wet. She carried an umbrella.

15 "Coming under?" she said to him, half raking him in with the umbrella. He avoided her.

"No. I don't want it all down my neck."

"All right. Stop where you are.—Goodness, aren't we late! I thought father Dixon was never going to dry up. Have you been waiting long?"

20 "No. I went to Lewie Goddard's."

"Did you! Isn't he soft? But I like Lewie."

They passed along the pavement for two hundred yards, till they came to the big dark windows of the Co-operative Stores.* In the midst of the range of dark buildings was a great closed doorway, where

25 on weekdays the drays entered to the yard and the storehouse.

Emmie put down her umbrella, and glanced along the road.

"Half a tick!" she said.

She went to the big doors, and pushed her finger through a round hole. A latch clicked, and she opened a sort of little wicket in the big

30 doors. It was left open for the bakers.

"Come on," she said.

And stepping through, she disappeared in the darkness. He stepped after her, and she closed the door behind him.

"All right here," she whispered, drawing him on.

35 He found himself in the wide passage or archway between the two departments of the stores, where the vans unloaded. Beyond was rainy darkness, brilliant lights of a smallish building in the near distance down the yard, lights which emanated and revealed ghosts of old packing cases and crates in the yard's chaos. Inside the passage it was

40 very dark.

Emmie piloted him to the further end, then she climbed a step into a doorway recess.

"Come up," she said, tugging his arm.

He came up, and they stowed themselves in the doorway recess, for the spoon.

He realised, whilst she was stuffing her velvet cap in her pocket, that there were other couples in the entry—he became aware of muffled, small sounds, and then of bits of paleness and deeper darkness in the dark corners and doorway recesses. They were not alone in their spooning, he and Emmie. Lucky they had found an empty corner. He liked the invisible other presences, with their faint, ruffling sounds. The outside light from the street-lamps showed faintly under the great doors, there was a continuous echo of passing feet. Away in the yard, the wind blew the rain, and sometimes the broken packing cases rattled hollowly, and sometimes a wet puff caught him and Emmie. There were sounds from the brilliantly-lighted bakery in the small distance.

Emmie, in her wet mackintosh, cuddled into his arms. He was famous as a spooner, and she was famous as a sport. They had known each other, off and on, for years. She was a school-teacher, three years his junior; he had seen her first at the Pupil Teacher's Centre.* Both having a sort of reputation to keep up, they were a little bit excited.

A small, wriggling little thing, she nestled up to him in the darkness, and felt his warm breath on her wet-frizzy hair. She gave a convulsive little movement, and subsided in his embrace. He was slowly, softly kissing her, with prefatory kisses. Yes, his reputation as a spoon would not belie him. He had lovely lips for kissing: soft, hardly touching you, and yet melting you. She quivered with epicurean anticipation.

As a matter of fact, he had that pouting mouth which is shown in Shelley's early portraits,* and of which the poet, apparently, was rather proud.

He was continually touching her brow with his mouth, then lifting his face sharply, as a horse does when flies tease it, putting aside her rainy, fine bits of hair. Soft, soft came his mouth towards her brow, then quick he switched his face, as the springy curls tickled him.

"Half a mo,"* she said suddenly.

She unfastened his wet overcoat, and thrust her hands under his warm jacket. He likewise unfastened her mackintosh, and held her warm and tender. Then his kisses began again, wandering along the roots of her hair, on her forehead, his mouth slowly moving forward in

a browsing kind of fashion. She sighed with happiness, and seemed to
melt nearer and nearer to him. He settled her in his arms, whilst she
clung dreamily to the warmth of his shoulders, like a drowsy fly on the
November window-pane.

5   Since the spoon is one of the essential mysteries of modern love,
particularly English modern love, let us clasp our hands before its
grail-like effulgence.* For although all readers belonging to the
upper classes; and what reader *doesn't* belong to the upper classes;
will* deny any acquaintance with any spoon but the metallic object,
10 we regret to have to implicate the whole of the English race, from
princes downwards, in the mystic business.

Dear reader, have we not all left off believing in positive evil? And
therefore is it not true that the seducer, invaluable to fiction, is dead?
The seducer and the innocent maid are no more. We live in better
15 days.

There are only spooners now, a worldful of spoons. Those wicked
young society people, those fast young aristocrats, ah, how soft as butter
their souls are really, tender as melted butter their sinfulness, in our
improved age. Don't talk of lust, it isn't fair. How can such creamy
20 feelings be lustful! And those Oxfordly young men with their chorus
girls—ah God, how wistful their hearts and pure their faces,
really!—not to speak of their minds. Then look at young colliers and
factory lasses, they fairly reek with proper sentiment.

It doesn't matter what you do—only how you do it.—Isn't that the
25 sincerest of modern maxims?—And don't we all do it nicely and *con
molto espressione?** You know we do. So little grossness nowadays,
and so much dear reciprocal old-beaniness!* How can there be
any real wrong in it? Old wives tales! There is no wrong in it. We are all
so perfectly sweet about it all, and on such a sympathetic plane.

30   Why bother about spades being spades* any more? It isn't the
point. Adam no more delves than Eve spins, in our day. Nous avons
changé tout cela.* Call a spoon a spoon if you like. But don't drag
in garden implements. It's almost as bad as the Greeks with their horrid
plough metaphor.

35   Ah, dear reader, you don't need me to tell you how to sip love with a
spoon, to get the juice out of it. You know well enough. But you will be
obliged to me, I am sure, if I pull down that weary old scarecrow of a
dark designing seducer, and the alpaca bogey of lust. There is no harm
in us any more, is there now? Our ways are so improved: so
40 spiritualised, really. What harm is there in a bit of a spoon? And if it

goes rather far: even very far: well, what by that! As we said before, it depends *how* you go, not where you go. And there is nothing *low* about our goings, even if we go to great lengths. A spoon isn't a spade, thank goodness. As for a plough—don't mention it. No, let us keep the spoon of England bright, between us.* 5

Mr Noon was a first-rate spoon—the rhyme is unfortunate, though in truth, to be a first-rate spoon a man must be something of a poet. With his mouth he softly moved back the hair from her brow, in slow, dreamy movements, most faintly touching her forehead with the red of his lips, hardly perceptible, and then drawing aside her hair with his 10 firmer mouth, slowly, with a long movement. She thrilled delicately, softly tuning up, in the dim, continuous, negligent caress. Innumerable pleasant flushes passed along her arms and breasts, melting her into a sweet ripeness.

Let us mention that this melting and ripening capacity is one of the 15 first qualities for a good modern daughter of Venus, a perfect sweetness in a love-making girl, the affectionate comradeship of a dear girl* deepening to a voluptuous enveloping warmth, a bath for the soft Narcissus, into which he slips with voluptuous innocence.

His mouth wandered, wandered, almost touched her ear. She felt 20 the first deep flame run over her. But no—he went away again: over her brow, through the sharp roughness of her brows, to her eyes. He closed her eyes, he kissed her eyes shut. She felt her eyes closing, closing, she felt herself falling, falling, as one falls asleep. Only she was falling deeper, deeper than sleep. He was kissing her eyes slowly, 25 drowsily, deeply, soft, deep, deep kisses. And she was sinking backward, and swaying, sinking deep, deep, into the depths beyond vision: and swaying, swaying, as a stone sways as it sinks through deep water. And it was delicious: she knew how delicious it was. She was sunk below vision, she swayed suspended in the depths, like a stone that can 30 sink no more.

He was kissing her, she hardly knew where. But in her depths she quivered anew, for a new leap, or a deeper plunge. He had found the soft down that lay back beyond her cheeks, near the roots of her ears. And his mouth stirred it delicately, as infernal angels stir the fires with 35 glass rods, or a dog on the scent stirs the grass till the game starts from cover.

A little shudder ran through her, and she seemed to leap nearer to him, and then to melt in a new fusion. Slowly, slowly she was fusing once more, deeper and deeper, enveloping him all the while with her 40

arms as if she were some iridescent sphere of flame half-enclosing him:
a sort of Watts picture.*

A deep pulse beat, a pulse of expectation. She was waiting, waiting
for him to kiss her ears. Ah, how she waited for it! Only that. Only let
5 him kiss her ears, and it was a consummation.

But no! He had left her, and wandered away to the soft little kiss-
curls in the nape of her neck: the soft, warm, sweet little nape of her
neck. His warm breath was among the most delicate fibrils of her hair.
She contracted with a sharp convulsion, like tickling. Delicious thrills
10 ran down her spine, before he gave her the full assurance, and kissed
her soft, deep, full among the fine curls central in the nape of her neck.
She seemed to be lifted into the air as a bit of paper lifts itself up to a
piece of warm amber.* Her hands fluttered, fluttered on his
shoulders, she was rising up on the air like Simon Magus.* Let us
15 hope Mr Noon will not let her down too sharp.

No! No! Even as she rose in the air she felt his breath running warm
at the gates of her ears. Her lips came apart, she panted with acute
anticipation. Ah!—Ah!—and softly came his full, fathomless kiss,
softly her ear was quenched in darkness. He took the small, fine
20 contours subtly between his lips, he closed deeper, and with a second
reeling swoon she reeled down again and fell, fell through a deeper,
darker sea. Depth doubled on depth, darkness on darkness. She had
sunk back to the root-stream, beyond sight and hearing.

Now surely it was finished. Occultists tell us that hearing is the most
25 radical of all the senses: that, at a crisis, all sensation can be summed up
in the perfected sensation of sound. Surely then it was accomplished.
At each new phase she felt she had melted, had sunk to the very
bottom. And every time, oh bliss of it, came a new crisis, and she
swooned downwards, down a deeper depth, to a new, fathomless,
30 oscillating rest. Oscillating at the deeps of intoxication, as now.

Yet still there was a tiny core of unquenched desire. She seemed to
melt and become tinier: and yet she swung in an immeasurable, hungry
rhythm, like a meteorite that has fallen through worlds of space, yet still
swings, not yet burnt out, caught in some unstable equilibrium between
35 the forces of the planets. So she hung and quivered in immeasurable
space.

For sometimes it seemed to her drunken consciousness that she was
high, high in space, yet not beyond all worlds, the net of the stars. And
sometimes it seemed she was sunk, sunk to immeasurable depths, yet
40 not quite to extinction.

His mouth was coming slowly nearer to her mouth; and yet not approaching. Approaching without disclosing its direction. Loitering, circumventing, and then suddenly taking the breath from her nostrils. For a second she died in the strange sweetness and anguish of suffocation. He had closed her nostrils for ever with a kiss, and she was sleeping, dying in sweet fathomless insentience. Death, and the before-birth sleep.

Yet, not quite. Even now, not quite. One spark persisted and waited in her. Frail little breaths came through her parted lips. It was the brink of ecstasy and extinction. She cleaved to him beyond measure, as if she would reach beyond herself. With a sudden lacerating motion she tore her face from his, aside.* She held it back, her mouth unclosed. And obedient down came his mouth on her unclosed mouth, darkness closed on darkness, so she melted completely, fused, and was gone.

She sank, sank with him, right away. Or rising, he lifted her into the oneness with him, up, up, and beyond, into the infinite. It seemed to him she was the heavier, rounded breath which he enwreathed in the perfected bubble flame of himself. So they floated as a perfect bubble, beyond the reach even of space. Beyond height and depth, beyond gravitation. Out in the beyond, suspended in the perfection.

Who knows if they breathed, if they lived!

But all the time, of course, each of them had a secondary mundane consciousness.* Each of them was aware of the entry, the other spooners, and the passers-by outside. Each of them attended minutely when one pair of spooners crept through the gap in the big doors, to go home. They were all there, mark you. None of your bestial loss of faculties.

—We have risen to great heights, dear reader, and sunk to great depths. Yet we have hardly fathomed the heights and depths of the spoon in the Co-op. entry. Don't you wish you were as good at it as Noon and Emmie? Practise then: and you too may swing suspended* in the heights, or depths, of infinity, like the popular picture we used to see over the railway bookstalls, winged spooners mid-heaven in the blue ether. Ah, we are all so clean, nowadays: fine clean young men, infinitely spoony, and clean young spoony maidens to match. Nothing earthy, not we. All in mid-air, our goings on.*

Till her mouth fell away, and her head fell aside. He turned his face aside from her, and they breathed their slow, inert breaths apart. They kept their faces apart from each other. And gradually conscious sight returned into the open mirrors of her eyes, gradually wakeful discrimi-

nation busied itself in the re-echoing cavities of her ears. Noises which
she had heard all the time, she now admitted into her audience.
Gradually. It could not be done, or should not be done, all in a smack.

—Ah, the spoon, the perfect spoon! In its mystic bowl all men are
5   one, and so are all women. Champagne and shoulders, poetry and long
scarves, loftiness, altruism, souls, hard work, conscience, sacrifice, all
fuse into perfect oneness in the spoon. All Whitman's Songs of Himself
and Other People* lie in the hollow of a spoon. If you seek the
Infinite and the Nirvana, look not to death nor the after-life, nor yet to
10 pure abstraction: but into the hollow spoon.*

Gilbert was staring down the opposite direction under lifted,
Mephistophelian brows. And seeing, of course, the ghostly chaos of
packing cases in the rain, and the strong beams from the bakery
windows.

15 The small sound of church chimes in the night! Emmie broke away
from him abruptly.

"I s'll have to be going. I s'll cop it from my Dad."

He lost his balance and stepped down from the step of the doorway
embrasure with a jerk, cramped. He felt rather vague and uncomfort-
20 able.

She was pushing at her hair, and pulling her cap on. There was a
flutter and rustle of her mackintosh. She stepped down from the step,
and shook herself. He would move towards the door.

"My gamp!" she said quickly, snatching the article out of a corner in
25 the recess. Then briskly she went forward to the dark wall of the doors.
The little round hole showed. In an instant he saw a framed picture of
wet pavements and passers-by, and a scarlet* cart, which he knew
carried the mail, splashing phantom through the mud.

Ah, dear reader, I hope you are not feeling horribly superior. You
30 would never call an umbrella a brolly, much less a gamp.* And you
have never so much as seen a Co-op. entry. But don't on this small
account sniff at Emmie. No, in that notorious hour when a woman is
alone with her own heart, really enjoying herself, ask yourself if your
spoon is brighter than Emmie's, if your spooner is better than Gilbert.
35 Nay, if you prefer *love* and *lover*, say love and lover to yourself. It all
amounts to the same. But in communion with your naked heart, say
whether you have reached Gilbertian heights and Emmelian profundi-
ties of the human kiss—or whether you have something to learn even
from our poor pair.*

Chapter III.

Gilbert Licks the Spoon.

Let none complain that I pry indecently into the privacies of the spoon. A spoon is an open mirror, necessarily a public concern.* I do but walk down the public road, past the Co-op. entry, and see Emmie and Mr Noon stepping guiltlessly forth through the aperture in the big doors, as integral a part of the Sunday night as is the darkness itself, or me in my after-service expansion of soul; and since all is told to me, in the innocent act of slipping through the Co-op. aperture, I tell all again including the innocence.*

Neither let the experts and raffinés* of the spoon object that my account is but the bare outline of what actually is. I insist that this is the summary and essence of all that is above-board* in spooning. There are variations on the spoon. There are tricks, dear reader. In the old days wicked black silk bed-sheets, for example. Ah, but mere interlarded tricks. Different seasoning, the soup is the same. I have heard too of Frenchy, and even of* Neapolitan spooning, which I should not like to speak of from hearsay. There are all kinds of kissings. Every nation, every city, every individual introduces a special and individual touch. There are dodges and peculiarities which I leave to experience and to other novelists. I concern myself with the essential English kiss, within the spoon. Yes, and with the basis of the essential: in short,* the radical Co-op. entry spoon of the common people, that has neither champagne and shoulders, nor yet cocktails and *fard** to embellish it and to obscure its pure simplicity. I am no dealer in abnormalities. Far from it.* I take the thing at its best, as one should. I speak of the spoon pure and simple, the spoon of our clean-minded age, from which we sip love's limpidest sweets. Ah infinite spoon-moments! dear spoon-memories!*

Mr Noon, however, was in no such complacent mood as ours.

"It's not raining so much, I shan't bother with the brolly," said Emmie, turning her Noon-kissed face to the dim moist heavens. "That was half-past I heard strike. I s'll be in a row with our Dad if I don't hop it."

She spoke rather breathlessly as she tripped along.

"Why what's the matter with *him?*" asked Gilbert irritably, turning traitor to the spoon-grail in the very moment when he had quaffed his dose.*

"Because he's a wire-whiskered nuisance, and I've got to be in by
5   quarter to ten,* because he's on night duty."

"What would he do if you weren't in by quarter to ten?"

"Ay, *you* ask me! Make my life a blooming hell.—Oh!—" and she stopped for a second in the road—"*now* I haven't got a book, and I told our Sis I was calling for one. Little fool! Little fool I am! *Drat*!" And she
10   stamped her foot. "You haven't got a book on you? He's sure to twig. Oh what a bally* nuisance!"

Gilbert fortunately had in his pocket a volume on Conic Sections, and this Emmie at once appropriated, hugging it under her arm.

She ran tripping forward, Gilbert strode beside her. She lived down in
15   the valley, about a mile out of Woodhouse. She was uneasy now because of her father, and had almost forgotten Mr Noon, at her side.

He, however, had not forgotten her. A black vindictiveness had come over him.*

"What time does your father go to work?" he asked. He knew that Mr
20   Bostock had a job on the railway.

"Ten. He's on duty at ten: and it takes him quarter of an hour to get there, or he says so. It would take me about five minutes. Like him to make a mountain of it."

"Come out a bit after he's gone," suggested Gilbert.
25   "Go on!"* said Emmie, with suggestive sharpness.

Now this was not the first of Emmie's spoons—even with Gilbert. And she was quite prepared for after-spoon developments—even naughty ones. So that when she said "Go on," she was merely non-committal.
30   She knew that young men would frequently follow up a nice innocent lovely spoon with a certain half-tiresome persistence in going further. Half-tiresome, because it is the last step which *may* cost. And yet rather wickedly nice, you know. Remember that Emmie is a sport, and that in defiance of fathers and stone tablets there is also bliss. And moreover the
35   man who is a true and faithful spoon makes this ultimate so dear, such a last clean sweep in sympathy! Ah, talk not of grossness in this soft and sympathising conjunction! Don't you agree, dear reader?*

"You'll come, won't you?" said Gilbert.

"Let's see how the land lies, first," she replied. "You needn't wait if I
40   don't come out and cooey."

By Cooey she meant call a soft, lurking *Coo-ee*! to him.

Gilbert was behaving in the accepted way—or one of the ways—of after-spoon, and she took no alarm. He was quiet, and seemed persuasive. His silence came suggestive and rather pleading* to her, as they hurried down the hill. She was a sport—and she liked a man who could come on: one who pressed fearless forward, a Galahad of sentiment, to the bitter end. Bitter! Well, bitter-sweet. Oh gentle joust of ultimate sentiment, oh last sweet throw of love, wherein we fall, spoon-overthrown! Shall I be Minnesinger* of the spoon?

But alas, there is a fly in the ointment. There is a snake in the grass. It is in Gilbert's mood. Alas, poor Emmie. She is mistaken about his soft, sweet, sinful coming-on. Instead of being in the melting stage, just ready to melt right down with her, the final fuse within the spoon, he is horrid. Ah, in the last coming on, how gentle is the Galahad of kisses, how subtle his encroachment to the goal! But Gilbert was a snake in the grass.* He was irritable, in a temper, and would not let her go though he did not really want her. Why he was in a temper, and why he hated her he did not know. Doubtful if he ever knew his own state of feeling. Beware, gentle reader! For if in the course of soft and kissy love you once get out of the melting spoon-mood, there is hell to pay, both for you and for her.

Emmie's garden gate opened from a little path between two hedges that led from the high-road between cottage gardens to the field stile. The two arrived at the bottom of the hill and crossed the road to where the path, called a twitchel,* opened between thick hedges.

"Don't come down the twitchel," she said to him in a low tone. "I'll bet he's watching.—If I can slip out when he's gone I shall cooey. Au revoy."

She disappeared between the dark hedges of the twitchel, and shortly he heard her gate clash. He loitered about again, and was in a temper because he was kept waiting. He was in a rage with himself, so turned his wrath against circumstances.*

He was in a rage. He did really like women—so he put it to himself. There was nothing he liked better than to have one in his arms—his own phraseology again. And Emmie was a regular little sport, a regular little sport. He admired her. And he fidgetted about in a temper waiting for her. Black devils frisked in his veins, and pricked him with their barbed tails. He was full of little devils. Alas, he had fallen from the white election of the spoon.* He plunged into the twitchel, saw the row of cottages, of which hers was the end one; saw the lighted window, heard voices; heard a man's voice from the back premises, from the back door, and plunged on. He clambered over the stile and went forward down the black, muddy field-path towards the canals. No good

5 going very far, however.

He heard a step behind him, and listened. Her father,* ten to one. He loitered on the dark, open field. The man came nearer. Glancing round, Gilbert saw the dark whiskers on the pallid face, and sent out a wave of hatred. He loitered whilst her father strode past him,

10 on into the night. Then he turned back towards the cottage.

He had been in a similar situation more than once. Nay, for the young fellows of the colliery-places like Whetstone and Woodhouse, for the young bloods who had a bit of dash of warmth about them, the situation was almost traditional. Bostock, Emmie's father, had done the

15 same, and worse, many a time in his day. So had old Noon, Gilbert's father. Gilbert was but keeping up a human* tradition. And yet he was in a temper about it. He sort of felt himself in a ready-made circumstance, going through a ready-made act, and he was thoroughly annoyed with everything. Yes, he was, in Woodhouse phraseology, a

20 womaniser: and he knew it: and he meant to be a womaniser. So why make any bones about his present situation? But his temper mounted. Yes, he *would* be a womaniser. He prided himself on it. Wasn't "Down Among the Dead Men" one of his favourite songs? Fine tune too.

"And may Confusion still pursue
25   The senseless woman-hating crew————"*

Alas, he would be a womaniser. Yet he kicked with fury against the universal spoon. He fought like a fly in oil.*

Meanwhile Emmie indoors was going through her own little act. She enjoyed play-acting. She had lied like a little trooper to her father,*

30 having a sulky innocence-suspected look which he exacted, and a pert tongue which he threatened with extraction. For Alf Bostock had been a womaniser both before and after his marriage to his mild, lax Jinny: and him a man with a swarm of little children. She had no rosy time of it. Till he got kicked out of his job; and suddenly became religious, with

35 all the ferocity of an old trotter. So he proceeded to put his children through the paces of narrow-pathdom.* His poor Jinny was always wax, but his own off-spring tended to bristle. And Emmie, who was perhaps his favourite—a pretty, taking, sharp-answering little thing,

with a way of her own—she was his special enemy as she grew up. A roaming bitch, he called her in his wrath. And it was curiously appropriate, for she had the alert, inquisitive, tail-in-the-air appearance of a bitch who has run away and finds the world an adventure, as she tripped the streets. 5

Once the tyrant was gone, Emmie was quite equal to any occasion. She had retreated upstairs, as if to bed, before his departure. Now down she came again.

"Hey, our mother, I'll have my supper now in peace," she said, taking a knife and going into the pantry for bread and cheese and cake. 10

"There's a bit of apple-pie if you'd like it," said her indulgent, easy mother.

Emmie walked out with the pie-dish, and sat scraping it with a spoon.

"I've got my lessons to do yet," she said cheerfully. 15

"Be ashamed," said her mother. "Last minute."

"Make use of the fag-ends of time," said Emmie.

"Ay, fag-ends," said her mother.

Emmie spread her books on the table under the lamp, to write the compulsory notes for the morrow's lessons. She pulled her hair untidy 20 on her brow as she did so.

"Go to bed, Mother Bostock," she said to her mother. "Don't sit dropping off in that chair. How do you think anybody can make notes, when they have to watch for your head dropping on to the floor. Get up. Go on." 25

"Ay," said her mother amiably. "How long shall you be?"

"About twenty minutes I should think. Go on now—go to bed. You know you'll get a crick in your neck."

"Ay, you'd like to think so," said her mother, weakly rising and obeying. "I shall listen for you, now," she added from the foot of the 30 stairs.

"Go on—I shan't be a minute if you leave me in peace."

And Mrs Bostock slowly mounted the creaky stairs. Emmie scribbled away in her flighty fashion for some time, pausing occasionally to listen. At length she shut her books and stretched her arms. Then with 35 startling suddenness she blew out the lamp. After which she stood in the darkness and listened.

All seemed quiet. She slipped to the back door and pushed away the bar. Closing the door behind her, she sauntered down the front path with all her leisurely assurance and bravado. The sense of danger was 40

salt to her. The rain was now only very slight. Glancing over the hedge
on the left, she could see, through the clearing darkness, the far-off
lamps of the station and the junction sidings where her father would by
now be safely occupied. So much for him.

5   She reached the gate and peered down the dark twitchel.

"Coo-ee!" she called, very softly.

And the dark shadow of Gilbert was approaching.

"Think I was never coming?" she said.

"I wondered," he answered.

10   They stood for a moment with the gate between them.

"How are you feeling?" she asked.

"All right. Coming out?"

"No, you come in." And she opened the gate for him to enter the
dark garden.

15   "Ma's put her light out. Sleeping the sleep of the nagged* by
now, I bet. My Dad's gone."

"I'm not going in the house," said Gilbert suspiciously.

"Nobody asked you."

She led him down the little winding side-path, in the wintry garden,
20   between the currant bushes, to a little greenhouse. The door was
locked, but the key was on the nail. She knew the greenhouse of old. It
was pretty small, but she knew how to move the plants and arrange
things. Luckily there were not many plants to move.

"Hold on a bit," she whispered to Gilbert, who hung in the doorway
25   whilst she made a place.

Meanwhile, we are sorry to say, the enemy was on their tracks. Alf
Bostock should not have been a railwayman, but a policeman. Now that
he was a reformed character, the policeman in him had no rest. Before
Emmie arrived home, at a quarter to ten, he had been in the back yard
30   listening for her. He had heard her voice speaking to Mr Noon, though
he had not caught what she said. But he had smelled a rat. And he was
a very keen rat-catcher these days.

Therefore he did nothing that could betray his suspicions, and he set
off to work a few minutes earlier than he need in order that he might
35   turn back and do a bit of spying. When he passed the more-than-
doubtful figure of Mr Noon in the field the smell of the rat was very hot
in his nostrils. Like the wicked, he exulted, and said Ha—Ha!* He
let Gilbert return towards the cottage.

And then the reformed parent swerved from his way to his work,
40   made a bend over the sodden field in the black darkness, and came to

the big hedge at the bottom of his garden, near the summer-house. There, among the old nettle-stalks, he crouched and watched. He heard Gilbert champing in the twitchel and away on the high-road, and prepared the net for the bird. He saw his wife's candle go upstairs, and at once supposed that she, poor thing, was conniving at her daughter's 5 shame. He saw his wife's candle go out—heard Mr Gilbert champ and chafe and light a pipe—and at last, Ah-ha!—saw the kitchen go suddenly dark.

Yes, there she was, the little bitch, prancing her shadowy, leisurely way towards the gate, and staring at the hedge where he crouched as if 10 she too could smell a rat. He ducked low, and watched.

"Coo-ee!"

He heard it, and his veins tingled. He'd give her *Coo-ee*, else his name wasn't Alfred.

Up comes the Johnny to the gate. Who could he be? But wait a bit. 15 Wait a bit. He'd follow soon and find out.

Hush! He strained his ears in vain to hear what they were murmuring. He rose to his feet, and cracked a stick. He would stalk them. Then all at once he ducked again under the hedge. Inside the garden, they were coming towards him. His nerves were keen on the 20 alert, to gather if they had heard him.

But they, poor darlings, were all unsuspecting. Alf Bostock crouched on his heels. His greenhouse! His little glass-house. She was opening the door with the key. Well of all the evil, low little bitches, if she wasn't a sly one. For a second his mind reverted to his own youthful 25 escapades, and the girls he despised so much for escapading with him. For it is a peculiarity of his type, that the more they run after sin, the more contempt they feel for their partner in sinning, the more insufferably superior they rise in their own esteem. Till nowadays, he would spoon with nobody but his Saviour. In religion he was still oh, so 30 spoony. So spoony, listening to the sermon, so spoony saying his prayers. Ah, such relish! With women he had always been rather gross. No wonder he hated Emmie for bringing it home to him again, now that his higher nature had triumphed.*

He'd kill her. He'd flay her. He'd torture her. Wouldn't he! My word 35 wouldn't he! What? Was she going to shame him, her father? Was he going to be shamed and disgraced by her.* His indignation rose to an inquisitorial pitch. At the thought of the shame and disgrace *he* might incur through her, he could have burnt her at the stake cheerfully, over a slow fire. *Him* to be shamed and disgraced by a 40

daughter of his! Was anything on earth more monstrous? The strumpet. The bitch. Hark at her clicking the flower-pots, shifting the plants. He'd give her shift the plants. He'd show her. He longed to torture her. Back went his mind over past events. Now he knew. Now he knew how
5 the pink primulas had been smashed and re-potted before he got home. Now he knew a thousand things. If his daughter had been the Whore of Babylon* herself her father could not have painted her with a more lurid striping of sin. She was a marvel of lust and degradation, and defamation of *his* fair repute. But he'd show her. He'd show her.
10   They had gone into the greenhouse and shut the door on themselves. Well and good—they had fastened themselves in their own trap. He straightened his creaking knees and drew himself upright. He was cold, damp, and cramped: and all this added venom to his malignancy.
       Lurching awkwardly, he shambled along the grass to the stile,
15 climbed, and went along the twitchel to his own gate. If it cost him his job once more, he'd settle this little game. *Wouldn't* he just. He'd show them. He'd show them.
       He was in such a rage, as he drew near the greenhouse, he went so slowly, on tiptoe, that he seemed to emanate in hate, rather than to walk
20 to the threshold of the poor little place. He got there, and stood still. He stood evilly and malignantly still, and listened: listened, with all his 'cute attention and shameful old knowledge.
       Poor Emmie. She thought she'd got a demon inside the greenhouse: she little suspected a devil outside. Gilbert did not make her happy any
25 more. Instead of being nice and soft and spoony, and pleasant in his coming on, he was rough and hard. She was startled, jarred in her rather melty mood. She hadn't bargained for this. If she had not possessed a rather catty courage, she would have cried out. But her soul rose against him, and she hated him.
30   And then, at an awful moment, the door slowly opened, and she gave an awful, stifled yell.
       "What's going on in there?" came a beastly, policeman's voice.
       Emmie heard it, and seemed to fall for a moment into a fit, paralysed. Gilbert was arrested, perfectly still.
35   "You're coming out there, aren't you?" said the voice. "Come on, let's see who you are."
       And there was a little rattling sound of a box of matches. He was going to strike a light. Emmie was making a funny little sound, as if she had fallen into icy water. Gilbert, on his knees, turned. He saw the
40 stooping figure, stooping policeman-like in the doorway, and black rage

burst his head like a bomb. He crouched and leapt like a beast, but aimed too high, and only caught the cap and hair of his assailant. The two men went with a crash down upon a gooseberry bush.

Emmie had leaped to her feet with another hoarse cry. The men were a confused heap. She heard gurgling curses from her father. She 5 gave a third, raven-like cry, and sped straight down the garden, through the gate, and away into the night.

A window had opened, and a frightened voice was saying:

"What's amiss? Who is it? Is it you Emmie? Who is it?"

Children's voices were calling "Mother! Mother!" 10

Gilbert had risen to his feet, but the other man clung after him, determined not to let him go, frenzied like some lurking creature of prey. In a convulsion of revolt, Gilbert flung the gripping horror from him, madly: flung himself free, and turned blindly to escape. He was through the gate, down the twitchel and over the stile in one moment, 15 making for the dark country, whereas Emmie had made for the lights of Woodhouse.

The disorder of his clothing impeded his running. He heard the other man rushing to the stile. He turned, in the darkness of the open field, and said loudly: 20

"Come on, and I'll kill you."

By the sound of his voice, he probably would have done so.

Women and children were screaming from the house.

The other man thought better of it, and turned back. Gilbert, standing there on the defensive, adjusted himself and waited. No one 25 came. He walked away into the night. He had lost his cap in the fray.

Chapter IV.

Aphrodite and the Cow.*

During the week that followed, Gilbert heard nothing of Emmie or of the Sunday-night affair. He was busy at Haysfall during the day, and during some of the evenings. He might have made an opportunity for running over to Woodhouse: but he didn't.

Sunday came again: a fine day for once, dim-blue and wintry. Gilbert looked out of his window upon it when he got up, and after breakfast went out into the woodyard. Tall yellow timbers reared up into the sky, leaning to one another and crossing in the air. Planks, correctly arranged in squares, with a space between each plank, stood seasoning. In the shed were planks and poles in solid piles. Near a chopping-block was a pile of split faggots, while huge trunks of trees, oak and elm, stripped of branches, lay aside like swathed corpses. Gilbert noticed the star-shaped cracks that ran from the centres of the trunk-bottoms, thought of the plant-histology, and in a dim sort of way calculated the combination of forces that had brought about the fissures. He ran his finger over a heavy-grained oak surface, and to him it was an exquisite pleasure, vibrating in his veins like music, to realise the flexible but grandly-based rhythm in the morphological structure of the tree, right from the root-tip through the sound trunk, right out to a leaf-tip: wonderful concatenation and association of cells, incalculable and yet so genetic in their rhythm, unfolding the vast unsymmetrical symmetry of the tree. What he loved so much in plant morphology was, that given a fixed mathematical basis, the final evolution was so incalculable. It pleased him to trace inherent individual qualities in each separate organic growth, qualities which were over and above the fixed qualities belonging to the genus and the species, and which could not really be derived by a chain of evolutionary cause-and-effect. Could they? Could the individual peculiarities all derive from the chain of cause and effect? He mused abstractedly. The question piqued him. He had almost decided not. The one little element of individuality, not attributable to any cause, fascinated him always in plants and trees. He longed to make quite sure of it. He longed to feel it musically. In plants it seemed to him so profoundly suggestive, the odd aloneness* of

34

the separate self in each specimen. He longed to hear the new note of
this in music. But his longing was vague, far removed from the
intensity of action.

He dawdled the morning away, with his pipe. There were things he
ought to do. But he could not begin. He sat in the kitchen by the fire,   5
glancing over the large pages of *Lloyd's Weekly*,* the lurid Sunday
paper, whilst the woman made pies and an apple dumpling, and
continually pushed past him to the oven: whilst the saucepans bubbled
and sent off first a smell of pudding-cloth, then a scent of vegetable
steam: whilst the meat sizzled in the oven, and his father came and   10
went, fidgetty, and drank a glass of beer between-whiles.

Between father and son there was not much correspondence. The
old man was mean, and he kept his heart also to himself. He looked
with a jealous eye on his son, half-scorning him because he did no
real work, nothing in the woodyard, for example, and in the other half   15
admiring him for being so clever. At the bottom he was domineeringly
gratified* to have the lad at home, though he found every manner
of fault with him. His only other child, a girl, a woman now, was
married with children of her own, and because she needed a little
more money, the old man was secretly determined to leave all to   20
Gilbert.

A few instincts Gilbert had of a gentleman so-called. He could not
bear to sit down to dinner unshaven and with no collar on, as his
father did. So, judging from the smell of the sirloin that it was nearly
done, he went upstairs to his room and shaved and dressed. His   25
bedroom was bare and tidy. There was not a picture, not a book.
From the window he looked down on the woodyard. But next to his
bedroom was a sort of study, with many books, and a piano, a violin
and music-stand, piles and sheets of music. This room too was tidy
and clean, though Gilbert tidied and cleaned it all himself.   30

Being dressed, he went and touched his violin: but he did not want
to play. He turned over a sheet of music: but did not want to look at
it. He waited for the woman to call him to dinner.

After dinner, he had still his mind to make up. He went out to his
motor-cycle and got it ready. He went indoors and put on his rubbers.   35
He pushed off, and was running noiselessly down Whetstone's steep
main street, past tram-cars and saunterers, before he knew where he
was going.

And then, after all, he turned towards Woodhouse. In half an hour
he was there, and had put up his cycle. Coming out brushed and tidy   40

on to the Knarborough Road, he hesitated which way to turn. Therefore he did not turn, but walked forward.

And whom should he see but Patty Goddard walking down the rather empty street: it was too soon for the afternoon chapel people, and the men were having a last drink before half-past two. Patty, in a dark, wine-coloured coat ånd skirt and dark silk hat, with grey gloves and very carefully-chosen shoes, walking by herself with her pale, full, ivory face towards the afternoon sun! She smiled across the road to him, and nodded. He strode over to her.

"Oh—! I thought you might come this afternoon or evening," she said, and he felt* a touch of significance in her voice, and was uncomfortable.

"Is Lewie there?" he asked, jerking his head in the direction of the house.

"No. He's gone to an I. L. P.* meeting in Knarborough. I expect him back about six. Did you want him?"

Again her dark eyes seemed to glance up at him with a certain mocking spite.

"No—no," said Gilbert.

"Another appointment, perhaps?" smiled Patty maliciously.

"No, I haven't. I've got nothing to do."

"Oh well then, if you'd care to take a walk. I'm just enjoying the sun while it lasts."

"Yes, if you don't mind."

And he took his place at her side. She was pleased. But today her pleasure was qualified, though she kept the qualification a secret. She made no more mention of the previous Sunday, and the conversation between them was rather lame.

They descended the hill in the pleasant afternoon, and came to the damp, mossy old park wall, under the trees. Patty stopped before the unimposing, wooden park gate.

"I thought I'd walk across the park,"* she said. "Lewie has managed to get the key."

So Gilbert opened the gate, and they walked along the pink-coloured drive, between the greenish winter grass. The old hall was shut up, everywhere seemed abandoned in the wintry sunshine of the afternoon. Just before they came to the second gate, the gate of the forlorn garden, Patty went to a huge beech-tree, and smilingly took out a pair of rubber overshoes.

"We keep all kinds of surprises here," she said. "But I love to walk

across the grass past the brook. I love the sound of water so much, and
the berries are so beautiful this year."

It was true. The dark, shaggy, hairy hawthorn-trees had a
purplish-burning look, they were still so heavy with haws. They stood
about fairly numerous in the near part of the park. Gilbert and Patty
walked along the crest of the stagnant, artificial ponds, that lay
melancholy in their abandon below the old house. Then Patty led the
way across the rough grass, to the brook which rattled and clucked
under deep hedges. Gilbert helped her to pick scarlet rose-berries, and
black privet berries, and white snow-berries from the bushes that grew
rampant down by the brook. Patty flushed with exercise and pleasure.
She was happy gathering the wet, bright, cold berries on their twigs and
branches, she was excited being helped by the young man near her. It
was such a pungent chill isolation, this of theirs down in the hollow of
the forsaken park, the open country, pathless, stretching the dim
beyond.

"Aren't they beautiful! Aren't they lovely!" said Patty, holding out
the bunch between her white hands. The scarlet and black and white-
heavy berries looked well in her hands. Her pale face was almost like an
ivory snow-berry itself, set with dark, half-tired, half-malicious eyes.
Her mouth set in an odd way, a slight grimace of malice against life.
She had had such a happy married life, such a perfect love with Lewie.

She stepped forward over the grass, a cloud on her flushed, strange
face of a woman of forty who has been married for twenty years in what
she considers an ideal happiness.

"Tell me now," she said to him, with her intensive seriousness of a
franchised woman,* "how *you* look on marriage." And she glanced
at him furtively, a touch of unconscious, general malevolence between
her brows.

"Marriage? Me? Why I don't know," came Gilbert's gruff voice.
Then he stood still, to ponder. She watched his face. He looked
forwards and upwards, into space. "I shall marry some day," he said.

"You will? But what sort of woman? What sort of marriage will it be?"
He pondered still.

"Why," he said, "a woman with brains, I think. A woman who could
stand on her own feet, not one who would cling to me. I shouldn't
mind, you know, what she did. If she liked another man, all right. We
could be good pals. Oh, I should want a woman to do as she liked."

Patty watched him sardonically, then strode on a few paces.

"You would? You think you would?" she replied, and the sardonic touch sounded in her voice. She was thinking how young he was, and how full of mental conceit. He glanced down at her, and his full, dark blue eye met her brown, onyx-bright eye. A flush came over her face, and a doubt over his mind, or his spirit, rather.

5 "I think so," he said.

"Yes, you think so," she replied quietly, walking on. He followed in silence.

"Why?" he said. "Don't you?"

She stopped and turned round to him, smiling suddenly her face 10 seeming to flicker all over with a strange, ivory-coloured flame, amid which her eyes showed dark.

"Ah!" she said. "What a difference there is between what you think now and what you'll think afterwards!"

She was usually rather uncouth in expressing herself, and he, for the 15 moment, was dazzled, had lost his feet. He only looked at her, at her strange, changed, almost uncanny face, so tense in its laughing. Something stirred in his veins. Something completely unusual awoke in him.

He had never had any real contact with a woman: only with tarts and 20 bits of girls and sports like Emmie. Other women, such as Patty, had always been to him dresses with faces. And now, to his terror, something else seemed to be emerging from her face, a new Aphrodite from the stiff dark sea of middle-aged matronliness, an Aphrodite drenched with knowledge, rising in a full, ivory-soft nudity, infinitely 25 more alluring than anything flapperdom could offer. Some veil was rent in his consciousness, and he remained a moment lost, open-mouthed. Patty dropped her eyes, and her smile became small and a little weary.

She had *had* to try to beat the flappers and the sports. She had *had* to try to break the spoon spell: which was the spell of her marriage, alas. 30 And she saw the beginnings of victory. But she was frightened. After all, she too was very fixed in her old way of life, up to the neck in the stiff wave of her fine serge dress. And to rise like Aphrodite—ah, after all—! There were so many considerations. Perhaps she was more frightened even than he.

35 He remained bemused, suddenly realising the soft, full Aphrodite steeped in the old sea of matrimony, and ready to rise, perhaps: rise from the correct, wine-coloured coat and skirt of fine serge in all her exquisite fulness and softness of forty years, and all the darkness of a finished past in her eyes. A finished past. The sense of it came over him 40 with a shock. He looked at her—but she was walking slowly, with bent

head. He saw the outline of her forty-year-old cheek, full and ivory-white: he saw the bowed head. And in the flame that ran from his heels* to his head all the Emmies of the world withered and were gone like so many shavings.

"What do you think of marriage yourself?" he blurted out.　　5

"Ah!"—she only half looked at him, funking the question, and answering archly: "I *don't* think about it, for myself. I have it behind me. You have it ahead of you. There's a difference."

He watched her, puzzling over her. She would not look at him, except with a screwed-up, baffling sort of smile. He pondered in his　10 logical way.

"But what you have behind you, have I got that in front of me?" he asked, putting himself in Lewie's place for all the past years, and not feeling himself fit.

Patty was caught in the net of her own words.　　15

"No," she said, seriously, becoming again the clumsy, thinking-woman. "No! You're a generation younger than that. You're bound to start different from where *we* started. But you've *got* to start somewhere."

Her phrases came out clumsily.　　20

"Perhaps where you left off," he said, inspired.

She flushed suddenly like a red camellia flower. She was very like a camellia flower: usually creamy-white, now rose.

"Yes," she said, in her suffragette voice now. "Very probably where we leave off! Very probably." She was retreating on to safe ground: the　25 platform of Woman. He felt it: and still, in his one-sighted way, was looking for the full, soft, pale Aphrodite.

"Then I should want a woman who's been through it all," he said, logically infallible.

She winced, and retreated further on to the dry boards of the　30 theoretic platform.

"I don't know. I shouldn't like to be so sure. There are many kinds of women in the world: many more than you have ever dreamed of. You don't see them—but they're there. You see little—remarkably little, if I may have the impudence to say so."　　35

And she smiled at him in the old, matronly, woman-who-thinks fashion. But it had no effect this time, because, between the blinkers of his logical concentration, he was looking ahead along his own road.

"Yes—I think that's true. I think that's true. But you won't get me to believe that you can find me a girl, a woman under thirty, who can start　40

where a woman of your age and experience leaves off. You won't get
me to believe it."

"Why not?" she cried. "Can you judge, now? Can *you*, of all men
judge? Can you even have any idea where it *is* that a woman of my age
5   and experience leaves off? How do you know?"

Now she was fencing with other weapons, trying to flirt with him.
But she had reckoned without her host. She was not prepared for the
blinkers of concentration which shut out from this Balaam's ass of a
mathematician all the side-tracks into which she would cajole him, and
10 sent him straight ahead with his nose against the opposing angel.*

He looked straight down on her, with full, dark blue eye. And she,
suddenly caught as by an apparition, was so startled that she let the
crinkly smile fall from her face, and the fencing cunning drop like a
mask from her eyes. For a second she met his look of strange inquiry,
15 and it was more than she could bear. Her heart ceased beating, she
wilted backwards. Mercifully, he began to speak.

"I've just realised something," he said. "And you can't make me
believe different till I realise something else."

What she heard in this speech was that he loved her: loved not the
20 girl in her, nor the independent, modern,* theorising woman
Lewie had loved; not that, but the soft, full, strange, unmated
Aphrodite of forty, who had been through all the ideal raptures of love
and marriage and modern motherhood, through it all, and through the
foam of the fight for freedom, the sea of ideal right and wrong, and now
25 was emerging, slowly, mysteriously, ivory-white and soft, woman still,
leaving the sea of all her past, nay, the sea of all the extant human world
behind her, and rising with dark eyes of age and experience, and a few
grey hairs among the dark; soft, full-bodied, mature, and woman still,
unpossessed, unknown of men, unfathomed, unexplored, belonging
30 nowhere and to no one, only to the unknown distance, the untrodden
shore of all the sea of all the unknown knowledge. Aphrodite, mistress,
mother of all the worlds of unknown knowledge that lie over our
horizon, she felt him looking at her with strange* full eyes, seeing
her in her unguessed ivory-soft nudity, the darkness of her promise in
35 her eyes, the woman of forty, and desiring her with a profound desire
that seemed like a deep, far-off bell booming, or a sea coming up.

And her strength ebbed, it was too much for her.

"Hadn't we better be turning home?" she asked, wide-eyed and
pathetic.
40 "Ay, I suppose we had," he answered automatic.

And they veered on the wintry grass, in the pale-coloured wintry afternoon. They had walked to the far end of the park, where it was open like a wide, rough meadow. At this end some rather shaggy cattle were out to pasture, winter-rough creatures. Some rough horses were in a far corner, by the fence.

Patty was looking round her, with a sort of anxious look on her face. She wanted to get back, back on to the road: above all, back into her own pleasant room, with her feet on her own hassock.

"You don't mind cows, do you?" asked Gilbert, noticing her anxiety.

"No. I don't *like* them though—not too near. I didn't know these were here."

"They're all right," said Gilbert.

"Oh yes, I'm sure they are," she said. But she hurried rather nervously. Glancing round, she said anxiously:

"Do you think that one means mischief?"

He saw a heifer putting her head down.

"No," he said negligently. He had no natural fear of cattle.

"She *does*," said Patty vehemently. "She's coming."

"Not she," said Gilbert easily.

But Patty was looking round in fear.

"Where can I go?" she cried.

"Don't bother," he said.

But she glanced round and gave a cry.

"She's coming." And she started running forward, blindly, with little, frightened steps. Patty was making for the brook, as the nearest safety.

Gilbert turned round. And sure enough, the heifer, with her head down, was running forward in that straight line of vicious intent which cows have when they *do* mean mischief. Gilbert was startled. Patty's nervousness unnerved him also. His instinct was to take to his heels. But he remained where he was, in a moment of stupefaction.

The heifer was going for Mrs Goddard. She was a dark-red creature with sharp horns. Gilbert gave a shout, and running forwards to the vicious, disagreeable-tempered beast, he flung his cherry-wood walking-stick at her. It caught her on the neck and rattled in her horns. She wavered, shook her head, and stopped. Gilbert took off his overcoat, and whirling it by the sleeve, walked towards her. She watched—snorted—suddenly with a round swerve made off, galloping into the distance, her tail in the air, female and defiant.

"She's gone. Don't run. She's all right," he called to the speeding Patty.

Patty glanced round with a white face of anguish.

"No. She'll come again," she said, in a stifled voice. And she pressed forward.

"She won't. You needn't hurry," said Gilbert, hastening after the dark little form of the woman, who pressed forward blindly, with hurried steps. He followed at some distance behind her, having recovered his stick.

The cow had stopped, and was watching. When he looked again, she had her head down and was coming on again.

"Damn the thing!" he exclaimed, in nervousness and anger. And stick in one hand, overcoat in the other, he started walking towards the animal, like some nervous toreador.

The cow ran at him. He threw his overcoat right in her face, and turned and ran also for a few paces. When he looked round, the cow was galloping in a funny, jerky zigzag, with his overcoat hanging on one horn, stumbling, snorting, shaking her head. There went his overcoat.

Patty was at the brook, climbing down among the bushes. The cow was prancing and jerking in the near distance, floundering with the black overcoat. He stood with his stick, and waited. He wanted his coat.

So he set off after the cow. She was a rare scarecrow, plunging and ducking in fear and fury. He pursued her as she dodged, shouting after her. At last she trod on the coat and got it off her horn, and went galloping away. He recovered his garment and returned after Patty.

She had scrambled through the deep brook and up the other bank, and was leaning against a tree with her eyes shut, faint. Her feet were full of water, there was brown earth on her skirt at the knee, where she had scrambled, and her breast was heaving, she could not speak.

When he came up he was filled with consternation.

"Has it upset you?" he asked, not knowing what to do.

"Frightened me," she murmured, gasping. She was ill. She could not stand up. She subsided at the foot of the tree, with her head dropped.

He stood near, looking on in distress and anxiety. He did not know in the least what to do. He wanted to put his coat for her to sit on, but did not like to disturb her. Her head was dropped as if she was unconscious, but her bosom laboured.

He waited, in nervous, irritable suspense. Her breathing seemed to be quieter. At last she lifted her head. Her face was paper-white, there were dark lines under her eyes, her eyes seemed dimmed.

"I'm sorry to give you so much trouble," she said, rather ghostlily. "But it's my heart. It gives way—on these occasions."

She seemed a shattered, elderly woman. He felt pity, distress, shame, and irritation.

At last she put her hand on the earth to rise. He assisted her, and steadied her. He had seen her overshoes full of water.

"Let me take off your goloshes," he said. 5

She leaned against the tree as he did so. He saw her nice shoes were wet too. And he wiped her skirt with his handkerchief where it was soiled.

"Thank you! Thank you!" she said. "It's awfully weak of me. But I can't help it." She closed her eyes, haggardly. 10

"Don't you bother. Let me do what I can for you," he answered kindly.

"Thank you. I'm feeling better now."

He waited still for her, as she leaned against the tree.

"If it weren't for my heart—" she said, looking at him with an 15 abstract,* hopeless smile. She was scarcely aware who he was.

"Yes, you can do nothing when your heart goes," he said sympathetically.

At last she drew herself together, haggard-looking.

"I'll see if I can walk," she said, her mouth thin and pinched and 20 frightened. He held her by the arm to support her, and wished they were both out of the situation.

So they crossed the meadow, crept through a fence into a bit of an orchard, and through the orchard gate into the road. She suffered agonies of self-consciousness because people saw them, and agonies of 25 self-consciousness all the way home, because of her appearance. It seemed a cruel long way. And Gilbert at her side took step after step, and thought to himself his luck was out as regards women. As a matter of fact, the accident of the cow was rather a bitter blow to him, though he formulated nothing in his consciousness. Still, he felt that his heart 30 had wakened and risen, and been knocked back again with a mallet-stroke. But he took it rather for granted that life was like that.

As for poor Patty, she felt humiliated, and was rather petulant. She recovered from her shock as she walked home, but her face did not lose all its haggardness and its broken look. And she wanted Lewie. She 35 badly wanted Lewie to come home. She wanted him to be there. The presence of this other man was a strain on her. She wanted her husband.

Chapter V.

Choir Correspondence.*

This same evening, Emmie sat in the choir-loft in chapel and warbled with her pleasant little voice. She was looking rather nipped, having had a bad week of it. But tonight she was on the wing again, and perking up her indomitable little head under her jaunty brown velour hat. Still, it was rather an effort. The enemy sat below, inimical. His stiff, thin figure rose at the end of the family pew, he looked as if butter wouldn't melt in his mouth, he sat so meek and still, with such a pietistic look on his face as he gazed up to the pulpit. Anyone would have imagined that the plump minister in a black B.A. gown shed out some mild incandescent light as he fluttered his plump hands, such a wistful* effulgence seemed to linger on Alf Bostock's rapt, black-whiskered face. He looked almost lovely, the demon: he was rather good-looking. Emmie spitefully itched to throw things in his rapt mug. But her hate went deep just now—down to rebellion level. The poor mother sat next the father, rather reddish and mottled in complexion, of no particular expression at all, except that she appeared submissive and seemed to be taking a rest, just sitting still. Her lilac hat looked as if it had been in the weather: a look her hats were apt to get, in spite of all her daughters could do. After the mother came a row of Bostocks, dear little Fra-Angelico-faced girls and rather long-nosed sons. The biggest son sat at the remote end of the pew, a long lad of nineteen, mild-looking, balancing the sermon-imbibing father who sat next the aisle, with his hands folded in his black-trousered lap.

Emmie was struggling hard to spread her game little wings. But they felt rather numb, after the treatment she had undergone. She watched the little minister. He was very plump, and rather ridiculous, perched on a stool in the pulpit and gyrating his pretty hands, as his voice soared and sank in leisurely, elegant measure. He was rather a comic: but Emmie liked him. He was nothing if not indulgent and good-natured. She would almost have liked to flirt with him. He *loved* his preaching, seemed to be swimming like some elegant little merman in the waters of his eloquence. A spirit of mischief spread its spoiled, storm-beaten wings in her eyes.

Just in front of her, among the altos, sat Agatha Sharp, next to Alvina Houghton.* Agatha was one of Emmie's pals, a school-teacher like herself, but much better behaved. Tall and slim, the girl in the altos sat looking her best, her boy being in a pew away below, facing her.

Emmie twitched and fidgetted, glanced bird-like down on the   5
bonnets and parted hair in the chapel, and shifted on her seat like a fidgetty bird on a bough, looking down on a motionless congregation, sermon-drugged. She knocked down her anthem-sheet, and picked it up again: sat with it in her lap: took a hymn book, fished a stump of pencil from her pocket and began to scribble on her anthem-sheet, on   10
the back.

"Lovely spoon last week with G.N.—Eh, what do you think. Wire-whiskers came back from work and caught us. Oh my, Agatha, I nearly had a fit. G.N. and W-W. went for one another and I ran off—thought I was never going back home."   15

She folded down the anthem-sheet like a game of consequences, reached over and poked her friend in the back. Agatha looked round. Emmie gave her the paper and pencil. Agatha, flushing and looking demure, bowed her head to read the paper. Then she too put the pencil to her lips, scribbled, and put her hand behind her back without   20
turning round. Emmie fished up the paper and pencil.

"Do you mean after chapel? Wherever did you go?"

Emmie sucked her pencil and scribbled.

"About half-past ten. He caught us in our greenhouse. I'd got no hat on nor anything. I ran without knowing where I was going, to Lewie   25
Goddard's."

She poked Agatha in the back. Instead of looking round, Agatha curled her hand behind her. Emmie deposited the paper in the fingers of her friend. Alvina Houghton, who disapproved of Emmie, looked round rather snappily. Emmie turned up her nose.   30

Back came the paper.

"You bad wench. How did you go home. Have you seen G.N. since."

Emmie snatched up the paper, sucked her pencil and scribbled hastily.

"I stopped all night at Goddards'. Mrs G. rather snipey. Lewie went   35
down home and told our Dad a thing or two. I was awfully bad*—they thought I was going to be really badly. So did I. I didn't go to school Monday—stopped in bed at Goddards, and went home in the afternoon. Our Dad hasn't spoken to me since."

Again Agatha felt a poke in the back. Again she curled her hand   40

behind her. And again Alvina Houghton glanced round frowning
coldly, while Cissie Gittens* glanced inquiringly over her shoulder. The choir was beginning to concentrate upon this correspondence. Even some of the audience were noticing a new centre of
5 disturbance. And the clergyman, poor man, was becoming decidedly
irritable in delivery, fidgetting on his footstool.

Back came the paper from Agatha.

"You *are* an awful bad catamaran.* Haven't you seen G.N.
since?"

10 Emmie got the paper, and industriously popped her pencil to her
lips.

"No, I've never been out. He wouldn't let me. Never saw you
Wednesday. He's trying his hardest to get G.N.'s name. He's got his
cap. But he's never asked *me*. He bothers our mother, and the others.
15 He'd better not ask *me*."

The paper went and returned.

"This will be a lesson to you, my lady. What will he do if he gets
G.N.'s name? Did they really hit one another? Didn't he see
G.N.—Oh I *do* think it's awful."

20 Emmie seized this message, and wrote:

"They were down in a gooseberry bush when I scooted for my life.
Look at the scratches on W-W's ear. It was pitch dark. He says I'm
never going to be out again after dark. *Aren't I*? I'm not frightened of
him. But he's not going to get Great Northern's* name. Our
25 mother doesn't know either. They're all trying to guess. Do you think
he'll come tonight. Can't see him if he does. You'll have to tell him
Agatha. He's the best spoon out. But tell him not to come again—not
just yet. I'm going to be a reformed character, and stick to Walter
George. What? See me—"

30 A poke in Agatha's back.

And at the same time the minister raised his fat, near-sighted,
pince-nezzed face, that was red as a boiled shrimp. Agatha was reading
in sublime unconsciousness, when the whole congregation woke from
its sermonial somnolence with a shudder as if someone had*
35 scratched on a slate a long shriek with a screeching pencil. So did the
changed note in the minister's sweet-oil voice set their teeth on edge
like vinegar.

"I should be glad if the interruptions from the choir could be
brought to an end. I have continued as long as I could without
40 observation, but further continuance is impossible. Either the unseemly

correspondence in the choir-gallery must cease, or I must close for this evening—"

A moment's pause and readjustment.

"*Please* let the passing of papers cease," continued the allforgiving minister. "I should be extremely sorry to hurt any individual feelings. 5 But I speak out of painful necessity, after considerable endurance. I* cannot continue under the strain of the previous distraction."

He was nettled, but with christian forbearance already rubbed dockleaves on the sting, adjusted his eyeglasses, looked down at his notes, and, still red as a boiled shrimp, picked up his oratorical voice, 10 which somehow he seemed to have dropped and left in the distance. The sermon began to trickle its suave flow again.

But the congregation! The congregation was electrified. Every eye was on the choir-gallery, except only the eyes of those who sat in the rather select pews beneath the said gallery. And these, the nobs, so far 15 forgot themselves as to screw their necks and look up at the sloping roof near above them, as if their X-ray eyes could pierce the flooring and distinguish the offender by his, or her, shoe-soles. Sternly and indignantly they stared at the little roof over their heads, above which roof, they knew, were perched the choral angels of the chapel. Fallen 20 angels indeed.

In the choir itself consternation and indignation struggled in every breast. As the Roman emperors were jealous and suspicious of any society which leagued itself together within the body politic, so are christian ministers obliged to beware of the wheels within wheels of 25 their church. A choir is an unpaid, independent body, highly oligarchic and given to insubordination. For music, said to be a soothing art, produces the most wayward members of the christian community. If the army caused the fall of emperor after emperor, how many christian ministers are unpleasantly thrown from the pulpit in these self- 30 governing churches by the machinations of the obstreperous choir. So little Daddy Dixon, as he was half-affectionately called, had better beware how he rushes with his angry lamb's bleat of expostulation into this mountainous nest of bears and she-bears.

From consternation the choir quickly passed to indignation. Poor 35 Agatha sat with her crimson face buried in her bosom, screened by her broad black hat. Emmie, the impudent, sat with her nose in the air, looking guilty. Alvina Houghton and Cissie Gittens kept glancing round at her, damnatory. The other members glanced at Emmie, and then turned their indignant looks to one another, before they directed 40

them in a volume against the little minister, perched there just beneath them on his little stool, continuing his little sermon, mildly flourishing his deprecating, plump hand out of the black wing of his gown. Emmie might be guilty of slight misdemeanour. But then, was she not an old
5   member of the sacred choral college. And was this privileged body to be submitted to the injury and ignominy of a public rebuke from the pulpit? From Daddy Dixon, moreover, that plump lamb! Bears and she-bears uttered inaudible growls, and flounced on their seats, crackled their music sheets, and altogether behaved like a mutiny on
10   the upper deck.*

Alf Bostock, however, sat with a wolf's eye glaring greenly up at his perky daughter. Mrs Bostock's brows were knitted with ancient perplexity as she too looked upwards, on her right. The boy Bostocks had gone red to their ears, of course. They seized every available
15   opportunity of going red to the ears.

Came the closing hymn, sung by the choir as if they had grit between their teeth. Meanwhile the poor parson sat in the pulpit with his brow in his hand, drawing upon himself the full and viscous flow of sympathy from the congregation, the extra venom of the choir, who stood upright
20   in their dimmish loft like a crowd of demons on the war-path.

Poor Norman Dixon prayed, in the final prayer, that hearts might be kept from anger and turned away from wrath, and oh, if we, whose sacred duty it is to guide the way along the path of Right, if we should stumble and catch our feet against the stones of passion, may we in our
25   humble repentance before Thee, beseech that our stumblings shall not cause others to fall, but shall rather show them the difficulties of the way, and assist them to walk in uprightness and love, remembering that each has his own burden to bear along the difficult journey of life, and that he who adds weight to his brother's burden does not thereby make
30   lighter his own, but brings weariness and sorrow where before was joy. For oh, let us beware of our own thoughtlessness——

This homily, though intended of course for the Almighty, the choir set down to their own account, and determined not to be mollified all at once. No indeed. If Norman Dixon stumbled, it was his own toe he
35   must blame, not somebody else's stone that lay in the way. Let him pick his way through the stones.* What else was he a minister of the gospel for?—And the congregation half agreed. After all, he could have spoken later on, in private, and not have caused a public scandal. Everybody is so eager to pull the chair of authority from under the poor
40   devil whom they have chosen to sit down in it.

Only one member of the congregation agreed and more than agreed with plump Norman in the pulpit. We know who this member was. He proceeded to gnash his teeth in preparation.

Emmie knew well enough the fat was in the fire, and therefore she was dumb when the choir rather grittily moaned the emotional vesper. 5

> "Lord keep us safe this night
> Secure from all our fears
> May angels guard us while we sleep
> Till morning light appears."*

The bass curved up and the treble curved down in the luscious melody, 10 and Emmie tried to gather her wits. Things were already at a breaking point between her and her pa.

As the choir trooped down the stairs after service, venting their indignation, Emmie hurried and caught her friend by the arm.

"Oh I say Agatha, damn Norman Dixon. What had *he* got to go and 15 put his foot in it for.—I say, if he's waiting—you know—you'll tell him, won't you? Oh an' I say, I've got a book of his. Tell him I s'll leave it for him at Lewie Goddard's, shall you. I fair forgot it till tonight, when I was thinking of last week. Oh I'm fair sick of things, Agatha. I'm sure I wish I was dead, I'm that persecuted. You know my Dad's made my 20 mother swear she'll tell him everything what I do. She told me herself he had. And what do you think, he can wring anything out of her, the inquisition devil. He'd better not try it on me though, or he'll get more than he's bargained for. I tell you what, Agatha, I could fair jump in the cut, I could, I'm that harassed and tormented. And all by that old fool. 25 And what's more, what right has he! I'm over twenty-one. I hope his rabbits'll die, for I hate him.—Eh, Agatha. And tell *him*—you know—that I can't get his cap back for him. My father's got it, trying to get a clue from it. But he won't then, because it was bought at Parkers* in Knarborough, and hasn't got a name or anything in. I 30 got it out of my mother, all that. But Lewie Goddard'll stand by me. An' I shall run away to our Fan's if he gives me any more bother—"

They had reached the needle's eye gate by which the choir emerged from the chapel precincts. Emmie glanced swiftly round. Yes, there was Gilbert on the opposite pavement. She pinched Agatha's arm excitedly. 35

"He's come, Agatha. You tell him. And if he wants to see me, tell him—"

"You're coming, there, aren't you?" said a policeman-like voice. We know whose.

"Yes I am," said Emmie sullenly. Then: "Goodnight Agatha. Hope I shall see you Wednesday."

And she followed her irate parent, who joined her forlorn mother at the big gate, and the family trailed off in a disconsolate Sunday-night crowd.

Agatha meanwhile went across the road.

"Good-evening Mr Noon. Excuse me. Emmie can't come tonight. She told me about last week. You know, don't you—?"

"Yes," said Gilbert. "Mr Goddard told me about it. Hasn't she been to Chapel then? Wasn't that she?"

"Yes. Her father made her go home. He's in another of his tantrums now. Oh—here's my boy! Can I introduce you—?"

And Agatha went on to communicate all Emmie's commissions.

"All right," said Gilbert. "Give her these when you see her. I shall go to Goddards' for the book."

He gave Agatha the inevitable packet* of chocolates, and turned away. Ah spoony chocolates! 'Tis you who have made the cocoa fortunes. And now Gilbert will buy no more. Lewie had given him a lively description of Emmie's plight on the previous Sunday night, how she had seemed to be losing her reason; and all the things *he*, Lewie, had said to her father, first oil then vinegar; and how Bostock had been brought to promise to say nothing to the girl; how he had kept his promise, but had been up to Patty to find out if *she* could tell him what the fellow's name was. Of course she couldn't. Of course Emmie hadn't mentioned the name to *them*.—This with one of Lewie's side-looks, which told Gilbert that the Goddards knew only too well. Moreover he remembered that Emmie was going to leave the book, for *him*, at Lewie's. Whereupon he had something else to put in his pipe and smoke.—And Alf Bostock was a nasty customer, Lewie said, one of your reformed ones.

Chapter VI.

The Sack.

Meanwhile a pretty kettle of fish was preparing for Mr Noon. He smelled nothing of it for some days. Neither did he go over to Woodhouse, but let matters remain where they were. He was annoyed and irritated by the whole business. The thought of Emmie now gave him a prickly unpleasant sensation in his skin, and made him knit his brows irritably. He had been relieved that he could not see her on the Sunday evening, and after receiving her message he hoped the whole affair was finished. Never would he start such a mess again: never. For the whole world of spooning, bits of fluff, jolly good sports, bits of hot stuff and the like he now felt a prickly repulsion, an irritable distaste. No more of that for *him*.

But wait a bit. Let him not holloa till he is out of the wood.

He did not go to the Goddards' either, because he felt that Patty had been making a butt of him. Yes, while he was feeling such a hero in the park, she was laughing up her sleeve at him.

"While from the dark park, hark——"

The ridiculous Tom Hood line* ran in his mind. Yes, he was a fool, a born fool and a made fool, both, and he felt in a state of intense irritation against everybody he knew and the whole circumstance of his life.

To crown which, on Thursday he received a note, at school, requesting him to attend a meeting in camera of the Higher Grade Committee, at Knarborough, at seven in the evening*—signed M. Britten.

Haysfall Technical School was under the control of the Education Committee, which had its seat in the county town of Knarborough. *M. Britten* was Minnie Britten, secretary for the above: and secretary for everything else into which she could poke her nose. Gilbert knew her: a woman with grey hair and a black hat, in a tremendous hurry of mental responsibility and importance, always scuffling in when she wasn't wanted and setting all the leaves fluttering with her strained sense of duty and her exaggerated sense of importance. Heaven knows how much she cost the County in petrol, for she was not out of the

official motor-car ever for a longer space than half-an-hour. Her superior, Jimmy Blount, a youngish bald man with an eyeglass, Clerk for Education for the county, let her flutter the dovecotes at will. He, poor devil, was harassed by the officious interference of the innumer-
5 able little gods who have education at heart and can make an official's chair uncomfortable. Mrs Britten then—we forgot to mention she was married—darted about the county wherever she felt she was in request, like some spider dashing from the centre of its web along the lines every time it feels or imagines it feels a disturbance. Of course
10 Mrs Britten did actually rush into a lot of educational bothers: which proves, of course, that the bothers existed. Whether her rushes made matters any better, we leave to the imagination of any individual who has ever had the misfortune and humiliation to be connected with our educational system.

15 Mrs Britten then: she was a B.A. also, and felt that her education was unquestionable. She wrote pamphlets on Education, and was sur-prised, yes surprised, if at least every *head* teacher in every school did not show an acquaintance with their contents. She was Secretary for the Children's Holiday Fund, and an assiduous collector therefor. A
20 foot-pad, even a burglar with a revolver is answerable. But Mrs Britten was unanswerable, especially to poor quaking elementary school-teachers, to whom she was the Dea ex machina.* She forced the reluctant sixpences out of them, and let her sun shine on schools whose contribution to the Fund was highest. She was an opponent of Feeding
25 the Children—we must refer to her pamphlet on the subject for the reason why. In fact she was for or against innumerable things, so that it was a wonder her hair hadn't all disappeared, instead of being merely stone grey at forty. She was honest, of course. She was kind, as goes without saying. She had lots of brains. She was hard and straightfor-
30 ward and downright enough. Wonderful what a lot of virtues she managed to have in a hurry. Though she wasn't at all a new broom, she swept the dust from pillar to post, and left everybody spitting, till some poor devil got the dust-pan and collected the dirt.

Mr Noon knew her. We've all known her. Such conscientious people
35 don't let themselves remain unknown. She rather approved of Mr Noon—because he was so clever, and had brought the remnants of such a reputation with him from Cambridge. She even rather toadied to him—in a mental kind of way. Spiteful female teachers said she wouldn't at all mind setting her black hat at him: but this isn't true. Mrs
40 Britten was merely Minerva extending her grace and craving a little

adulation in return. She heard—oh yes, she heard of his peccadilloes. What escaped her? But, curiously enough, she was rather more indulgent to him because of them. If he had been so brilliant and impregnable, her wing might not have covered him. But if not her intellectual, at least he might be her moral chicken.

Therefore Gilbert felt no particular qualm when he received the note summoning him to the meeting in camera. Rather he poured a little ointment on his prickly, nettle-rashed vanity, and concluded they were going to consult him, privately, upon some matter connected with the school, probably the fitting up of a laboratory for technical chemistry.

So he put his best suit on, tied his tie to his taste, and whizzed over on the motor-cycle to the county town. When he arrived at the town hall, the porter told him the meeting was already sitting. He went to the waiting-room, and there sat cooling his heels. Doubtful if even now he smelled the above-mentioned fish, which were stewed and nearly ready for him in the next room.

A bell rang. A clerk went into the meeting-room, returned, and ushered in Mr Noon. Mrs Britten was at the head of a long table round which were seated the various members of the committee, mostly fat fossils and important persons of complete insignificance. Mrs Britten rose to her feet.

"Ah, good-evening Mr Noon. Will you sit *there*—!"—and she indicated a chair at the doorwards end of the table, opposite herself. Gilbert said Good-evening, and looking very fresh and spruce, seated himself in the chair indicated. Meanwhile, down either side of the black-leathered table the members of the committee, their faces very distinct owing to the shaded lights that hung over the table and cast all the glow down on them, looked steadfastly and mutely at Mr Noon, as if they had expected some inhabitant of Mars to make his appearance. Gilbert suddenly felt like a baby that has fallen to the bottom of the sea* and finds all the lobsters staring at him in the under-sea light. So they stared, like inquiring lobsters, and he felt like a baby, with his fresh face and pouting mouth.

But Mrs Britten had seated herself once more, and stretching out her arms on the table in a very-much-herself fashion, she held certain papers within the full glare of the lamp, and began:

"We are sorry, Mr Noon, to have to call this meeting tonight to consider the subject in hand. Yesterday a formal report was made and signed in my presence which, although it does not directly affect the concerns of this Committee, yet may prejudice your successful work in the Haysfall Technical School seriously. Is not that so, gentlemen?"

The lobsters buzzed and nodded in the submarine glare. They no longer looked at Mr Noon, but studiously away from him. He sat
5 looking rather wonder-stricken and stupid, with his pouting mouth a shade open.

"Therefore we have decided to put the matter before you openly, and hear your account. We are sorry to have to intrude on your private life, but we do feel that the interests of the school where you are doing
10 such good work are at stake."

"Quite!" said one of the lobsters distinctly and emphatically. Gilbert's eye strayed wonderingly to him.

"We are met here in camera, even without a clerk. If we can clear the matter up satisfactorily, nothing more shall be heard of it. We are
15 prepared to forget all about it."

"Oh certainly, certainly," barked a couple of lobsters.

At this time Mr Noon's attention was interrupted by his recalling the story about a certain French poet who was seen slowly leading a lobster by a blue ribbon along one of the boulevards. When a friend asked why,
20 why?, the poet replied wistfully: "You see they don't bark."*

Gilbert wondered if they really did never bark, or if, under-water, they rushed out of their rock-kennels and snapped and yapped at the heels of the passing fishes. This fancy caused him to hear only a wave-lapping sound for a few moments, which wave-lapping sound was
25 actually Mrs Britten's going on. He came to himself when she flapped a paper to attract his rather vacant-looking attention. He stared alert at the paper, and heard her portentous reading.

"I wish to make known to the Members of the Knarborough Education Committee that Gilbert Noon, science-teacher in Haysfall
30 Technical School, has been carrying on with my daughter, Emma Grace Bostock, and has had criminal commerce* with her. He has got my daughter into trouble, and ruined her life. I wish to know whether such a man is fit to be a teacher of young boys and girls, and if nothing is going to be done in the matter by the Knarborough
35 Education Committee. Signed Alfred Wright Bostock—"

Mrs Britten's level voice came coldly to an end, and she looked keenly at Mr Gilbert. He sat staring at some invisible point above the middle of the table, and was quite inscrutable.

"We feel," said Mrs Britten, "how delicate the matter is. We wish
40 above all things not to trespass. But we find* we must have an

answer from your own mouth. The meeting is private—everything will be kept in strictest privacy. Will you tell us, please, whether this statement by the man Bostock is altogether false?"

Gilbert still stared at the invisible point and looked absent. There was a dead silence which began to get awkward.

"Yes or no, Mr Noon?" said Mrs Britten gently.

Still the vacant Gilbert stared at a point in space, and the lobsters began to squiggle in their arm-chairs.

"We have your interest at heart, Mr Noon. Please believe it. But we are bound, *bound* to have the interest of your school and scholars also at heart. If the matter had not been formally forced upon our attention, as I may say, we might have let gossip *continue* its gossiping. But the man Bostock seems to be a determined individual, capable of creating considerable annoyance. We thought it best to try to settle the matter quietly and as privately as possible. We have the greatest possible esteem for your services: we would not like to lose them. And so we are met here tonight to do what we can.

"Answer then simply, yes or no. Is this statement made by the man Bostock utterly false, or must we consider it? It is completely false?—yes?—"

The lobsters glued their eyes on Mr Noon's face. He looked up and along at Mrs Britten: surely she was a Jewess by birth. A thousand to one on it she was a benevolent Jewess by birth.

"All right then," he said gruffly, leaning forward on the table and half-rising, pushing his chair scraping back: "I'll send in my resignation."

He stood leaning forward for one second at the table, looking at the confounded lobsters.

"No no, Mr Noon! Please! Please sit down! Please! Please! Do sit down. Please do! Please!" Mrs Britten had risen to her feet in her earnest agitation. She seemed really *so* concerned for his welfare that he wavered, and half sat down.

"Certainly! Take your seat, young man," said one of the lobsters, who evidently owned employees.

"I'll send in my resignation," barked Gilbert, sending his chair back with a jerk and opening the door before any lobster could disentangle himself from his lobster-pot of a round official chair.

"Oh *don't* let him go!" cried Mrs Britten, with a wail of distress. There was a clinking and scraping of lobster-pots and one lobster-voice shouted—"Here! Here you!" But Gilbert* was going down

the wide, dim stone stairs three at a time, not running, but lunging down, smack, smack, smack, three steps at a time. He bumped aside the porter and took his hat and coat, and in another second was going out of the front doors of the Town Hall, hearing the last of Mrs
5   Britten's voice wailing from the semi-darkness up aloft the stairs:
"Please, Mr Noon! *Please* come back!"

All her nice little game of that evening was spoilt. Oh, what a temper she was in, and how she longed to box the ears of all the lobsters, particularly the one who had "young-manned" the truant. Oh how she
10 hated the lobsters, over whom she queened it so regally. Oh how she itched to smack their faces and tell them what she thought of them. A Jewess born!

But she did none of these things. She only said:
"He will send in his resignation tomorrow."
15 "And it will be accepted," barked a lobster.
"*Sine diē*," yapped another, though nobody knew what he meant by it, or whether it was English which they hadn't quite caught.

Chapter VII.

Jaw.

Gilbert's kettle of fish had been all lobsters but one: but that didn't make it any the sweeter.

The next day was Saturday: half-day at school. His one fear was that Mrs Britten would pounce on him. If she did, he would put her off with vague promises and sweetnesses. For he was determined to have done with Haysfall, Whetstone, Woodhouse, Britten-women, Goddard-women, Emmie-women, all his present life and circumstance, all in one smack. Men at some times are masters of their fates, and this was one of Mr Gilbert's times. The wonder is he did not break his neck at it, or get locked up, for he rode his motor-cycle at many forbidden miles an hour, so anxious he was to get home. He was so anxious to have between his fingers the Lachesis shears of his thread of fate,* in the shape of a fountain pen. He could snip off the thread of his Haysfall life in about three strokes—"I beg to resign my post in Haysfall Technical School, and wish to leave at the very earliest opportunity." That was all he would say. And he was itching to say it. His motor-cycle fairly jumped over the dark roads from Knarborough to Whetstone.

He arrived, wrote out his resignation, and sat down to think.

In the first place he was clearing out. He was going to Germany, as he had often said he would, to study for his doctorate.*

That was settled.

But—

And there were rather serious buts.

Criminal correspondence with Emmie had *got her into trouble* and *ruined her life*. Did that mean she was going to have a baby? Lord save us, he hoped not. And even if she was, whose baby was it going to be? He felt in no mood at all for fatherhood, but decided, since he was running away, he had better see Emmie again and make it as square with her as possible.

Which meant also going to the Goddards.

And would that damned Mrs Britten fasten on him tomorrow? He knew she would on Monday if not tomorrow. Saturday morning, he knew, she was busier and fuller up than ever, if that were possible. The thing was, to get away without seeing her. Could he clear out after tomorrow morning? Not put in any further appearance at the school after the morrow?

That remained to decide.

5   Then money. He had no money. He never had any money, though his father said that when *he* was his age, meaning Gilbert's, he had saved a hundred and seventy pounds out of thirty shillings a week. Gilbert would have been glad of the hundred and seventy pounds if he'd saved them, but he hadn't. How was he to clear out with about 10 fifty-five shillings, which was all he had.

He must get something out of his father, that was all. And sell his motor-cycle. Ay, sell his motor-cycle. Leave that also for the morrow. Sufficient unto the day etc.*

Of course he'd brought it all on himself. And he didn't seriously care 15 either. One must bring one thing or another on oneself.

There was his father just come in from having half a pint at the Holly Bush. Down he went. His father was sitting in the many-staved arm-chair, almost a lobster-pot, the throne of the house. Gilbert sat on the sofa opposite. The father began to unfasten his boots.

20   "Father," said Gilbert. "I'm chucking Haysfall Technical."

"Oh ay," replied his parent.

"I'm thinking of going to Germany."

"Are you!"

"I'm going to work there for my doctorate."

25   "Doctorate? Oh yes."

"Doctor of Science, you know."

"Ay! Ay!"

"It would do me a lot of good, you know."

"It would, would it?"

30   "I should get a much better job than ever I can get now."

"Yes—yes."

"The only thing is funds."

"Funds. Yes."

"It'll cost me a bit at first, only at first."

35   "Where? In Germany? Oh yes."

"Yes."

"Ay."

This passionate conversation between father and son was drawing to an inevitable close.

40   "You don't see your way to helping me a bit, Dad?"

"Helping you, child! I'm always helping you."

"Yes, but a bit extra."

"Nay, how can I help you if you go to foreign parts."

"By setting me up with a few quid."

"A few quid. Why—you can stop at home an' have board an' lodging   5
for nothing. What'st want to be goin' to Geermany for!"

"For my doctorate."

"Doctrat be—hanged."

"Nay father."

"Thou'rt doin' right enough as t'art."   10

"No, I'm going to Germany."

"Tha* art?"

"Yes."

"Oh—all right."

"You see father, I want a few quid to start off with."   15

"Save 'em then, my boy."

"I haven't saved them, Dad, and you have. So you give me a few."

"Tha does talk."

"Ay—what else should I do!"

"Save thy wind."   20

"Like you save your money?"

"Ay—t'same."

"And you won't give me any?"

"Tha'lt get th' lot when I'm gone."

"But I don't want you gone, and I want a little money."   25

"Want. Want. What art doin' wi' wants? Tha should ha'e th' fulness,
not th' want."

"So I should if you'd give it me."

"Nay, I can niver put th' fat off my own belly on to thine."

"I don't want your fat—I want about fifty pounds."   30

"That *is* my fat."

"You know it isn't."

"I know it is."

"Won't you give them me?"

"Tha'lt get all when I've gone."   35

"I want it now."

"Ay, me an' all.* I want it now."

Whereupon Gilbert rose and went upstairs again. His father was a
lobster.

The next morning passed without any descent of Mrs Britten. He   40 got on his bicycle and left Haysfall for good, taking his few personal possessions with him from the big red school.

Arriving at Whetstone at one o'clock, he immediately went and bargained with an acquaintance who, he knew, wanted his motor-cycle. The man offered fifteen pounds. The thing was worth a good forty.

"Give me twenty, or I'll ride it to London and sell it there."

It was agreed he was to have his twenty, and hand over the cycle the next day, Sunday. So he went home for dinner, did not speak to his father, with whom he was angry, hurried through his meal, and shoved off with his motor-bike again.

Chapter VIII.

His Might-have-been Mother-in-law.*

At Woodhouse, Patty opened the door to him. She started, and looked embarrassed.

"Is it you Mr Noon! Come in." Then in a lower tone: "I've got Mrs Bostock here. Poor thing, I'm sorry for her. But perhaps you'd rather not see her?"

"What do you think?" he said.

Patty pursed up her mouth.

"Oh—as you please. She's quite harmless."

"All right."

He took off his hat and marched into the room. Mrs Bostock fluttered from her chair. Patty came in wagging herself fussily as she walked, and arching her eyebrows with her conspicuously subtle smile.

"What a coincidence, Mrs Bostock! This is Mr Noon."

Mrs Bostock, who at a nearer view was seen to have a slip-shod, amiable cunning in her eyes, shook hands and said she hoped she saw him well. Patty settled herself with her ivory hands in her dark-brown lap, and her ivory face flickering its important smile, and looked from one to the other of her guests.

"How remarkable you should have come just at this minute, Mr Noon! Mrs Bostock has just brought this book of yours. I believe you lent it Emmie."

Gilbert eyed the treatise on conic sections.

"Yes," he said, "I did."

"It was my mistake as did it," said Mrs Bostock, with that slip-shod repentance of her nature. "I picked it up and said 'Whose is this book about Comic Sections?' I thought it was a comic, you see, not noticing. And our Dad twigged it at once. 'Give it here,' he said. And he opened it and saw the name. If I'd seen it I should have put it back on the shelf and said nothing."

"How very unfortunate," Patty said. "May I see?"

She took the book, read the title, and laughed sharply.

"A mathematical work?" she said, wrinkling up her eyes at Gilbert. Not that she knew any more about it, really, than Mrs Bostock did. She saw the Trinity College* stamp, and the name, Gilbert Noon, written on the fly leaf.

"What a curious handwriting you have, Mr Noon," she said, looking up at him from under her dark brows. He did not answer. People had said it so* often. He wrote in an odd, upright manner, rather as if his letters were made up out of crochets and quavers and semibreves, very picturesque and neat.

"If I'd opened it I should have guessed, though I didn't know the name any more than he did. But our Dad was too sharp for me. I tried to pass it off. It was no good though," said Mrs Bostock. She had a half-amused look, as if the intrigue pleased her.

"So it all came out?" asked Patty.

"Ay, I'm sorry to say. As soon as our Emmie come in he showed it her and said 'I'm goin' to Haysfall Technical with this.' And she, silly like, instead of passing it off, flew at him and tried to snatch it from him. That just pleased our Dad. I said to her after: 'Why you silly thing, what did you let on for? Why didn't you make out you knew nothing!' And then she flew at me."

"You must have had a trying time between the two," said Patty, wrinkling her brows at Noon.

"Oh, I have, I can tell you. He vowed he'd go up to the Tech. with the book, and she said if he did she'd jump in th' cut. I kept saying to her, why don't you pass it off with a laugh. But she seemed as if she'd gone beyond it. So he kept the book till this morning. She told me she'd promised to leave it here."

"You knew," said Patty; "that Emmie had run away?"

"No," said Gilbert.

"Gone to our Fanny's at Eakrast," said Mrs Bostock. "I had a letter from our Fanny next day, saying she was bad in bed. I should have gone over but I've got Elsie with measles."

"You have your hands full," said Patty.

"I have, I tell you. I said to our Dad, you can do nothing but drive things from bad to worse. Our Fanny had had the doctor in to her, and he says it's neuralgia of the stomach. Awful, isn't it! I know neuralgia of the face is bad enough. I said to our Dad, well, I said, I don't know whether she's paying for her own wickedness or for your nasty temper to her, but she's paying, anyhow."

"Poor Emmie. And she's such a gay young thing by nature," said Patty.

"Oh, she's full of life. But a wilful young madam, and can be snappy enough with the children. I've said to her many a time, you're like your Dad, you keep your smiles in the crown of your hat, and only put 'em on when you're going out.* She can be a cat, I tell you, at home. She makes her father worse than he would be."

"I suppose she does," said Patty. 5

"Oh, he gets fair wild, and then tries to blame me. I say to him, she's *your* daughter, I didn't whistle her out o' th' moon. He's not bad, you know, if you let him be. He wants managing, then he's all right. Men doesn't have to be told too much, and it's no good standing up to them. That's where our Emmie makes her mistake. She *will* fly back at him, 10 instead of keeping quiet. I'm sure, if you answer him back, it's like pouring paraffin to put a fire out. He flares up till I'm frightened."

"I'm afraid," laughed Patty grimly, "I should have to stand up to him."

"That's our Emmie. I tell him, if he will make school-teachers of 15 them, he must expect them to have tongues in their heads.—" Then she turned to Gilbert. "He never did nothing about your book, did he?"

"Yes," said Gilbert. "I've got the sack."

"Oh how disgusting!" cried Patty.

"Ay, a lot of good that'll do," said Mrs Bostock. "It's like him though. 20 He'll pull the house down if the chimney smokes."

"When are you leaving?" said Patty.

"This week-end."

"Can you believe it!" said Mrs Bostock.

Patty mused for a time. 25

"Well," she said, "I must say, your husband has caused a marvellous lot of mischief, Mrs Bostock. He's fouled his own nest, indeed he has; done a lot of damage to others and no good to himself."

"No, it's just like him—but there you are. Those that won't be ruled can't be schooled." 30

"What is Emmie going to do then?" Gilbert asked.

"Don't ask me, Mr Noon. She'll come back when she's better, I should think: silly thing she is, going off like it."

"What is her address?"

"Were you thinking of going over on your motor-bike? Well, I'll 35 back* she'll be pleased. Care of Mrs Harold Wagstaff, School House, Eakrast. He's one of the schoolmasters, you know, Fanny's husband. A clever young fellow, come out first class at college. I'm sure you'd get on with him. It's the fourth house down the lane after the church—house and school combined. You can't miss it. But it's a very 40 quiet place, you know. I bet they're not sorry for a bit of company."*

Gilbert looked down his nose rather, for Mrs Bostock continually glanced sideways at him, approvingly, and he knew she was quite comfortable, assuming in him a prospective, or at least a possible son-in-law. Not that she was making any efforts herself towards the status of mother-in-law. But there was never any knowing what the young people would do, and she was quite willing, whichever way it was. She was quite ready to be agreeable, whichever way things went.

And this was almost as disconcerting to Mr Gilbert as the old man's tantrum of hostility had been. Moreover that neuralgia of the stomach was worrying him. How easily it might mean an incipient Noon—or, since it is a wise father that knows his own child—an incipient little Emmie, an Emmeling. The thought of this potential Emmeling was rather seriously disconcerting to our friend. He had certain standards of his own, one of them being a sort of feeling that if you put your foot in it, you must clean your own shoe, and not expect someone else to do it. At the same time he was determined to clear out of the whole show.

Mrs Bostock rose, and must be hurrying back to her home. Gilbert rose too.

"Oh but you'll stay and have a cup of tea," Patty cried. "You're sure you can't stay, Mrs Bostock?"

"I can't, thank you. I s'll have our master home at half-past five, and the children's teas to get, besides our Elsie. Thank you all the same, I'm sure. I'm sure you and Mr Goddard has been very kind to our Emmie. I'm sure I don't know what she'd have done without Mr Goddard."

"Oh he's a friend in need," said Patty, with a curl of the lip.

"He is, bless him."

And the mother of the Bostocks took her leave.

Patty rang at once for tea, and sat herself down by the fire in the twilight. Gilbert had remained. It was too late to get to Eakrast that night.

"Well," said Patty, settling her skirts over her knees in a way she had: "you've had quite an adventure." And she smiled her wrinkled smile. She reminded Gilbert for a moment of one of those wrinkle-faced ivory demons from China. But that was because he was in a temper, and rather in a funk.

"If you look on it as an adventure," he said.

"Well—how else? Not as a tragedy, I hope. And not altogether a comedy. Too many people have had to smart. I guess Emmie Bostock feels anything but comic at this moment." This in an admonitory tone.

"Why?" said Gilbert.

"Why!" replied Patty, curling her lip in some scorn of such a question. "I should have thought it was very obvious. A poor girl lying ill—"

"What of?"

"Well—neuralgia of the stomach, they say. I expect it's some sort of gastritis—"

"You don't think it's a baby—"

Even Patty started at the bluntness of the question.

"No. I can't say. I've had no suggestion of such a thing. I hope not, indeed. That *would* be a calamity. Did you say you were going over?"

"Yes. I'm going to ask her."

"Yes. So you should. And if it were so—would you marry her?"

"What do you think?"

"I don't know. What do you *feel*?"

"Me? Nothing very pleasant."

"No—so I should imagine, so I should imagine. You've got yourself into a nasty position—"

"Not I. If a lot of fools make a lot of fuss, why should I blame myself for something that's only natural, anyhow."

"Natural—yes—maybe. But if Emmie Bostock is going to become a mother, and you're not going to marry her—or perhaps you are—"

"No I'm not."

"No, you're not! Well then!"

"I can't help it," said Gilbert.

"That is no solution of her problem," said Patty.

"I didn't invent the problem," said Gilbert.

"Who did then?"

"Her father, society, and fools."

"You had no hand in it, then. You had no finger in the pie?"

"Be hanged to fingers," said Gilbert.

"Well then!" said Patty, starting and looking round as the woman came in with the tray.

"Do you mind lighting up, Mrs Prince!"

Then, changing the subject slightly, she spoke of Lewie and his doings, until the woman went out of the room.

"Mind," said Patty, pouring out the tea. "I'm not so foolish as to think that you *ought* to marry the girl, if she is in trouble—"

"Thank you," said Gilbert, taking his cup.

"No. I think that would be throwing good money after bad, so to speak. But surely *some* of the responsibility is yours. The woman isn't going to be left to suffer everything."

5 "What a damned lot of fool's rot it is," said Gilbert, becoming angry as he felt the crown of fatherhood being pressed rather prickly on his brow.

"Yes, it is! It is! There should be a provision for the woman in these matters. There should be a State Endowment of Motherhood,* 10 there should be a removal of the disgraceful stigma on bastardy. There *should* be. But there isn't. And so what are you going to do?"

"Find out first," said Gilbert, rising and buttoning his coat.

"Oh, but finish your tea," said Patty.

"I've done, thank you."

15 "But you can't ride to Eakrast tonight."

"Yes I can."

"Dear me. But leave it till tomorrow—do. Wait till Lewie comes."

"No thanks. I'll go and make sure, anyhow."

As a matter of fact, State Endowment of Motherhood and the stigma 20 on bastardy had done for him. The wind had gone all out of his sails as completely as if Patty had put two cannon-balls through him, and the ship of his conversation could make no more headway on the ruffled waters of her tea-table. Was he to lie there like a water-logged hulk? Was he to sit in that smothering arm-chair with his cup on his knee and 25 a scone in his fingers, sinking deeper and deeper through the springs of the chair like a leaky wreck foundering? Thank Goodness his legs had taken the matter into their own hands—pardon the Irishism—and had jerked him on to his feet.

Chapter IX.

Emmie at Eakrast.

Emmie, we had forgotten to say, was engaged to Walter George all the time she was carrying-on with Mr Noon. The fact so easily slipped her memory that it slipped ours. We ought to have mentioned it sooner, for the sake of Alfred Bostock even.

To be sure, Emmie had been engaged several times. She got engaged in peace-time as easily as other women do in war-time. On every possible occasion she accepted a ring: varying in value from ten shillings to three pounds. Almost every time she sent the ring back when the affair was over. Twice the young men had generously said she could keep it. Hence the three ornaments which decked her fingers, and of which she was justly proud.

One she wore ostentatiously on her engagement finger. It was one of those re-made rubies, quite red and nice, and Emmie felt she could honestly say it was a real stone. It tied her to Walter George quite closely. She had shown it with pleasure to Gilbert, and told him its history. And he had wondered if he was bound by the laws of Emmie-gallantry to offer himself as an engagee. There wouldn't be much harm in it. And Emmie would so lightly commit pre-wedding bigamy, and there is safety in numbers.

But he hadn't gone so far, and Emmie had no ring of his. These rings, she loved them, they were her trophies and her romances, her scalp-fringe* and her forget-me-not wreaths, her dried roses pressed into sound £. s. d.

Walter George was a quite nice boy: we are going to make his acquaintance. He was a clerk, and quite a gentleman. Let us say it softly, for fear of offending a more-than-sacred institution, he was a bank-clerk. He had walked out with Emmie all the time he was in Woodhouse, and she had hardly found an opportunity for a stroll with anyone else. Cruel authority, however, had moved him to the newly-opened branch of the London and Provincial bank in Warsop.* He departed, deeply regretting the soft and cuddly Emmie, who made love an easy and simple path for him. For the ease and simplicity of his paths of love he was wise enough to be thankful. Therefore, when rumour

whispered poison-gas in his ear, he looked at other maidens, and imagined himself cuddling with *them* in a dark entry, and wiped his ears. Emmie was Emmie. So far, she belonged to herself. His nature, being easy like hers, though less flighty, comprehended her sufficiently
5   to realise that she was sipping all the flowers of love in her singleness in order to store the honey-jars of connubial felicity for him. The honey might be no more than golden syrup, but he would never know the difference. And therefore, so* long as Emmie had the decency not to offend him too openly, he had the sense not to peep round the
10 corner after her when she left him.

Some men want the path of love to run pleasantly between allotment gardens* stocked with cabbages and potatoes and an occasional sweet-william: some men want rose-avenues and trickling streams, and so scratch themselves and get gnat-bitten: some want to scale unheard-
15 of heights, roped to some extraordinary female of their fancy—*chacun à son goût.** Walter George was born in the era of allotment gardens, and thus Providence had provided for his marital Saturday afternoons. Which is saying a good deal. He was a bank-clerk too, and wanted to have an easy conscience and a dressy spouse. Church parade every
20 Sunday morning was an institution to him. And he had quite a lot of cuddly lovey-doveyness. If anyone can mention to me a better recipe for a husband, I shall be glad to write it down.

Emmie took him seriously. Roses and rapture* were good fun, but the cauliflower was the abiding blossom.* Co-op. entries might
25 have their thrill, but she was not one of those whose fanatic idealism insists on spending a life-time in such places. No, she would rather forfeit her chances of heaven than her chance of a home of her own where she could keep warm like a cat, and eat her cauliflower of a Sunday dinner.

30 In short, Emmie was *au fond** very sensible, much more sensible than her father. She knew even better than he that the cauliflower is the flower of human happiness, and that rose-leaves act like senna. All very well to purge off the follies of youth with red, or better still with pink roses.* And she was sooner purged than her father. If only he had
35 understood, he would have slept better in his bed. But, seeing his own more frenzied colics revived in the vagaries of his Emmie, he reacted more violently than he need have done, and that largely from fear. Once his daughter had run away he began to realise this.*

Having thus apologised for our characters, and demonstrated that
40 they have a bed-rock of common-sense; having revealed their

acquaintance with the fact that rose-leaves bring belly-aches, and that cauliflowers are delicious, and that Sunday dinner is the key-stone of the domestic arch, on which repeated arches all society rests;* having proved, in short, that the Bostocks are of the bulldog breed, full of sound British sense; let us go on with our story with more 5 self-satisfaction than heretofore.

Emmie arrived at her sister Fanny's with real pains rending her. She knew it was rose-leaves, but blamed her father. In fact she was in a state of subdued hysteria. So she took to her bed, and decided to turn over a new leaf. No, not a rose-leaf. She decided, if possible, to 10 open the last long chapter of a woman's life, headed Marriage. She intended it to be a long and quite banal chapter, cauliflower and lovey-doves. Having at the moment a variety of pains in her inside, dubbed neuralgia of the stomach, she developed some of her own father's reactionary hatred against the immortal rose. And though her 15 hatred would lose its violence as the pains passed off: though it would decline into mere indifference, like her mother's, except she would retain a little crisp flirtiness of manner, to show she kept her end up: still, this sound and sensible emotion, this fundamental detestation of rose-leaves because she knew what rose-leaves were (just like her 20 father: a piece of impudent assurance too); this dislike of the immortal rose, and a consequent exaltation of the solid cauliflower would henceforth be the directing force of her life.*

Warsop—and with this word the story gets on its feet again—lies but ten miles from Eakrast, across the forest. After two days of 25 temper, hysteria, neuralgia of the stomach, after-effect of rose-leaves, or whatever it may have been, Emmie began to recover her common-sense. She had eaten the rose, and would make an ass of herself no more. So she lay and plotted for settling down in life.

The school and school-house were one building. In the front, the 30 long school-room faced the road: at the back, the house-premises and garden looked to the fields and the distant forest.

Fanny, Emmie's sister, was a dark, rather big-nosed girl, very good-natured. She had been married for a year, and had a baby. She received Emmie without too much surprise or consternation. In 35 Fanny's sky the weather always blew over.

"Don't bother. It'll blow over," she said to Emmie as she said all her life to herself.

She put her sister on the sofa, covered her up, and gave her a hot cup of tea; then she* waited for Harold to come in. Emmie could 40 hear Harold, on the other side of the wall, talking away at the scholars.

"Now then, Salt, what river comes next? Witham Welland Nene and Great Ouse—what comes after that? Don't you know? Do you know what your own name is? What? Oh, you do, do you. What is it? What? Salt! And if the Salt hath lost its savour?* You don't know, do you. No, you wouldn't. Tell him what river comes next, Poole."

Emmie guessed it was Geography: therefore probably near the end of the afternoon. Listening, she could occasionally hear a shrill word from the assistant teacher, a girl, who was apparently taking sewing. There were only about forty-five scholars in the whole school.

The itch came over the rose-leaf-griped girl, to be down in the school-room taking a lesson. She longed to begin with a "Now then—." Fanny had been a teacher, and had helped Harold till the advent of the baby. When the baby was a bit older, she would get a servant and go into the school again with Harold. It was so handy. You could just pop in and turn the pudding while the children were doing their drawing. You could pop in and put the kettle on at half-past three, and at four o'clock you would find it singing nicely.

Emmie envied Fanny her little school and school-house. As for Harold, he was all right. He was very respectable and a bit of a mardy,* perhaps—but he was all right.

"Hello Emmie. We weren't expecting you," he said when he came in from school and found her at tea with Fanny and the baby. He talked in the rather mouthing fashion which teachers often have in the Midlands. "Have you got holidays at Woodhouse then?" he continued, his first thought of course, being school.

"No, I've come away from our Dad for a bit."

"Oh! I thought perhaps you'd closed for measles. We've twelve absent this afternoon.—What's amiss then."

"Oh, same old song. Our Dad nagging the life out of me till I can't put up with it. I thought I'd come here a bit if you'd have me."

"Yes, you're welcome. But won't your Dad be more wild than ever? What about school?"

"I've sent to tell them I'm bad. And I am an' all. I'm feeling damn bad, Harold!"

"Are you, why what's wrong?"

"I've got a cramp in my inside till I don't know what to do with myself. I had to sit down about six times coming from the station."

"And she's not eaten a thing," said Fanny.

"Looks to me as if she'd better go to bed," said the sympathetic

Harold. "*I've* had a sore throat for this last week. I've been thinking, Fanny—have you got that linseed in th' oven?"

Fanny had.

"You'd better look at it an' see it's not too dry. I sent Bentley for a stick of Spanish juice.* You'd perhaps have some of that Emmie. I know it's an old-fashioned remedy, but it does me more good than these modern preparations like aspirin and camphorated chlorodyne and such."

Fanny meanwhile was at the oven looking into a steamy stew-jar, from which came a strange odour of flax-seeds. She stirred the brown, pulpy, porridgy mass, and Harold came to look.

"It would do with a drop more water, dear, don't you think it would?" he said to Fanny, putting his arm round her neck as they both stared into the stew-jar, she crouching on the hearth-rug.

"Just a drop," said Fanny. "Take it from the kettle."

And between them they concocted the mess.

On the other side of the tall range which prevented, or which was to prevent the baby from walking into the fire, in future days, the bedding was airing.

"Should you like to go to bed now, Emmie?" asked Harold in concern.

"Oh, I can wait," said Emmie.

"You needn't wait," said Harold, disturbed to see her sitting there mute with a pinched-up face, doubling herself over as twinges caught her.

"I'll make your bed directly I've fed baby," said Fanny, picking up the infant that was crying crossly for food.

"I can do it," said Harold. Like a good economical soul and husband, he had taken his jacket off when he came in, and was in his shirtsleeves. "I'll take th' oven shelf up, Fanny," he added.

"Take the bottom one," said Fanny, who was faintly squeezing her breast between two fingers as she directed the nipple to the infant. "It's not so red-hot as the top one."

Harold wrapped the oven shelf in an old piece of blanket, and took it upstairs with him and the candle, for a bed-warmer. In the spare bedroom he went methodically about, making up the bed.

"I tell you what," he said as he came down, "I'll put that oil-stove up there a bit, to warm the air. It comes rather cold."

And he rubbed his arms, through his shirtsleeves.

Another half-hour, then, saw Emmie in a warm bed, in company of

the oven shelf against which she knew she'd knock her toe. She screwed herself up upon her pains, which, though genuine enough, seemed to proceed from a sort of crossness which she could not get over. The little paraffin oil-stove shed its low light and its curious flat,
5 oil-flame warmth across the atmosphere. Harold appeared with a cup of the brown, slimy steaming linseed-and-liquorice stew and pressed her to drink it.

"I take a lot of it, and find it does me worlds of good. I think it's the oil, myself. I'm sure it's better than cod-liver oil. Your skin gets so nice
10 and soft if you take it regular."

But Emmie, her naturally fluffy hair rather astray over the pillow, her little brows rather tense, would not look at it.

"Don't come near me, my lad. I don't want to be looked at," she said, half hiding her crossness in a sort of gruffness.

15 "Is it all that bad. I'll go down and make you a bran-bag,* should I?—You've not lost your good looks, anyhow.—But should I make a bran-bag for you?"

"Ay—" said Emmie.

Down he went, found there was no bran, put his hat and coat on and
20 went down the lane to borrow some: returned, and stuffed it into a flat flannel bag, put this between two plates in the oven, to heat, and finally carried it, piping hot, up to Emmie, who gratefully hugged it against her.

"Thank you, my old chuck,"* she said to him. "It's rosy, that is."
25 "Perhaps that'll shift it," said Harold.

"Ay—perhaps."

But she had her pains all through the night, and said in the morning she hadn't slept a wink. She looked peaked, and Harold was bothered, so he sent a note for the doctor: much against Emmie's will. The doctor
30 said it was neuralgia of the stomach, and Emmie said it felt like it. Harold made Fanny write to Woodhouse, and in the school-room from time to time he would raise his voice a little and say:

"Less noise there down at that end! You know what I've told you. You know how poorly Miss Bostock is, in bed in the house. Think of
35 others besides yourselves."

And the scholars duly hushed themselves, and felt important, having somebody poorly in bed in the school-house.

That evening Harold came up to Emmie for a fatherly talk.

"What's wrong between you an' Dad more than usual?" he asked.
40 "Oh nothing," said Emmie.

"Nay, come, it's not nothing. It must be something rather special, if you've not told Fanny yet."

"I don't feel like talking, either," she said.

"You'd better tell us. You'd feel better if you got it off your chest."

"There's nothing to tell," said Emmie.

"Nay," expostulated the young man. "If that's the way you feel towards me and Fanny, then we know how matters stand."

Emmie sulked in the bed with her new bran-bag, and Harold sat in the chair beside the little oil-stove—there was no fireplace in the bedroom—and felt offended.

"Oh damn you," said Emmie. "You're an old nuisance."

"Ay, I know I'm an old nuisance, if I don't just please you altogether," said Harold, rather flattered than otherwise. "But it's for your own good I ask you. It's nothing to me personally—except I always want to do my best for you and for all of you, for Fanny's sake. Though it isn't so very much I can do. Still, I'll do my bit whenever I get a chance."

There was a slight pause after this oration.

"I had a walk with Gilbert Noon, if you want to know," said Emmie.

"What, with Gilbert Noon from Haysfall Technical? I should have thought he'd have known better. And did your Dad catch you?"

"Yes."

"And what did he say?"

"He knocked Gilbert Noon's cap off, and had his own cap knocked off back again, and they both fell down in the dark in a gooseberry bush, and all the blame laid on me, of course."*

"You don't mean to say so! Did they go for one another?"

"I didn't stop to look. Our Dad's a devil—an interfering spying devil. He'll kill me before he's done."

And Emmie pulled the sheet over her face and blubbered underneath it. Poor Harold, who was in a whirlpool of emotion, sat pale as death in the chair, and felt like offering himself up as a burnt offering, if he could but find an altar with a fire going.

"Well now," he said at length. "You shouldn't let it get on your nerves. Dad means well, I suppose, only he goes a funny way about it. What do you take it to heart for? You can stop here for a bit till things blow over. Have you written to Walter George?"

He waited with beating heart for an answer. No answer: though a certain stilling of the under-sheet waters.

"Have you written to Walter George, Emmie?" asked Harold once more, in an excruciatingly gentle and pained voice.

A sniff from under the sheet.

"No"—from under the sheet.

5 Harold watched the sheet-top, which had grown damp during the bad weather, and, to its mournful blotting-paper blankness he said, tender, anxious, treading gingerly on the hot bricks of emotion:

"And aren't you going to?"

No answer from under the sheet.

10 "You're going to, aren't you Emmie?"

No motion from under the winter-landscape of a sheet.

"You're not in love with Gilbert Noon, are you Emmie? You'd never make such a mistake."

"No I'm not, fat-head."

15 This barked out from under the sheet gave Harold hopes of the re-emergence of the crocuses and scyllas of Emmie's head. Surely a thaw had set in beneath the damp snow-scape of the sheet.

"Well I'm glad to hear that, at any rate. Because I'm sure it would be a mistake. I'm sure Walter George is the man for you, Emmie; though I 20 must say your treatment of him is such as most men wouldn't stand. I know I shouldn't. But he hasn't got a jealous nature, and that's why he's the right sort for you.—My word, if your Fanny treated me as you treat him, there'd be some fat in the fire, I can tell you. Somebody would have to look out. But different men, different ways. He's not a jealous 25 nature, thank goodness."

Out popped crocuses, scyllas, christmas roses and japonica buds in one burst from beneath the wintry landscape. In short, Emmie's head came out of the sheet, and her nose was so red with crying that we felt constrained to make the japonica flower too early.

30 "Different men have different ways of showing it, you mean," she snapped. "He won't have any occasion to be jealous, once he isn't a hundred miles off. So there! I know what I'm doing."

"Well, I've always said so. I've said to him more than once, 'she'll be as true as wax once the knot is tied, Walter George, but she's not the 35 one to leave at a loose end.' And he sees it plain enough. Only he doesn't think he's in a position yet—

"But I tell you what! Why don't you come here and help me? Miss Tewson is leaving at the end of February. You come here and help me, and you could see a bit more of one another while you make your minds 40 up."

Harold had his little plan. Indeed, life is made up of little plans which people manufacture for one another's benefit. But this little plan Emmie had fore-ordained herself. It had occurred to her when she heard Miss Tewson's treble chiming after Harold's baritone in the school beneath. She wanted a little peace.

And so she began to feel somewhat better, and the pains began to diminish.

"You write him a note," said Harold, "and I'll ride over tomorrow night and take it him, and ask him to come over for the week-end. How about that, now? Does that suit?"

"I'll see," said Emmie.

But Harold knew the victory was won, and he went to bed with his Fanny as pleased as if all the angels were patting him on the back. And his Fanny was quite content that the marigolds of his self-satisfaction should shed themselves in her lap.

In the morning Emmie wrote to Walter George.

"Dear old bean-pod

Lo and behold I'm at our Fanny's, and bad in bed, and that mad with myself I could swear like a trooper. Come over and cheer me up a bit if you can. If you can't, come over to the funeral. Ollivoy! E.B."

Ollivoy was Emmie's little pleasantry, substituted for *au revoir*. Sometimes she wrote *olive-oil* instead.

The day was Friday. She listened to the business of the school, and at last felt happier in bed. She felt what a luxury it was, to lie in bed and hear school going on: hateful school. She heard the children go shouting out, at midday, into the rain. There was rain on the window and on the wet bare creeper stalks. She wondered if Harold would ride ten miles through the weather.

Listening, she heard thud-thud-thud, and realised it was Fanny knocking with the poker on the fire-back downstairs, to summon Harold in from the school-room. This was Fanny's wireless message to her overdue schoolmaster. Presently the sister, rather blowsy but pleasant-looking, came up with stewed rabbit and a baked onion. Harold had thought out the baked onion. It was such a good receipt for earache and neuralgia of the face—a hot onion placed against the ear: therefore why not just as good taken internally, for neuralgia of the stomach. Nourishing as well. He explained to the two sisters, who had been school-teachers as well as he, what proportion of sugar there was in onions, and what proportion of other matter: something very encouraging, though we forget exactly the ratio. So Emmie plunged her fork into the nutritious bulb, which sent its fumes wildly careering round the room, and even tickled the nostrils of afternoon scholars, so that they became hungry again at five past two. We little know the far-

5   reaching results of our smallest actions.

Chapter X.

Introduces Walter George.

The afternoon, thank goodness, cleared up, and Harold prepared his
acetylene lamp till the whole village knew he was going to ride out on
his bicycle, and wondered if Miss Bostock was taken worse, you know. 5

He reached Warsop by half-past six, having ridden against the wind.
Walter George did not come in till seven, because the bank was doing
overtime. When he came, Harold greeted him as man to man, and met
with a similar greeting back again.

Walter George—his family name was Whiffen, since trifles 10
matter—was a nice, well-built, plump lad of twenty-one, with round
rosy cheeks and neat hair cut rather long and brushed carefully
sideways: *not* backwards: who looked exactly like a choir-boy grown
into a High-School boy, and a High-School boy grown into a bank-
clerk, and a bank-clerk just budding for a nice, confidential, comfor- 15
table-looking, eminently satisfactory manager of a little bank in some
little industrial place in the provinces. Already he inspired confidence,
he looked so like the right kind of choir-boy grown into the right kind
of high-school boy, the kind that mothers find so satisfactory as a
product of their own. 20

And indubitably he was gone on Emmie. We prefer the slang, as
having finer shades than the cant though correct* phrase *in love
with*. In-love-with means just anything. But to be gone on somebody is
quite different from being smitten by her, or sweet on her, or barmy
over her. Walter George was gone on Emmie, and he was neither 25
smitten by her nor barmy over her.

"Hello Harold! You're a stranger."

Walter George Whiffen was just a tinge patronising towards the
bicycle-bespattered, wind-harrowed young schoolmaster.

"You've not ridden over from Eakrast?" 30

Why, you bank-clerk, do you think he'd flown over, with bicycle clips
round his trouser-ankles and spots of mud on his nose.

"Yes, I've come with a message for you."

"For me?"

Immediately Walter George's rosy face looked anxious. 35

"We've got Emmie bad at our house."

The choir-boy—he was no more at this moment—looked with round eyes on Harold.

"Bad!" he re-echoed. "How long?"

5   "Oh, since Tuesday. She's been in a rare way, I tell you: awful amount of pain."

"Where?"

"Why, the doctor says neuralgia of the stomach, but I say it was more like cramp of the stomach. We were up half the night two nights with

10 hot bran-bags. I thought she'd go off any minute, as true as I'm here I did. She couldn't speak, and her face went that funny. Cramp of the stomach catches you and you die like a fly, almost before you know where you are. I was thankful when she came round a bit, with hot bran-bags and hot water-bottles to her feet, I can tell you."

15   The choir-boy stood with his mouth open and his eyes blue and round, and did not say a word for some moments.

"Had she got it when she came?" he asked at length.

"Bad, she had. She'd got it bad when I came in and found her at tea-time. It took her I don't know how long to walk from the station.

20 She had to keep sitting down by the roadside, and going off in a dead faint.—It's a thousand wonders she ever got to our house: our Fanny says so an' all."

The choir-boy's pleasant mouth, that still looked more like chocolate than cigarettes, began to quiver, and he turned aside his face as his eyes

25 filled with tears. Harold, also moved too deeply, turned his pale and hollow face in the opposite direction, and so they remained for some minutes like a split statue of Janus, looking two ways.

"Did she ask for me?" quavered the choir-boy's voice in the east.

"She did," sounded the schoolmaster's voice from the west. "She

30 sent you a note." And he took the missive from his pocket.

Then the two halves of the Janus statue turned to one another as if for the first time, and the choir-boy wiped his eyes with a dashing and gentlemanly silk handkerchief which he had bought for himself at the best shop in Warsop. Having wiped his eyes he took the letter. Having

35 read the contents he looked at the envelope. After which he kissed the note-paper, and let Harold see him do it. Harold approved heartily, and knew that was how he himself would feel if it was Fanny. The hearts of the two young men beat as one.

"Poor little child," said the high-school boy, wiping his eyes again.

40 "How did she get it?"

"It's nerves, you know. She's a bundle of nerves—*I* know from Fanny. She lives on her spirit, till her nerves break down. And she'd had a row with her father again. He doesn't understand her a *bit*." This last from the psychological schoolmaster with some spleen.

"Had he been tormenting her?" asked the bank-clerk. 5

"Why he makes her life a misery," said the schoolmaster, with a curl of the lip.

The bank-clerk, almost a man now, looked aside and became red with profound indignation.

"She's only a bit of a thing you know," he said brokenly. 10

"I tell you," rejoined Harold. "She ran away to Fanny and me for a bit of protection."

"Damned devil," murmured the bank-clerk, making his brows heavy against the bugbear.

"Oh but she's a king to* what she was," said Harold. "And that's 15
one thing, she'll be better nearly as sudden as she got bad: I'm hoping so, anyhow. She's eating a bit today. She seemed fair comforted when I told her to ask you over for the week-end, and when I said she could stop with us and take Miss Tewson's place. Don't you think that would be better all round?" 20

"Yes—" but the young gentleman wasn't listening. "I'll ride back with you tonight."

"Oh I shouldn't," said Harold. "Can't you come tomorrow and stop over Sunday? That's what we were counting on."

"Yes, I shall be only too glad. But I'll see her tonight." 25

The high-school boy had no sooner uttered this resolve, and was fixing his clouded brow like another Roland,* than his landlady tapped at the door and hovered half way into the little parlour. She was a nice old lady with a lace cap.

"Your pardon, young gentlemen—but tea is ready for you." 30

"Oh!" and the high-school boy became the incipient bank-manager. He put his hand lightly through Harold's arm. "Come on. We have dinner at one o'clock here, and a late tea. Mrs Slater can't cope with dinner at night. We'll sit down, shall we?" And he led the half-willing Harold to the door. 35

"No thanks," said Harold. "I'll be off. I had my tea before I came. I'd better be getting back."

"Oh no you won't—not till you've had a cup of tea." And he led his friend hospitably across the little hall or entrance passage, to where his landlady stood hovering in the doorway of the little dining-room. 40

"Mrs Slater—you know Mr Wagstaff, don't you?"

"Indeed I do. Indeed I do. Come and sit down both of you."

She spoke in a small, piping voice, quite briskly for the sake of the young men. But her face looked remote, as if she hardly belonged. She
5 seemed to be looking across the gulfs which separate us from early Victorian days, a little dazedly and wanly.

Walter George, of course, did not dream of going without his tea. He ate large quantities of toast and bloater-paste and jam and cake, and Harold tucked in also. And the little woman in a lace cap looked at
10 them from far away behind the tea-pot—not that it was geographically far away, only ethnologically—and was glad they were there, but seemed a little bewildered, as if she could hardly understand their language.

Harold, as appetite began to be appeased, demonstrated methodi-
15 cally to the bank-clerk that it was no use his, Walter George's, riding to Eakrast tonight, that he would only knock himself up for tomorrow and spoil Emmie's chance of a perfect recovery and her bliss in a perfect meeting. Of which the young gentleman allowed himself to be convinced. Therefore he begged to be allowed to write a line in answer
20 to Emmie's. Therefore Harold sat on pins and needles while the young Tristan* covered much paper. Harold, of course, was thinking of Fanny and the baby, and how they'd be getting nervous etc. etc.

But at length Walter George sealed his letter and addressed it to Miss E. Bostock. He wrung Harold's hand in the high-road, and
25 watched the acetylene flare elope down the hill.

Chapter XI.

Lovers' Meeting.

"My precious, poor little thing,
    I felt my heart was breaking when Harold told me the news. Little was I expecting such a shock as I came in late from the bank, where we are doing overtime for the next fortnight. Little did I think you were so near, and in such a condition. I almost broke down completely when Harold told me. I wanted to come at once, but by the time I had had my tea and given Harold a cup it was after eight o'clock, and he said you'd be settling down for the night before I could get to Eakrast. Not wishing to imperil your night's rest, I have put off coming to my own little angel till tomorrow, but oh, I don't know how I keep away, for I feel my heart torn for you. I have never had a greater shock than when I heard of your illness. I picture you so small and fragile, with your beautiful baby face, and could kill myself to think of all you have had to suffer. Why these things should be, I don't know. I only know it shall not happen again if I can help it.

Well, my darling little treasure, Harold is waiting for this, so I must not keep him. What a splendid fellow he is. How thankful I am to heaven that you have his roof to shelter you and his arm to sustain you. He is indeed a man in a thousand, in a million I might say. I shall never be sufficiently grateful to him for taking care of you at this critical juncture. But when I think of your father I feel that never can the name of father cross my lips to him. He is not my idea of a father, though unfortunately his type is only too common in the world. Why are children given to such men, who are not fit even to have a dog?

Oh, my little child-love, I long to see your flower-face again. If I am not unexpectedly detained I shall be at Eakrast by three o'clock tomorrow, but don't be anxious if I am a little later. Man proposes, God disposes*—unless there is really the devil having a share in the matter, which I believe sincerely there is, otherwise you would not be suffering as you are. I hope the pains are gone, or at least diminished by now. I cannot bear to think of you in agony, and am afraid Mrs Slater may see in my face what I feel.

Well goodbye my own sweetest little kitten and angel. I feel I can't

wait till tomorrow to fold you in my arms and tell you once more how I
love you. Oh if we could only unite our perfect love and be as happy as
Harold and Fanny. I feel we must risk it very soon, funds or no funds.
This kind of thing must not and shall not continue.

5   With one last kiss from your unhappy lover, and one last hug before
you go to sleep

> I am your own ever-loving
> Walter George Whiffen."

Emmie read this effusion once more when she woke in the morning,
10 and was satisfied. It was what she expected, in the agreeable line, and
what can woman have more? What can satisfy her better, than to get what
she expects? Emmie, moreover, knew what to expect, for she had had
various such letters from various authors. Walter George was perhaps
the most elegant of her correspondents, though not the lengthiest. She
15 had known one young collier who would run to six pages of his own
emotions over her baby face etc. Oh, she knew all about her baby face
and "our perfect love." This same perfect love seemed to pop up like a
mushroom, even on the shallow soil of a picture-postcard from the seaside. Oh, we little know, we trembling fiction-writers, how much perfect
20 love there is in the post at this minute. A penny stamp will carry it about
hither and thither like a dust-storm through our epistolary island. For in
this democratic age love dare not show his face, even for five minutes, not
even to a young tram-conductor, unless in the light of perfection.

So Emmie took her perfect love with her breakfast bacon, and
25 remembered that morning had been at seven some little while back, at
which hour God is particularly in His heaven, and that hence, according
to Mr Browning, all was well with the world.* Like any other
school-teacher, she had a number of "repetition" odds and ends of
poetry in her stock-cupboard. So why shouldn't she, as well as some
30 Earl's daughter, enrich the dip of her bacon with Browning, to borrow
Hood's pun.*

The day was fine, and her only problem was whether to get up or not.
She would have had no problem if only she had brought her sky-blue
woolly dressing jacket along with her. Failing this, how would she
35 manage in a white shetland shawl of baby's, and Fanny's best nighty? She
decided she would manage.

The morning was fine. Harold went pelting off on his bicycle to buy a
few extra provisions. Emmie had the baby in bed with her, and smelt
Fanny's cakes and pies cooking down below. Dinner was a scratch meal
40 of sausages, and Emmie had an egg instead.

Harold brought her some sprigs of yellow jasmine to put by her bed, and tittivated up the room a bit, according to his and her fancy. Then he left her with her toilet requisites. She was a quick, natty creature. She washed and changed in a few minutes, and did her hair. When Harold tapped, to carry away the wash-water, asking if he could come in, she answered yes, and went on with her job. 5

She was propped up in bed, with a silver-backed mirror propped facing her, against her knees, and she was most carefully, most judiciously powdering her face and touching up her lips with colour. Harold stood with the pail in his hand and watched her. 10

"Well if you don't take the biscuit!"* he said.

"Which biscuit?" she said absorbedly. "Hand me the towel."

And she concentrated once more on her nose, which was her Achilles' heel, her sore point.

"You fast little madam," said Harold. His Fanny never "made up." 15
He wouldn't have stood it. But he quite liked it in Emmie. And he loved being present during the mysteries of the process.

"Go on," she said. "I feel so bare and brazen without a whiff of powder on my nose."

He gave a shout of laughter. 20

"I like that," he said.

"It's a fact though. I feel as uncomfortable without a bit of powder as if I'd forgot to put my stockings on."

"Well it never struck me in that light before. We live and learn. I bet you think other women barefaced hussies, if they don't powder." 25

"They are. They don't know how to make the best of themselves, and then they show the cheek of the Old Lad."*

She put her head sideways, screwed her mouth a little, and carefully, very carefully put on a stroke of rouge.

"You think it improves you, do you?" he asked, standing with the pail 30
in his hand, and watching curiously.

"Why," she said, not taking her eyes off the mirror. "What do you think yourself?"

"Me? Nay, I'm no judge."

"Oh well, now you've said it. People who are no judge generally do 35
the judging."

He felt pinched in his conscience.

"Ay, well—I think I like the genuine article best," he said walking away.

"Go on, you're no judge," she said coldly. 40

She finished her toilet, disposed her shawl carefully, and proceeded to the last task of polishing her nails. She looked at her hands. How beautiful they had become whilst she was in bed: how white and smooth! What lovely little hands she had! She thought to herself she had never seen such beautiful hands on anybody else. She looked at them, and polished her small finger-nails with consummate satisfaction. Then she tried her rings first on one finger and then on another, and thought the bits of gold and colour showed up the loveliness of the skin. She enjoyed herself for half an hour, fiddling with her own hands and admiring them and wondering over their superiority to all other hands.

We feel bound to show our spite by saying her hands were rather meaningless in their prettiness.

While thus engaged she heard a loud prrring—prring of a bicycle bell outside in the road. Heavens! And it was only a quarter to four. She hastily dropped her scissors into the little drawer, and took the sevenpenny copy of the *Girl of the Limberlost** into one hand, and her best hanky in the other. So equipped, and framed behind by the linen and crochet-edging of one of Fanny's best pillow-slips, she was prepared.

She heard voices, and heavy feet on the stairs. It was her Childe Rolande to the dark tower come, ushered up by Harold.

She looked for him as he came through the doorway, and he looked for her as he crossed the threshold. Never was so mutual a greeting of tender faces. He was carrying a bunch of pheasant's-eye narcissus and mimosa: luckily it was Saturday, and he could get them at the shop.

"Hello old thing!" sounded his overcharged voice.

"Hello!" her deep, significant brevity.

And he bent over the bed, and she put her arms round his shoulders, and they silently kissed, and Harold in the doorway felt how beautiful and how right it was. We only wish there might be a few more *ands*, to prolong the scene indefinitely.

But Walter George slowly disengaged himself and stood up, whilst she gazed upward at him. His hair was beautifully brushed and parted at the side, and he looked down at her. Their looks indeed were locked. He silently laid the flowers at her side, and sank down on one knee beside the bed. But the bed was rather high, and if he kneeled right down he was below the emotional and dramatic level. So he could only sink down on one poised foot, like a worshipper making his deep reverence before the altar, in a Catholic church, and staying balanced

low on one toe. It was rather a gymnastic feat. But then what did Walter
George do his Sandow exercises* for in the morning, if not to fit
him for these perfect motions.

So he springily half-kneeled beside the bed, and kept his face at the
true barometric level of tenderness. His one arm was placed lightly   5
around her, his other gently held her little wrist. She lay rather
sideways, propped on her pillows, and they looked into each other's
eyes. If Harold had not been there to spectate they would have done
just the same for their own benefit. Their faces were near to one
another, they gazed deep into each other's eyes. Worlds passed   10
between them, as goes without saying.

"Are you poorly, my love?" asked Walter George Whiffen, in a tone
so exquisitely adjusted to the emotional level as to bring tears to the
eyes.

"Getting better," she murmured, and Harold thought that never,   15
never would he have thought Emmie's little voice could be so rich with
tenderness.

He was turning to steal away, feeling he could no longer intrude in
the sacred scene,* and the two dramatists were just feeling
disappointed that he was going, when fate caused a rift in the lute.*   20

Fanny, like a scientific school-teacher, polished her bedroom floors.
The mat on which Childe Rolande was so springily poised on one foot
slid back under the pressure of the same foot, so his face went
floundering in the bed. And when, holding the side of the bed, he tried
to rise on the same original foot, the mat again wasn't having any, so his 25
head ducked down like an ass shaking flies off its ears. When at last he
scrambled to his feet he was red in the face, and Emmie had turned and
lifted the beautiful flowers between her hands.

"I tell our Fanny we shall be breaking our necks on these floors
before we've done," said Harold, pouring his ever-ready spikenard.   30

"Don't they smell lovely!" said Emmie, holding up the flowers to the
nose of Walter George.

"They aren't too strong for you, are they?"

"They might be at night."

"Should I put them in water for you?" interrupted Harold.   35

"Ay, do my dear," said Emmie benevolently to him.

And he went away for a jar, pleased as a dog with two tails. When the
flowers were arranged, he spoke for the last time.

"You don't feel this room cold, do you, Walter George?"

"Not a bit," said Walter George.   40

"Then I'll go and see what Fanny is doing."

Now the perfect lovers were left together, and tenderness fairly
smoked in the room. They kissed, and held each other in their arms,
and felt superlative. Walter George had been wise enough to take a
5   chair, abandoning that kneeling curtseying-knight posture. So he was
at liberty to take Emmie right in his arms, without fear of the ground
giving way beneath him. And he folded her to his bosom, and felt he
was shielding her from the blasts of fate. Soft, warm, tender little bud
of love, she would unfold in the greenhouse of his bosom. Soft, warm,
10 tender through her thin nighty, she sent the blood to his head till he
seemed to fly with her through dizzy space, to dare the terrors of the
illimitable. Warm, and tender, and yielding, she made him so wildly
sure of his desire for her that his manliness was now beyond question.
He was a man among men henceforth, and would not be abashed
15 before any of the old stagers. Heaven save and bless us, how badly he
did but want her, and what a pleasure it was to be so sure of the fact.

"I tell you what," he said. "We'll get married and risk it."

"Risk what?"

"Why everything. We will, shall we. I can't stand it any longer."
20 "But what about everybody?" said Emmie.

"Everybody can go to hell."

And here we say, as Napoleon said of Goethe:

"Voilà un homme."*

He held her in his arms. And this was serious spooning. This was
25 actual love-making, to develop into marriage. It was cuddly rather than
spoony: the real thing, and they knew it. Ah, when two hearts mean
business, what a different affair it is from when they only flutter for
sport! From the budding passion in the Eakrast bedroom many a firm
cauliflower would blossom, in after days, many a Sunday dinner would
30 ripen into fruit.

The lovers were very cosy, murmuring their little conversation
between their kisses. The course of their true-love was as plain as a
pike-staff. It led to a little house in a new street, and an allotment
garden not far off. And the way thither, with kisses and the little
35 plannings, was as sweet as if it had led to some detached villa, or even
to one of the stately homes of England. It is all the same in the end: safe
as houses, as the saying goes. Emmie was now taking the right turning,
such as you have taken, gentle reader, you who sit in your comfortable
home with this book on your knee. Give her then your blessing, for she
40 hardly needs it any more, and play a tune for her on the piano.

"The cottage homes of England
How thick they crowd the land."

Or if that isn't good enough for you:

"The stately homes of England
Are furnished like a dream."*   5

Play the tune, and let that be your portion, for you are not going to take any part in the burning bliss of buying the furniture, or the tragedy of the wedding-presents.

"There's a little grey home in the west."*

Pleasantly the hours passed. The party gathered for a common chat   10
in Emmie's bedroom before supper. The table was laid downstairs, and there was polony as well as cheese and cocoa, all waiting invitingly: the cocoa still in its tin, but standing at attention on the table. The clock ticked, the baby was in bed, the kitchen was a cosy feast, if only they would come down and tackle it. The clock struck ten.   15
And still the party in the bedroom did not break up. Still the supper waited below. Emmie was making her droll speeches, Harold was exercising his dry wit, and the high-school boy was laughing out loud, and Fanny was saying: "Oh my word, what about baby?" Whereupon they all lifted a listening ear.   20

Chapter XII.

The Interloper.

In one of these moments of strained attention a motor-cycle was heard slowly pulsing down the road outside. It came to a stop. The strength of its white lights showed under the bedroom blind, in spite of Emmie's lamp. She knew at once what it was, and restraint came over her.

In another minute there was the crunching of a footstep on the path below, and a loud knock at the back door. The company in the bedroom looked at one another in consternation, even affright. Harold summoned his master-of-the-house courage and went downstairs. The three in the bedroom listened with beating hearts.

"Is this Mr Wagstaff's?"

"Yes."

"Is Miss Bostock here?"

"Yes."

"Can I see her?"

"She's in bed."

"Ay, her mother told me she was bad. Is she asleep?"

"No, she's not asleep."

"Can I speak to her a minute?"

"Who is it?"

"Gilbert Noon."

"Oh! Is it anything particular?"

"No. But I just want to speak to her. Just tell her, will you?"

Harold was so flustered he went upstairs and said:

"Gilbert Noon wants to see Emmie."

Childe Rolande and Fanny stood open-mouthed.

"All right, let him come up then," said Emmie sharply.

"Should I?" said Harold.

"Don't look so ormin'.* Let him come up," repeated Emmie in the same sharp tone.

Harold looked at her strangely, looked round the room in bewilderment. They listened while he went downstairs. Gilbert still stood outside in the dark.

"Shall you come up?" said Harold.

88

And after a moment.

"There's the stairfoot here. Let me get a candle."

"I can see," said the bass voice.

The light of the little bedroom lamp showed on the landing at the top of the stairs.

Heavy feet were ascending. Emmie gathered her shawl on her breast. Gilbert appeared in his rubber overalls in the doorway, his face cold-looking, his hair on end after having taken his cap off.

"Good-evening," he said, standing back in the doorway at the sight of the company.

"Do you know Mr Whiffen, Mr Noon?" said Emmie sharply. "My elect, so to speak."

Gilbert shook hands with Childe Rolande, then with Fanny, whom he knew slightly, and then with Harold, to whom he was now introduced. Harold had gone rather stiff and solemn, like an actor in a play.

There was a moment's pause.

"Well, how are we?" said Gilbert rather awkwardly to Emmie.

"Oh, just about in the pink, like," she replied. She was cross, and showed it.

He was rather disconcerted.

"I saw your mother this afternoon," he began.

"Where?" she snapped. "Sit down some of you, and make a bit of daylight. It's like being in a wood."

Fanny handed Gilbert a chair, Childe Rolande sat assertively on the bed, at the foot, and Harold went to the next bedroom and was heard bumping the legs of a chair as he carried it in, while Fanny looked agonies for baby.

"Where did you see mother?" asked Fanny pleasantly.

"At Lewie Goddard's."

"And she was all right?"

"Yes—seemed so. Worried, you know."

"What, about Emmie?"

"Yes—and one of the children with measles: but getting better, I believe."

"Tissie hasn't got them then?" asked Fanny.

"I didn't hear your mother say so."

"Because when they start, they usually go through the house. I hope baby won't catch them."

"There's no reason why she should, is there?"

"Oh, they're very bad in Eakrast——"

And Emmie, Walter George, and Harold sat like stuffed ducks while this conversation wound its way through all the circumstances of measles in the Warsop Vale region.

5   Emmie had not told Walter George about Gilbert and the *fracas*. She had warned the other two not to speak of it. And now she was in such a temper she could not, for her life, think of anything to say. She sat propped up in bed, looking very blooming, but with a frown between her little brows. She twisted and twisted her ring with its big ruby,

10   round and round her finger, and grew more tense as she felt the Fanny–Gilbert conversation running down. She had asked Harold to bring Gilbert up because she always preferred to trust rather to her ready wit than to her powers for inventing a plausible lie in answer to troublesome questions. And now she was as stupid as a stuffed

15   owl,* and couldn't say a word. The conversation died, there was an awful vacuum of a pause. Meanwhile Emmie sat in the bed with her head dropped, twisting and twisting her ring. In another minute she would be flying into tears: and Walter George sat near her feet worse than a monument.

20   Harold Hardraade* lifted his head.

"You came on a motor-bike didn't you, Mr Noon?"

"Yes," said Gilbert.

"I thought I heard one come up the lane."

"I lost my way the other side of Blidworth and got to Sutton before I

25   knew where I was. And then coming through Huthwaite I had something wrong with my engine, and had to stop and have that seen to."

"My word, you have had a journey. What time did you start?"

"Why I was coming down Woodhouse hill at a quarter to six."

30   "My word, and it's after ten. You've been out of your road some."

"I have. I don't know these roads round here, and it's like riding in a puzzle."

"Oh, the roads through the forest and round-about, they're very misleading. You'd best have come through Thoresby,* you know.

35   It's a bit longer, but it's a better road. What made you go Blidworth way?"

Started an itinerary conversation between the motor-cyclist and the push-cyclist, whilst Emmie still turned her ring, and Childe Rolande stared inquiringly and rather mortified at the newcomer. He resented

40   the intrusion deeply. Not only was he forced to smell a rat, but even he

must have the rat thrust under his nostrils. He sat rather stiff on the bed, and turned the side of his rosy cheek unrelentingly towards the bothered Emmie.

The itinerary conversation slowed down, and Fanny felt she must get out of it. She couldn't stand it.

"I'll go and make the cocoa," she said, rising. "You'll have a cup of cocoa, won't you, Mr Noon?"

"No thanks, I won't trouble you."

"Yes do. It's no trouble. I'll make you one then. Harold you'll go to baby if he cries."

"All right," said Harold.

And when Fanny departed a hoar-frost of silence once more settled on the dislocated party. Harold began to get a resigned martyr-at-the-stake look, Walter George was becoming thoroughly sulky, and Emmie was breathing short. Gilbert sat looking rather vacant—a trick he had when he was ill at ease.

Suddenly came a thin wail from the unknown.

"There's baby," said Harold, and with all the alacrity of a young husband he quitted the room.

The frost now became a black frost. It seemed as if each of the three of them remaining in the bedroom would have been killed rather than utter a word to either of the others. A deadlock! Lips and hearts were padlocked. The trinity sat as if enchanted in a crystal pillar of dense and stupid silence. Emmie felt the pains coming on again, Gilbert felt how cold his feet were with the cycling, and Walter George felt that a can-opener would never open *his* heart or lips again. He was soldered down.

From the next bedroom they could hear all the soothing sounds of the young husband, sounds anything but soothing to one who is not a first-born and an infant in arms. From below they heard the clink of tea-spoons and smelled the steam of stirring cocoa. And suddenly Gilbert lifted his head.

"What ring is that?" he asked.

Emmie started, and stared defiantly.

"What, this? It's my engagement ring."

"Mine," said Childe Rolande, with a sulky yelp. Whereupon he became nearly as red as the re-composed ruby.

And immediately the frost settled down again, the padlocks snapped shut, and the solder went hard in the burning lid-joints of Walter-George's heart. For a few seconds, Gilbert went to sleep, the cold air having numbed him. Walter George sat on the edge of the bed and looked over blackly at his toe-tips. Emmie tried to scheme, and almost got hold of the tail of a solution, when it evaded her again.

A soft, very soft, fear-of-waking-baby voice floated like a vapour up the stairs.

"Cocoa's ready."

Gilbert woke and looked round at the door, but did not stir. Childe Rolande did not bend his gloomy looks, but stretched his neck downwards over the bed-edge and stubbornly contemplated his nice brown shoes as if he had heard no sound.

"Go and have your cocoa," said Emmie, speaking to t'other-or-which, as the saying is. But she was completely ineffectual. Gilbert sat dreamily, vacantly on, and Childe Rolande sank his chin nearer and nearer his knees, as he perched on the edge of the bed like some ungraceful bird.

Emmie now gave way to resignation. Was she not the base of this obtuse-angled triangle, this immortal trinity, this framework of the universe? It was not for her to break the three-cornered tension. Let fate have its way. If Gilbert had not given himself to vacancy the problem might seriously have concerned him: how to resolve an obtuse-angled triangle into a square of the same dimensions. But he was glotzing,* if we may borrow the word.

But eternity has rested long enough on this tripod footing, the universe has been framed quite long enough inside a triangle, and the doctrine of the trinity has had its day. Time now the sacred figure, which magicians declare to be malevolent, dissolved into its constituents, or disappeared in a resultant of forces.

Oh Deus ex machina, get up steam and come to our assistance, for this obtuse-angled triangle looks as if it would sit there stupidly forever in the spare bedroom at Eakrast. Which would be a serious misfortune to us, who have to make our bread and butter chronicling the happy marriage and the prize-taking cauliflowers of Emmie and Walter George, and the further lapses of Mr Noon.

So, Deus ex machina, come. Come, God in the Machine, Come! Be invoked! Puff thy blessed steam, or even run by electricity, but come, oh Machine-God, thou Wheel of Fate and Fortune, spin thy spokes of destiny and roll into the Eakrast bedroom, lest Time stand still and Eternity remain a deadlock.

Is our prayer in vain? We fear it is. The God in the machine is perhaps too busy elsewhere. Alas, no wheel will incline its axle in our direction, no petrol will vaporise into* spirit for our sakes. Emmie, and Childe Rolande, and Mr Noon may sit forever in the Eakrast bedroom.

Well then, let them. Let them go to hell. We can at least be as manly as Walter George, in our heat of the moment. 5

Gentle reader, this is the end of Mr Noon and Emmie. If you really must know, Emmie married Walter George, who reared prize cauli-flowers, whilst she reared dear little Georgian children, and all went happy ever after.

As for Mr Noon! Ah, Mr Noon! There is a second volume in store 10 for you, dear reader. Pray heaven there may not be a third.

But the second volume is in pickle. The cow in this vol. having jumped over the moon, in the next the dish, dear reader, shall run away with the spoon.* Scandalous the elopement, and a decree nisi for the fork. Which is something to look forward to.* 15

PART II.

Chapter XIII.

High Germany.

The sun was shining brightly when Mr Noon awoke in his bedroom in the ancient and beer-brewing city of Munich, capital of Bavaria, queen of the lovely southern lands of Germany. Does not the Marienkirche lift her twin brown cupolas capped with green copper over roofs and palaces* and look pleasantly round her this morning? For behold, the snow is melting, and is piled in heaps in the thawing streets. Behold, the sun is shining, and the time of the singing of the birds has almost come. Behold, the long, watchful line of the ice-pale Alps stands like a row of angels with flaming swords* in the distance, barring us from the paradise of the South. Behold the land of the thawing snow stretches northward and westward to the lakes like chrysoprase this morning, and the foothills of more Alps, and the rolling plains of Germany, and the islands of the west. Yes, the islands of the west, meaning the British Isles. We will say Islands of the Blest, if you wish it, gentle reader.

Well then, here you are———and the rolling plains of Germany, and the islands of the Blest. Yes, the islands of the Blest, meaning the British Isles. Now you've got it.

After which I hope I can say what I like. For if that sop doesn't sweeten Cerberus,* I hope it'll choke him.

No, I'm not going to tell you how Mr Noon got out of the Eakrast bedroom; I am not. Eat the sop I've given you, and don't ask for more till I've got up the steep incline of the next page and have declined like a diminished traveller over the brow of the third.

You'll not hear another word about Emmie. In fact there is no Emmie. I saw someone coming down the street when I was in Woodhouse last Christmas, and I thought I knew her walk. She was in a pale-coloured fur coat and a cap of black-seal-fur, and she had a little girl by the hand, a little girl clad in a white curly-woolly coat and white woollen gaiters. "Dear me," thought I, "what a lot of gentry crops up in Woodhouse nowadays."

So I crossed the road, beaming becomingly.

"Why how are you E———"

But the child raised its round blue eyes, and I saw a chorister hovering.

97

"Mrs Whiffen," I concluded.

"Quite well thanks. How are you?"

How brisk, how sharp, how rapped out, how coined in the mint of the realm! If the head of King George* had been embossed on
5   every one of her words, as it is on pennies, it could not have given a sounder ring of respectability and genuine currency. I felt like a man who is caught trying to change a bad shilling, and hurriedly fished a few half-pence of well-worn small-talk out of my purse, and rushed the risky shilling back to cover. I wouldn't have pronounced the name
10 Emmie, not for worlds, in the presence of that fur coat and infant.

There! I said you wouldn't hear another word about Emmie, and you haven't. If I have mentioned Mrs Whiffen, as she sauntered down Knarborough Road in a pale-coloured fur coat and a black seal-coney cap, leading a little woolly-curly, gaitered girl by the hand, I have done
15 so designedly, to prevent your thinking, gentle reader, that I have no presentable acquaintances at all.

And Mr Noon! You have heard that he awoke in his bedroom in the ancient, royal, and beer-brewing city of Munich. Well, and what by that? Is there anything wrong with it? I expect you are waiting for me to
20 continue that the bedroom was a room in a brothel: or in a third-rate and shady hotel: or in a garret, or in a messy artistic-bohemian house where a lot of lousy painters and students worked their abominations. Oh, I know you, gentle reader. In your silent way you would like to browbeat me into it. But I've kicked over the traces at last, and I shall
25 kick out the splashboard of this apple-cart if I have any more expectations to put up with.

Mr Noon awoke in none of these places. He awoke in a very nice bedroom with a parquet floor and very nice Biedermeier furniture* of golden-coloured satin-wood or something of that sort, with a couple
30 of handsome dark-red-and-dark-blue oriental rugs lying on the lustrous amber polish of the parquet floor. He awoke with his nose trying to emerge over the white cumulous cloud of his swollen but downy overbolster.* He awoke with the sun coming through the double windows, with a handful of gentian looking very blue on his round
35 Biedermeier table, and a servant in a dark-red cotton dress entering with a cup of eight-o'clock tea. He sat up quite comfortably in bed to take his tea, and said Guten Morgen to Julie. I say he sat up comfortably because the air in the room was dulcet and warm, for the house had central heating.
40 Now, gentle reader, I had better give you time to readjust yourself.

You had better go upstairs and change your dress and above all, your house shoes. You had better tell the maid to light the drawing-room fire, or light it yourself if there is nothing else for it. In the Isles of the Blest every house has its drawing-room, and the drawing-room fire is always lighted to receive company.   5

"Let your light so shine—"*

And while you are changing your dress let me explain that we stand upon another footing now. Not that we have lost a leg in Badajos's breaches,* but that we have gone up a peg or two. Man is mercurial, and goes up and down in the social scale like a barometer in   10 the weather. This I hope you will allow, gentle reader, even if you be at the moment perched high upon Mount Batten, or on that Windsorial eminence which you share with nothing but soap.*

What is man, his days are as grass. Though he rise today above the vulgar democratic leaves of grass as high as a towering stalk of fools-   15 parsley, tomorrow the scythe of the mower will leave him as low as the dandelion. What is a social status nowadays? The wind passeth over it and it is gone, though the place thereof may see it again next summer,* even the crown of the cow-parsnip soaring above the herd of green.   20

While you are changing your dress, gentle reader, don't get in a stew because you have never heard of Biedermeier or because you don't know what Bavaria is doing in connection with such a disreputable land as Germany. Bavaria can't help it, and Biedermeier doesn't matter. We can't all be born in the Isles of the Blest; only a few of us fortunate   25 ones: Te Deum laudamus.*

Let me re-introduce you, by your leave, to Mr Noon. Kindly forget that it ever rhymed with spoon. In German a spoon is a Löffel, and Noon is *now*.* It isn't my fault that Noon is Now in German—but so it is. So pray cast out of your mind that spoon association, and be   30 prepared for the re-incarnation of Mr Now. Noon is Now. That is, he is at his zenith, and you, gentle reader, may even belong to the afternoon.

"Gentle reader, may I introduce you—Mr Noon."

Bow, gentle reader, bow across space to Munich, ancient capital of   35 ancient kings, known to the British youth on the beautiful postage-stamps. Beautiful postage-stamps of Bavaria, Bayern* so beauti-fully lettered, do they now stamp black ink words of obliteration across you? Ah well, they didn't in Mr Noon's day. And therefore, gentle reader, be on your best behaviour at once, for the ancient and royal   40

court is only just round the corner, and who knows what Kammerjunker* or what Lady in Waiting may be casting a supercilious eye
over your manners.

"The Herr Professor is already there," said the maidservant, tapping
5   and entering once more as Mr Noon tied his bow tie: the identical tie
he had tied for Patty and for Emmie.

"Right," said Mr Noon.

And in another moment he was striding across the amber flooring of
the hall, to the breakfast room.

10   "Ha! There you are. Julie! Julie!" sang the Herr Professor,*
covering his fretful impatience with a certain jocularity. He was a
smallish man with white hair and big white moustache and little white
imperial and very blue eyes and a face not very old. In fact he was just
over fifty, and restless and fidgetty. He had spent ten years in England,
15   so spoke English well, if in the rather hard-breathing, German fashion.
How Gilbert came to be living in his flat I shan't tell you. I am sick of
these explanations. Sufficient that the Herr Professor was called Alfred
Kramer, and that he held a chair in the university.

He had brought various little English fads with him to Munich, and
20   one of these was Quaker Oats. Julie appeared with the plates of Quaker
Oats, and the two men sat down opposite one another. The
professor—we will call him Alfred and so spite all titled Germany—
seemed to be pondering. He tucked his napkin under his chin and ate
his porridge without saying a word. Catching sight of a spot on the
25   linen table-cloth, he poked it with a carefully-manicured finger-nail,
like a child. His eyes had a petulant look.

Gilbert, who was not to be outmatched in a game of silence,
contented himself with his own thoughts. He half-divined the petu-
lance and fussiness of his host, and therefore withheld his attention.
30   Though he lived with the professor house-free, he gave certain
valuable assistance with a book his host was providing, and felt he
earned his salt. He knew that Alfred at the bottom was glad of his
presence. For the fretful, petulant professor was one of those Germans
who find the presence of an Englishman soothing and reassuring, seem
35   to derive a certain stability from it. And therefore Gilbert took no notice
of moods, and Alfred was careful not to be really offensive.

He was a sensitive soul, really, the fussy, rather woe-begone looking
little man. And he was by nature liberal. But, in spite of his moderate
riches and his position, he felt himself at some sort of disadvantage
40   before the world, and so was often irritable and tiresome.

This was one of his mornings of tiresomeness. Gilbert had a faculty of abstraction or of vacancy, whichever you like, which made him the most feasible companion to such a man. He said nothing, but dreamed, or mused, or abstracted, whichever it was, and took his egg in its little silver cup, and helped himself to honey, and handed his cup to the professor without further thought. And if Alfred in his spirit was mortified because Gilbert's cup came too soon, and took a bigger proportion of the coffee than the little man liked, and if his sense of proprietorship writhed to see his guest make so free in the matter of honey, still, the host with his little imperial under his thickish mouth managed to expend all his exasperation inside himself, which was a relief, really. It was a relief that the small brimstone fires of his irritable meannesses set nobody else's corn-ricks alight. He begrudged the unearning Englishman his bigger share of coffee, and he almost wanted to snatch the honey dish off the table. Yet all the time he knew so well that such irritability and such small meanness and grudging were beneath him, beneath his *intellectual* temper if not his housekeeping one, that he only bounced on his chair and spied out the spots or flaws in the fine linen cloth, or the scratches on the silver. So did the poor professor keep the smallness of the flesh in check by the greatness of the restraining mind. He told himself quite plainly that if his guest ate a pot of honey every morning—which he didn't—what were the odds to a man with an income of two-hundred-thousand marks. No odds at all. And yet, poor Alfred, he twitched on his chair at every spoonful after the third, and the mongrel dogs of the flesh almost jerked the leash out of the controlling hand of the mind.

But not quite. Which was always a great cause of self-satisfaction to poor Alfred. He was pettyfogging in his blood, and he knew it. So he admired Gilbert's *sang froid* with the honey more even than he hated it; for in the mind, at least, the little professor was a free soul, even if he had never found a *von*.* In the mind he was superior, and he knew that it behoved him to be superior somewhere, he, with his queasy spirit. If he had given way to his own littlenesses, then he would have condemned himself to the society of natures as little as his own. Which, to a man of his squeamishness and intellectual intelligence, would have been a worse mortification than death itself. So he put up with the pin-pricks of his stingy flesh, for fear of the sword-thrust in his freer spirit. Almost he loved Gilbert for administering the pin-pricks with so cool and unconscious a hand. He loved his own little whippings, for he knew they were good for him. Perhaps if he lived to be a hundred he

would be able to sit sunnily in his chair while the guest scraped the
dish and licked the honey-spoon. Perhaps he would even tell Julie to
put a new pot on the table. Who knows the ductibility of human
forbearance.

5   In one direction, however, poor Alfred's idealistic forbearance had
been drawn out too fine, almost to breaking point. It is curious how
much easier it is to be idealistic over big things than over little: how
much easier it is to give a hundred pounds for the Home for the
One-legged, than to see a guest take ten spoonfuls of honey: how
10 much easier it is to die a heroic death than to get over one's foibles.

    How thin Alfred's idealism had stretched his human sensibility at
one point, and that the most important, the following conversations
will show.

    "Na!"* said the professor suddenly, breaking the spell. "What
15 are you going to do today?"

    The day was Sunday, when everybody must do something.

    "Nothing in particular," said Gilbert. He had a few acquaintances
with whom he might talk his head off, in the Court Brewery or the
Hahn Café. Or he could go to Pinakotheks or Glyptotheks* or to
20 music. All remained to be seen.

    "I am going to work," said the professor crossly.

    "You don't want me, do you?" said Gilbert.

    "No—no. No—no. I have something prepared in my *mind*—" the
professor emphasised this word in a fine resonant voice, and put his
25 finger-tip to his fine forehead, as if the something prepared was a rare
old cup of tea for the universe. But alas, the professor was only
nervously joking. Though he worked and fussed and wrote and
theorised and popped up hither and thither like some unexpected
rabbit in the warren of learning and theory, it was all artificial to him.
30 He was missing something. He was missing something. What was it?
It was life. He was missing life, with his books and his theory and
papers. The mental part of him was overstrained and ennuyé, and yet
what was he to do. He was damned to theorise.

    For sure he had a drop too much of Jewish blood in his veins, and
35 so we must not take him as typical of the sound and all-too-serious
German professors for whom the word is God, though the Word is
not with God,* but with them, the professors thereof.

    Alfred—we can't help saying poor Alfred—boomed out the *Word*
with the best of them. And since he was a very shrewd little person,
40 with generation after generation of Rabbinical training behind him, he

could lick the usual German professor with his left hand, at intellectualising. And he knew it. Hence the boom of his voice:

"I'm going to *work*."

But Gilbert belonged to his private life, and so he did not mind letting Gilbert hear the half-jocular frisky boom, he did not mind revealing to his young acquaintance that he was going to let himself off in a whoop of self-importance, and that he knew it.

So off he trotted to his study, after having informed Julie that he was working, and that niemand and nichts,* nothing and nobody should disturb him. For the Word was with *him* that morning.

Once in his study the frisky jocularity and importance fell from him. Out of his depression he had worked it all up, for Gilbert's sake. The whoop would not come off. Alas, he felt dry and anxious. Books, books, books! Blotting paper, and paper, and gold pen. The neat and spotless and roomy writing desk, the date calendar, the nibs, the reference books, the god-knows-what of a rich learned man in his study. Ach Gott, there it all was, and he was missing something.

Alfred looked at it all, and the little tense pleat came childishly between his forehead. He sighed, and said: "Ach! Ach jeh! Wo ist——?"* And he fiddled among the pens and among the papers, though he had lost nothing and was looking for nothing. His nervous anticipation of authorship was all a fraud. Now he was in the study he seemed to have shrunk, to have gone littler: for he was little to start with. A great nervous weight was upon him. Books, paper, pens, ink. Books! walls and bastions, buttresses and gables of books!

Imagine it, for a white-haired little man of fifty-three, who has booked it all his life, and who has moreover twenty-three Rabbinical ancestors in a straight line behind him! For a little man who suddenly imagines Life to be something and the Word a mere bauble in the hands of buffoons like himself. Finds himself strangely anxious, books showering down on his head like the ruins of Carthage, while all the time he wants life, life, whatever life may be. Finds himself anxious—to be with young people, to share their existence, their youth.

He sighed again and dipped his pen, seated himself like a little boy in his chair, and drew his paper to him. He arranged it, he squared it, he settled it in the centre of his blotting paper with the nicest precision, touching it along the edges with his nervous, fussy fingertips. That was life. To take a sheet of paper, to arrange it, to settle it, to open the inkpot, to put the sealing-wax in its right place—all that was life. But to write, to put down words! Alas, to the poor professor this was anti-life itself, the most foolish of papery illusions. That Life with a big L was also an illusion of his, he had not yet realised.

So he fidgetted and sighed and scribbled a dozen words in his bad handwriting and reached for a reference book and it wasn't there 5 because it never was there but on the fourth shelf of the B block and so he frowned and felt he might get in a temper with Julie and he got up and hunted for the book and found it where he knew it was and busily rattled the leaves over looking for his reference: found it, and hastily scribbled it down on his paper. And that was the only bit of his 10 morning's work which he enjoyed.

He was scribbling a few more irritable words when he heard a step in the hall. Yes! And the clink of a walking-stick being taken from the hall-stand. Ach!—the unbearable—there was Gilbert going out: going out to the morning, and to life.

15 "Gilbert! Gil—bert!" he sang, in his resonant, musical voice. And he listened, his blue eyes round and childish and vaguely desperate. We must mention that he was the youngest child of elderly parents.

He was just starting out of his chair when he heard Gilbert's step on the polished parquet floor, so he settled himself and poised his pen, like 20 a man torn between two desires. The serious thought-line was adjusted in his brows.

"Ach Gilbert, weiss' du—?"* he began in his breathless, anxious German. Then he changed to English. He liked flourishing his English. "Ach, I can't find the second volume of Ammermeister's 25 *Theorie des Unbewussten*.* It ought to be on the second shelf. Do you know where it is?"

Gilbert was dressed for out-doors, overcoat and stick and hat on his head. Life—life!

He strolled to the second shelf of the D block and produced the 30 book.

"Oh yes! How silly of me. Thank you. Thank you!"—and then the anxious-theoretic-author voice changed to one more flippant: "Where are you going?"

"A walk."

35 "Where will you go?"

"Just a stroll."

"In the country—or in Munich?"

"Oh, I shan't go out into the country. Isn't there too much snow?"

"We-ell!" the professor pursed his lips. "For young and adventurous 40 persons like *me*—" he boomed jocularly—"there is not too much. I tell you, I like it. I like these days when the snow is melting, and you have patches, patches of the world coming through. I like it. I like the sun, even when it makes me feel my rheumatism. Ah, when we get old, we like even our Schmerzen*—Well? Don't we? You are young still. Only wait—only wait.—But seriously, I like these days among the best 5 of the year. The snow is going, going, the sun is come, come, and gentian and the pink flowers are on the patches. Ah—"—and here he looked through the double windows at the trees of the Ludwigshöhe* as they stood bare-twigged in the sunshine—"I am tempted. I am tempted. What do you say? What do you say to my lazy 10 and unworthy suggestion? My lazy and unworthy suggestion! What?"

"I've not heard it," said Gilbert.

"No, you haven't," said the professor. "But you *shall*. What do you say if we go into the country and look at my little piece of land where I am going to build my little wooden house, my dog-kennel I shall call it. 15 I shall call it the dog-kennel. I shall call it Vow-Wow. Vow-wow-wow!" and the professor rubbed his hands and imitated a dog barking. Then he glanced again brightly at Gilbert.

"What? What do you say? Shall we run away from *work*—" boom that word as he did—"and go and look at my house? Yes? Shall we?" 20

"I should like to," said Gilbert decidedly.

"Yes, you would! Then we will go. We will go and look at the land for my little Vow-Wow—" He fell into a sort of students' chant as he jumped from his chair and pressed the bell for Julie.

"But now then, when is there a train?" 25

He darted his nose into a time-table.

"Sonntag—Sonntag—Sonntag—Isartalbahn—Isartalbahn—Ommerhausen—Ommerhausen—Yes, we have it—halb-neun*—a quarter to eleven—a quarter to eleven—Sundays—yes. Will that do? Yes? Will it?" he looked up excitedly at Gilbert. 30

"Just right," said Gilbert.

"Yes."

Enter Julie. The professor countermanded dinner, and ordered boots and wraps.

"We will run away from work like two bad boys—" boom the word 35 boys—"and we will look at the seat for my little Vow-Wow. Seat you say?—or site? Site of course. And we'll be *Off to Philadelphia in the mo-orning.*"* Chant the last words all out of tune.

They set off, the professor in knee-breeches and cloak, Gilbert in mountain-boots and English leather gaiters. Alfred was as happy as a 40

school-boy. He rattled away in English as they sat in the little train
running down the Isar valley. They travelled third class, in those
wooden carriages where one can see the heads of one's fellow-
travellers in the other compartments. Students were there with guitars
5 and little accordions, there were snatches of song. Soldiers in Bavarian
blue leaned out of the carriage windows in spite of the cold air, and
with frost-reddened faces watched the landscape and shouted in
Bavarian dialect the length of the carriage.

The train ran comfortably beside the high-road, whose snow was
10 melted, or lay in mounds at the road-side. Students in groups were
strolling down the road, between the high, wind-tired pear trees and
apple trees. Men from the mountains, in short leathern trousers and
bare knees, like footballers, short little embroidered jackets, and a
chamois-tail in their green hats, jumped on the train at the station.
15 There was a sparkle and crackle of energy everywhere on the sunny
Sunday morning after the winter.

And Gilbert loved it: he loved the snow-ruddy men from the Alp
foot-hills, so hardy-seeming, with their hard, handsome knees like
Highlanders, and their large blue eyes, and their curiously handsome
20 plastique, form and mould. He loved the peasant women trudging
along the road from church, in their full blue dresses and dark silk
aprons and funny cup-and-saucer black hats. They all stood to look at
the little train, which rattled along beside the road, unfenced and
unhampered, as tram-cars run in England, and everybody made jokes
25 to them or about them.

Alfred and Gilbert got down at Ommerhausen and quickly left the
muddy village. The peasants, pious catholics, were coming from mass,
from the church which reared high its white neck, capped by a small,
black, Byzantine-looking cupola. The churches are so characteristic
30 that the sight of one will send the whole violent nostalgia of the
Bavarian highlands into the heart even of a stranger. So Gilbert, in the
midst of Bavaria, was seized with the strange passion for the place. He
went with Alfred across the levels, where the snow lay only in pieces
here and there: over the rushing little streams, towards the nestling
35 village of Genbach, whose white farms with their great roofs and low
balconies clustered round the toy-looking church. It was a tiny
village—not more than a dozen houses on the slope of a hill, near the
edge of the forest.

The sun was hot. Alfred had taken off his cloak and slung it through
40 his little knapsack. Gilbert did the same with his overcoat—and took

off his cap and stuffed it in his pocket. Then the two men turned round
to survey the world.

The great Isar valley lay beneath them in the spring morning, the
pale, icy green river winding its way from the far Alps, coming as it
were down the long stairs of the far foot-hills, between shoals of   5
pinkish sand, a wide, pale river-bed coming from far off, with the river
twisting from side to side between the dark pine-woods. The mountains, a long rank, were bright in heaven, glittering their snow under the
horizon. Villages with the white-and-black churches lay in the valley
and on the opposite hill-slope. It was a lovely, ringing, morning-bright 10
world, for the Englishman vast and glamorous. The sense of space was
an intoxication for him. He felt he could walk without stopping on to
the far north-eastern magic of Russia, or south to Italy. All the big,
spreading glamour of mediaeval Europe seemed to envelop him.

"Na! Isn't it beautiful?" said the professor.   15

"Beautiful," said Gilbert.

The bigness: that was what he loved so much. The bigness, and the
sense of an infinite multiplicity of connections. There seemed to run
gleams and shadows from the vast spaces of Russia, a yellow light
seemed to struggle through the great Alp-knot from Italy, magical Italy, 20
while from the north, from the massive lands of Germany, and from
far-off Scandinavia one could feel a whiteness, a northern, sub-arctic
whiteness. Many magical lands, many magical peoples, all magnetic
and strange, uniting to form the vast patchwork of Europe. The
glamorous vast multiplicity, all made up of differences, mediaeval,   25
romantic differences, this seemed to break his soul like a chrysalis into
a new life.

For the first time he saw England from the outside: tiny she seemed,
and tight, and so partial. Such a little bit among all the vast rest.
Whereas till now she had seemed all-in-all in herself. Now he knew it   30
was not so. Her all-in-allness was a delusion of her natives. Her
marvellous truths and standards and ideals were just local, not
universal. They were just a piece of local pattern, in what was really a
vast, complicated, far-reaching design.

So he watched the glitter of the range of Alps towards the Tyrol: he   35
saw the pale-green Isar climbing down her curved levels, coming
towards him, making for Munich and then Austria, the Danube, the
enormous meanderings of the Danube. He saw the white road, which
seemed to him to lead to Russia. And he became unEnglished. His
tight and exclusive nationality seemed to break down in his heart. He   40

loved the world in its multiplicity, not in its horrible oneness, uniformity, homogeneity. He loved the rich and free variegation of Europe, the manyness. His old obtuseness, which saw everything alike, in one term, fell from his eyes and from his soul, and he felt rich. There were so
5   many, many lands and peoples besides himself and his own land. And all were magically different, and it was so nice to be one among many, to feel the horrible imprisoning oneness and insularity collapsed, a real delusion broken, and to know that the universal ideals and morals were after all only local and temporal.
10   Gilbert smoked his pipe, and pondered. He seemed to feel a new salt running vital in his veins, a new, free vibration in all his nerves, like a bird that has got out of a cage, and even out of the room wherein the cage hung.

He trudged with the professor up a slope to a brow of the hill. And
15   there, in an angle of the forest, was Alfred's new bit of land. It faced the south-west, looked right across the wide valley to the hills and the high peaks in heaven. Behind, on two sides, was forest of fir and great beech-trees. A snug place with a great scoop of the world in front.

"You know," said the professor, as they paraded round the split-
20   wood fence, "I have one hobby, and that is houses. My brother has the same. I have a house in Göttingen and a house in Maulberg and a house on the Starnbergersee. Now I am going to have my little Vow-Wow. And I shall have it here."

They walked through a tuft of snow to a spot on the brow of the
25   slope.

"Here!" said Alfred. "What do you think?"

Gilbert stood and looked out at the snow peaks that bounded the far horizon, one looking over the other's shoulder in the remote sky. And as he looked he seemed rooted to the spot.
30   "Yes," he said. "Build it here."

"You know," said Alfred, "it is a model I saw at the exhibition—a little model wooden house. I have signed the contract, and everything will be complete by June, and it will cost ten thousand Marks. It is not cheap, but not so very dear. Hein? And it will be my little Vow-Wow."
35   "But what will you do with it?" asked Gilbert.

"What shall I do with it? I shall use it for a summer-house* for myself, and the children will stay with me, and my wife—and it will be very nice. What? Don't you think? Eh?"

"Yes," said Gilbert. "I do."
40   "And if you like you can stay here too."

"I wish I may."

"You wish you may—Well, you shall. In June: in June all will be ready. I shall give you a room of your own."

Gilbert had spied sparks of blue in the steep bank facing the sun, just below where he was standing. He went down and saw, for the first time in his life, blue gentian flowers open after the snow. They were low in the rough grass on the bank, and so blue, again his heart seemed to break one of its limits, and take a larger swing. So blue, so much more than heaven blue: blue from the whiteness of snow and the intensity of ice. He touched the perfect petals with his finger.

"The first gentian! Yes?" said Alfred, coming jerkily down and picking a few buds. "I must take them to show Marianne."*

Gilbert heard a noise. He looked up. A deer was running across the little clearing. It must have leaped from out of the fir-trees over the split-wood fence. Now it ran swiftly, on slender legs, straight to the fence on the beech side of the forest. It put its head back, and with the swift, frail feet ran along the side of the fence, seeking a way out. It started as Gilbert rose, twitching with alarm, and turning on its light haunches, ran quickly, almost without weight, back along the fence. It was puzzled finding no exit.

"Na, a Rehbock!"* said Alfred. "You see, it must have jumped over the fence. There! I thought the fence was high enough. But the children will like it. Won't they, don't you think?"

Gilbert was watching the animal, the delicate white marking of the rump, on which the tail lay in a pattern; the flatness of the haunches, the beautiful softness of the ruddy fleece. The little stag swerved, became frightened at the continual obstacle, turned, and came running forward again.

"Shall I open the gate for him and let him out?" said Alfred, going forward.

The deer was now terrified. It laid back its head and bounded by the fence. In a sudden gust of terror it sprang like the wind at the fence, showing its whitish belly, lifting its little feet clear, and alighting with a jerk like a puff of wind in the free forest, where it galloped away through the great beech-trunks, scarcely visible over the beech-leaves patched with snow. It was gone like a bit of magic, and Gilbert felt himself possessed.

The two men went back into the village to the inn, where they sat at the bare wooden benches and ate boiled pork and sauerkraut and good black bread and mountain butter and a delicious ring of cake, and drank beer, while the peasants and farmers and foresters smoked big pipes and talked, and were festive.

After dinner they rose again.

"Now we will walk to the Starnberg lake* and see my wife and
5   my mother-in-law. Yes? Shall we do so? Can you walk so far?"

"How far?"

"Oh, about eight miles, eight miles. But in the wood there will be snow."

So they set off. In the wood, as Alfred said, there was snow. Going
10 between the great beech-trees, some of which lay prostrate, there were only patches of snow. But on the paths between the great, dry trunks of the firs there was deep snow still, heavy walking. The fir-woods were dark and vast, impenetrable, and frightening. Gilbert thought of the old Hercynian forest,* and did not wonder at the Roman terror. For in
15 the dark and bristly fir-trees, in their vast crowded ranks, the dimness and the subtly crackling silence, there was something as it were of anti-life, wolvish, magical.

Both men were tired by the time they came to the top of the last hill and looked down on the long, pale lake of Starnberg. They wound
20 down past one of the royal castles, or villas, and waited on the little landing-stage for the steamer which was to take them to their destination. The afternoon was fading towards evening, lights were beginning to twinkle by the pleasure-lake, the cafés were already lighted up, and Alfred and Gilbert were growing cold and tired by the
25 time they had their place on the steamer. They were going only two stations down, to pay a visit to Alfred's mother-in-law.

It was dusk by the time they arrived and rang the bell.

"Ho Marta!" cried the professor to the maid who opened to him, a handsome girl. "Is the Baroness at home? Is anybody here?"

30 "Yes, Herr Professor. The Frau Professor and the Herr Professor Sartorius."

"Ach, are they also here? Ach—so! All right. All right. We will go up. Are they taking tea? So! So. We have just come right. Two more cups. Ach! Ach! We are rather tired. We have come on foot from
35 Ommerhausen. Yes, I will take off my shoes. I will take off my shoes. Ach! Ach!" and the professor seated himself wearily and a little stiffly in a chair in the hall, while the maid, who had taken his hat and cloak and knapsack and stick, now hurried away for shoes. "Ach! If I don't have my rheumatism tomorrow!" The professor spoke in English now,
40 and put his hand on his hip. "I fear it! I fear it! Oh!" and he gave a

twinge with his face. "Ach, Marta, my rheumatism!" he lamented as the
girl came back with patent-leather shoes. So she kneeled to unfasten
his thick shoes. She was a dark, lovely girl with thick black eyebrows
and a plait of black hair going right round her well-shaped head. She
wore a peasant-dress of mid-blue colour with sprigged roses, close   5
fitting at the breast, full skirted, and a fine white apron, bib-less. She
quickly drew off the professor's heavy boots, hurried away with them,
and came back with a pair of heelless pantoffles.*

"Shoes there are no more," she said, dangling the pantoffles. She
had a rich, mantling colour under her dark skin, and that curious   10
fecund virginity of a mountain-catholic peasant.

"Ach! Ach! Only pantoffeln! Well—what do you say?" and the
professor turned boisterously to Gilbert, changing into English. "It is a
choice of evils. Which do you choose? Boots or slippers with no heels?
Hein? Say the word, say the word."   15

For once Gilbert was embarrassed. Marta was looking at him, and
dangling the Japanese slippers. She had beautiful large grey eyes, slow
and steady. He was rather carried away by her. Her brightish blue dress
with the rose-sprigs was so telling. He looked at the professor, who,
rigged out in neat patent-leather shoes, was rather pleased with his   20
advantage.

"Well, what do you say? Say the word! Say the word!" sang the little
professor in his resonant voice, his tired pale-blue eyes looking jocular.

At that juncture they heard a door open upstairs, and looking up, saw
a woman* in a dull-green silk dress leaning over the rails.   25

"Ach, is it you, Alfred!" she said, in an odd, cultured voice, half
familiar, half excited.

"Ho Louise! Ho, you are there," sang the little professor.

"Ja! Ja! We didn't expect you."

"I didn't expect myself—ha-ha. Nor did I expect you. Ludwig is also 30
there? Yes. Ha! Well! How is everybody? Thou? The children."

Louise was coming down the stairs, slowly. She was a very beautiful
woman, with rich, pomegranate colouring and a beautifully chiselled
face. Her soft dark-brown hair hung rather loose over her ears, coiled
in a simple knot behind. She wore a long, beautiful scarf, frail and full 35
of dull glimmers of greens and black and dead white. She was one of
the women who naturally have a long scarf draping the shoulders, a
look of wearing a robe rather than a modern dress.

"Ja—all well. You too? Good!" and Louise reached the bottom stair.
She was looking at Gilbert. He had no more eyes for Marta, now   40

Louise had come. The beauty of the mistress, rich in colour as that of the maid, had a lovely, pure, soft-cut form, outdazzling the more oxen charm of the peasant girl. Louise knew her power.

"Mr Noon," said Alfred in English. "You have never met my wife.
5   Well, she is here. Louise, you know of Mr Noon, I told you of him in my letter to Dresden."

"How do you do?" said Louise, in slow, but very charming English, giving her hand to Gilbert, and narrowing her beautiful grey eyes in an odd way of scrutiny she had. "And so you come all the way on foot?—Oh,
10 my English, it is very bad, but you will forgive me.—Well then, come and have some tea. And bread and butter. Yes, I know you Englishmen, you want bread and butter with your tea. Come then."

She turned to Marta, and saw the straw slippers.

"Aber—!* But what are you doing with the pantoffles, Marta?"
15 she laughed mockingly.

"The gentleman will change his boots," said the grave-eyed peasant girl.

"Ah—yes! Yes!" said Louise, looking at Gilbert's wet and muddy boots.

20 "I'm not fit to come up either way," said Gilbert.

"Not fit? Oh yes. Take the pantoffles. Oh, what does it matter? Yes, take them. We are simple people here.—Yes Marta," she added in German—"take the gentleman's boots."

And Marta kneeled beautifully at Gilbert's feet. He blushed to his
25 ears, and Louise saw it.

"No—no," he said in his German. "I will do it."

"Oh let her! let her!" cried Louise. "What does it matter? She is used."

And so Gilbert sat confused whilst the beautiful, still peasant girl unfastened his thick boots and pulled them off. He pushed his feet into
30 the straw slippers.

"And now come," said Louise. "More cups, Marta, and some bread-and-butter—do you know?"

Gilbert paddled up in the heelless sandals, and felt a rare fool. He found himself in a long, yellow-amber-coloured room. A handsome
35 white-haired lady* with an arched nose rose from her chair and looked at Gilbert under her white, raised eyebrows, whilst she addressed Alfred in German, in a rather high voice.

"Oh yea, Alfred, and hast thou come all the way on foot, thou young fellow, thou! Hast thou no respect for thy white moustaches and little
40 beard? Ach, the man, he runs across the land like a ferret."

With which she turned to Gilbert. She was rather stout and handsome, in a black silk dress with a jabot of Venetian point, flaky, old lace.

"How do you do," she sang, in slow, high-pitched English, on a note of lament. "And must we speak English? No—it is too difficolt—I can it no more. You will speak Gairman.—Come, my son-in-law has brought you through the country in the weather. Oh yea! Sit down please."

But there was a third occupant of the room—Professor Ludwig Sartorius,* from Bonn. He was a middle-aged man with a dark-brown beard streaked with grey, a bald forehead, and little, nervous, irascible dark eyes. He was well dressed in the English manner, in grey, carefully tailored and booted: and he wore a handsome tie of an orange colour. Evidently something of a gallant: but of the irascible sort. He shook hands with Gilbert, and seated himself abruptly, only getting out the usual "How do you do," pronounced very German.

The party now settled themselves. The Baroness was at the tea-table, lighting the spirit under the silver kettle. Professor Sartorius sprang up to do it for her, as if a gun had gone off, and fumbled wildly in his well-flattened pockets for matches.

"Oh sit still, sit still, Professor Sartorius," said the Baroness, striking her matches calmly. "I am old enough to light my own tea-kettle, at my age—" And she peered with shrewd, rather screwed-up blue eyes at the spirit-flame. It was evident there was no love lost between her and the gallant professor. He sat down looking crosser than ever, whilst poor little Alfred, with his pink face and white hair, shone like a daisy.

"Ah, Ludwig," said the Frau Professor, "tell Alfred about Wendolf."*

The younger professor turned and began in German in a rather snarling voice. The Frau Professor—we will call her Louise, because she is Alfred's wife, and it is shorter—settled her skirts and turned her low chair towards Gilbert. The softened light fell from behind her, and threw a shadow from her soft dark hair and her long dark lashes, upon her cheek. Marta came in with a tray, and Gilbert again turned fascinated to the full, dark, motionless face of the girl, with its unspeaking closed lips and meeting dark brows, as she stooped with the tray full under the rim of the lamp which stood on the tea-table. Mediaeval, remote, and impressive her face seemed, banded above with the black plait of hair.

Louise, sunk in her low chair, her dark-green dress with its pale, metallic lustre falling rather full round her feet, shaded her brow with her hand and watched Gilbert's face. It looked to her young, and alert, and self-possessed, with its narrow, fine brows, and full dark-blue eyes, and pouting mouth. She watched him closely.

5   "You look at the maid," she said in a mocking voice. "Is she not beautiful?"

Gilbert had been vaguely watching, not criticising, so it was in a hadn't-thought-of-it tone he answered:

"Yes, I think she is."

10   "Quite a beautiful type. She is a peasant from the mountains, and she is in love with a young forester, and she will soon marry him. She has been with me since she was almost a child, and we lo-ove her."

Gilbert turned to Louise. She spoke the word lo-ove as if it were difficult to say, dragging it out and breaking the vowel. And she was

15   looking up at him from under her shading hand, half-laughing, half-wistful, her grey eyes with their dark light looking soft and vulnerable. She was really very beautiful. The warmth of her colouring and the softness of her hair seemed to give her a warm, almost winsome glow. Odd, the half-laughing winsomeness, with a touch of irony and a

20   touch of pathos. Gilbert watched her with round eyes.

"Is this your house then?" asked Gilbert.

"No, it is Mama's. And Marta is lent. My house is at Maulberg,* and my children. Today I have come to see Mama, and so I meet you.—Well—I shall be very banal, and ask you if you

25   like Munich. Yes, you do? Oh, I am glad. Yes, I like it as much as any town in Germany, though I like Dresden almost as much. And you get on with your work?—Oh, I am glad. Yes, I am sure you will do well at Munich for a year, then I think you must go to Göttingen. Yes, Göttingen will be better for you in a year."

30   "I must find some way of earning money," said Gilbert.

"Ach, money. Do not bother, it will come."

"What makes you know?" laughed Gilbert.

"Ah—" and she made an odd gesture of reckless indifference—"it always comes in these days.—And when you have your doctorate, you

35   will write?—yes? You will write, and go to England to be a professor?"

"I don't know," said Gilbert. "What should I write—unless I try music?"

"Music! But music! But music is not pure mathematics, nor applied

40   mathematics." She laughed in a quick, girlish way, ironical too. "You

will write music for England?—Well do! do!—And what will you write? An opera to begin with, I am sure."

"No," said Gilbert.

"Oh, you are joking! Everyone who writes music writes an opera in the first place. When he is an old man perhaps he will try to write just a song to sell to the music-hall, and so make money. Yes? Isn't it so?"

"I don't know," said Gilbert.

"Perhaps you will begin with writing a song for the music-hall, out of your mathematics? Yes? Do you think? 'Just like the ivy on the old garden wa-all.' So!"

"No," laughed Gilbert. "I'll do the opera in preference."

"Ach yes! And then the ivy. I must sing English songs in French, and then I know they are funny. Before this I am troubled, you know. But I like the ivy—

> 'Et comme le lierre
> Je vous grimperai—'"

"Ha-ha-ha!" rattled out Professor Sartorius, and he said in German: "That is a famous song, Louise, 'Et comme le lierre je vous grimperai.'" He tried to put some tune to it, but was tuneless. So he rattled with laughter, and added: "But where have you found it?"*

"Oh, it is English. But I am so unsure, I feel I may be moved by English, so I must put it in French to be sure."

"What is the English, what is the English?" cried Alfred, speaking up.

"Mr Noon will sing it to us, yes?"

But Gilbert shook his head.

"Then shall I sing it? You would like?—Ya, Mama, don't look down your nose at me.

> 'Jost like the ivee
> On the old garden wa-all
> Cling-ging so tightly
> What e'er may befall—'

Nein! Nein! I can't sing any more."

"What e'er may be—what?" cried Alfred.

"Be-fall!" said Louise, full-sounding.

"Yes—yes. Be-fall."

"But finish the chorus," said Gilbert.

"There is no *je-vous-grimperai*," said Alfred, professorial.

"Ah, it is later.

> 'As you grow older
> I'll be constantly true
> And jost like the ivy
> I'll cling to you.'"*

The professors burst into laughter.

"Nein!" said the Baroness. "No, it is too stupid. Louise, du Papagei,* we are all highly-educated people here, God be praised. Mr Noon—a-nother cup of tea. Yes—Yes."

"Aren't German music-hall songs funny?" asked Gilbert.

"Oh yes! Oh yes! But only, you see, the funniness is different. But they are as bad. Oh yes.—You must forgive me for laughing. Only the song was told me in Dresden—" and she began to laugh—"and I thought it was so funny—"

"Yes—yes—" cried the Baroness, knitting her brows and crooking her fingers—"'I'll cling to you.'"

"Yes, like ivy," cried Louise, laughing till tears came to her eyes.

"On an old wall, ach yea!" cried the Baroness, also shaking with laughter.

"Constantly true!" cried Louise, suffocated.

"Constantly true!" repeated the Baroness, her fine, mephistophelian white eyebrows going up her forehead in sardonic laughter as her sides shook.

"Constant *and* true," said Gilbert.

"Oh—I am wrong—I am wrong. Mama—Constant *and* true, do you hear," and after making a mock-solemn face, she again laid her hand on the arm of her chair and sat weak with laughter, while the Baroness rocked behind her tea-table.

The men were more uneasy.

"Really comic," Ludwig was murmuring in German, looking cross.

"Silly! Silly! They are too silly!" said Alfred.

And Gilbert sat and looked with round eyes at the two women.

"Yes, yes," sighed Louise. "It is too silly——" Then she changed her tone. "But you don't mind, Mr Noon, if we laugh. Ah, one must laugh sometimes. Does it matter what at?"

"Not a bit," said Gilbert.

"No, I think not."

The conversation now lapsed into German, and Gilbert followed with a little difficulty. The big professor theorised on the one hand, the little professor theorised on the other, and they wrangled with a noise like tearing calico, whilst the Baroness sat in impatience, throwing in a curt phrase now and then, and Louise sat in her low chair like a lovely Athena balancing the professorial scales* first this way, then that, and seeming passionately interested and looking very beautiful. Gilbert 5 watched with wondering eyes. It all seemed so strange. And why did Louise care whether the immature manuscript of Faust, which the great Goethe had commanded to be burnt and which his tender friend had not burnt,* why should anyone care whether the world saw this manuscript or did not see it? Care ethically, at least. Why should 10 this moral debate be raging between the two professors, balanced by the beautiful woman who was all the time stealing from Athena to give to Aphrodite, or stealing from Aphrodite to give to Athena.

Gilbert sat on ignored, and began not to hear. The women were soon sensitive of this. 15

"Now—enough! Enough!" put in the Baroness. "Goethe should burn his own old papers. And if he didn't, then let him not mind who scrubs the pans out with them. Let every man burn his own rubbish."

"No, Mama, it is a genuine question," said Louise.

"Yes, Mother-in-law," said the little professor. "My work is my 20 intimate property—etc. etc. etc." We won't hear them out, as we agree with the Baroness.

"Oh yea, one can say so much about nothing," protested the Baroness. "Are you eating here?"

"No," cried Louise, rising. "We must go." 25

"No thank you," cried Alfred. "We must catch the seven-fifteen train. Louise, how are you going home?"

"We came in a motor-car," said Louise, whilst Ludwig stood with drawn brows, his little eyes darting from side to side.

A maid was sent to summon the car. Alfred and Gilbert watched 30 Louise drive away with Professor Sartorius. Then they two prepared to catch the train for Munich.

"Ah, the Sartorius," sang the Baroness in her high, lament-voice, "he talks so much. Alfred, when you come to tea with me please do not climb up from the ivy on the wall to the godlike Goethe. Goethe is so 35 beautiful in himself, but not when he is torn to pieces between you and the Sartorius. Let the sartor stick to his patching, or we will call him snipper and Schneider—*Sartorius*."*

It was unfortunate that the "ius" of the Bonn professor's name should always get on the nerves of the Baroness: but so it did. 40

Chapter XIV.

Snowflower.

Looking back over the last chapter, I become aware of an unkept promise. No one will have noticed it but myself, and nobody will care a straw even when it is pointed out. Confess, gentle reader—I call you gentle, as a child says "Nice doggie" because it is so scared of the beast;—confess that you don't know what promise I mean. Oh, I am not offended.

But I am exact. Now my critic in the *Observer* of December 1920 says I am out on the quest of some blotched lily of beauty, some *fleur du mal*, like the defunct Aubrey Beardsley. We live and learn, and I am very pleased indeed to shake hands with the *outre-tombe* Monsieur Beardsley.* On the other hand, I am told that I am *not* like Swift. I am *not* out on the search for truth. So the infernal Dean can call me a Yahoo if he likes. I parade with my spangled lily* down the avenues of time.

Yet, gentle reader—don't bite then, don't bite—I am really quite fond of truth: and even of keeping my word. Which is more than can be said of a certain Dean. And therefore, I recall to you a promise I made.

I said I would indicate, in the following conversation,—or conversations, I forget which—what was the reason of the tenuity of the scarlet thread of human feeling binding the little professor Alfred Kramer to his fellows. That scarlet thread is thin: very thin: spider-web thin. And why?—In professor Alfred, I mean—

Why? That's what I promised to reveal in further conversations. As a matter of fact I thought the professor was going to unbosom to Gilbert Noon. And he never unbosomed, which is rather a let-down for me.

Pray excuse the unbecoming word *let-down*,* gentle reader. That's what it is to come of humble origin: these abominable hyphenations rear their flattened heads from among the nettles of the unchastened vocabulary. How a *Times* critic dropped on me for using the word *toney*!* I'm sure I never knew it wasn't toney any more to say toney. Because once it was quite toney, I'm sure. Perhaps I even meant then. But now I'm being almost modern, so I shall eschew *toney*, and yet not eschew *let-down*. I tell you, gentle reader, it was a let-down.

In the Orient Express, which in those paradisal days ran to the

Morgenland* via Munich and Vienna, sat a lady* who ought
to have got out at Frankfort. Why then is she spinning on towards the
Austrian frontier?

The answer is simple. At dinner, on the train, she sat at a tiny table
face to face with a little Japanese. The lady was fair and fresh-faced and   5
just over thirty: the Japanese was a Japanese, presumably about the
same age as herself, discounting the aeons of his ancestors. Over the
Moselle wine, the two talked in English. Useless to repeat what they
said. Sufficient that they talked in English, and as they talked, the face
of the woman shone like a flower in the sun, and flashes of strange light   10
seemed to go over the little Japanese face opposite her. Why this
strange and electric connection should suddenly have started across a
tiny table in an express train, who knows. Suffice that by the time the
oranges and apples and nuts were bounced on to the table, the woman
had felt a quiet, strangely powerful, hand grip her knee under the   15
board, and linger with a slow, intense, magnetic pressure. She was so
startled that her will-power deserted her for the moment, and she sat
gazing with transfixed bright eyes into the face of the little Japanese,
which was bent down near the white cloth, as the young man stooped
ostensibly to pick up his table-napkin.   20

The sad, almost saurian eyes of the Oriental gazed fixedly into the
green-grey eyes of the woman, till she felt she would do anything,
anything for him. Then came coffee, and the soft voice of the stranger
inviting her to drink a liqueur with him. She would take a Benedictine.
Yes, she would take a Benedictine. And as the waiter filled her little   25
glass she felt the two legs of the stranger pressing her knees between
his own, under the table, a long, slow, invidious pressure, with all the
Japanese magnetic muscular force, while the sad, saurian, oriental face
still watched hers. She drank her Benedictine in a little throatful, and
by the time it was swallowed she had lost all sense of her surroundings.   30

The Japanese invited her to go down with him to the saloon car. She
went, and sat by him, and he talked to her with his slow quiet voice, and
she answered with her bright voice. And the train flew on, and still they
sat side by side in the saloon, and still they talked.

Till she felt the jar of the brakes: and she heard the porters yelling   35
München. München—how was that possible? She gave a cry, and
collected her wraps and her valise.

"Are we in Munich?"

"Yes, in Munich."

In dazed bewilderment she was climbing out of the train, and the   40

Japanese was following in his slow oriental fashion, watching. He decided not to leave the train.

And so it was that Gilbert, reading in bed just after midnight, heard the bell ring in the distant kitchen—and ring again—and again. Till he
5 became uneasy, and went into the passage. And heard a desperate peal. So he shouted for Julie: and got no answer.

The Herr Professor was away: so, apparently, was Julie, in this carousing city of Munich. So Gilbert, who didn't possess a dressing-gown, went in his pyjamas and opened the door of the flat. And there
10 stood the above-mentioned lady, bright-faced, with her furs and wraps and her valise.

"Ist der Herr Professor Kramer nicht zu Hause?"

The question came in German.

"Isn't Professor Kramer at home?"
15 "No—he is in Göttingen for three days."

"And is no one there? Julie?"

"She doesn't seem to be here."

"Oh dear!" A hesitation on the doorstep. "Professor Kramer is my cousin. I forgot to get out at Frankfort, and it took all my money. Can
20 you lend me ten Mark for the taxi?"

"Yes," said Gilbert.

"Oh dear," said the woman, "I am such a fool." And sighing wearily she came into the hall and threw her wraps and valise on to a seat, whilst Gilbert, in his faded flannel pyjamas, went into his room for the
25 money.

"Ah thank you," she said. "I must go down and pay! Ah me, I am such a fool."

Whereupon she ran down the stairs, and Gilbert heard her speaking first to the night-porter, then outside to the taxi-man. He remained in
30 the doorway, and saw her rise like a Wagner Goddess* through the floor, in the lift.

"Oh danke!" she cried to the night-porter, and came rushing into the flat again. She shut the door behind her.

"Ah Gott sei dank!* Aren't I hopeless? But who are you? I don't
35 know you, do I?"

All this in German.

"No," said Gilbert. "I am staying with Professor Kramer."

"But are you German?"

"No—"
40 "Ah, you are English—!" and here the conversation breaks into

English. "I come from America. I am going home to my parents—they are in Frankfort expecting me now. Ach, what a fool I am, I came straight through. Poor papa—I know he is at the station. Oh dear, I hate myself. I just slept and didn't wake."

This, as we see, is a complete lie: but then how can a woman confess   5
to a knee-pressing Japanese in a dining car?

Poor Gilbert still stood in the hall in his pyjamas, and felt not so frightfully uncomfortable.

The woman was already so flustered, he did not matter very much. She took off her hat and dropped it unheeding on the couch in the hall,   10
and lifted her soft, dark-fair hair from her brow with her fingers.

"Poor Papa, he will be in such a rage."

"Perhaps I can telegraph to him," said Gilbert.

"Can one telegraph now?—Or telephone perhaps? But I don't know the number. Perhaps we could find it. Oh yes."   15

The two went into the study and hunted the telephone books. They found the address—and succeeded after a while in getting the connection.

"Ach Papa—is it you? Oh, I'm in Munich. Think of it. Yes, I slept! Yes! And you were there all the while! Oh dear! No—no—I didn't   20
have any dinner. I was so tired. No—no. Ach, I hate myself. What? What? Yes. Tomorrow. But I must sleep. When? Yes. No—no, it's no good. No—he's not here—only the servant.—Ach, Papa, you dear Papa, I hate myself. No, but I could cry. And were you *fearfully* disappointed—no—no—you?—yes. Dear Papa, and how are you?   25
And Mama?—Good—Good! I'm awfully glad.—I'm dying to be with you—dying.—Yes.—" A pause. "Ah Mama, are you there? Ah, what am I for a stupid ass!* Yes, yes, I know how you'll scold me. Never mind, I deserve it. I do. What? What? You can't be as cross as I am. Yes, good. No, only Julie. You were in bed—yes—Papa still   30
waiting? Oh dear. No, don't be too cross. No—you're not surprised. No—No—No——" The conversation drifted to an end, and the woman hung up the receiver. Then she rose from the chair, and for the first time looked at Gilbert. He, for modesty's sake, had put on his overcoat. She was wearing a dark-blue coat and skirt.   35

"Well!" she said, in English, scrutinising him.

"Are you hungry?"

"Rather. But where is Julie."

He spread out his hands in a faint gesture.

"When the cat is away the mouse will play.* Is that it?" said the   40

woman. "Poor Julie, she *will* feel dropped on. I shall have to promise not
to tell Alfred. What did you say your name was?"

"Gilbert Noon"—and he spelled it.

"Gilbert Noon—rather nice," she said. "Mine is Mrs Johanna
5 Keighley. My husband* is an American doctor, and I am just come
home to see my mother and father. And this is how I bring it off."

"Bad luck," he said.

"Isn't it! And just like me."

"Like you, or your luck?" asked Gilbert.

10 "Me! Me! I'm afraid it's me. I'm awful, I really am. My husband would
be so disgusted. Ach, but it's lovely to be back. We live in Boston, and I
hate it. So dull, so dull. I'm always pining to be here again. I'm German,
and I love Germany——Do you know where the pantry is? My husband
is an Englishman too, but we went to America the first year I was
15 married.—Oh America—I don't know what to say to it."

Gilbert in his overcoat, the full-breasted woman in her delicate,
dark-coloured blouse went down to the kitchen quarters, switching on
lights till the whole flat was aglare. As they were making a collection of
cold meat and sausages and cheese and sweets a form suddenly appeared
20 in the open doorway. It was the truant Julie.

"Ach, Frau Doktor—!"*

"Ja, Julie! Ja! Yes! What time is this to be coming in, you? I come from
the train and the strange gentleman must let me in. Good for you that the
Herr Professor is far enough away. But I want to eat—I am so hungry.
25 Make me an omelette, will you—with four eggs: or with six, and the
gentleman will eat some."

"No," protested Gilbert. "No."

Julie, who looked flushed and guilty, with her hair astray, flung off her
things and darted into her apron. Her kitchen was spotless: not only
30 clean, but of that purity of texture as if the very cast iron of the stove had
never known the common, contaminating earth, but had been born out
of a black, clean cloud of the sky.

When the two returned to the long drawing-room, Julie darted round
switching off the lights. Whatever would the Herr Professor have said to
35 such a mass of brilliance.

"And what are you doing in Munich?" Johanna asked of Gilbert.
Whereupon he told her, as briefly as possible. He looked rather a comic
figure, sitting there buttoned up in a thick dark-brown overcoat, which
would keep sliding apart and exposing his pyjamad knees, so that he was
40 as self-conscious as an elderly woman with short skirts.

"And are you happy here?" asked Johanna.

"Oh yes—very."

"And is Alfred nice with you, and not too fussy?"

"Very nice."

"And do you have a good time with the Hebers and the Wolf-stangels* and Alastair and all those?"

"Yes—quite. I've got no money you see, except the little bit I make one way and another—nothing. So I have to go gently, you know."

"Oh, but in Munich one doesn't need money. It's the loveliest town [in] the world for that. Don't you think? You can be at court and have a pink flannelette petty, and nobody minds."

"Why should they?" said Gilbert.

"Well it *is* rather horrid, pink flannelette. Oh, but it if weren't for my children, I'd come and live in Munich like a shot."

"Have you children?"

"Two lovely little boys. They *are* dears."

"In America."

"Yes—so far away."

"Couldn't you bring them?"

"No, it's such a bother dragging children about."

"Don't you miss them frightfully?"

"No—not unless I start thinking about them. They're there, you know—like the sun or the Frauenkirche."

"Yes, I suppose they're all right."

"Yes. I've got a perfect German nurse for them. I believe she's much better with them than I am, though I rather hate her bossy little ways. Let's go and eat."

They returned to the dining-room, and Julie carefully switched off the light after them.

So, instead of facing the little white-bearded professor, Gilbert sat facing a young and lovely, glowing woman. His double-breasted overcoat was buttoned over his breast, his fresh face and pouting lips perched above inquiringly. The woman was glowing with zest and animation, her grey-green eyes laughed and lighted, she laughed with her wide mouth and showed all her beautiful teeth. Her hair was soft and brownish and took glints, her throat, as it rose from the fine texture of her blouse, that was dark blue-and-red frail stuff transparent over white, rose like a lovely little column, so soft and warm and curd-white. She was full-bosomed, and full of life, gleaming with life, like a flower in the sun, and like a cat that looks round in the sunshine and finds it good.

Now Gilbert was an impressionable young man, who never left off being smitten. Whether it was the fluff and cuddliness of Emmie, or the ivory irony and slowness of Patty, or the dark-browed peasant passivity of the catholic Marta, or the glow of the learned and wistful and
5 uncertain Louise, he was sure to be smitten. Now he was struck all of a heap, so much so that he did not even know he was smitten at all, but only watched and listened, was all eyes and ears and soul-attentiveness, with no saving afterthought to steady him.

Johanna liked him. Women did like him as a rule, with his full,
10 dark-blue eyes, his pouting lips, and his musician's hands.

"Tell me about your home, in England," she said.

He told her about his father, and Whetstone.

"Oh," she cried, "I know those Midlands. They are a dark, dreary hole in the face of the earth. And did you never have a mother, then?"
15 "Not to remember."

"Well I think you're lucky. Mothers are awful things nowadays, don't you think?"

Gilbert had not been accustomed to think so, therefore he inquired "why?"
20 "Don't you think they all want to swallow their children again, like the Greek myth?—who was the man?*—There isn't a man worth having, nowadays, who can get away from his mother. Their mothers are all in love with them, and they're all in love with their mothers, and what are we poor women to do?"
25 "Do you do so badly?" asked Gilbert.

"Yes! Yes! You don't believe it!" She made round solemnish eyes at him. "But it's true. It's true."

"In what way," said Gilbert.

"One wants a man to oneself, and one gets a mother's darling.—*You*
30 don't know what it means. They're all Hamlets, obsessed by their mothers, and we're supposed to be all Ophelias, and go and drown ourselves."

"But you're not on the way to the water, are you?" asked Gilbert.

"No," she cried, with a shout of laughter. "No, I'm not. Neither am I
35 going to put rue and rosemary in my hair, though they'd all like to make me.—Ha—mother-love. It is the most awful self-swallowing thing."

"You've got a mother-in-law, then?"

"Yes, but she's a dear, really. She loves her husband. She's quite beautiful, really. No, my husband isn't like that. He wants to set me on
40 a throne and kiss my feet. You don't know how uncomfortable I feel."

"I can believe it," said Gilbert.

"Can you? Can you? Well I'm glad you can. I hate a throne, it's so hard and uncomfortable. And I *don't* think I'm a white snowflower,* do you?"

He looked at her across the table.

"I shouldn't say so," he said.

"No by Jove! Anything but. Oh, if he knew.—Do you know, he is quite capable of killing me because I'm not a white snowflower. Don't you think it's absurd? When I'm a born dandelion. I was born to get the sun. I love love, and I hate worship. Don't you agree?"

"Yes, quite," said Gilbert, shaking his head solemnly.

"To sit and be worshipped all my life by one solemn ass—well, it's not good enough. There are lots of men in the world—such lovely men, I think. There was a little Japanese in the train. Don't you think they're fascinating—so quick and on the spot."

"Yes—!" said Gilbert doubtfully.

"I should love a little Japanese baby: brown and solemn and so different. I think they're dears."

"Have you ever seen one?"

"Yes, haven't you? The first I saw was when I was quite a girl—you know I'm thirty-two, and have a son of twelve. And it was the dearest little thing—a father and a mother Japanese in awful European clothes, carrying this dear little brown baby. It was in Florence, and the people ran after them in crowds, perfectly fascinated. So that they had to get a carriage and drive off. Oh I can remember them so well. And I always knew after that that I wanted a brown baby. Yet there I've got an honest English husband and two sweet boys, and I'm adored for being a white snowflower. Don't you think it's strange?"

"Very."

"No you don't! You think it's quite right, I know you do, you Englishman. You all want a white snowflower in your button-hole. Say you do, now."

"Well, I don't know much about white snowflowers, so perhaps it's no good my saying."

"Oh you cautious Engländer. And aren't you in love with anybody now?"

"No, nobody in particular."

"Nobody in particular! *That* sounds just like you. When you can't have a snowflower you have some perfectly impossible *horizontale.** Oh, the English and the Americans, with their snowflowers and their

saintly mothers and their unmentionable incidents in the background!
It's all such a lie."

"Nay," said Gilbert. "I never have anything to do with *horizontales*. No,
I left England because of a girl."

5 And he told the story of himself and Emmie.

"It *does* sound awful," she said. "So common and unrelieved. I don't
like it."

"No, neither do I," said Gilbert.

"But you *did* it, and therefore you must have liked it. Oh, I can't bear to
10 think of love made so low."

"You like love on a high plane?" said Gilbert.

"Yes! Yes! There must be something ideal about it."

"Japanese?" said Gilbert ironically.

"Yes. I think they're so wonderful."

15 "Perhaps I think Emmie wonderful," said Gilbert.

"Oh no! Oh no! How can you. Such a common little thing, and rather
a minx, I'll bet."

"And what about a Japanese? Isn't he common? Isn't he an ugly toad?"

"No! No! It's an ugliness that fascinates me.—No! No! I hate
20 commonness. The commonest man I've ever had is my husband,
really.—No, I had a wonderful lover*—a doctor and a philosopher,
here in Munich. Oh, I loved him so much—and I waited for his
letters—"

"When, before you were married?"

25 "Oh no. It is only two years ago. He was Louise's lover first. It was he
who freed me, really. I was just the conventional wife, simply getting
crazy boxed up. But he was wonderful, Eberhard. Ah, I did love him."

"And don't you any more?"

"No—no! I knew it was no good. When I'd been with him—I was only
30 with him two weeks—two separate weeks—here, and in Utrecht.*
He was a marvellous lover—but I knew it was no good. He never let one
sleep. He talked and talked. Oh he was so marvellous. I once went with
him to a zoo place. And you know he could work up the animals, by
merely looking at them, till they nearly went mad."

35 "A psychiatrist."

"Perhaps! Perhaps! He took drugs. And he never slept. He just never
slept. And he wouldn't let *you* sleep either. And he talked to you while he
was loving you. He was wonderful, but he was awful.—He would have
sent me mad. Perhaps I am a bit mad now.—But he was my first
40 lover—four years ago."

"And where is he now?"

"I don't know. In Berlin or somewhere. He simply lives on drugs. And he was so beautiful, like a white Dionysos.* He never writes. But Louise will know. She was his wife's best friend. But Wilhelmine never tried to keep him. You couldn't try to keep a man like that.—The only thing I couldn't quite stand, was that he would have two women, or more, going at the same time. And I couldn't bear it."

"No," said Gilbert, who was becoming depressed. "But why did you think he was so wonderful."

"Oh, he was a genius—a genius at love. He understood so much. And then he made one feel so free. He was almost the first psychoanalyst, you know—he was Viennese too, and far, far more brilliant than Freud.* They were all friends. But Eberhard was spiritual—he may have been demoniacal, but he was spiritual. Which Freud isn't, don't you think."

"I don't think Freud is spiritual," said Gilbert. "But what was it that Eberhard taught you, that made you feel so free?"

"He made me believe in love—in the sacredness of love. He made me see that marriage and all those things are based on fear. How can love be wrong? It is the jealousy and grudging that is wrong. Love is so much greater than the individual. Individuals are so poor and mean.—And then there can't be love without sex. Eberhard taught me that. And it is so true. Love *is* sex. But you can have your sex all in your head, like the saints did. But that I call a sort of perversion. Don't you? Sex is sex, and ought to find its expression in the proper way—don't you think. And there is no strong feeling aroused in anybody that doesn't have an element of sex in it—don't you think?"

These theories were not new to Gilbert. How could they be, in the professor's house? But he had never given them serious attention. Now, with the gleaming, distraught woman opposite him, he was troubled by the ideas. He was troubled, and depressed. It all saddened him, and he did not agree, but did not know what to say.

"I never know quite what you mean by sex," he said.

"Just sex. It is the kind of magnetism that holds people together, and which is bigger than individuals."

"But you don't have sexual connection with everybody," said Gilbert, in opposition.

"Not directly—but indirectly."

"Nay," he said. "I don't see that. Sex is either direct sex, or it is something else which I don't call sex."

"But don't you see," she said, "sex is always being *perverted* into something else—all the time."

"Ay," said Gilbert. "And perhaps something else is always being perverted into sex."

5   "Yes," she said. "Yes."

It was evident she was all distraught, bewildered, roused, and yet not having any direction.

"Of course," she said, "I daren't tell Everard. When I try to tell him, he sneers. I tried to tell him about Eberhard. But he wouldn't let me.

10   He didn't want to know. And he would kill me rather than know. Isn't it strange.—And yet the secrecy almost sends me mad.—Why can't I tell him?"

"It isn't a pretty thing for a man to hear—from his wife," said Gilbert.

15   "But why? It isn't unnatural. And he's my husband. And he lets me do what I like. He lets me come to Germany for three months at a time, and he is *quite* happy there in Boston, with his work, and his love for me as a snowflower. Why won't he let me tell him I'm not a snowflower? I do tell him that. But why won't he let me tell him about Eberhard? He

20   *knows*, at the bottom. He *knows*. In his unconscious, he knows I'm not faithful to him. But he would kill me rather than let me tell him. And that is what is so awful to me. I feel it is awful—I live in a lie, and it sends me mad. But what am I to do?"

"Write to him, and tell him."

25   "Yes, but it seems cowardly. And one writes all the wrong things. And then he's one of the people who make it just impossible. He would never face it—never. He would just make horrors for himself and me and the children, and it wouldn't be faced at the end. He might commit murder, but he would funk facing what I've done and what I *am*. You

30   see it's what I *am* that he's got to see, and which he never will see. Whatever Eberhard was, he was something which Everard, my husband, never *could* be: something wonderful, something beautiful, and something so much more *intense* and *real*. Well, I can't help it that I needed that, can I? I did need it. I was just arrested without it.—And

35   Everard would just either kill me or show off in some other way like a maniac, if I tried to tell him. Why will men never know their own limitation?"

"Will women?" said Gilbert.

"Oh much sooner.—You see I could always be friends with Everard:

40   even be married to him. I am fond of him, really. But I did *love*

Eberhard—and my husband would have to admit it. I *loved* Eberhard. And I rather love Freyling and Berry.* I do, and so I do. It's no use denying it. And I won't deny it. Why should I deny them any more than Everard? Why should I?"

Gilbert sat with his head dropped, and did not answer. Johanna watched him.

"Ah!" she said, with a distraught, reckless sigh. "It is all so complicated, I feel sometimes I might go mad. Why is it all so complicated? Why can't we admit love simply, and not go into paroxysms about it?"

"Perhaps it isn't natural to be simple about it," said Gilbert. "Perhaps it would be unnatural if Everard, your husband, let you do as you do and *knew* about it."

"But why can it be any more natural, his just refusing to know? He only refuses to know. And if that is natural, well, better be educated beyond nature."

"Probably," said Gilbert.

"You know that's what makes me hate him. I don't hate him. I'm fond of him really. And it sends me mad to have to hate him, when I'm fond of him. But I shall go mad if I have to live with him. Because I've got to keep it all secret, and that just does for me."

"Why don't you tell him, then?"

"I've tried. Ha, haven't I tried, God knows. But he'd expect me to be a weeping Magdalen, which I'm not: repenting at his feet, which would be just a lie. I loved Eberhard, God knows I loved him: and I'll never go back on it. And I love Berry and Freyling, but not so much. And I'm fond of Everard. And they're all true, so I shan't deny any of them. But I hate Everard, really, for making me lie. I hate him for it, with a deep, deep hatred. He has made me lie, and I can't do it any more. I can't do it."

"Then don't," said Gilbert. "Write and tell him."

"I don't know what he'd do to the children."

"Nothing," said Gilbert. "Be tragic over them."

"But I don't want him to be tragic over them.—It might all be so simple."

"While you've got people, things never will be simple," said Gilbert.

"No, I suppose they won't.—But I'm not going to be self-sacrificing. Since Eberhard, I can't even if I want to. I can't, I *really* disbelieve in it."

"So do I," said Gilbert.

They relapsed into silence.

"Well—" she sighed after a while, looking up with her bright, reckless, rather pathetic smile again. "There it is!"

"Yes," said Gilbert. "There it is."

"Goodness!" she cried, looking at the clock. "It's nearly three."

"It is," said Gilbert.

She rose, letting her serviette drop on the floor, and turned towards the door.

"Well goodnight," she said, holding out her hand.

"Goodnight," said Gilbert, shaking hands.

"You wouldn't like to come to me?" she said, looking direct at him.

"When?" he asked, looking back into her eyes.

"Tonight," she said.

He was silent for a moment, looking unconsciously at her.

"Yes," he said, and was surprised that his lungs had no breath.

"In about ten minutes," she said, turning away.

Chapter XV.

Jupiter Tonans.*

To say that Johanna and Gilbert found that famous first night of theirs
a success would be false. It was not a success for either of them. The
passion did not get free in either, and therefore neither of them felt
satisfied or assuaged or fulfilled. And yet in the morning they were
rather happy. They were happy just being together. The very fact that
the attempt at passion had failed for the moment kindled a deeper
gratification in companionship. They were delighted like two children
at being together.

"What are you doing today?" cried Johanna at breakfast—which was
at half-past ten.

"Alfred is coming back this afternoon," said Gilbert.

"Oh dear! And tomorrow I must go to Frankfort. Isn't it
maddening!—Shall we go out?"

"Yes," said Gilbert—though he should have gone to the university.

Therefore they wandered through the streets of the town till midday,
then took the train to the mountains. They went to Kochel, to the
Kochelsee. It is a little, deep, dark-watered lake. The day was sunny,
with a vivid radiance enhanced by the not-far-off flashing of many
snows and spear-heads of mountains. At the foot of the Alps, among
the foot-hills, there are bogs where the peasants cut turf. The two
walked across the bogs, picking blue gentian and delicate pink primulas
and bog-flowers like violets. In the village they bought food and
oranges—which Gilbert liked because the peasant woman who sold
them called them Apfelsinen, applesses, feminine apples. By the side of
a little white shrine they sat in the sun, listening to the Alpine gurgling
of running waters, smelling the tang of ice and bog in the sunshine, and
eating the black bread, which is so very good with mountain butter, and
the slices of rare good sausage, and sipping the Schnapps from a tiny
shilling bottle, and hearing the cow-bells tong-tong-tong, behind the
fir-trees at the back, and seeing the mountains in heaven pale and
radiant.

"If I were you," said Gilbert, "I shouldn't go back to America."

He was holding her hand quietly in his.

"When, never? Oh, I must."

"But I should write and tell Everard."

"What?"

5   "That you won't come back."

"But he'd want to know why."

"Because you are staying with me."

She was quite still, whilst the cow-bells clonked from the slopes above, and a peasant far off yodelled in the spring air.

10   "But I must go back, mustn't I?" she said wistfully. "I'd love not to.—But I must."

"Write and tell him you are with me."

"Must I?"

"Yes."

15   "I am frightened."

"What's the good of being frightened.—It would be better if you told him to his face. But you can't. So write. Write tonight."

"And say what?"

"That you are with me."

20   "But shall I?"

"Yes. Write openly. Then let things develop."

"I'm afraid to."

"But you must."

"Are you sure."

25   "Yes I am."

"I'm frightened."

And she clung to his fingers. He stared away into the marshes of the foot-hills, where clumps of birch-trees balanced magically in the air, on silver stems, radiant almost as the mountains are radiant, yet near, and

30   alive.

"Are you sure I must?" she said. His face, so still, looking into the distance and seeming devoid of feeling, frightened her.

"Yes, you know I am."

But she knitted her woman's brows, and thought of things he did not

35   think of: her children, her many years of married life in England and America, her parents: all the old scheme of things. She knew he thought of nothing: only he looked away into the distance. And she didn't remind him. She let his far-awayness decide.

As the afternoon wore on they rose and went to the lake. It was deep

40   and dark blue, dark green, heavily ice-cold. There was a little pier, a

little wooden jetty near a small bathing establishment that was shut. They sat on this jetty and dipped their feet in the heavy, clear water, and watched the light on the steep slopes opposite, and the deep shadows infolded in the encroaching mountains. They seemed quite alone—there was nobody else. 5

After a while she got up and went away, through the shrubby walks by the water—a sort of hand-breadth of deserted pleasure ground. He stayed fastening his boots.

She drifted on alone, with head dropped, brooding. It was her instinct to get away and be alone. She came to the mountain high- 10 road. Bullocks with a load of wood were slowly swinging along. Some soldiers passed. And she walked towards the infolding of the mountains, and still did not look up.

Then suddenly she remembered she was alone. She looked along the white, lost road, that ran between birch-trees. She turned. The 15 soldiers were looking back at her. The scarlet band of their round caps showed so plainly above their ruddy, rude, peasant faces. She was frightened. Always fear took possession of her when she found herself alone in lonely places: a strange fear of men, of being attacked.

Why didn't Gilbert come? Why wasn't he in sight? She hurried 20 towards the little pleasure ground. But the seats were bare. She went round the paths between the shrubs. But there was no sign of him. The world seemed strangely empty, void, and fear overcame her.

Bewildered she hurried to the little jetty. There she had left him, sitting at the end with his feet dangling over, not touching the water. 25 Now it was empty. There was nobody. The sense of emptiness in the air was overwhelming.

Could it be possible he had slipped in and was drowned? She went forward trembling along the jetty, and peered into the deep, ice-heavy water. Oh god, was he gone? Was he gone down then? Terror 30 mounted into her heart. She kneeled on the end of the jetty and peered down into the water. Could she see something down there? Could she?

She started up and looked round in horror. The sombre mountains stood almost upon her. She looked back at the little pleasure grounds. 35 Empty. It was all empty, empty. He was drowned in the dark, still water of the Kochelsee, and there was a terrifying absence in all the chill air. She stared round. She called, and called again. No one answered.

Wildly she hurried towards the station. She asked a peasant woman 40 if she had seen her husband—Mein Mann. But the woman had not seen Gilbert. Johanna arrived at the small terminus station. Nobody there. She asked a porter. Nothing.

5 And she felt sure he was drowned. She felt sure he was drowned. He was drowned, and she was alone, and what should she do. She felt a thrill of horror, and somewhere else, a pang of relief that the great solitude surrounded her again. In the midst of terrible fear, an awful void, there was a tiny motion of gratification that she was free. For in a way, she feared him—she had an incomprehensible small dread of
10 him.

But her chief feeling was one of bewildered terror. As yet she spoke to no one. But she raced back along the white, empty high-road towards the lake. That was where he was: in the lake at the end of the jetty. It fascinated her, drew her on.

15 And as she raced in the frenzy of her heart, she saw him coming, a solitary figure, along the high-road towards her. Ah! All the tension dropped from her. He was there. And yet her heart was still aching from its strain.

"Where have you been? I thought you were drowned," she cried
20 almost angrily, as he approached her.

"Drowned! Why? I've been looking for you."

"But where? Where? I've been nowhere? What have you been doing?" Her voice was peremptory and rather angry still.

"I came out on to the road and turned towards the village, thinking I
25 was following you. I can't have been two minutes behind you—not two minutes. Which way did you go?"

He too was rather angry, having been wandering in bewilderment and fear, looking for her. And neither of them could believe that such a small thing should have shattered them as this half-hour's evasion had
30 shattered them. The effect was by no means in proportion to the cause. And as they stood looking at one another in angry relief, there on the high-road, they knew it.

"I thought you were drowned. I was *sure* you were drowned," she insisted.

35 "But why should I be drowned?"* he answered irritably.

"I thought you'd fallen in the lake."

"Am I such a fool?"

"Heaven knows. But I was *sure*."

"Ah well then, you had no need to be sure."

40 They walked slowly towards the station, a curious couple. But once

in the train, she was glad again of his presence. He relieved her from the world. She was afraid of the world: terrified of its sentence on her. It seemed to emit a horrible police-suspicion of her, which maddened her with fear and unease. And this man seemed to relieve her of it—though she did not know why. He made her feel quiet. And he too rested within her presence, and looked out from the little inaccessible conning-tower of his submerged spirit upon the world, as if the world were some endless streaming phenomenon. Without noticing one another, they gave each other a strange ease in the midst of a life that was alien to them both.

They arrived at the flat in town to find Alfred irritably expecting them, waiting for dinner.

"Ho! Johanna! You are a nice girl. You are a nice girl!" he cried in English. "So you slept in the train while your father and mother were waiting for you! Well, you are a dutiful loving daughter. You are a nice vestal. Ho! Julie told me. And where have you been? Do you know Mr Noon?"

"Quite well," laughed Johanna significantly.

"Quite well! Quite well! Well, that is quick work. And behind my back! And when do you go to Frankfort?"

"Tomorrow."

"Tomorrow! Well, it is lucky, because Professor Hartstein is coming and I shall want your room."

"Don't you like it that I came here and settled myself in?—But I had no money—I spent it all and hadn't enough to pay the auto."

"Ach, what a girl, what a girl! What should you do if you had no relations to go to? Well? What? Ha! What would you do without your relations?"

"Ya, Alfred, in a world where all men are brothers, you know—"

"And all women sisters! Yes, I know. I know! Well. And where have you been? What have you been doing with yourself? Well? What? Have you been to see Louise? Have you been to see your cousin. Because I am only your cousin-in-law, remember. I am only your cousin-in-law.—How do you say that in English—?" he turned to Mr Noon.

"The same," said Gilbert.

"Well! Well! You haven't told me where you have been, and what you have been doing."

"Ach, *du guter Alfred**—we've been to Kochel."

"To Kochel? To Kochel! But why? And who is we? Did Louise go?"

"No. Louise doesn't know I'm here. Mr Noon and I went."

"So! You two! You two! And what would your dear husband say?—your dear forsaken husband.—Ach, you know, Gilbert—" said the professor, turning to Noon, "these women have no conscience AT ALL. It is an awful family of women: an awful family for women: I don't know which. I married one, so I know. I know, who am a-telling of you. Well—well! Well—well!—And how goes it with you then, Johanna? Eh? Eh?"

"Well, thank you," she said mockingly.

"Well, eh? Ah well, all I can say, Gilbert, is that I am sorry for you. I am SORRY for you."

"Green grapes, green grapes, you old fox, you!" cried Johanna. The conversation, if such it can be called, had lapsed into German.

"Ah well, we shall see who pulls the longest face when he's eaten the grapes,"* said Alfred. Then rather pettishly, pantingly. "Ach! Ach! I've got such a headache. Ach, such a head-ache."

"You want your dinner," said Johanna, "and so do I."

"No! No! I have had it all day. Ach, such a head-ache!" And he rested his head on his hand and made miserable eyes.

"Ja, *du armer Alfred*!" said Johanna, in a tone of commiseration, as to a spoilt child. "Go and wash thy face in hot water—really hot water—and then let us have dinner."

"Nein! Nein! Hot water won't do it any good," lamented Alfred peevishly.

"Perhaps senna," said Johanna brightly, going away.

Alfred was in one of his pets. He was very much put out at arriving home and finding no one there. He thought he was angry at the way people appropriated his hospitality, and never gave him a thought. So he said ach!, and turned his shoulder to Gilbert, and would not speak; thus betraying his displeasure. So Gilbert also went away.

Johanna was hovering in the doorway of her room as he went down the passage. A bright, roused look was on her face. She lifted her eyelids with a strange flare of invitation, like a bird lifting its wings. And for the first time the passion broke like lightning out of Gilbert's blood: for the first time in his life. He went into her room with her and shut the door. The sultriness and lethargy of his soul had broken into a storm of desire for her, a storm which shook and swept him at varying intervals all his life long.

Oh wonderful desire: violent, genuine desire! Oh magnificence of stormy, elemental desire, which is at once so elemental and so intensely individual! Oh storms of acute sex passion, which shatter the soul, and re-make it, as summer is made up out of the débâcle of thunder! Oh cataclysm of fulminous desire in the soul: oh new uprising from the cataclysm. This is a trick of resurrection worth two.

The cyclone of actual desire—not mere titillation and functional gratification—or any other -ation—broke now for the first time upon Gilbert, and flung him down the wind. Not, dear moralist, to break him against the buttresses of some christian cathedral which rose in his path. Not at all. It flung him smack through the cathedrals like a long-shotted shell. Heaven knows where it did not fling him. I'll tell you later on.

But for the moment, I insist on apostrophising desire, intense individual desire, in order to give my hero time. Oh thunder-god, who sends the white passion of pure, sensual desire upon us, breaking through the sultry rottenness of our old blood like jagged lightning, and switching us into a new dynamic reaction,* hail! Oh thunder-god, god of the dangerous bolts—!—No, gentle reader, please don't interrupt, I am *not* going to open the door of Johanna's room, not until Mr Noon opens it himself. I've been caught that way before. I have opened the door for you, and the moment you gave your first squeal in rushed the private detective you had kept in the background. Thank you, gentle reader, you can open your own doors. I am busy apostrophising Jupiter Tonans, Zeus of the thunder-bolt, the almighty Father of passion and sheer desire. I'm not talking about *your* little messy feelings and licentiousnesses, either. I'm talking about desire. So don't interrupt. Am *I* writing this book, or are you? Let me tell you, even if, gentle reader, you happen to be a wonderful, chirping, gentle, soft-billed gosling of a critic, gentilissimo,* *I* am writing this book, and it is *not* being chirped out by you. That is the mistake you make, gentle critic. You think I ought to write down what you chirpingly dictate to me. But you're wrong, you fluffy little thing. I'm writing this book myself, and nobody is chirping it out to me like a piece of dictation.—Oh Jupiter Tonans, oh God of great desire, oh Storm-Father, I pour out my wine to you! Let the lightning play in my blood, let the—

"Johànná! Jo—hàn—náh—h—h!"

That is the voice of Alfred, calling from the door of the drawing-room in long-drawn musicality, high-low.

"Dìn—nérff! Esséńńń! Kòmḿḿ!"*

"Jà—áh—h!" piped the shrill voice of Johanna from behind the ever-closed door. "Kòm—mé—e—!"

And in two more minutes she appeared, bright, a little dazzled, and very handsome. Alfred still stood waiting in the doorway of the drawing-room; a small, correct figure with a white imperial.

"Where is Mr Noo—oon?" he asked, still singing.

"Mr Nòo—oó—n!" sang Johanna in antiphony. And she led her
5 cousin-in-law into the dining-room.

Critic, gentle reader, I shall not say a word about Mr Noon's movements. Suffice that he walked in a dignified manner into the dining-room, wearing a neat bow tie, just as Julie was removing the soup plates.

10 "Late! Late!" cried Alfred. "Has your toilet taken you so ló—òng?" Pray reverse the intonation of the last word: start low, and go high.

Gilbert seemed not to hear, but sat and ate his soup quickly. He too was fresh in the face.

"He *looks* very clean and nice," said Johanna.

15 "Yè—és! Quite a nice young man," said Alfred, whose attention was now, fortunately, attracted by the good brown lump of larded venison on the dish before him.

Chapter XVI.

Detsch.*

The home of Johanna's parents was not in Frankfort, but in Detsch, a small but important military city where her father, Wilhelm Freiherr von Hebenitz,* held a moderately important office under government. 5

In Frankfort the family assembled, and moved on to Detsch: at least the Baron and Baroness and their daughter Johanna arrived in the home city shortly after the events related in the last chapter. Johanna was scolded and spoiled, and all the delicacies of south Germany—— 10 whose name was legion*—were set on the table for her.

Detsch was much warmer than Munich. So Johanna sunned herself, and flirted with her old friend Rudolf von Daumling,* a rather wistful cavalry officer with a decided wife. Rudolf was thin and pleasant-looking, and still, at the age of thirty-eight, wrote little poems 15 for his own delectation. Johanna had a certain fondness for him: *der gute Rudolf*. He was one of the men who didn't fit the army. Now he is dead: killed in action the first month of the war.

We mention him gently. He was not happy with his wife, who wounded his over-sensitive spirit. Therefore, though he lived under 20 the same roof as she, he did not live with her actually. He was sad and wistful, and did not know what he lived for.

Johanna, of course, who took her sex as a religion, felt herself bound to administer the cup of consolation to him. He had thought his days of love and love-making were over. 25

"Ah, you!" cried Johanna to him—but not in his wife's hearing. "You are a young man, and awfully good-looking. You might give any woman a good time. Why do you sit moping?"

So he told her, and she pooh-poohed him. And so the fires began to beat up in Rudolf's breast, the sun came out on his brow, faintly. 30

"But you don't love me, Johanna," he said.

"Yes, I do; why not?"

Which is one way of putting it. Why not?

But in Detsch Johanna was well known, and Captain von Daumling even better. Moreover there was his unhappy, lynx-eyed wife, with 35

whom he lived and did not live. But Johanna sailed bravely on. She
found occasion to draw her old Rudolf to her breast, and even further.

"Ja *du*!" she said to him, teasing. "*Du*! *You*! You, to say you can't love
any more."

5   And he laughed, and blushed, and was restored in his manliness.
For, in spite of Tolstoi and chastity,* he had found his own
impotent purity unmanly, and a sense of humiliation ate into him like a
canker. Now that Johanna had demonstrated his almost splendid
capabilities, he felt he had been rather a fool. And he was rather
10 pleased with himself.

But—! But—! He wanted love. And Johanna only loved him
because—why not? Well, and why not?

It *ought* to be a sufficient reason. But alas, Rudolf, although a cavalry
officer, belonged to the wistful of this world. And why-not? wasn't
15 enough. He wanted flaming affirmation. Therefore he blew this little
why-not fire faint-heartedly.

And so on for a week. Oh, things go quickly! On the seventh day
Johanna was waiting in the station at Detsch, all agog. In whizzed the
train for Paris, out stepped Mr Noon, in a new suit and with a gladstone
20 bag.

"I was awfully afraid you wouldn't come," said Johanna.

"Here I am," said Gilbert.

After which Johanna felt a perhaps even purer compassion for her
poor Rudolf. And he, to his credit, found compassion even more
25 humiliating than impotence. Whereupon he wrote quite long poems, in
which Gilbert all-unwitting fluttered as a dark *Unglücksrabe*,* raven
of woe.

Now my latest critic complains that my heroines show no spark of
nobility: never did show any spark of nobility, and never do: perchance
30 never will. Speriamo.*

But I ask you, especially you, *gentle* reader, whether it is not a noble
deed to give to a poor self-mistrustful Rudolf substantial proof of his
own virility. We say substantial advisedly. Nothing ideal and in the air.
Substantial proof of his own abundantly adequate virility. Would it have
35 been more noble, under the circumstances, to give him the baby's
dummy-teat of ideal sympathy and a kind breast? Should she have said:
"Dear Rudolf, our two spirits, divested of this earthy dross of
physicality, shall fly untrammelled." Should she once more have done
the pure and pitiful touch? Should she have proceeded to embrace the
40 dear depressed Captain of the fifth regiment in the spirit, to whoosh

with him in unison of pure love through the blue empyrean, as poor Paolo and Francesca were forced to whoosh on the black winds of hell?* Would this have been noble? Is the baby's dummy-teat really the patent of true female spirituality and nobility, or is it just a fourpence-halfpenny fraud? Gentle reader, I know *your* answer. But unfortunately my critics are *usually* of the sterner sex, which sex by now is so used to the dummy, that its gentle lips flutter if the indiarubber gag of female *spiritual* nobility is taken away for one moment.

That is why I am continually addressing myself to you, gentle reader, and not to the sterner sex. The sterner sex either sucks away at its dummy with such perfect innocent complacency, or else howls with such perfectly pitiful abandon after the lost dummy, that I won't really address the darling any more.

Gentle reader, gentille lecteuse, gentilissima lettrice,* don't you agree with me that Magdalen had only *one* fall, and that was when she fell to feet-washing. What a pity, what a thousand pities! However, it can't be helped. Fall she did, and spilt her spikenard. No use crying over spilt spikenard either. But let me help you up, dear Magdalen, and let everybody wash his own feet.* That's sound logic, I believe.

The poor Hauptmann* Rudolf von Daumling, however, was crying. He was crying for a dummy, and to have his not-particularly-beautiful feet washed with spikenard and long hair. Poor Johanna—how we throw that little adjective of condolence from side to side: poor Johanna had gone to the wrong shop with her wares. The above-mentioned substantial proof only proved a larger thorn in the flesh of the poetic captain, a thorn which had ceased to rankle, and now rankled again. Therefore his poetry, like pus, flowed from the wound. We are sorry to be distasteful, but so it strikes us. Fortunately the war came in time, and allowed him to fling his dross of flesh disdainfully down the winds of death, so that now he probably flies in all kinds of comforted glory. I hope really he's not flying in our common air, for I shouldn't like to breathe him. That is really my greatest trouble with disembodied spirits. I am so afraid of breathing them in, mixed up with air, and getting bronchitis from them.

Well, my dear Johanna has so far showed no spark of nobility, and if I can help it, she never shall. Therefore, oh sterner sex, bend your agitated brows away from this page, and suck your dummy of sympathy in peace. Far be it from me to disturb you. I am only too thankful if you'll keep the indiarubber gag between your quivering,

innocent lips. So, darling, don't *look* at the nasty book any more: don't
you then: there, there, don't cry, my pretty.

No one really takes more trouble soothing and patting his critics on
the back than I do. But alas, all my critics are troubled with wind.

5 Now Mr Noon had a new suit on, grey with a brown thread in it: and
a new grey hat: and he looked quite laa-di-dah. Johanna eyed him with
approval. This is still in Detsch station, with a porter standing holding
the bag.

"Where am I going to put up?" asked Gilbert.

10 "Will you go to the Wolkenhof?* They know us there. We
always put friends up there. It's a sort of family hotel place, not
expensive."

"It had better not be," said Gilbert; "for I've got just a hundred and
twenty Marks—just six pounds sterling."

15 "In the world?" said Johanna.

"In the universe, till my father dies—and probably even then."

"Well," said Johanna, "I can give you some. Everard sent me a
hundred dollars."

"Wait a bit," said Gilbert.

20 They drove to the Wolkenhof, a big, dull, brown place. Gilbert had a
big attic under the roof, and looked down on streets and soldiers and
drill-yards.

"I shan't have to know you very well," said Johanna. "You're only just
an acquaintance—or a friend, but not very intimate, you know."

25 "All right," said Gilbert.

Whereupon she left him.

He wandered about the old town. It was full of soldiers and officers:
an endless parade of blue, waspy officers with swords and cloaks, who
put his back up. They seemed to have favorite restaurants, and our

30 Gilbert was always wonderstruck, when by accident he found himself in
one of these restaurants and sat eating his asparagus—very good
asparagus—and heard the clash of spurs in the doorway, saw the
martial and supercilious salute. It did not occur to his north-country
innocence that they were despising him and being in some way

35 offensive. But he felt uncomfortable, and rather angry with everything.
Up and down his spine went a creepy uncomfortableness and unease.
But still, to him the brilliant blue officers were only wonder-figures, he
had no human connection with them. Their heel-clicking, their
super-martial salutes, their silver sword-points and their flowing

40 cloaks—all this was a sort of spectacle to him, upon which he looked

with curious wondering detachment. If they eyed him down their noses, from under the brim of their super-martial caps, well, he thought, this is only correct military deportment. He was himself so remote and civilian that the officers might have put fingers to their noses at him, with both hands, and he would only have found it some novel correctness in military deportment. If they had flourished naked swords before his blinking eyes, he would have smiled and bowed, thinking it all an essential part of the military mystery. Those were days of unblemished civilian innocence.

Yet he was uncomfortable in Detsch. The German language seemed to strangle in his throat. He couldn't get it out. And he seemed not to be in his own skin. Which is a nasty feeling.

Johanna met him in the cathedral square and took him to the Wilhelmgarten,* where her mother was waiting. The Baroness von Hebenitz was pleasant and curious about him. She kept glancing at him, as women of fifty-five will glance. She knew he was Johanna's latest gallant, and wondered what to make of him. She summoned all her English, and asked him to take coffee there in the gardens.

The Wilhelmgarten was lovely with masses of lilac and laburnum in full bloom. The cathedral with its many spines, like a hedgehog pricking its ears, was in the background. Away down on the left wound the river, through the ancient houses of the old town. It was sunny and lovely and four-o'clock. But Gilbert was somewhat bewildered. He ate apple-cake and rich cream, and drank his *café au lait* there with the two women in the open air, whilst a military band played not far off, and elegant waspy officers paraded with super-elegant ladies in enormous Paris hats and glove-fitting dresses of lace or silk.

It was all so strange—the sunshine was so strong, the lilacs were like wonderful cathedrals of blossom, so full and massively in flower, the officers glittered and clicked in their pale blue and silver and scarlet.* The Baroness talked in English and German, catching her breath oddly between the words. Johanna, in a dress of dull, smoke-coloured gauze stuff, with a delicate black hat, looked somehow strange to him. She was so shining, so assured, so *super*. There was no getting away from that curious German exaggeration.

Gilbert had noticed, at the entrance to the gardens, a board which said that it was forbidden to speak French in the Wilhelmgarten. There was a strange sense of unreality: intense, marvellous sunshine, massive, amazing flowers, and people all gleaming and assertive as if they sent out little flashes. It was uncomfortable and intensified, as if everything

were focussed here under a burning-glass. The German language
seemed to sparkle and crackle like fireworks going off. The women—it
was so near to France—all looked so French and yet not French, so
curiously definite. Everything was assertive—so assertive that Gilbert,
5　with his sensitive musician's tissue, felt often that he could not breathe.

He let the Baroness pay for the tea, and wondered afterwards if that
was wrong. Johanna seemed assertive and self-brilliant like everybody
else. She left him, saying she would call at the Wolkenhof next morning
at ten.

10　So he roamed round the old, debated town, which all the time
glittered with the military as with pale-blue glass. He was at a hopeless
loose end, and not himself, not in his own skin. At nine o'clock he was
thankful to climb upstairs to his big attic. And then he stood for a long
time at the window, looking down at the strange, tiny marionette
15　threading of people in the street below, far below, the lights glittering,
and listening to the bugles and strange sounds from the barracks
opposite.

The next day was Sunday. He would not see Johanna till after
lunch.* So he watched the amazing military parade of pale-blue
20　officers and dazzling women, hard-souled, strange, either inhuman, or
super-human men, not like men at all—all showing themselves off like
splinters of bright-coloured opaque glass, there in the open place
before the ancient, dark-grey cathedral. It was after mass, so Gilbert
went in and looked at the shadowy, incense-perfumed interior—tall
25　and gothic, tall like a forest of stupendously tall trees, from the low-
stranded floor. It was all rather too much for him.

Johanna met him, and they walked into the country: flat, fortified,
depressing country. They walked along a canal, and saw squadron after
squadron of blue infantry thresh heavily, with that awful German
30　rhythm of march, along the white road coming in from the country.

Johanna was important with news. She had a cable from Everard.
"Believe you have gone with Berry. Wire *ganz richtig* or *nicht wahr*."

Gilbert looked a little pale. To be sure he wasn't Berry, but he feared
that Noon would smell no sweeter.*

35　"Have you answered?" he asked.

"No," she said. "Why should I hurry!"

"Shall you wire ganz richtig?"

"How can I?"

Now *ganz richtig* means *quite right*, and *nicht wahr* means *not true*.
40　Poor Everard was not *quite* right.

Gilbert asked about Berry:* and Johanna told him all about the American: a fair, pleasant young business man, in the same matrimonial situation and of the same age as Rudolf, but of the mercurial rather than the despondent form of idealism.

"We were always motoring away into the country—but he's the kind of irresponsible, all-above-board man people don't talk about. He's awfully nice, really. I hope you'll meet him one day. We did awfully nice things. One day, deep in the forest, I took all my things off and ran naked through the trees. He said I was Daphne.* I believe he loved it. But I was too much for him, really: though he *loved* me as a *friend*, he loved me quite wildly as a friend. But I was too much for him otherwise."

"So you've not come away with Berry!"

"No I haven't, have I," she laughed.

"Why don't you wire—Nicht Beere aber Mittag?—Not Berry but Noon?"

"Yes. It would be all up," she said.

"Let it be all up. Don't you want to?"

"I'm not so sure," she said.

"Cable halb richtig—half right," he said.

"Oh, I can't," she said.

She decided she would not cable till the morrow. Louise, her school-sister, was coming from Munich, arriving that evening: and Lotte, Johanna's own sister, was arriving from Vienna next day.

Gilbert was now becoming rather depressed. He could see it was impossible for Johanna to go back to Boston: and it seemed to him inevitable that she should stay with him. And it depressed him—the tangle and nastiness of it all. He felt in a shabby and questionable position, hanging on there unacknowledged in that unnatural military town. And whether he would or not, he suffered from the peculiar assertive German callousness, he felt he was always being bumped. He rather blankly hung on, being of the bulldog breed.

The next morning Johanna came to his room at the Wolkenhof at ten in the morning. He heard a tap—opened—and there she was, radiant on the doorstep. They felt remote in that high attic. He locked the door.

Later on, talking almost to herself as she tidied her hair before his mirror, she said:

"Do you know, I was rather frightened that you weren't a good lover. But it isn't every man who can love a woman three times in a quarter of an hour—so *well*—is it—?" and she looked round at him with a radiant and triumphant face, holding his comb in one hand. He almost blushed.

"How should I know?" he muttered, turning aside.

5   "I assure you it isn't," she said.

Vaguely through his mind went the thought—That's the price she takes me at. Which thought was followed by a second: Yes, and I'd rather.

And yes, gentle reader—I hope to heaven the sterner sex has left off
10 reading before now, so that I may address you alone—Yes, gentle reader, and at what better price can a woman take a man for good? A woman may have the most marvellous pure esteem for a man: but *is* that any reason why she should sleep with him? She may feel her soul carried away to mid-heaven by him: but *does* it therefore follow that she
15 should unfasten her garters? They may behold in each other all sorts of spiritual, aesthetic, ethical, and intellectual miracles: but will this undo one single unrelenting button? It won't. Then why on earth urge people to marry in Tolstoyan spiritual rapture, when as far as marriage goes, spirits, like angels, *n'ont pas de quoi.**

20 I can see absolutely no sounder ground for a permanent marriage than Johanna's—three times in a quarter of an hour, and so *well*. Then you know what you're in for. Then you're down at the bed-rock of marriage. And why, gentle reader, the sterner sex—I won't accuse you yourself;—why the sterner sex should have such a craving for the wings
25 the wings of a dove,* far away, far away from the bed-rock of marriage to fly, I really don't know. Why he wants to soar in mid-heaven with a dummy in his enraptured lips, I cannot tell. It is one of the many mysteries.

"Bing—bang—bump goes the hammer on the anvil."

30 Well, and life is a thing which is hammered out between the hammer and the anvil, it isn't a feather wafted downwards from the flight of some soothing, sanctified dove. Man is a smith, and it behoves him to smite while the iron is hot, if ever he is to get any shape into life, or any sharpness on his plough-share.

35 Johanna and Gilbert went downstairs a little timorously. The Wolkenhof, where Baron von Hebenitz put all his guests, was quite famous as a semi-religious kind of family hotel—a tiny touch of the Y.M.C.A. about it. Johanna did *not* want to meet on the stairs the old Countess Kippenkegel, a chronic family friend and bygone lady-in-
40 waiting of the Saxon court.

However, she met no one worse than the rather severe Swiss manageress, whom she greeted in her most innocent, naive, disarming fashion.

Johanna had agreed to meet Louise* at the cathedral. The three were to talk-it-over.

Louise in the sunshine of the cathedral square, wearing a dress of fine, pale-purple cloth, was evidently about to rob Athena to pay Aphrodite.

"How do you do?" she smiled to Mr Noon. "I had not expected to meet you here in *soch* circumstances! Yes?"

Her manner was decidedly ironic.

"Hardly," said Gilbert.

"Hardly, you say!" laughed Louise, knitting her brows in a cogitating way she had. "That is very nice. I like your hardly! Now, where shall we go to have a quiet talk. Shall we have chocolate at Beltrand's—yes?"

"Nein," said Johanna. "Kein chocolat,* Louise."

"No! Oh very well. Then let us go into the French park."

So they went into the old, deserted, rather depressing park, and Louise took matters into her own hands. That is, first she took from her bag the cablegram.

"Now then," she said, "we must settle this difficolty.—Believe you have gone with Berry. Wire ganz richtig or nicht wahr.—Well—"

And she looked up at Gilbert and smiled her odd, wicked, sisterly smile.

"Well—" she repeated, with all the irony of Athena cum Aphrodite—"I think you are not this Berry—this black berry, whoever he may be—"

"Nein Louise—er war nicht schwarz," said Johanna. "He wasn't black. He was beautiful like ripe wheat."

"Ach, you simple soul, you! Ach, ripe wheat! What next! Ach—this cran-berry.—But we are very wicked, to joke over this serious business. Ach—poor Everard. I am sure it is very dreadful for him."

She knew Everard well: he and she detested one another. They understood one another too well. They had worked together at Heidelberg.

Louise smoothed the telegram once more on her knee, with her well-gloved hand.

"Ganz richtig oder nicht wahr," she repeated musingly. "But it is certainly *not true*: you are not this Berry. Ach, best cable not true. Best cable not true. Think of the life that is coming. Think of Johanna's children. Ach, all the years which are before you. Best cable *nicht wahr*—much better—much better."

"No," said Gilbert. "She can't go back. There'd be a catastrophe."

"But why! But why! Why should there? Ach, he does not *want* to be
told anything except *nicht wahr*. He does not want the truth. He wants
only to be—to be assured, made sure. And for this he does not want
the truth—not all the truth—only just the little bit which is komfort-
able—ha—!" and she laughed an odd, half bitter, half pathetic laugh.
"You are so young, Mr Noon. When you are older you will not ask for
the wolf's head. You will not wish it—ha! You will want only three little
hairs from his tail, to prove to you that he is a dead wolf.—Ja, Johanna,
das ist wirklich so—" and again she laughed her brief, hot, tired,
cynical little laugh.

"Yes, I believe it," said Johanna. "He wants to be told the comforting
lie. But what about me?"

"*Eben!*"* cried Louise. "He wants the comfortable lie—and with
that you are caught."

"Wire," said Gilbert, "wire *not quite true, name wrong*—"

"Yes," laughed Louise. "That is very nice. Wrong name—wrong
Berry—not bil-berry but cran-berry. That is very nice—"

She mused to a moment's silence, then resumed:

"But we must not joke. It is not a laughing matter. Ach, you poor
Johanna, how can I think of your years in front. Ach, it is so difficolt.
There are the children—there is money—there is everything."

"Oh," cried Johanna, "there is quite as much on the other side."

But there was a dismal silence in the park, whilst Gilbert looked at a
massive horse-chestnut tree in full flower. What was life but a
complication of artificial difficulties.

"I think," said Louise, "it is best to cable *nicht wahr*, and wait for a
time. Later—later—"

"Yes perhaps—" said Johanna.

"Don't you think, Mr Noon?" said Louise.

"No," said Gilbert. "It's not a bit of good going on that way any
further. Best make a clean cut. Best wire *ganz richtig*—it will save a
calamity. There will only be a calamity later on."

"Yes—yes—you think—" mused Louise.

"But it isn't *quite right*," said Johanna. "There isn't any Berry."

"There is me," said Gilbert.

"Yes, there is you," said Louise, with doubtful intonation. Gilbert
flushed, and went pale.

"Wire that it is another man," said he, with his immovable, pale-faced obstinacy.

"But think—think what it means!" cried Johanna.

"I know without thinking. There's nothing else to do. Say another man."

"Shall I?" wavered Johanna.

"Ach—but you don't know what you are doing!" cried Louise. "You are so young—you are so young, Mr Noon. You are younger than Johanna. Think what will happen—ach—I can't think of it. You have no work—no money. Let there be time. Let Johanna have time. You must not hurry her in such a thing. Let her take time."

There was silence. Gilbert became paler and paler. He hated the park, and the morning sunshine, and the chestnut-trees in flower. They all looked to him like cardboard.

"Yes, is it not better so?" persisted Louise.

"No," said Gilbert. "She must wire the truth."

"Ach *must—must*. There can be no must," said Louise, rather cuttingly. "And the truth is *nicht wahr*. It is so simple." She laughed cynically.

"Yes," said Gilbert. "The truth isn't true."

"The truth isn't true," repeated Louise. "No—the truth is never true, Mr Noon. You are so young, you do not know what it means." She laughed hollowly.

It is a stagey thing to say. But then Louise had a queer, tired, devilish hollow little laugh of her own.

"Wire *another man*," said Gilbert to Johanna.

"Must I?" she said.

"Ach Hannele, du bist so dumm!"* cried Louise. "There can be no *must*."

She seemed to be brooding a bitter end of meditation, as she sat with her knee crossed, her veil loose on her brow, looking across the park.

"I think you must," said Gilbert to Johanna.

"And shall I do as you tell me? What shall I say?" asked Johanna.

"Say *another man*—" said Gilbert.

Louise had listened in silence to this little dialogue, almost as if she did not hear. Now she put in.

"*Another man!*" she laughed. "Oh, it sounds so nice. I like it very much. *Another man.*"

"Shall I say that?" said Johanna.

"Yes, say that," said Gilbert.

"Must I?" said Johanna.

"Yes."

Louise rose to her feet.

"Oh you young people!" she said. "Come, I must go. Mr Noon, I
5 must take Johanna away to our mother."

"You will telegraph before you go home?" said Gilbert to Johanna.

"Yes—yes—" said Johanna nervously.

"And you'll say what I told you?"

He looked into her eyes.

10 "Yes, I promise," she said, still waveringly.

"Come! Come!" said Louise. "Ach what are you doing? You do not
know."

They walked across the hateful park, into which wild horses would
not have dragged Mr Gilbert again. He loathed everything he was in
15 for. And yet he was in for it, so there was nothing to be done.

Louise got a taxi, and drove off with Johanna. Both had lowered their
veils. Both waved to him triumphantly as they drove off between the
avenue of trees. And if anything can be more hateful to a man than to
have two females driving triumphantly off in a taxi, and waving to him
20 as they leave him stranded in uncertainty, hanging at a loose end, then
tell me what it is.

He rambled round the attractive but to him hateful old town of
Detsch, and in perfect misery had his hair cut. The barber was French,
and talked anti-German.*

25 With a trimmed head Gilbert looked for luncheon—found a little
place where working men ate, and where he had Frankfurter sausages
and sauerkraut and felt horribly conspicuous. Then he went home and
lay down on the bed. Johanna was coming some time during the
afternoon. And he felt wretched, and not in his own skin. He felt
30 thoroughly humiliated, and now knew he was embarking on a new little
sea of ignominy. He writhed under all the ignominy.

There was a tap at the door. It was Johanna. She entered in silence,
looking worried.

"Did you wire?" he said.

35 "Yes."

"What?"

"I said *Nicht Berry—Schreibe—Not Berry, am writing*."

"You sent that?"

"Yes, I sent it before I got home—from the Friedrichstrasse post
40 office.*—Oh, Mama is in such a state. She wants to see you too."

"And have you written?"

"No—but I'm going to today."

"What is the address? I'll write too."

"Will you? To Everard?" she said doubtfully.

"Yes. What is the address?"

"What will you say?" she asked.

"Exactly what is."

"And what is? Tell me what you'll say."

"That you will stay with me—that you are living with me now—and that you won't go back."

He was anything but happy and assured. But a strange, pale fixity was on him. He said what he had to say, without giving it thought. In a process of strange abstraction his mind had decided without thinking. And this seemed to mesmerise Johanna.

"Will you say that?" she said wistfully.

"Yes—what is the address?"

He went to the table and took a piece of paper. He stood there in his shirtsleeves. Johanna, in a lovely dress of dull reddish cashmere, wearing a close toque made all of darkish bird's breast-feathers, stood in the light of the window, wondering and half wistful like a child. He looked at her, from his pallid, gloomy face.

"What is the address?" he repeated.

"Dr Everard——" and she answered automatically, whilst he wrote what she said.

"I shall write to him tonight," he said, laying down the pencil.

"Shall you?" she said wonderingly.

He looked at her, then he locked the door.

"Do you want me?" she said.

"Yes."

"Do you want me always?"

"Yes."

"Are you sure?"

"Yes."

"You don't say it very brightly."

"No."

"My love—"

She could see the sombre fire of passion in his eyes and his clouded brow. He resented so bitterly all the complication and humiliation. No man felt the sting of humiliation more keenly than he, or resented it more deeply and lastingly. He resented the rising tide of black, sewer-like ignominy that was just going to envelop him. He was heavy with deep, sullen resentment. And yet, like fate, his soul was fixed. Johanna was going to stay with him. She was with him now. In the midst of it all he was to enjoy her, she him.

5   She was quite ready to enjoy him—far more ready than he was to enjoy her. She could soon abandon herself to passion and delicious pleasure. But he came dense and crude.

None the less she admired him.

"What a wonderful shape you are here!" she said, running her
10   fingertips over the front contour of the big hip bone. He was rather bony. He wondered over her appreciation of him: something very unexpected in it. But he liked it, and his desire spread new wings.

The course of true love is said never to run true.* But never did the course of any love run so jagged as that of Johanna and Mr Noon.
15   The wonder is, it ever got there at all.

And yet, perhaps, a jagged, twisty, water-fally, harassed stream is the most fascinating to follow. It has a thousand unexpected thrills and adventures in it. Let those who love peace seek peace and pursue it. We are not so keen on peace. To be a fat cow in a fat pasture is not our
20   ideal. Away with your stodgy and suety peace. Let us have a continual risk and tumble and the unceasing spur of jeopardy on our flank to make us jump and fly down the wind. None of your fat grazing-grounds for us. If we are to have yon tasty tuft of grass, or yon patch of sweet-herb, we've got to hop perilously down a precipice for it. And that is
25   what we prefer. God, I don't want to sup life with a spoon. I'd rather go lean-bellied till I'd caught my bird.

Which all goes to prove that the critic who says I am on the search for beauty rather than truth may be right. He can read this book and make certain. He says I am Aubrey Beardsley rather than Swift. So that all
30   you have to fear, gentle reader, is some exquisite tail-piece to Salome. I'll do my best for you. If you have misgivings, leave off now.

> "Quick, sharp, on the alert
> Let every gentleman put on his shirt!
> And, oh, quick if you please
35   Let every lady get on her chemise!"*

Never was such a pair of unfortunate interrupted lovers. As in *Macbeth*, there came a knocking at the door. Johanna, in the arms of Gilbert, gave an awful start. He sat up and listened, with visions of husbands, police, incensed official Barons and what-not coursing through his mind.

"Bang-bang-bang-bang!" came the double knock. Whoever it was, they would have heard the voices of the guilty pair. The door-handle gave a little squeak of protest as the unknown horror tried it from outside. Luckily the door was locked.

"Bang-bang-bang!" came the officious knock. And still dead silence in the room, where the guilty pair lay on the bed with beating hearts.

"See who it is," whispered Johanna, pushing him from her.

And then he saw her, *in puris naturalibus,*∗ flee swiftly, white and naked, behind a curtain which hung across a corner, huddling there with her feet, and the tip of her shoulder, and then, as she stooped, that exquisite *finale* of Salome showing round and white behind the curtain, before the dazed eyes of Gilbert.

He was in no better plight than she: not a rag, not a stitch on him, and there he stood in the middle of the room listening to that diabolical knocking and vacantly watching the come and go of the exquisite tail-piece to Johanna, as she stooped to unravel her stockings.

And why, under such circumstances, should she be putting on her grey silk stockings, and routing for her garters with rosebuds on them. Why oh why, in the shipwreck of nudity, cling to the straw of a grey silk stocking.

Rap-rap-rap! This was not to be borne. The vacant Gilbert was man enough upon necessity: necessity it had to be, however: and necessity it now was. Therefore he reached down his double-breasted brown overcoat, and wrapped it round him as far as possible. It went round him well enough, but it left his bare neck sticking out at the top, and half a yard of bare shins sticking out at the bottom. No help for it. He unlocked and opened the door, holding it and barring the entrance of—that damned Swiss manageress. His hair was ruffled and on end, he looked at the precise female with his vacant, unassailable eye.

"Die gnädige Frau ist da?—Is the lady there?"

"Wie?—What?"

"Die Frau Doktor is da?—The Mrs Doctor is there?"

"Wie?—What?"

"Madame, est-elle ici?—Is Madam here?"∗

Gilbert shook his head solemnly.

"Non, elle n'est pas ici."

Heaven knows why he chose to answer the French and not the German.

The Swiss woman looked at him: he looked at her.

"Elle n'est pas ici?" she repeated.

"Non. Non!" and Gilbert looked into the room behind him, vacantly. He saw Johanna's now stockinged ankles behind the linen curtain.

5   "Non! Elle n'est pas ici," he said with the innocent "pipe of half awakened bird."* He looked into the hard black eyes of the venomous manageress mildly.

The manageress looked various volumes and daggers back at him, but as she did not proceed to throw them he let her look.

10   "Merci," she said reluctantly: very reluctantly. She had lost the battle. And she turned away.

And as he saw her back, Gilbert became aware of his own hairy shins, and agonies of confusion went over him. He locked the door stupefied with confusion.

15   "Oh God, I must get out of this!" cried Johanna, springing from behind the curtain in her grey silk stockings, rose-bud garters, and cambric chemise. Gilbert, still clasped in his brown overcoat, watched her as she flew into her lacey-white knickers, her pretty, open work French stays, her grey silk petty and her reddish dress. She tied the

20   tapes and snapped the press-studs like lightning. In a moment she was tying her shoe-laces. And then she had only to poke her hair more or less under the dusky-lustrous feather toque, and fling the lace scarf over her shoulders, and she was ready.

"Goodbye!" she said, looking at him with wide scared eyes. "I hope

25   before God she won't make a row.—I'll go down."

She was much more scared than Gilbert would have thought. But in a moment she was gone—her red dress and white scarf and soft-feathered head flashed across the landing and was gone.

He proceeded to dress himself, feeling a new rage at his new mess.

30   But there was nothing for it but just to go on. And when there is nothing for it but just to go on, why, one goes on.

So he went downstairs—without mishap. And at the bottom he heard loud laughing talking voices from the lounge. Johanna for certain. Yes, there was Johanna talking to a handsome, ultra-fashion-

35   able woman* who had daring dark eyes and looked like a cocotte.

This was Johanna's sister Lotte, descended from the *chic* of Vienna.

"Ja Lotte—le voilà—le faux Monsieur Berry."

"Bonjour M'sieur," said Lotte, holding out an elegant white-kid-gloved hand. "Vous n'êtes pas Berry, alors!"

40   Gilbert bowed, and his eye caught a spark from Lotte's.

"Safe—safe!" cried Johanna to him in English. "Oh, I had the fright of my life."

"Ai-dà!" said Lotte. "I doan spik English. Je vous ai fait un mauvais tour, hein? Mille pardons!* I did you a bad turn. I asked the woman if Johanna was here, and she said she thought she was upstairs. 5 So I said Tell her please. Of course, if I had *known*—" Lotte made dark, wicked eyes at Gilbert—"I should have said Pray don't disturb her." She put on an engaged look, and smoothed her gloves like a woman just going out, and arched her eyebrows in a rather becoming pantomime. "But I have made a serious *faux pas*." 10

And she bridled, displeased with herself.

"However," she continued, "all can be finished in the next chapter. I am going."

She once more made eyes at Gilbert, and held out her hand.

"I come with you, Lotte," said Johanna. 15

And once more Gilbert watched two women sail off in a taxi-cab, whilst he was left stranded in that accursed, blaring, military town. And what was worse, he had lost another of his skins now, and felt more raw than he cared to admit even to himself. He loathed the black-eyed Swiss manageress, with her face like a pair of scissors. And he hated 20 her hotel: family indeed!

The twilight of the same day saw Johanna walking sentimentally with Captain von Daumling, who was sparkling in his blue and pink uniform, but whose heart was veiled in a grey chiffon of tears. They strayed unconsciously to the spiney cathedral. 25

"Let us go," said Rudolf, "and light a candle to our love, on the altar of the Virgin."

"Yes, do let us," cried Johanna, thrilled to her soul.

Now that the candle of Rudolf's brief passion was drooping and almost spent, its ruddy light dwindling to the smallest pale wick-glow, 30 Johanna was thrilled to her marrow to stick up a good stout candle of wax to burn on the altar of the Virgin. In the dusk of the tall, forested cathedral, with the gorgeous windows glowing but shedding no light, they crept on the low strand of the floor, and the captain's spurs tinkled melancholy, a tiny sound low on the floor of the vast, branching shadow 35 of the interior. Johanna was not a catholic, but she loved her cathedral. Its slender, shafted upsoaring affected her deliriously. She crept across the forlorn floor to the flickering altar of the Virgin, whilst the Captain of the Fifth trod softly, holding the stout wax candle between his fingers, at her side. 40

It was a hushed moment. He lighted the wick of his new pale candle at one of the candles already burning, and then stuck it, like a new pale tree, a new wasting column of life, on one of the expiring sockets. After which he came and kneeled at Johanna's side, and they knew a perfect
5   unison.

Oh white, oh waxen candle of purified love, how still, how golden the flame of the spirit hovers upon you, while the wax lasts. Oh beautiful tall erect candle of chastened aspiration, how soothing is the sight of you to a soul perplexed and suffering. Nay, quench the dusky,
10 crimson-burning torch of unhallowed passion, scatter its lurid blood-flame, crush it down to next to nothingness, put* it in your pocket and forget it. And light a six-franc waxen candle upon the altar of uplifted aspiration, and pray a little prayer to the Virgin and the Unbegotten.

15 And prepare to consume this six-francs-worth of material wax, this mundane flesh: prepare, oh prepare to struggle as a guttering flame struggles with the wick, for release. For release into the infinite. Rudolf watched the sunken, flapping flame of somebody else's candle beating its wings to escape into the boundless eternity, and he pressed his
20 hands to his breast. To escape—ah, to escape from the limitations of this five-franc mould of a corpus!

Johanna meanwhile watched the same sunk flame flapping and fighting for life, fighting, sipping, sipping avidly at the spent wax, and yet, in spite of all its struggles forced to go, forced to leave the lovely
25 warm place of presence, to be driven over the threshold of existence into the howling wilderness of infinite chaos, where the world is void and dark.* So there she knelt with luxurious tears in her eyes. I say luxurious. For after all it wasn't her candle, it was only the cavalry captain's. And he was no longer indispensable.

30 They were both sad, but for different reasons. They both saw the candle-flame shuddering in its frail mortality, and felt the vast shadow of eternity branching overhead. And they both had pangs: widely differing pangs.

So, gentle reader, before you light your next candle to the Virgin,
35 make up your mind which emotion you're going to get out of it: whether you're going to see the immortal soul escaping at last into freedom and bliss, on a strong draught of uplift; or whether you're going to lament "Alas, gone out, gone out!"

Let us invoke the great spirit of Uplift. Oh Uplift, Uplift, that which
40 carries us beyond ourselves, how much bigger we are than ever we were

intended to be when we whirl with thy wind in our skirts, heavenwards.
Oh mighty rushing wind, oh universal Uplift, carry us above our own
high-water-mark and make us boundless. Blow us into the mid-heaven's
zenith till this poor earth is no more than a speck of dust in our eye, and
we are so god-almighty elevated that there's nothing either here nor in   5
kingdom come* but we can look down on it. Dear draughty uplift,
bellow out our skirts and trouser-legs like zeppelin balloons, till we whirl
straddling up into the sky, whence we can look down on our fellow-men.
Oh holy uplift, let us look down on our fellow-men: in love of course! Let
us look down on our fellow-men, as pathetic, tearful Gods look down on   10
mankind, pitiful, all pitiful and all benign. Oh, as we straddle in mid-
heaven with the sanctified wind of Uplift bellowing up our trouser-legs
and ballooning our trouser-seat so that we float butt-end uppermost, oh
then, then oh then we spread our arms to mankind away below there, we
gather humanity like a tray of silk-worm cocoons to our beneficent   15
bosom, and we fairly reel in mid-air with charitable feeling. Of course
our trousers are sound, so we are safe. We are none of your arse-patched
mundane sitters. We are the uplift-wooshers,* who dribble the
Pluto-drizzle of charity* over the world. It's a risky thing to do, of
course, if your trouser-seat is worn a little thin. The balloon of the   20
spiritual inflatus might then burst and let you down flop on that same
pathetic mankind, which will not welcome you at all if you come cropping
down like a brick-bat. In fact, in these days of risky tailors, it isn't half
such a safe thing as it used to be, to go wooshing up in the air on the
draught of sanctified Uplift. In fact I should warn people to beware of   25
entertaining charitable and benevolent feelings just now, till they are
quite sure their material gas-envelope is quite sound. Let them rub and
feel their trouser-seat and their backside carefully, to make sure it is a
sound vacuum, and that it will act as a trustworthy float when it is filled
with the spirit of uplift, most vacuous of all vacuosities. I say the trouser- 30
seat, because of course that is the obvious pouch or inflatus-bladder of
Uplift. Ah humanity, humanity, let your posterior forever not exist, save
as a vacuum. Queens of Spain have no legs, but all lofty mankind has no
backside: not a bit of it. Nothing there. Nothing twin-protuberant and
kickable. Only the float-void.   35

But dear me, we become lyrical. Let us return to our muttons; Johanna
of the golden fleece, and poor dear shorn lamb of a Gilbert, who lost
another skin in his encounter yesterday with the Swiss Manageress. I
think that Swiss Manageress ought not easily to be forgiven: for sure she
was an upliftress.   40

But it was yesterday. And now surely, surely the wind is going to be tempered to the shorn lamb.* Tempered indeed. Damned ill-tempered.

In Detsch at that moment the May fair* was being held, the
5 Maimesse. It had great attraction for Gilbert. He went and stared long at the booths, the woman in red satin with six monkeys; the prize-fighter who had such horrible bulk of arm-flesh in his shapeless, folded arms, and such a rudiment of a face, and no back to his head, a sickly object; at the dancers in sequins and the pictures of La Belle Turque
10 and the family of jugglers; and the rather old-fashioned round-abouts. It was not like an English fair: nothing of our mechanical spick-and-spanness and superior vulgarity. There was here a deeper, more suggestive, more physical vulgarity, something ancient and coarse. The language was either French patois—which was more frequent—or
15 crude German.

Since Monsieur Gilbert was uneasy, wretched inside his remaining skin in this town of Detsch, all on edge and bored, at a loose end, and semi-stupefied, he found this fair a sort of god-send. He could stand staring like any boor, for hours: not really attentive, but at any rate not
20 so acutely burdened with himself. And the ancient pagan grossness, something Mediaeval and Roman even, in the brutality of the fair, interested him. It was as if the modern squeamishness had hardly affected this last remnant of coarse old Europe.

So he stared and strolled, and felt for some reason less of a stranger
25 here than in the town itself. Some sort of Latin or Gallic crudity in the fair gave him a sense of familiarity, old blood-association, whereas the purely Germanic influence seemed always to put him outside his own skin, and make him so ill at ease he could not remain still for a minute.

As he strolled, behold, Johanna and Lotte coming brilliant and
30 laughing and elegant through the fair. He rushed up.

"This is all right," he said. "Are you going to any of the shows?"

And he put himself at their side.

Lotte gave him her hand and said *Guten Morgen* in her deep, nonchalant voice. But Johanna said fiercely, in a half whispering voice:
35 "Go away! Go away, Papa is just behind! Go away, he is not to see you! Go away, you don't know us."

Gilbert went pale and looked at Johanna.

"Allez! Allez donc!" said Lotte, in her deep, sardonic voice. "Et au revoir. Mauvaise occasion!"* And she nodded her head, and made
40 eyes at him.

Fumbling with his hat, he stepped back. And glancing round he saw Louise with a smallish man in a German crush-hat and upturned moustaches. Louise made frightened eyes at him that he should withdraw. The Baron had not noticed him.

He left the fair-ground at once, and walked straight out, and out over the bridge, and up the hill, and away from the town, through the vineyards where peasants were working, through the deep lane, uphill, uphill towards a village.

On a sort of platform or wide terrace on the brow of the hill he sat down. Below lay the town and the canals and the fortifications and the plain. He did not look out. Black rage was in his heart.

The wide level place on the brow of the slope was the real centre of the village. Horse-chestnut trees, deep in new leaf and flower, made flat shade. A blue soldier was exercising a bright brown horse in and out of the horizontal shade. Other greyish soldiers stood near the parapet, looking out. Down on the high-road below, where they were looking, some artillery was rattling along far away, a cavalcade.

Gilbert felt it was all strange—just strange. In the old vineyards on the slope out here in the country there was a strong sense of Rome—old Rome. This was old Roman territory. But in the school beyond the chestnut trees he could hear the children saying their lessons in German—a queer sound to him.

The soldiers made him feel uneasy. He went across the place into the village—an old, French seeming village, where still he felt the old Roman influence. He went into a clean, old-fashioned inn. A tall, black-eyed man, peasant-farmer and inn-keeper, brought him wine and bread and sausage. And they talked in slow French. And in the black eyes of the inn-keeper was a sort of slow, implacable malice. He had a son—in France, and a daughter—in France. With his laconic, malicious smile he said that they spoke no German. His children were educated in France: if they were educated here, they would be forced to speak German. He did not intend that they should speak German. He smiled slowly and maliciously.*

And Gilbert sympathised sincerely. This rampant Germanism of Detsch was beginning to gall him: a hateful, insulting militarism that made a man's blood turn to poison. It was so forcé,* unnatural too. It wasn't like the quiet lovely German villages of the Black Forest, or the beery roisterousness of Munich. It was an insulting display of militaristic insolence and parvenu imperialism. The whole thing was a presumption, a deliberate, insolent, Germanistic insult to everybody, even to the simpler Germans themselves. The spirit was detestably ill-bred, such a mechanical heel-clicking assumption of haughtiness without any deep, real human pride. When men of a great nation go a bit beyond themselves, and foster a cock-a-doodling haughtiness and a

5　supercilious insolence in their own breasts, well, then they are asking for it, whoever they may be. There is such a thing as passional violence, and that is natural: there is such a thing as profound, deep-rooted human pride, even haughtiness. But that self-conscious conceit and insolence of Detsch had nothing to be said for it, it was all worked up

10　deliberately.

In a temper Gilbert went back to town. Far from having had the wind tempered to him, the wind had taken a bit more skin off. He was angry, and rawer than ever. But at evening he sat in his room, so remote and still, and gradually he recovered somewhat. And then, on a large sheet

15　of paper, he wrote a letter to Johanna's husband.

"Dear Doctor X,

I hope you will not mind if I write to you direct.

I am here in Detsch with Johanna, and I have asked her to tell you everything openly. I love her. It is no use making a calamity of things.

20　What is done is done, and there remains only to make the best of it. Johanna is in a queer state, mentally and nervously. I know it would be fatal for her to come back to America. You must know yourself that her state is not normal. One day you will be perhaps grateful to me for saving you from something worse than this————"*

25　So Mr Gilbert ran himself down his sheet of foolscap, saying what he actually thought and felt, without imagining the husband at the other end of the communication. He did not talk about love and tears: only that this was something which had come to pass, and which, given Johanna's state of mind, was bound to come to pass, and which coming

30　to pass might have taken a far more painful form, bringing far more nastiness and misery than at present. Therefore it remained for him, Everard, and for himself, Gilbert Noon, to work for the best solution of the difficulty, and to try not to make further disaster.

Which screed of half-innocent earnestness Gilbert signed, and

35　sealed, and addressed, and went out into the night and posted. Which was another finality secured. It is just as well to have a faculty for intense abstraction and impersonality, but it is very dangerous to use it. However, Gilbert poured out this private effusion from his abstracting soul, and committed it to fate and the international post.

40　We shall notice a few little gusts of uplift. Our young mathematical friend could not be English without being a bit of a St. George. Behold, Johanna posing as the fair Sabra,* with a huge dragon of nerves and theories and unscrupulous German theorisers just about to devour her, all unbeknown to her fatherly husband, when up rides St. George in the shape of Mr Noon, and proceeds to settle the brute. How very 5 agreeable! Yes, he saved his own moral bacon when he waved that red-cross flag of greater disaster under Everard's far-off nose. And yet, he was right. The fair Johanna was in the dragon's mouth, and the brave Saint Gilbert hadn't half settled the reptile yet. In fact he hadn't begun. But he spoke as heroes speak before the fight: as if it was 10 finished.

The next morning he met Johanna—and what did they do? Ah friends, you would perhaps expect them to go into the cathedral and light a still fatter ghostly candle. No, Gilbert was not in a candle-lighting mood. The dark red torch of his wicked passion was feeling a 15 bit quenched for the moment, but he was prepared to blow on the spark. Therefore he drifted with Johanna away from the town, down across the river. There at the side of the high-road were green thick trees, and narrow paths into the seeming wood. It looked very quiet and still, even forbidding, this dark bit of close woodland almost in the town 20 itself.

"Shall we go down there?" said Gilbert, pointing to the path that went straight from the high-road rather sombrely under the trees and into the unknown. To be sure there was some sort of not-very-new-looking notice-board: but why notice notice-boards. 25

"Yes," said Johanna. "It looks nice."

So they strayed down the narrow, tree-crowded, sombre path, on and on till they came to an opening. It was rather romantic. There was a smooth greensward bank, very square and correct, and a sort of greensward dry moat, and a high greensward bastion opposite, all soft 30 and still and lovely, with a spot of sunshine shining on it, and the trees around. So in this green seclusion the two sat down, looking at the romantic velvety slopes and moated formality of their quiet nook, and feeling very remote and nice, like Hansel and Gretel, or the Babes in the Wood. 35

Johanna put her hand in his as they sat side by side in the spot of sunshine, and musingly, gently he turned the jewelled rings on her soft finger.

"I wrote to Everard," he said.

"Did you! What did you say?" 40

Gilbert told her.

"I wrote to him too," she said.

"And what did *you* say?"

"I said I didn't think I could ever go back."

5   "You should have said you were sure," said Gilbert.

"Oh, but one must go gently."

"Do you call this going gently?" he asked.

"With Everard. I mustn't give him too great a shock."

"But you won't go back."

10   "No," she said, rather indefinitely. "Don't you want me to?"

"You know all about that. What *are* we going to do?" He seemed indefinite now.

"Why—shall we go somewhere—later?" she said.

"Where?"

15   "I thought to Munich. We might go to Louise. I love the Isar valley—don't you?"

"I do," he said. "Go there as man and wife?"

"Dare we?" she said.

"Yes."

20   "But they know I've got a husband in America."

"Let them know. I can be he."

"It would be rather fun," she said.

"And we could find some little place, and live cheap."

"Oh, cheap as dirt in Bavaria. I don't mind what we do so long as I
25 can get away from all that awful Boston business. Oh, you don't know how I suffered being a correct, highly-thought-of doctor's wife among all those good middle-class people. Ah the agony, when I think of standing on deck and seeing that town again—seeing Everard waiting for me there! No, I couldn't do it. It is real agony."

30   "Weren't they nice with you?"

"Oh, they were! They were awfully nice. That made it all the more horrible. I never felt I could breathe among them. I *never* felt I could breathe—*never*—not till I was on board the ship and coming to Germany. All the rest of the time I simply couldn't get a deep
35 breath—I don't know why."

She put her hand on her breast and breathed to the depths of her magnificent chest.

"Oh, you don't know what I suffered. Because they *were* all so nice to me. I used to think—Oh, if they knew, if they knew about me!—That
40 was after Eberhard. I'm sure I wonder I'm not mad. I got into such a

state of terror. I *am* terrified. I'm so terrified I know I shall go mad if ever I set foot on Boston dock again. I'm not the sort that gets ill, I'm the sort that goes mad. Everard says so himself."

Gilbert looked at her. Fortunately for him he simply could not understand it. He could not understand her terror—her almost criminal terror, that would drive her to unknown lengths and horrors.

"Well, you needn't go back," he said.

"No, I don't think I can."

"But we shall have no money."

"Ah, I don't mind about money. I don't care. I'd rather live in a *cave* than in one of those houses. Yet I loved my house. It was called *Marvell.** It was so sunny, and I loved the garden. I loved making it all myself.—But the *terrors*, the *horrors* I've felt in that house are indescribable.—I don't *want* to live like that. I don't *want* to live like the middle classes. I'd rather live in a cave. If we have no money, let's find a cave and live there."

"We can't," said Gilbert.

"Why not. People used to. Why are you so damned civilised. I should love it."

"No you wouldn't," he said.

"How do you know? I should love it. Anything to get out of that horror."

"You might negatively love it: but you wouldn't positively. No, if we've got to live, we've got to be moderately comfortable, moderately decent."

"What an old stager you are! What a conventional civilised creature! Ha, I could fling it all away. I *could* live in a cave."

"I couldn't—not in this climate," said Gilbert.

"Why not? It could have a door.—But oh, if we do go right away together, let us be like tramps. I feel such an outcast, such an outcast. And oh, how I hate them for making me feel it. I hate them. They like to make you feel a pariah."

"Then why give in to their likings. They'll never make me feel a pariah," said Gilbert.

"You wait. Wait till you've been as I have been—all of them loving you and admiring you, and you *knowing* what they'd do to you if they found out."

"What would they do?"

"What *wouldn't* they!—And they were so nice on the other hand. His parents—they are such dear old people, in England. I love them really. I do hope they'll never know, it would break their hearts."

"Pah," said Gilbert. "Nice people have the toughest hearts as a rule."

"Why? Why do you say that?—But it is all so horrible! The awful things I've done—how I've lied. It has nearly sent me mad. I *am* a bit
5   mad."

"Well, then make an end of it. Break it clean off—and we'll go right away together."

He was holding her hand between his.

"Ah, it would be lovely!" she sighed. "It would be lovely.—Let us
10   go right away—let us disappear. And never, never let us have a house and live among people again—never, never. Never let us be among people as if we were one of them—never. I couldn't bear it all over again."

"Don't bother about them—they don't matter," said he soothingly,
15   kissing her soft fingers.

"Ah but they *do. How* they matter when one is penned in among them. Think of it, I've been married and penned in with them for twelve years. And it's four years since Eberhard. He showed me one could be free. But he didn't take me away—he didn't take me away.
20   And how I waited—ah God, how I waited for him.—And then I really believed that one shouldn't wait for one man. *That* is the mistake. I believe he is right there. One should love all men: all men are loveable somewhere."

"But why love *all* men? You are only one person. You aren't a
25   universal. You're just a specific unit."

"Why aren't I universal? I've got two hands and two feet, like all women. And I *do* understand something in every man I meet—I *do.* And in nice men I understand such a *lot* that I feel *forced* to love them—I feel forced."

30   "Oh Good God!" he said. "Do you love for what you can understand?"

"Yes!" she cried. "Why not?"

"I usually hate what I understand. If I love it must be something I can't understand."

35   "Well," she said, "and there's something in everybody. In every man there's something I can understand—sometimes so deeply. And that *makes* me love him. And there's something I *can't* understand. And that makes me go on loving him till I do understand it."

"My sacred God!" exclaimed Gilbert irreverently. "Your love is a
40   blooming understood affair. I'd rather have mathematics."

"It *is* something like mathematics—except that it's *life*. Something to know in every man—and something to solve. One can do an awful lot for a man through love."

"You might as well call youself Panacea—,"* he said sarcastically.

"Well—why not? I *am* something of a Panacea—I know I am. And I know love is the only panacea—and where we make a mistake is that we don't use it or let it be used."

"A damned patent medicine that poisons more than it cures."

"Don't you believe in love?" she cried, snatching away her hand.

"Not in general love."

"What in then?"

"In particular love I may believe."

"Oh may you!" she mocked. "And what do you mean by particular love? Just keeping one person all for yourself! Ah, I know the horrors of that. It is all based on jealousy. I think the noblest thing is to overcome jealousy."

"I don't," said Gilbert. "Jealousy is as natural as love or laughter. You might as well overcome everything and have done with it all straight off."

"No! No!" she said. "Jealousy is mean and horrible—and marriage is vile and possessive. I *do* believe in love: in all love. And I believe one should love as much as ever one can. I do. Eberhard taught me a great deal. He was wonderful!"

"Do you believe you can be here and in Boston at one and the same time?" asked Gilbert.

"In a way, I *am*."

"In a way! In a way! Damn your ways. Damn your spirit. You may be here and in Boston in the spirit, all at once. But I can't do with spirit. Can your body be here and in Boston at one and the same minute? Can it?"

"No—that's its limitation."

"Ah! Then I'm all for limitation."

"You would be: like the rest of men."

"All excepting the wonderful Eberhard!—You can't be here and in America, *physically*, at once. Limitation or not, you've got to abide by it. And it's the same with physical love. You *can't* be *physically* in love with more than one man at the same time. It can't be done. You can be spiritually in love with everybody at once, and take all men under your skirts in the same instant, like a Watts picture.* But that's not physical. That's merely spiritual. And there's a difference."

"There isn't a difference unless we make it."

"Can you be physically in Boston and Detsch at the same moment? *Can* you physically take two men at once? If there is *physical* love, it is exclusive. It *is* exclusive. It's only spiritual love that is all-embracing. And I'm off spiritual love. I *don't want* it. It stinks. I want exclusive
5 physical love.—There may be aberrations. But the real fact in physical love is the exclusiveness: once the love is really *there*."

"But I thought I loved Everard—"

"Thought! Thought! You've thought too much. I should leave off thinking, if I were you."

10 "Yes, you're just like all men. You'd like me to."

But at this point a brutal interruption.

Ah, gentle reader, however you may disapprove of Johanna and Mr Noon, be a little gentle with them, they have known so many brutal interruptions.

15 A fellow in a blue uniform and a peaked cap and carrying a gun, creeping forward with the loathsome exultant officiousness of all police or soldier individuals on duty, and of German specimens in particular.

"Was machen Sie hier?"

20 Imagine the foul sound of the German officious insolence the lump of a police-soldier put in these words, as he looked down his nose at the offending couple. They had jumped to their feet seeing him creep on them.

"What are you doing here?" said the sergeant.

25 "What are we doing here!" said Johanna, her pride of birth and authority springing like flame to her eyes. "And who are *you*, to come asking. What do you want?"

Gilbert was staggered by the sudden authoritative fury with which Johanna towered and flared at the lump of a sergeant. But he, in all
30 the majesty of his duty, was not to be abashed.

"Ja, was machen Sie hier!" he repeated with calm insolence. "You know these are the fortifications." He spoke as if he had two culprits in his power.

"Fortifications! What fortifications indeed." cried Johanna. "We
35 walked here two minutes from the high-road."

"You are two foreigners. I have heard you for the last quarter of an hour."

"What a beast!"

"Foreigners! Take care what you say. I am German, and my father
40 is Baron von Hebenitz—"

"And the gentleman—?" sneered the sergeant, a cunning, solid lump of a fellow.

"The gentleman is English," said Johanna.

"So!—Have you any papers?"—he turned now to Gilbert. But Gilbert was looking with such a pale face and such dark round eyes that he did not understand.

"He wants to know if you have any papers," said Johanna.

"Papers—" said Gilbert, feeling in the pocket of his new suit. "No—I've only this—" and he took out a letter addressed to a friend of his in the Rhine province.

The soldier or police individual, whatever he was, took the letter and scrutinised the address.

"It is forbidden to enter the fortifications," he said, looking up with his impertinent officiousness. "You saw the notice. And since you are foreigners—"

"Do you *know* that I am no foreigner!" cried Johanna in a flame of fury—the sergeant almost cowered—*almost*. His sacred duty saved him. "Have I not said my father is the Baron von Hebenitz. Do you know the Baron von Hebenitz? Have you never heard of him?"

She lapsed now into jeering sarcasm.

"Yes, I have heard of him," said the creature.—"And the Herre is Englishman?"

"Yes—and what does it matter!" She proceeded to swallow some of her fury.*—"Cannot one sit and talk. What harm does it do?"

She was breaking into a flirtatious, cajoling laugh, after having been white at the nose with fury.

"Yes—how does one know," said the sergeant. "I have my orders to arrest anyone within the fortifications."

"Oh, how stupid!" said Johanna. "We didn't know at all that we were in any fortifications—"

"There is the sign-board—"

"Ach, why don't you paint it orange and violet, so that one could see it!"—She was smiling a little tenderly at him. He was not really such a bad-looking young fellow, apart from his dummified duty.

"Ja, that is not my affair—" he said. "It is my duty to arrest you both—"

"Oh yea!" cried Johanna. "And we are still so young.—But it is absurd—we have done nothing but walk six yards and sit down and talk.—You can refer to my father—and to Captain von Daumling—they will give you guarantees." She was rather frightened.

"Yes," said the sergeant. "Your address?"

And he drew forth a paper and pencil, and wrote Johanna's address. "And the address of the gentleman?"

This also he wrote down.

5   "And inquiries will be made from the Herr Baron," he said—rather mollified, and a little pleasanter, but still duty-bound like a brass-bound time-piece.

Johanna and Gilbert took themselves off, whilst the dutiful soldier followed them down the little path.*

10   Once free in the high-road Johanna began to exclaim:

"What fools! What fools we are! Of course I ought to have known. Now there'll be a hell of a fuss, and they will go to Papa."

"But there is nothing to make a fuss about," said Gilbert. His English innocence still seemed to him unassailable. Alas, he has learnt

15   better—or worse.

"Ha—you know what fussers they are, with their damned fortifications. Why do they leave them open to the public! Why don't they put some notice! Oh what a curse!—You will have to meet Papa."

To Gilbert it all seemed rather a mountainous mole-hill. But he had

20   a creepy feeling down his spine that anything uncomfortable might happen in this beastly Detsch. The grating sound of officious, aggressive militarism was getting on his nerves and making him feel almost guilty of something—perhaps of being a mere civilian. He began to look behind him, as if he really were going to be arrested. He was half

25   afraid to go to his room for fear it might be under military seal. He felt suspect, and whoever feels suspect feels infect, as if he were infected with some mysterious indefinable disease.

However, his room was all quiet. Johanna called for him in the afternoon to take him to call on her mother and father. Very stiff, badly

30   at a disadvantage, he climbed the stairs.

The Baron and Baroness were both in the drawing-room.

"Oh, you are so seelly, to go there," said the Baroness, in her fragmentary English.

The Baron bowed stiffly, military fashion, and shook hands. Gilbert

35   never had a bow in him. And as for kissing the Baroness' hand—you might as well have asked him to kiss her toe and have done with it. Hence a little added stiffness in the Baron's salute.

"Sie   sprechen   Deutsch—oder   französisch?—Vous   parlez français?"*

40   "Oui," said Gilbert, monosyllabic.

The Baron put him down as an ill-mannered lout with no breeding. Gilbert, tongue-tied, and everything-else-tied, felt that these grating German good manners were apish showing-off. But alas, he was at a disadvantage.

The Baroness called him to take his tea, to ask if he would have meelk. He said he wouldn't, and went with his cup to the window. There the Baron, who scorned tea, joined him.

"Vous fumez?" said the little gentleman, offering a cigarette-case.

"Merci," said Gilbert, taking a cigarette and getting most hopelessly entangled with it and his tea-cup. The Baron gave him a match, and with tea-cup shivering nervously in his left hand our young friend lit his cigarette.

"Vous êtes longtemps en Allemagne?"* asked the Baron.

Poor Gilbert stumbled with his French. The two men eyed one another. The Baron was rather elegant and *comme il faut*, with his hair and his moustaches on end. He was small, but carried himself as if he were big. His manners had that precise assertiveness of a German who is sure of himself and feels himself slightly superior. These manners always petrified Gilbert into rigidity. Only his eye remained clear and candid. He looked at the Baron with this curious indomitable candour, and the Baron glanced back at him rather fierily and irritably. So, like two very strange dogs, they stood in the window and eyed one another, and Gilbert stuttered hopeless French. He *sounded* a hopeless fool: he behaved like an unmitigated clown: only the insuperable candid stillness of his dark-blue eye saved him at all. But the Baron was impatient.

"Vous êtes à Munich, ma fille m'a dit. La Bavière vous plaît?"

"Oui! Oui! Beaucoup. Et la peuple est très intéressante."*

"*Le* peuple—oui," said the Baron.

And that put the stopper on it. Our friend stood corrected, and not another sound would come out of him.—Oh these weary dreary banalities in a foreign language!

Johanna came to the rescue, and ended the ridiculous interview as soon as possible. And now Gilbert was carted off to interview dear Rudolf. He felt like an image of the Virgin being wheeled round.

Rudolf was in undress uniform, smoking a cigarette—a fresh-faced, ingenuous fellow gone somewhat bald in front, prematurely, and, thank goodness, wearing his moustaches quite short and unassuming. Altogether he was unassuming. Johanna, in her bright flirtatious way—gentle reader, *do* forgive words like flirtatious, they are so

apt—told the story with laughter, and once more the œillades, or
fusillade of glances went on between the two gentlemen. Rudolf had
large blue eyes—really rather nice. But he eyed his supplanter and said
nothing. It seemed to Gilbert that neither himself nor Rudolf said one
5   single word during the interview. Probably that was an illusion. But
certain it was that Johanna was almost ignored, whilst the two males
exchanged this series of looks.

Now Gilbert had this one saving advantage. He went so stiff and
absent in wrong company that he seemed an absolute imbecile. No one
10 can blame the Baron for calling him, when affairs grew hot, later on, an
ungebildeter Simpel, a gewöhnlicher Lump: very nasty things to be
called: *uneducated simpleton*, and *common lout*. *Common lout* is especially
nasty; yet it was not, from one point of view, unapt. And still, though in
every other bit of him the young gentleman became a semi-imbecile,
15 still, in the middle of his eye remained a certain impregnable self-
possession, candour, and naturalness. Now the Baron had long lost his
own candour and naturalness, therefore when he saw it so quiet in the
middle of Gilbert's dark-blue eye, like the evening star showing on a
stormy sky, he was unsettled, he felt he must call names. And poor
20 Rudolf had so absolutely lost *his* self-possession, that he saw in Gilbert
a strange menace: this thin, this silent individual, this raven of woe, as
the poem later on put it.

Well, the raven of woe said Guten Abend to the blue-eyed, bald-
fronted young captain, and took his departure. A solitary and hopping
25 raven, he went through the Frenchy, raspingly-Germanised streets of
the city till he found a restaurant where he could go in and eat. And
even then, when at the end of the meal the waiter said Fruit ou
fromage?—he only answered with a troubled stare.

"Fruit ou fromage?" repeated the waiter, raising his voice.
30 A troubled, anxious stare from friend Gilbert.

"Obst oder Käse?"* snapped the waiter.

A look of greater bewilderment.

"Obst oder Käse? Fruit ou fromage? Obst oder Käse?" shouted the
waiter in exasperation.
35 Two consternated blue eyes and a slightly open, pouting mouth, and
a brow of agony, for answer.

"Imbécile!" muttered the waiter, and flounced away.

Gilbert understood this.

Back came the waiter, and bounced a piece of gorgonzola uncom-
40 promisingly under imbecile's nose. And then Gilbert heard it all—

Fruit ou fromage—Obst oder Käse—He heard it all, and he recognised the appalling sounds as perfectly familiar words. But something had gone wrong with his works, and he only just had enough wits to remember that the word *café* meant a black substance, usually liquid, in a small cup.

He hurried away from the restaurant, feeling that he was really going beyond himself in the direction of idiocy. Detsch was really taking off a skin too many.

So he wandered through the horrible, wide, new desert avenues or boulevards which the Germans had made round the old town, and felt like a lost soul. And then if an old woman with a huge bundle didn't stop him and ask him something.

To his infinite relief, he realised that she wanted the railway station. He pointed and said:

"Darunten—links."

"Danke sehr,"* said the old woman, and off she lugged with her bundle.

Gilbert faced his hotel. His room, thank heaven, was untouched. He stood at the window and looked at the lights of the great barracks, and at the tiny officers in cloaks, far away under the street-lamps below. It was raining. Tiny umbrellas swam like black unicellular organisms through the zones of lamp-light, taxi-cabs jarred their brakes almost like a Prussian officer speaking.

Next morning came Johanna with that infallible diplomat, Louise.

"Yes—!" Louise's cogitating, brow-wrinkled manner. "It would be best if you should leave Detsch. You will not go far. We think Trier. We think if you go to Trier, then Johanna can join you in a few days. It is only two hours in the train. Johanna will come to you. She will come."

Gilbert looked at Johanna.

"I shall come. On Tuesday I shall come," she said.

"And stay?" said Gilbert.

"Yes," said Johanna. "I shall come and stay."

"Ach! Hannele!" exclaimed Louise, putting her hand to her brow. "It is so difficolt. You see, it is such a peety that you had to go to her father—" Louise turned to Gilbert. "Now he asks so many questions, and it is difficult to make him quiet. And then the military authorities! Ach yes! Ach yes! It is better you go to Trier, much better. It is not far, and Johanna will come. You will go? Yes? Tomorrow morning?"

"Yes," said Gilbert.

"That is good. That is good. Better that you are alone also for a few days, to know your mind. Ach, you will see things all so much clearer.—And we, we shall decide something."

"You will come on Tuesday?" said Gilbert to Johanna.

5   "Yes, on Tuesday. I shall come to you on Tuesday."

"Yes! Yes! On Tuesday," said Louise. "And we must all do what we can to find the right way. Ach, it is so difficult. There are so many things to consider—ach, so many, many things. We must take time.—And you will go by the half-past-ten train in the morning? Yes?"

10   "Yes," said Gilbert.

"I shall come and see you off," said Johanna.

"Ach, it is such a peety that Johanna's father had to be told of you. Now he suspects so much, and he will not be made quiet. He is afraid that Johanna leaves her husband. He is very much against such a thing.

15   So you will see we have a great deal of trouble at home. Yes! You understand?"

"Yes, I understand," said Gilbert stubbornly.

Louise smiled at him from narrowed eyes. She could be queer and winsome and sympathetic: sisterly, so close and sisterly. But his face

20   was still too stiff to relax. He felt he was on toast. They had got him on toast. Perhaps Louise loved to torture him—and loved him because she could torture him.

Next morning Johanna was at the station. She gave him seventy Marks—seventy shillings. Lotte, who was rich, had given her a

25   hundred Mark note. Gilbert took the money, since he hadn't enough, and he knew it would be merely futile to make more fuss. So he took the money: and again Johanna promised to come on Tuesday—the day was then Friday.

And so he sat in the third-class carriage and drew out of the station,

30   watching Johanna's face retreat into the distance. She seemed isolated in the world—as he knew himself to be isolated in the world. And he loved her. And destiny seemed inevitably to unite him to her. It was so inevitable that he did not question it. It was so. Only it was all taking place rather jaggedly. But then destiny was like that: rather a jagged

35   unpleasant business: even love. He accepted it as such, and sat still with his fate, whilst the train ran on through the wonderful, so Roman regions of the Moselle valley, which gave him a keener sense of the Roman Empire of great days than ever Italy could do. And he was leaving Detsch: which place he hated with so deep a hatred, with all its

40   uniforms and its *verbotens*.*

Chapter XVII.

Lily of the Valley.

"Well!" thought Gilbert to himself. "This is a love affair, by Jove!" And he wished himself joy of it.

He was settled in a little, comfortable enough hotel in Trier,* on the main street leading from the station: a small place for commercial travellers.

The morning after his arrival he went out into the town. It was sunny, and Saturday. In the old market-place the peasant women sat under the great umbrellas, like grasshoppers under toadstools, and sold their produce: green vegetables and pinkish carrots and white asparagus, eggs and butter, such a bursting abundance of everything, and everything so dirt cheap. There were also bunches of lilies of the valley—round bouquets of wild lilies of the valley, the pale greenish grains of the buds floating on the whiteness of the dense-packed flowers. And some had fringes of slipper orchids. How lovely they were.

Gilbert stood in the market-place looking at them and smelling the perfume, which was perhaps his favorite: at any rate, for the moment. When one smells violets, there is no scent imaginable more lovely: when one smells jasmine, again perfection. So he sniffed the watery fragrance of the clusters of lilies of the valley, and thought of love affairs and delicate romance, and rather longed to flutter into amorous ecstasies like a true young lover. But alas, even in the lily the scent, not only of tears, but of soap that smarts in the eye.

Ought one to be like a lily!—a lovely ethereal presence? Much of a lily *his* life was! Much of a lily he was himself. Not even a rank tiger-lily.

Man is born to ponder.

"Alas!" thought Gilbert. "My lily is Johanna, and in some ways she's more like a blunderbuss."

And then he began to imagine the true lily-maid: the virgin, the pure, the modest, the pale. Heaven above save us from any more Lilies.

He strode manfully out of the market, with his pipe between his teeth. No, damn it all, what was the good of love that wasn't a fight! What was the good of anything that wasn't a fight. Be damned, he did not care to fancy mingling with a woman, as if he and she were two spoonfuls of honey put into the same pot.

Lily! A lily has a ferocious tangle of roots underearth. Ach, in the cold, horrible earth its roots probe and fight and suck. He didn't want
5 his lily a plucked blossom, all very nice and fair. No, good heaven, let us have the whole party: the tangle of deep, unspeakable passions, the rage of downward shooting desires! Ah, all the terrible and unspeakable things that happen to a lily of the valley as it wrestles and writhes in the corrosive sod. Right then! He was ready for the fight and writhing and
10 wrestling in the soul's underground. Passion is always a fight, desire is always a strife. Hurray then for the fight and the strife. Let it never end, or we are picked blossoms.

The thought came to him on the cathedral steps. It is a massive, heavy round-bowed Dom,* much more congenial to Gilbert than
15 the soaring of Detsch's singing stone, as somebody has called the cathedral. Our mathematical hero loved the heavy, downward-plunging masses of the ancient building, the for him gorgeous, ponderous return to earth, the down-thrust, and again the down-thrust.

This was like roots again. And this was what he wanted. Damn it, he
20 didn't want to be a picked blossom, like the rest of cultured civilised people. Picked blossoms, stuck in a nice aesthetic jar: there they are, while the water goes stagnant and rots. Picked blossoms! Myriads of sweet lilies—in blue vases. Damn the female lilies in blue vases. He wanted a lily with her roots deep down in the muck, fast, gripped,
25 triumphant rooted in the muck. Then she could wither and grow old, and yet not die. Unlike one of these picked, spiritual, cultured lilies, that wither once and for all in a vase of putrifying water. Pah.

No, he was not going to try and idealise his love. Heaven save us. We pick it in the bud, and achieve its undoing. He was going to wrestle with
30 it in the dark, down under-ground, in the damp, rotting, pungent earth. Long live the roots in the muck! The fight, thank God, is for ever.

Oh, you may have your blossom. But humanly, you mayn't pick it: or even force it. There's the blossom right enough. Even he, Gilbert, had written a bit of real music these last days. Even he felt great
35 lovelinesses. But he felt the acrid, deep-down battling under the sod still more strongly. Rooted in battle he was. So be it. Thank God the battle is never quite won. It always has a new phase tomorrow. No Nirvana, thank you. God is very good to us. Supposing we *were* given our imbecile Nirvanas and heavens, what mugs we should look. Luckily
40 we get a kick in the backside from a sane deity, if we try and sit too long

on our raptures. Get on then! Get off that rapture! Enough of that
lovey-dovey eternity stunt. And if you won't, take a kick in the backside.
For in spite of all rhapsody, there is no man breathing but has a
posterior, and no man breathing can abstract and spiritualise a well-
kicked bottom into song. Thank the Lord for that, and give us a strong 5
toe-cap.

Gilbert's host at the Grünwald was very inquisitive about Gilbert.
The host was young—not more than thirty-three. He and his wife ran
the hotel between them. He spoke English: had been Steward on the
Nili boats, and on the Nord-Deutscher-Lloyd boats.* And, 10
although rather a nice young fellow, he was curious about his visitor.
Not many people, foreigners, came to Trier: and none of them put up
at the little Grünwald.

What was Gilbert doing there? This was the question rampant in
Fritz's mind. So much so that our innocent friend felt called upon to 15
give an explanation.

And this is how he did it.

"I am waiting for my wife."

"Your wife!"

"Yes. She is in Detsch." 20

"Your wife is in Detsch?"

"Yes, with her mother and father."

"Oh, then your wife is German?"

"Yes, she is German. But she has been a good many years in
England." 25

"Ah yes! You have been married a good many years?"

"Well—some."

"So! And your wife will join you *here*—?" which meant, in the
Grünwald Gasthaus.

"Yes," said Gilbert. "She is coming on Tuesday." 30

"Ah—*so*! On Tuesday! And shall you want another room?—or
better a room with two beds?"

"A room with two beds."

"And shall we put them together—" Fritz closed his two
hands—"Or apart"—and he sundered his prayer-joined palms. 35

"Together," said Gilbert.

"Ah together! Good!"

So do we count our chickens before they are hatched. Or rather, so
do we build our nest before we have a hen to sit in it.

Gilbert wrote to Johanna and said how he was waiting for her and 40

they must not part again, and Johanna wrote and said how she was
dying to come.

He waited for Tuesday. He played his fiddle, he stared into the
Moselle, he raced over the hills. More soldiers. Bolting out of the town,
5 musing, he came to a dead halt one morning hearing men's martial
voices singing—God Save the King! His heart quite stood still. Never
had it had the same sound.—

So he made out a barracks, and a drill-ground,* and a company
of soldiers marching to the solid, ominous tune.

10   "God save our Gracious King
             Long live our noble King."

The Englishman stood and felt quite faint. Heavy, male, massive
voices plunging out the rhythm with strange, deep force, march-
rhythm, but not meant for the feet, meant for the heart's stroke. Was it
15 possible the banal tune could come out with such a terrible, ponderous,
splendid heart-stroke, stroke after stroke welding the deep heart into
black iron! Men's voices in terrifying martial unison, like some great
tolling bell.

For a few moments Gilbert stood stunned. And then he gathered
20 courage to listen. And then he realised the words.

"Heil Dir im Sieger Kranz—"*

Strange! Something seemed to knock at his consciousness—something he refused to admit. Wherever he was in Germany, the soldiery
made a deep impression on him. But he did not take them quite for
25 real.

They frightened him. Another day, just outside Trier he met a long
cavalcade of horse-soldiers with guns coming down a little hill
between yellow earthy banks. And he stood aside under the bank as
they rode by—a long time. And he watched them all. And for some
30 reason, fear knocked also at this inner consciousness, though he
would not admit it.

They were handsome, on the whole, the cavalry: so strong, so
healthy looking, powerful, with that strange military beauty which one
never saw in England. How far they were from him! What a gulf! Yet
35 he almost envied them, he, in his incurable civilian innocence. So
clatter-clatter-clatter he watched them retreat, and looked after the
strong retreating backs. Ah, the man's world! The fighting world. The

strange glamour of the string of cavalry riding through the vineyards towards the Moselle.

"Will you come and see your room?" said the young host Fritz when Gilbert returned.

Gilbert went. It was a pleasant big room with a large bed. And our hero actually went out and bought a bunch of the above-mentioned lilies.

"But you will stay where you are till tomorrow?" said the host.

"Oh yes," said Gilbert. And he sat reading *Jugend** and waiting for tomorrow. There was a joke about a mouse-trap and the bait.

"What is *Speck*?" asked Gilbert.

"*Speck*?" said the host, coming and bending over the paper. "Oh—*Speck*! That is bacon."

Gilbert never forgot the German for bacon. Let us hope, gentle reader, you may also remember.

On the morrow arrived Johanna, the Baroness in a black silk coat, and Lotte in Parisian black and white, made substantial by Vienna.

"Bonjour!" cried Lotte, making dark, flashing eyes. "Moi, je ne suis pas de l'ambassade. Je m'en vais. Je viendrai te trouver, Mère."*

And she jumped into a taxi, and drove off to see the sights.

Gilbert was somewhat taken aback by the family arrival: and Johanna in a new rose-coloured erection of a Viennese hat, that didn't suit her, and no more luggage than a pocket-handkerchief.

"And how do you like to be in Trier? It is a nice town. You have seen the Dom and the——" so the Baroness made polite conversation as the three walked towards the Grünwald—three or four minutes walk from the station. He felt he could hardly speak to Johanna in that rose-pink erection of a bishop's mitre.

"You will have coffee!" said Gilbert.

So the three sat at one of the little tables just outside the hotel door, in the sunshine of the street.

"Would you like to see the room first?" said Gilbert to Johanna.

"Oh—" she stammered. "I'm not staying."

He looked at her.

"I had to promise Papa to come back with Mama and Lotte. He'd never have let me come if I hadn't. Oh, I've had an awful time of it with them."

Gilbert sat down.

"Ja! Wissen Sie—"* began the Baroness, in a quaint, plangent, lamentoso voice. "Yes, you see, her father can't allow it. He can't allow

his daughter to go off in this way. You must excuse her. She must go
back tonight. I must take her back tonight—"

Fritz brought coffee and sweet cakes. The Baroness interrupted
herself, but immediately resumed in her high, crying voice, sometimes
5 German, sometimes English.

"Her father is a gentleman and an officer. Hee fears very much for
his daughter's name and all the trouble and the shame. Ah, you do not
know. You have not thought of it all. Ah, you must think much more.
You cannot begin this thing in such a way, like a glass of wine. It cannot
10 be done so. It is a dreadful thing for Johanna—"

The Baroness sipped her coffee and straightened her hat, which had
a disposition to go sideways.

"You know how hard, how ha-aarrd it is for her here in Germany.
You know the divorce is three years—hier in Deutschland die
15 Scheidung braucht drei Jahren, three years, drei Jahrelang.* And
in America it is much quicker. Ach, yes! If she does not go back to that
Boston—ach, poor Hannele, she doesn't like it at all there—then she
must wait, the divorce must be in America. It takes much shorter, only
six months, only three months even. Only three months! And here it
20 takes three years—three ye-ears! Ja!"

Fritz was hovering in the background drinking in every word.
Johanna was rapidly eating the sweet cakes, one after the other, like a
goat nibbling leaves. The Baroness' hat went on one side, and she
resumed:

25 "Yes, he must make the divorce in America. Yes, her husband must
make her a divorce. He must make her a divorce. Yes, he must. That is
what you want, is it not so? You want that she should have the divorce?"

"Yes," said Gilbert.

"Yes! Oh yes! Oh yes, he must. Her husband must make the divorce
30 over there in America. It is much easier. And much queecker! Only
three months. And here in Deutschland three years! Three years! Drei
Jahren! Ach, it is too lo-ong, too lo-ong."

The three years, drei Jahren rang through and through Gilbert's
brain. But still he did not see the point.

35 "But in the meantime?" he said.

"Ja—in the mean time—she must come back to Detsch to her
father—and we must think of the best way. You are young, you do not
think. You do not know what you are doing.—She is a mother with two
little children—Oh yea, it is dreadful. Ach, afterwards! Afterwards! It
40 is this we must think of."

This was just what Gilbert did not intend to think of. Indeed, he did not intend to think at all. In his mind, or soul, Johanna was predestined to stay with *him*, and there was no thinking to be done. If one must reckon the costs, at least let us have the dinner first and reckon afterwards. No matter what the cost is, if we've once had the dinner 5
nobody can take it from us. And life is often called a feast. But society is a mean host, the modern world is a paltry kind of inn.

Now the poor Baroness felt very much as Gilbert himself felt. She would much rather have left her daughter comfortably behind with her young lover. But oh dear, was she not saddled with a mother's duties. 10
And having had all her life to enjoy an unfaithful, gambling husband, she naturally felt that a legal position was the only sure thing in a woman's life. It was the only sure thing *she* had had. And here was Johanna going to play skittles with her legal surety: and for what?—for an escapade with an unknown young fellow of the lower classes, 15
without money. Oh dear oh dear—the man was right enough. The Baroness quite liked him, and if he had been no more than a transient lover she would have winked quite gratefully at him. After all, she did not wish her daughters to know nothing but the long tied-up widow-hood she had known herself. 20

But afterwards! afterwards! The money, the never-ending irritation of moneylessness—money was always lacking in the Hebenitz house-hold.—And then the children—the two little children! Ach no, no, it was too hard for the Baroness. Why should all this misery and distraction take place! So, like a floundering swimmer who has lost his 25
nerve, she lectured Gilbert, rather pathetically, and Gilbert got into a bull's rage.

"You are young, ach, so young! You do not know the world, you do not know to keep a woman. Ach, you have all your life before you, and you would take a woman who has two children and a husband! Oh yea! 30
Oh yea! Think what you do. Think what you do! You will spoil your life. You will spoil your life. And also Johanna's life! Oh no! Ach, nein, es ist zuviel.* Better you should go back to England."

And she looked at him under her black eyebrows, and he scowled heavily in response. She could see he had no intention of going back to 35
England.

"Better you go to England," she insisted.

"No," he said.

"You don't want? Ach! Well, you must go somewhere and wait for her. You must wait—" 40

"There's Lotte!" cried Johanna. And sure enough there was Lotte coasting by gaily in her taxi, waving a handkerchief to the party at the little table.

"Gleich! Fünf Minuten!"* called the Baroness in a quaint, high
5 shout, after the retreating car. Then, her face all lifted in upward-tending wrinkles of worry, she resumed to Gilbert.

"And Johanna's father must write to her husband, and ask him for the divorce, if still she will not go back. And the divorce must be in America. But what will you do? How will you keep a woman? Where
10 will you find the money?"

She looked at Gilbert from under her knitted brows, and he scowled back. "Ach, all things are against it. All things.—So you must wait. You must wait. I must take her back to her father tonight, and you must wait. You must go away somewhere where you can forget this.—And
15 then her husband must give her the divorce—"

So she went on, round and round in the same wheel, till Lotte appeared once more in the taxi.

"Shall we go for a walk?" said Johanna to him.

"Yes," he answered.

20 "And you will bring her back at four o'clock—please? Yes? You will promise."

"Yes," he said.

"Oh thank you. Thank you. Her father is promised that she shall come home with me. Danke! Danke! Ja, auf wiedersehen—Vier
25 Uhr,* weiss du, Hannele."

Johanna moved off, and Gilbert, glancing round, saw the Baroness' ample rear climbing into the motor-car. In another moment she drove by, looking like a child that has just got out of a row, and is going to enjoy itself.

30 Gilbert and Johanna walked away into the country, and she told him what a life they were leading her at home. Her father was dead against any breach with her husband.

"Poor Papa," she said. "He is so unhappy. He said to me, 'My Child, I know the world.' But I said to him, 'Not the best, Papa. Not the best.
35 You don't know that.' And he didn't answer. Poor Papa!"*

"I don't see what the world, or knowing the world has got to do with it," said Gilbert.

"Ah, but they get so upset. And they are so frightened. I believe poor Papa sees a lost woman in me. Poor Papa, with his Elena in the back-
40 ground, and his illegitimate son!* How else could he see it."

"Then why should he look! It's not his affair."

"Oh yes. Poor Papa. He does love me, in a way. And he was awfully fond of Everard.—Ach, it is all such a bother."

"What shall you do then?"

"Oh I don't know. Go back and let them talk.—But you—what shall you do?"

"I shall go to Joseph Heysers at Wensdorf, and wait."

"Shall you wait? And will you come to me when I tell you?"

"Yes. But don't be too long. How long do you think?"

"Ah!" she sighed. "I don't know. They give me a hell of a time. I'm almost out of my mind. Ah, and they all say they love me. Ah—it is too much. What am I to do?"

"Let us go away together."

"Yes! Yes! I know. But I've promised to go back tonight."

"In a few days then. Don't stop long, or God knows what will happen to you."

"I know. They will drive me mad."

"Then don't stop long. And I will come whenever you let me know—and wherever you tell me."

"Yes! Yes! If only I could get away."

They walked away into the country, she holding his hand. In a world of floating straws he seemed for the moment solid.

So they stayed and kissed and made love in a dry ditch under a beech-tree. This was not the matrimonial bed Gilbert had prepared. But still, it was something. And that is always better than nothing.

So Johanna returned to Detsch, and saw the look of relief come over her father's face when he caught sight of her in the railway carriage. He had come to the station to meet the train.

Gilbert returned to the Grünwald.

"So the gnädige Frau is not staying?" said Fritz.

"No! She has had to go back to Detsch with her mother."

"But I have changed all your things, and prepared the big room." The inn-keeper's tone was rather aggrieved, and there was a touch of impertinence.

"Yes. I know that. But she couldn't stay."

Gilbert closed so definitely, that the man said no more.

"I shall be going away tomorrow," said Gilbert.

"In the morning?"

"Yes."

"Very well."

And so our hero went up to the room that smelled of lilies of the valley. And he slept alone in the big matrimonial bed. And next day he sat in the train and wound that wonderful way all along the Moselle valley to the Rhine at Coblenz—where he changed, and crossed the
5   river—and changed again, and caught the train north for Cologne.*

Chapter XVIII.

The First Round.

Dear Gilbert was not in one of his brilliant moods. He sat in a third-class carriage gazing vacantly out of the window of the Cologne express, while the peasants eyed him curiously. The ticket collector came slamming the doors. He glared at Gilbert's ticket—then glared at Gilbert—and broke into a torrent of abuse in a vile Rhenish accent: again, we must say, like the tearing of badly made calico. Snarling and flourishing in the pretty Prussian official manner in front of the offender's nose, whilst all the others in the carriage looked either virtuous or rebuked! Snarl snarl snarl went the beastly person—and Gilbert's brain turned to cork. He heard objectionable noises, but like a drowning man with the roar of eternity in his ears, he made out no earthly sense.

Till at last, *fünf Mark fünfzig.** Five and sixpence!—the damned fellow wanted five-and-sixpence! Out came the money, scribble went the ticket collector, and pushed a scrap of paper in the offender's face.

"Ich verstehe gar nicht," said Gilbert, like a turning worm. "I don't understand at all."

The ticket collector looked as if he would eat him in silence.

"Zuschlagen—zuschlagen—" he snarled—and names of stations—Ehrenbreitstein, Niederlahnstein.

"Was meint zuschlagen?"* said our innocent.

The ticket collector turned up his nose as if he meant to take Gilbert's scalp with it. Then he departed, slamming the door. The peasants made round eyes, and Gilbert tried etymologically to extract some meaning out of the marvellous word zuschlagen.

Since he was destined to live and learn, he learned later that if when changing trains you take a Swift-train, whereas the previous train was but a Hurry-train, then you must present your ticket at the ticket-office of the change station, and zuschlagen—pay the transfer. All of which is system—wonderful system.

We would here offer an address to System, and German system in particular, if it weren't already a thing of the past. Ah System, thou fallen but not yet shattered god of a mechanical age.

Dear Gilbert mused on the god-almighty ferocity of Prussian officials. Nay, the shabbiest porter was an olympic—or at least a Wotan God*—once he had put his holy cap on. And all the mere civilians grovelled before a peak-official-cap as before some nimbus. What a
5 funny world! They saw in it the symbol of Germanic Over-Allness.*

Gazing on the great Rhine—Rhenus Flux—with its castles and its cardboard scenery, our hero thought of Rome and the naked great Germanic tribes: of the amazing Middle Ages: and then of Luther and
10 the Thirty Years War—and then of Frederick and the great Goethe.

Oh Goethe, what a fool you were. If only someone had given *you* a good kick in your toga-seat, when you were godlifying yourself and olympising yourself and setting up the stunt of German Godlikeness and superhumanness, what a lot it would have saved the world, and
15 Germany in particular. If only Napoleon had not been taken in. If only that usually sensible person had exclaimed, not *voilà un homme!* but *voilà un dieu gratuite!,** and given the gratuitous God–Goethe a good old Napoleonic kick in the rump! Oh weh! Oh woe! When will mankind learn the right use of toe-caps and posteriors! It would save so
20 many cannons later on.

Musing somewhat in this strain, our friend changed once more, and once more got into a simple Hurry-train. It was six o'clock when he changed for the last time, at Hennef. Every time he changed he seemed to metamorphose.

25 Hennef was a station in the midst of water-meadows. There was a stream of full, swift, silent water, and marsh-plants, and evening beginning to glow over the remote Rhineland.

He sat by the stream* under the evening, while some birds swung past, and he felt himself in the middle of nowhere. And a great
30 peace like an annunciation seemed to settle on his soul. He looked at the glowing west, the lush green water-land beneath. And he thought of Johanna, and felt filled with peace and an assurance that surpassed anything he had known: such a lovely sense of fulfilment in the future: peace like a full river flowing, flowing far-off, into the sunset. He sat
35 quite still, near the station, waiting for his connection. And he felt a beautiful calm, a glamorous, holy calm, as if a sacred light were in the evening air.

And when he clambered into the mere Person-train, the Bummel-zug* that trotted in the open by the road-side, he was quite still
40 and happy. There was the high-road in the twilight—and a

stream—and the thick trees of the forest. And a lovely peace and bigness and breathing-room, such as he always imagined in the Middle-Ages: a peace not made up of quietness or of lovey-doveyness, but of room, room to move and breathe.

And now, gentle reader—aha, I feel you shy at those two words. Yes, 5
I admit it, they are my *Dilly-Dilly-Dilly, come and be killed.** Yes, I am going to apostrophise or moralise: and why shouldn't I? If you don't want to read, turn on to page

Gentle reader, I am going to let the cat out of the bag. I am going to do so, because I never ask anyone, even the most desirous, to buy a pig 10
in a poke. After this very nice little peace-like-a-river touch, I am going to let the cat out of the bag. For I'm sure if I don't, you'll be yelling and saying I promised you two turtle-doves in a cage. Gentle reader, I have *not* got two turtle-doves in a cage for you. I'm sorry, but I'm not a dove and pigeon merchant. 15

An anonymous lady—she may even be yourself, gentle reader— once wrote to me thus: "You, who can write so beautifully of stars and flowers, why will you grovel in the ditch?" I might answer her—or you, gentle reader—thus: "You, who wear such nice suède shoes, why do you blow your nose?" 20

However, gentle reader, I must invite you to grovel in the ditch with me. I am not a dove and pigeon merchant. Out of this very promising-looking bag of a story, which I have this minute shown you tied with a pretty blue ribbon of peace, I am going to let out,—what?—the cat! I am going to let the cat out of the bag. Or even two whirling, fur-flying 25
cats, all claws and sparks.

Gentle reader, this peace was not the peace of the amorous coo of the ring-dove. Gentle reader, it was not the silent bliss of two elective affinities* who were just about to fuse and make a holy and eternal oneness. It was the bridal peace—surely we are entitled to a little 30
Wagnerian language here: it was the bridal peace of Gilbert and Johanna. It was the grail hovering before our hero, shedding its effulgence upon him.

It was the peace, gentle reader, of one who has found his opposite, his complementary opposite, and his meet adversary. The pleasant 35
darling, he didn't know it. And he wasn't going to tumble to it till he'd had so many tumbles he was quite knocked out of his original shape. But whether he knew it or not isn't the point. I know it, and I'm telling this history. And I like to let my cat out of the bag right off, so that nobody shall think it's a chaste unicorn or a pair of doves in a cage. 40

Dear Gilbert, he had found his mate and his match. He had found one who would give him tit for tat, and tittle for tattle. He had found his soul's affinity, and his body's mate: a she-cat who would give him claw for claw, a bitch who would give him snarl for snarl, a falcon who would 5 demand an eye for an eye. Here's to them!

The love of two splendid opposites. My dear—I mean you, gentle reader—all life and splendour is made up out of the union of indomitable opposites. We live, all of us balanced delicately on the rainbow, which is born of pure light and pure water. Think, gentle 10 reader: out of the perfect consummating of sun and rain leaps the all-promising rainbow: leap also the yellow-and-white daisies, pink-and-gold roses, good green cabbages, caterpillars, serpents and all the rest. Out of what, gentle reader? The moment's matching of the two terrible opposites, fire and water. The two eternal, universal 15 enemies, you call them? I call them the man and the woman of the material universe, father and mother of all things. If you don't believe me, that's your affair.

Tell me, why are all royal things brindled: the tiger with his pointed flames of black and fire, the eagle with his bars of dusk and glow, the 20 golden lion with his mane of smoke? It is, gentle reader, the eternal opposite elements lying side by side in him, magnificently juxtaposed, royally wedded, as man and woman lie like fire and smoke in the marriage bed, or like dark-rippled water.

Opposites! The magnificence of opposites. Not the horrible sticky 25 merge of like things. The fight, gentle reader, the fight! Up boys, and at 'em!—'em, of course, meaning the women. Up boys, and at 'em!

Oh heaven, save me from a morass of people all alike to one another. The sharpest divergencies possible, the most miraculous of superb differences.

30 Opposition! Wonderful opposition! The whole universe rests on the magical opposition of fire and water, sun and rain. Is not every plant brindled?—dark and damp below earth, sunny above. Do not the watery thread-tender streams run forward to touch the thread-tender fiery beamlets of the sun, in every growing plant and every unfolding 35 flower. Is it not a lion running out of the fiery desert, to meet a lioness of shadow? And is not the mating always half a fight. At least half a fight. Is not the very embrace at least half a fight. At least half a fight. Before a plant adds one new cell to its growing tip, has it not been the living battle field and marriage bed of fire and water: *both*. Is not the 40 marriage bed a fiery battle field, as well as a perfect communion, both

simultaneously. Till we know this, we know nothing. And till we fight
our fights like splendid royal tigers, in the wonderful connubial rage,
we are nothing. We are at a dead-lock: either water-logged, or gone
woody and dry. Water-logged and fat, or woody and dry and sapless.

Beautiful brindled creatures of fire and darkness, sun and smoke. 5
What is your darkness but shadow, and what is your shadow but watery
intervention, the cloud in the sun, against the sun.—Beautiful brindled
creatures, snakes and tortoises, fish and wild-geese, tigers, wolves,
trees. Only men are all white or all black. But then mankind itself is
brindled. Never forget it. 10

Our Gilbert arrived at Wensdorf* late at night, and was received
and feasted by his friend and his friend's wife Ulma.* Joseph was a
small official for the district.

And Gilbert was happy in the little flat over the village street where
the oxen-wagons trundled slowly, far away in the Rhenish hinterland. 15
He listened to the bells in the pointed steeple of the Lutheran church
playing hard against the bells of the white catholic church. He saw the
streams of peasants flowing in opposite directions and turning up their
noses at one another. He drank beer in the vaulted chamber, where
Joseph smoked his long pipe and talked in dialect and got mellow with 20
the cronies of the inn. It seemed almost like the Middle-Ages: save of
course for the recurrent stridency of Deutschland Über Alles which
crept out.

He liked Ulma, and her traditional German housekeeping. He liked
the great basket of different breads, white bread and black bread and 25
grey bread and Pommeland bread and Pumpernickel and
Kringeln:* always a choice of five different sorts of bread. Then
the lovely linen and silver in abundance, in the quite small flat.

Then the long walks between the old, ragged, blossoming pear-trees
of the unknown high-roads, to villages* that never were and never 30
will be known, lost behind great woods or great arable stretches: the
sense of being in an upland region, yet having no big hills: the sense of
the great lands going on and on, and not coming anywhere: the feeling
of the ageless Rhine, some forty miles away. They drove in a little
carriage far off: and always the same country. They went to a fair, and 35
drank all manner of Schnapps and bought all manner of wonderful
cakes, hearts and houses and horses and angels and children, every
imaginable thing in sweet, spicy honey-tasting cakes. On a Sunday they
went down to the Rhine and sailed on a steamer and went to some high,
famous castle.* And Gilbert did not like the Sunday crowd at all. 40

But he was really happy. So he wrote Johanna rather lofty and sweet letters,* saying he would wait till she was ready, and have faith in her. And that when she sent for him he would come. And that he would abide by her decision, and trust her through eternity. And that his life
5 was only a waiting, only a waiting for her. But he would leave her free to bid him stay or come.—And similar things he wrote in answer to the managing Louise, and to the troubled Baroness: very lofty sounding and nice.

Which was all very well for him, while he was having a jolly good time
10 with Joseph and Ulma far away from the scene of battles, in the Rhineland. He managed moreover to get twelve pounds from England.

Meanwhile Johanna was having no such rosy time in Detsch. Her father worried her—though what was the good! The first *cris de cœur*,* and the first volleys of abuse began to arrive from America.
15 There was no light and no clear counsel anywhere, none.

Till Johanna declared she would go mad. And the whole household in Detsch began to go off its head. And so Johanna escaped to Louise in Munich. Where she took to her bed and would not stir for two days.

After which she wired to Gilbert that he should come to Munich.
20 And he wired he would come next week. Next week!

However, till next week he would not come. So Johanna devoured her incertainty. Then next week came. He set his teeth, packed his traps, bade a lingering farewell to the Rhineland, and set off on the twenty-hour journey down to Munich.

25 He arrived at Munich late at night—there was Johanna shining in the crowd in the darkness.

"You've come!" was all she said.

And in the background little Alfred, Johanna's escort.

"Ha-ha! Ha-ha!" he said, shaking hands with his friend and pupil.
30 "The return of the truant! The return of the Bad Boy! Well I never! Well I *nevah!*"

And, accompanied by a porter with the luggage, they turned out of the station.

"Goodnight, you two! See you soo-oon!" sang Alfred, suddenly
35 waving his walking-stick and disappearing.

Gilbert looked in surprise, but the little figure was already disappearing under the lamps.

"We'll stay in an hotel tonight," said Johanna. "And tomorrow we'll go out to Louise. Do you want to eat?"
40 The hotel was near: they were soon installed: and soon launched on

the wild seas of the bridal bed. It is usual in books to avoid such topics, so we will merely mention them. We wish to hint that Gilbert, in spite of his various gallant adventures, was but an acolyte at the Dionysic or Priapic altar. He was a raw hand.

Now in no field of human activity is so much rare adjustment and   5
well-balanced niceness required as in the service of the great Priapic god. Your libertine, with his thousand experiences and his many dodges, your Don Juan and Doña Juanita, they are always only apprentices: life-long apprentices. Your Don Juan is a life-long apprentice, who could never master his craft.   10

Should a man really become a master, then, in the Priapic craft? Ah yes, gentle reader. Ah yes! When all is said and done, the Father of life is a passional begetter, not an ideal. The ideal is but a nice little end in itself. But the creative cycle is one strange, incalculable, passional round, eternal.   15

Let us confess our belief: our deep, our religious belief. The great eternity of creation does not lie in the spirit, in the ideal. It lies in the everlasting and incalculable throb of passion and desire. The ideal is but the iridescence of the strange flux. Life does not begin in the mind: or in some ideal spirit. Life begins in the deep, the indescribable   20
sensual throb of desire, pre-mental.

What is the soul, gentle reader? What is your soul, what is my soul? It is not some evaporated spirit. Ah no. It is that deep core of individual unity where life itself, the very God, throbs incalculably, whose throbbing unfolds the leaves and stem of the body, and brings forth the   25
flower of the mind and the spirit. But the spirit is not the soul. Ah no. The soul has its deep fibrilled foliage in the damp earth, has its dark leaves in the air, it tosses the flower of the spirit like a bauble, a lovely plaything, on to the winds of time. Man can live without spirit or ideal, as dark pine-trees live without flowers: dark and sap-powerful. But   30
without the deep sensual soul man is even inconceivable. This angel business, this spirit nonsense! Even spirits, such as really exist, are potent sensual entities.

If you would like to get at the secret of tree worship*—Druid and Germanic, nay, universal—then realise the dark, sap-powerful,   35
flowerless tree of the mindless, non-spiritual, sensual soul.

Gentle reader, our era has landed in the *cul de sac* of the spirit and the ideal. And I, poor darling, grope my way back to the tree of life, on which Jesus was crucified.* He did so want to be a free, abstract spirit, like a thought. And he was crucified upon the tree of the eternal,   40 primal sensual soul, which is man's first and greatest being. Now I, gentle reader, love my tree. And if my mind, my spirit, my conscious consciousness blossom upon the tree of me for a little while, then sheds its petals and is gone, well, that is its affair. I don't like dried flowers, 5 *immortels.** I love my tree. And the tree of life itself never dies, however many blossoms and leaves may fall and turn to dust. I place my immortality in the dark sap of life, stream of eternal blood. And as for my mind and spirit—this book, for example, all my books—I toss them out like so much transient tree-blossom and foliaged leaves, on to the 10 winds of time. The static, written-down eternity is nothing to me: or rather, it is only a lovely side-show, almost a bauble: but lovely. Yes I love it—the spirit, the mind, the ideal. But not primarily. The primal soul I see in the face of the donkey that is tied to my gate, and which shifts its long ears. The dark, sensual soul, and that gorgeous mystery 15 of sensual individuality.

Enough! Basta! Revenons à nos deux moutons.* Let us return once more to our two sheep, Mr Gilbert and Mistress Johanna. We left them in the Priapic bed, and there we find them again, you will no doubt be glad to hear.

20 "Man survives earthquakes, epidemics, the horrors of disease, and all the agonies of the soul, but as long as time lasts his most excruciating tragedy is, has been, and will be—the tragedy of the bedroom."*

Pray note the inverted commas. I am quoting the great Leo Tolstoi, 25 who, in such matters—matters of didactic judgment, I mean—seems to me a quite comical fool.

Friends, let us put our money on the tragedy of the bedroom. I could do with tragedy if it weren't so very sorry for itself: if it would only admit *how* it enjoyed itself in its throes.

30 To return to our two tragedians.—The Priapic mysteries are not tricks. They can't be learned with the head, nor dictated from the mind, nor practised by deliberate intent. You can no more bring about, deliberately, a splendid passional sexual storm between yourself and your woman than you can bring about a thunderstorm in the air. All 35 the little tricks, all the intensifications of will remain no more than tricks and will-pressure. You have got to release from mental control the deep springs of passion: and after that there has got to be the leap to polarised adjustment with the woman. And these two things are deep mysteries. It takes us a long time, us, to release the profound desires 40 from all mental control. Even the young animals, it is terrible to them,

and difficult. And as for the leaping into the chasm to pure connection with the woman, that needs a basic courage and a strange concerted unison between the two protagonists, which life alone can give. It is absolutely useless going to a prostitute or a libertine. The deep *accustomedness* of marriage is the only way of preparation. Only those 5 who know one another in the intricate dark ways of physical custom can pass through the seven dark hells and the seven bright heavens of sensual fulfilment.* And this is why marriage is sacred. And this is perhaps the secret of the English greatness. The English have gone far into the depths of marriage, far down the sensual avenues of the 10 marriage bed, and they have not so easily, like the French or Germans or other nations, given up and turned to prostitution or chastity or some other *pis aller*.

But now alas the English adventure has broken down. There is no going on. There is *cul de sac* and white-livered fawning. 15

Mr Gilbert, therefore—we *will* get back to our tragedians—was no very wonderful experience for Johanna, though she was a wonderful experience to him. To tell the truth, Johanna had had far more sensual satisfaction out of her husband, Everard, than out of her other lovers. Everard was a dark-eyed, handsome man, rather stiff and marquis-like, 20 learned and a bit sarcastic. He loved his Johanna violently: and he loved his learning with an almost mediaeval passion.

There you are, then. As a husband he was darkly, furiously sensual—in his hour: and, in his hour, deeply satisfying to the woman. Yet here she was, racing round and looking for sexual love, and taking 25 it from men who could not give her half the passional gratification and fulfilment Everard had given. Which is the perversity of women.

But hold a minute. Women are not so perverse as men would like to find them.

Everard's nature was basically sensual. But this he *hid*—though 30 mind you, he was *au fond* proud of it. Secretly, almost diabolically he flattered himself on his dark, sensual prowess: and not without reason. But he had to keep it lurking in secret. Openly: ah, openly, he was all for the non-existence of such things.

He had a terrible passion for Johanna—and he craved madly that it 35 should remain a tacit secret even between him and her. Let it remain in the dark. He kneeled before her, he kissed her feet in a frenzy of craving sensual desire. If she would give him his tremendous gratification, he would sacrifice his very soul for her. Truly. He would sacrifice his individual male soul for her. 40

So you see, he did not ask and take his terrific sexual gratification as if it was something natural and true to marriage. He asked for it, he craved for it as if in some way it were a *sin*. The terrific, the magnificent black sin of sensual marriage: the gorgeous legal sin, which one was proud of, but which one kept dark: which one hated to think of in the open day, but which one lusted for by night.

Ah, he could not bear to be consciously reminded of it. And so he called Johanna his snowflower, his white snowflower. He liked to think of her as an eternal white virgin whom he was almost violating.

So that she should continue in this wise, he kneeled before her, he gave her everything. He gave her all the money he had, and perfect, perfect freedom. Nay, he would gladly have borne that she had lovers, if only she would have pretended it was not so.

This is typical of him. In the daytime, he had no lower man. In the night-time, he had nothing else. He was madly sensitive about this. Though he would read his Rabelais, and make risky jokes, and admire his Maupassant*—though he seemed the very freest of the free—yet he had a weak horror of any sensual or really physical reference by day.

For example, a water-closet was a place which really must not exist for him, in his world. There was an end of it. We may well call it Number O, or even doubly nought, Number OO.* It is twice nought.

Now Johanna, in her reckless and unEnglish way, instead of with circumspection looking if the coast was clear, would dash off recklessly to this OO, this non-existent place. She would seize the door-handle, and if it would not open, shake the door fiercely. For of course, if one wants to go somewhere, one wants to go. An Italian, finding the non-existent door locked, invariably puts his shoulder to it and proceeds to burst the hinges. But this aside.

There would Johanna seize this nameless door-handle and twist and pull, till from within came the snarl of a wounded and enraged tiger.

"Oh, are *you* there!" she would exclaim, and stand aside.

And presently would emerge Everard, handsome and white with rage, trembling with fury.

"Are you mad, woman!" he would snarl as he passed her.

"But why? Are you the only man in the world that never must go to the W?" she would jeer.

He would only grind his teeth. At such moments his hate of her was diabolical, inhuman.

Now perhaps we may judge Everard: the darkly-passionate, upright,

unmercenary man, noble enough, whose sensual secrecy and weakness in this direction prevents him from ever being quite loveable. Whatever we are, this we must stand by. If we are sensual, and deeply, utterly so, then let us not be humble about it. Man has his native right to his dark, flaming, sensual fulfilment. It is incumbent upon him, and upon his 5
honour he must get this fulfilment. Shall he creep then for it, and grovel for it: even under the permission of the law? Shall he? If he does, he will pay the price.

For the sensual humbleness in her husband threw Johanna off her balance. It made her distraught, and at last even vindictive. For is it not 10
a maddening thing for a woman to have the deep sensual relation so insulted, written Number O, like a W.C. Johanna turned against her husband, and because he was humble, she trampled on him. It is the fate of slaves. Because he was craving, she flouted him. Yet she feared him, as one fears a lurking beast. She feared him as one fears a cringing 15
beast, that may fly at one's throat.

Look you then! Everard was a true Englishman. Milton, Wordsworth, Dickens, Hardy, even Tennyson, these are the truly sensual poets of England: great men they are, perhaps the greatest. But they are the great sensual *non-admitters*. There is a doom on them. 20

And of such non-admitting, cowering sensualists, Tolstoi is the flagrant example.

There are the other people—the non-sensual, quite spiritual poets like Shelley. These, having nothing much to admit, admit it openly. Even Swinburne. But the true dark ones have much to admit, therefore 25
they are the more convulsive in their retention.

What is to be done? Are we to fly off at the spiritual tangent, like Milton or Tolstoi? or at the intellectual, like Everard and very many more?—or at the romantic and fantastic?—or at the sensuous like Keats?—or at the hopeless tragic, like Hardy. Hardy is the last word, 30
and reaches the verge of the ridiculous, which Conrad passes.*

We've got to start all afresh, and laugh at the W.C., and give reverence and honorable fear to the passional sensual fulfilment.

Now Johanna, after Everard, was aiming in the Shelley direction, at the mid-heaven spiritual, which is still sexual but quite spiritually so. 35
Sex as open and as common and as simple as any other human conversation. And this, we urge, is a quite logical conclusion of the spiritual programme. If *In the beginning was the Word*—then sex is a word also.—And we know that the Word is one word for all of us. Therefore why not free sexual love, as free as human speech? 40

Why not? Because the *a priori* are all wrong. In the beginning was *not* the Word, but something from which the Word merely proceeded later on. Let us stick to the first and greatest god, and let the Logos look after itself. The first, great, passionately generating God.

5   So Gilbert seemed a really lovely and spiritual lover to Johanna. He was really frightened, like Everard. But gathering his courage in both his hands, he managed to look on the naked woman of his desire without starting to grovel. Which, if you have profound desire, isn't so easy. You either grovel or overween. Or else, grovelling, you overween.

10 To be neither more nor less than just yourself on such an occasion: well, that takes time and a sound heart.

In the morning they were happy. The coffee, the lovely new crisp rolls, the honey, the Alp butter—how good it seemed, all of it. Gilbert was very joyful to be back in Munich. And as they sat at

15 breakfast, they heard the strange, heavy thresh-thresh-thresh of marching soldiers. They went to the window. A squadron of blue Bavarian infantry marching heavily past. Strange and heart-penetrating the sound of their motion—so rhythmic, with a sound like a heavy lash.

20 They were not to stay in Munich. Alfred had appearances to consider. Gilbert would not go back to the university. He dropped all that. Johanna had promised to go out with Gilbert to Louise at Schloss Wolfratsberg.*

Therefore the two sauntered in Munich till after lunch, then took the

25 train towards the mountains. It was a dull day, rather cold, with some rain.

Louise sat in her rather dark, warm sitting-room, that had grey linen walls, and dark oriental carpets, and dark, shapely furniture, and many of the pale-yellow books that are current in France and Germany. She

30 was writing, but she put away her pen. She seemed to Gilbert like some spider spinning in a jewelled web: or like a dark, magical Lady of Shalott who never looked out of the window, but sat weaving* heaven knows what.

"So, you have come back again!" she gave her hand to Gilbert

35 and smiled at him oddly. Beautiful she was. She had lovely white, well-shapen teeth, small and attractive. And in her big, dark-grey eyes a half-laugh, mocking, yet as if misted with tears. In an instant Gilbert fell again under the fascination she had thrown over him before.

40 "And what will you do? Ach! What will you do-oo?"

She sat down and glanced at him wickedly from under her long
lashes—but with a half winsome wickedness, mingled with benevo-
lence and kindliness.

"What *shall* I do?" said Gilbert, abstract.

The fire went bright in her eyes.

"Ach, you ask *me*! You ask *me*! Come, that is strange. How shall I
know?—Now you have come back to Johanna—Ah, Johanna, I have a
letter for thee—from thine husband—"

Incredible irony in the last phrase.

"Oh yea!" cried Johanna. "Where is it?"

Louise produced the letter, Johanna went with it to a window. Louise
resumed her seat opposite Gilbert. He glanced at the proud figure of
Johanna, as she stood in the window-light—then back, abstractedly, at
Louise.

"And you will give up your studies?" she said.

"I think so. What good are they?"

"Yes, what good is anything, if you talk so! What good is your coming
with Johanna? Much bad, surely: and what good? Yes?"

Gilbert looked back at her. She could not get over a certain distant
untouchedness in his eyes.

"Yes," he said. "Nothing's any good unless you feel it is good."

"But your studies! Do you then feel they are no good?"

"Yes."

"Ach! But what will your life be?"

"I don't know."

"No! You don't know. You don't know!—And poor Johanna! I am
afraid it will be a tragedy for both of you."

He seemed to listen to what she said: and then to listen to something
inside himself. It was curious, how indifferent he felt about it.

"Oh," he said, "I'm not tragical. I don't believe in tragedy."

"You don't believe—But that is good! Can there be no tragedy
without a belief in tragedy?" She laughed hollowly and ironical.

"Perhaps not," he said. He had never thought of it.

Johanna came forward with a rather loud sigh.

"Ha-a! Poor Everard! Er ist doch so schwer."*

And she gave the letter to Louise.

"Shall I read?" said Louise, looking up at Johanna. Then she knitted
her brows.

"Ach, I remember this writing so *well*, Hannele: so tidy, so neat and
tidy! Is it not good to write so *plainly*!"*

And she curled her voice mockingly. She had hated Everard,
fourteen years before.

"Ja, aber er ist dumm—" she broke out in ejaculations as she read.
"That is good! Ha! Ha! But he is so stupid—so stu-upid! One does not
5 write such things to a woman.—What does he mean—when you accost
him in Piccadilly he will hand you over to the police? What does he
mean—Piccadilly?"

"When I am a prostitute—"* laughed Johanna.

"Ach nein! Ach nein! Das ist Frechheit.* The man is im-
10 pudent. Ach, I have no patience!—But do not trouble, Hannele—it
is words, words, words—!—No, to such a man thou canst not go
back. No, that is impossible. No, we must not think of it. Thou canst
depend on me. No, to such a person one does not give one's life. But
see what he says—the dustman! The dustman! To his own
15 wife—"

"But he is mad just now, Louise. We mustn't mind what he says,"
replied Johanna.

"Is he mad? Or is he not only bourgeois? Oh, he is impudent, with
his rights of a husband. Ach, you poor Johanna, to give your life to such
20 a man."

"But poor Everard!" said Johanna. "Think what he must *feel*."

"Ach!" cried Louise impatiently. "Is this the letter of a *man*? Does
he call himself *man*?"

"No, he's a mad beast just now," said Johanna.

25 "Ja, du gute Hannele! A mad beast!" Louise laughed her hollow little
laugh. "He is not mad but he makes himself so. Ach, men are not mad,
but showing off. Oh yea, all Englishmen are Hamlets, they are so self-
conscious over their feelings, and they are therefore so false. Ah, so
false! They flatter themselves they feel so much that they are mad. It is
30 a self-flattery, this madness."

"Not all of it," said Johanna. "And it is dangerous, I know."

"Yes—yes! Sometimes! Sometimes! Sometimes they make themselves so mad, in their fine frenzy, that they kill someone. But not often.
Not often, you good Hannele. Ach, you are such a good simple
35 soul.—If I have hysterics I am not going to jump in the river. It is too
cold.—And these men with their tragical man-hysterics!—ach, es ist
so saudumm.*—It is words, words, words—"

She concluded with her hollow, mocking laugh. Gilbert, who was at
the book-shelves, looking over the books, listened with one wide ear
40 open. He had found a book of folk-songs, a collection he had never

seen. These he was studying. But more, he was attending inwardly to the two women.

"Would you like to read the letter?" said Johanna to him.

"But Johanna! Why will you do such a thing? Why trouble him with such a—such a—" cried Louise.

But Gilbert had taken the letter. As he read it he turned pale. It was indeed a frenzy, full of abuse, madness, hate, and various other things. "I am going mad, and my children will be left fatherless to a depraved mother."

His eyes darkened as he read. A certain anger filled his soul.

"He is a fool!" he said bitterly, as he handed back the sheets. But poor Gilbert, he was white to the lips.

"Indeed he is a fool! How can a *man* write such things—ach!—and post it on a steamer to travel across the many many miles of sea!—No, I have not patience—"

Louise made a gesture of dismissal.

"But Louise, think how he must suffer!" said Johanna.

"Ach, yes! And think how much, how very much he thinks about his sufferings! So self-conscious and self-pitying! Does he think of *you*, of his own real self?—or of *anything*?—only his own foolish feelings."

"Feelings aren't so foolish."

"Yes—yes! Yes—yes! When people have feelings and must think about them—ach, I have not patience to hear another word. Enough! Enough! Basta! Take thy letter and thy husband away.—Mr Noon, what book have you found?"

He brought her the volume of songs.

"I am glad," she said, glancing at him winsomely and mischievously, "that you are not a tragical man. You have said it. Oh, you must not forget it. Johanna will be so very tragic, if you will let her."

Poor Gilbert tried to smile—but it was a pale effort. The other man's letter upset him profoundly.

Louise had decided that the best thing would be for Gilbert and Johanna to go to Kloster Schaeftlarn,* some few stations further up the line, and stay there for a while, since they were determined to live openly together. Evening saw them setting off once more. It was raining. They stood with their baggage on the station and waited in the dark and the wet, to carry them to the unknown destination. It was the last train.

When it arrived, it was nearly empty. So they sat in the bare third-class carriage, and Gilbert felt rather wan. They rattled through the

night, and arrived at Kloster Schaeftlarn. They descended at a tiny
station, in the midst of profound darkness and pouring rain. Complete
and staggering darkness enveloped the fragment of a railway-station.

"Where is the village? Where is the Post Hotel?" Johanna asked of
5   the porter.

It was about eight minutes away. There was no such thing as a
carriage. If they would wait while he put out the lights and shut the
station, he would accompany them and carry the bags.

They waited. Out went the station lights. Bang went the door. And
10   into the night they plunged, in the pouring rain. They walked across a
stone-flagged track through deep, dark, wet meadow-land: then past
the white gable and black balcony of a farm. Then there was a glimmer
of light—and a big building. It was the Inn of the Post—a country
public-house.

15   They found themselves in a big room where peasants sat at the tables
with huge mugs of beer. A sort of tramp was devouring food, his head
in his plate, in a corner. The landlady was a hard, large, cross woman.

Yes, they could have a bedroom with two beds—yes, for two shillings
a night. This was Whitsuntide charge. So Gilbert and Johanna followed
20   up the broad stairs, to a vast, dim passage or upper hall, a great place
full of varying smells—straw and beans among them. They were given
a large, rather bare room, with huge feather beds that seemed inflated.

And here the newly-wed, if we may use the adjective, couple stood
and looked at one another. A big, bare, farm-bedroom. A lurid
25   oleograph of Mary with seven swords in her heart. Darkness and rain
outside. And down below, heavy voices of the highland peasants.

"Well, here we are!" said Johanna, not very cheerfully.

"And here we're going to stop for a time," he answered, a little
gruesomely.

30   "We may as well change our shoes," she commented.

They went down and had dinner in the big public-room, that had
tables round the walls. Farmers and peasants stared fixedly. Two huge
dogs, and one little one, came prancing in and began to mouth Johanna
and Gilbert. A boy entered with a lantern. And then a young woman
35   brought a huge tureen of soup, spread a little cloth, and in the near
corner of the common room the young couple sat alone and ate their
meal, while the great dogs pranced round, and the big men shouted to
the creatures, and wiped the beer from their big moustaches with the
two front fingers.

40   Johanna was happy—it was adventure she wanted—and now she

had got it. She was free. As she sat in the great, old Gasthaus, the handsome farmer men of Bavaria looking over their pot-lids at her with the half-hostile, challenging mountain stare, and as she heard the uncouth dialect, felt the subdued catholic savageness in the indomitable atmosphere about her, she spread her wings and took a new breath. She had escaped. She had escaped. From Boston and her house and servants, from her husband and his social position, from all the horror of that middle-class milieu, she had broken free, and she sat in a big, common room in a half deserted old inn at the foot of the Bavarian Alps, and breathed the ancient, half-savage tang of snow and passion in the air. The old, catholic, untamed spirit of the Tyrolese! How handsome and how fierce these men could be! She was happy.

She and Gilbert crowded into one of the beds, under one of the great feather overbolsters, which rode upon them like a cumulous cloud. The darkness was intensely dark. There was a wild, strange scent in the air, a strange thrill. They held fast together like children in the darkness, and spent part of the night capturing the cumulous cloud, which showed a disposition to float away and leave some portion either of her or of him exposed to the cool air.

The morning was a dream of beauty. If you do not know the Tyrol in Spring, gentle reader, you don't, and there's an end of it. But Gilbert and Johanna stood at their window in the early morning and looked out in bliss. The mountains in the distance sparkled blue with snow and ice. The foot-hills were green-golden, and the wonderful meadows, a sea of blue and yellow flowers, surged nearer in the pure, transcendent light. The magic of it! A few great trees by the road, and two farmhouses with enormous sweeping roofs, white gables and black balconies! And then a pond, and a bridge downhill, and most lovely birchtrees standing translucent and gleaming along the wet, white way between the river-meadows. And everything crystal-pure, having the magic of snow-Alpine perfection. The crystal, paradisal calm of everything on such a morning is such as only the great snow-radiant north can offer: the sheer heavenliness that is in gentian flowers and the curve-horned chamois.

Ah the abundance, the wonderful abundance of those days—heaven and earth abundant. The various new little breads that smell so sweet with coffee, the hard clear butter, the mountain honey. For a moment of perfection, give me such a morning, such a world, and my new little breads.

Outside the inn-door was the village green—or village square. There

was the high-necked white church, like a bird, with the black cupola in
heaven. There was the white convent, where a few nuns still taught the
children and young women. There were three or four great farmhouses: and opposite the inn-door, big trees and little wooden tables. It
5 was all uplifted with pure morning-shine, warm, strong sunshine of
heaven's fountain. Three bullock wagons came slowly along the white
road through the open square, the drivers cracked long whips, and
looked with their sharp blue eyes at the two strangers. Softly swung the
necks of the pale cattle. It was morning in the world.

10   The village was tiny—just a few farms—no shop at all. It was very
still, now the convent was suppressed. It had had active mediaeval days.

Gilbert suddenly found himself almost transportedly happy. It was a
god-world: but strange northern gods. Nay, it was so wonderful,
crystal, high, and gentian-flowered! Was it not almost superhuman? It
15 went to the soul like a god-madness.

The river flowed full and swift, white-green, hissing from the
glaciers. The flat meadows from Schaeftlarn to Maierhof were a
miracle: deep, waist-deep in flowers, where the pale-gold spheres of
the great ranunculus floated like marvellous bubbles, lovely, heaven-
20 pale globe-flowers. It was hard not to believe in the old, white-skinned
muscular gods, whom Wagner travestied. Surely Siegfried tramped
through such spring meadows, breaking the god-blond globe-flowers
against his fierce, naked knees. Surely for him the birch-trees shook
their luminous green fleece in heaven, poised on a trunk-beam of icy
25 light.

How lovely the birch-trees were, on either side the road, and
loitering in clusters in the ice-shimmering distance! They cannot be
themselves beyond the smell of ice. Here they were glamorous with the
heroic light of the sagas, shaking and communing in the magical,
30 north-seeming air, flashing the ice-white brand* of their stems.

And then the foot-hills were tangled with bell-flowers, tresses and
tresses of myriad weightless blue bell-flowers among the gold and
green of the grass, the white and gold of great daisies, the pink of
evanescent flowers. Blue, blue, tangled, aerial blue, and white and gold,
35 among an evanescence of liquid green and pink. MacWhirter's picture
in the Tate, of *Spring in the Tyrol*,* would be correct if it had only
a little more of the sense of lightness, transfusion of cold luminousness,
nothing heavy: ice-colours gleaming in blossom.

Gilbert and Johanna would sit together in the sun, talking, watching
40 the flash of the mountains, hearing the magical tong-tong of the cow-

bells, and finding themselves outside the world, in the confines of a
northern heaven. Johanna wore a smoke-blue gauze dress and a white
hat, and was like the landscape. Gilbert watched and wondered, with
his soul unfolded and his mind asleep. A wonderful deep peace flowed
underneath his consciousness, like a river.   5

They would walk far off, sometimes up the hills through the woods,
sometimes across the bogs that were full of floating flowers, and cut
into dark-brown channels. The peat was stored in long dark heaps. In
the distance a broad-roofed farm seemed to settle its wings low over its
white walls. Sometimes they went by the river with their backs to the   10
mountains, and sat upon the great heaps of logs that had been floated
down, and now were piled beside the living birch-trees.

Returning at evening, the glow-worms were shining in the grass,
low-down, their strong, electric-green lights seeming to give off a
sudden joyous sound. There was a faint scent of birch-trees, and ice-   15
water, and spring in the dusky air. And everywhere, in the forest-tangle
of deep grass, the sudden jewel-lamps of the glow-worms, sending a
faint, smoky, witch-like gleam upon the surrounding grass-stems. So
that one could easily imagine oneself a tiny gnome, down in a jungle of
ferocious tall grass. Gilbert would stoop and watch them, sitting   20
crouched on his heels at the silent road-side, watching the living,
entangled stars emit their luminous fume, lighting up a tiny, tiny
grass-stemmed world of their own. He watched and watched, and was
bewitched. Meanwhile Johanna stood talking behind him, and the night
stars came out overhead. A half moon was in the sky.   25

They went slowly towards the dark, tree-clustered village. At the
bend of the road was one of the usual crucifixes, with the Christ spread
under the hood. Gilbert glanced up at the Christus. He too was pale,
lurking spread-eagled in the crucifix shadow.

"Good-evening, Mister," said the man on the road, looking up and   30
addressing the Christus in the crucified shadow.

"How are you?"

The air was dark and mountain-horrific around. Gilbert's voice,
addressing the Christ on the Cross, terrified Johanna.

"No don't!" she cried, catching his arm. "Don't! It frightens me."   35

"Why?" he said. "Can't I have a word with him?"

"No," she said. "Don't! I was educated in a convent."

"And I in a Board school." He turned again to the Christ. "How are
you, Mister? Glad to meet you," he continued. "Shan't you come
down? Come down a bit. You must be stiff. You give me the arm-ache   40

to look at you. Come down! Come and have a drink. You've been up there long enough. Come and have a drop."

"Heilige Maria!" said Johanna, crossing herself. Then to him: "I won't hear it. It scares me. No, I'm going."

5   And she set off up the dark road.

"What's the odds!" he said, going after her. "A drop of Dunkels* would do him good. He can't spend *all* time up there. I don't begrudge him a century or two—but there's a time to hang on a cross, and there's a time to get down and go your ways, it seems to me."

10   But Johanna only reiterated:

"It scares me. It scares me. I'm still too catholic."

At their bedroom window at the Post Johanna stood smoking a cigarette and looking out. The moonlight fell on a great horse-chestnut tree, on its white candles and black, palm-foliage. There was a pond

15   too, with reeds. And the frogs were singing loudly under the great, risen moon. They were whirring and rattling and simmering like a pot on a crackling fire. And Johanna was thinking of her children, as she stood there in her nightdress looking out, and smoking her cigarette. At last Gilbert came and stood by her.

20   "Think of my little boys!"* she said.

"Why think of them!" he said. "They are all right."

"Are they! Without their mother!"

"But you wouldn't go back till August, anyhow. You weren't due to go back till August."

25   There was a pleading in his voice. She flung away the end of her cigarette, into the night. The frogs simmered and rattled outside. She turned and threw her arms round his neck, and gave him a hard kiss. And they went to their narrow, passionate bed.

But in the night he woke with a click, to realise she was awake.

30   "Aren't you asleep?" he asked, in fear.

"These beds are too small for two," she answered, in a hard, wounding voice.

"Why, they haven't been! There's been room till now."

"Why should you have everything your way?"

35   It is amazing how wounding a woman can make her tone, like the cut of a blunt, horrible knife, irrespective of her words.

"My way?" He was a raw hand, and frankly puzzled.

"I can't stand this," she said, and with a horrible kick she kicked away the feather overbolster and got out of bed.

40   "Where are you going?" he asked.

"To the other bed."

"But why?"

"Because I want to be alone."

"Why?"

She vouchsafed no answer, but darted into the other bed and enveloped herself in the overbolster like a viper darting to cover.

He was now hard awake. The moon had set, and it was dark. It was very dark, so dark that he could not even see the window. He knew the direction of the other bed, where Johanna had gone. And from this direction he felt strange, terrible currents of malevolent force vibrating out on the intense darkness. The room was so dark, he felt it must be some dungeon, some awful prison. And the darkness seemed imprisoned and horrific, like being buried alive. He knew it was no use speaking to Johanna. She was as it were the spider at the core of the horror. Sometimes the darkness in the room bristled like a black wolf's hide. He lay in horror. Then he became semi-conscious.

Then again he woke with horror. There was a pallor—something horrible was coming. Something pallid and fearful was coming from the distance. He lay staring, while his heart felt ruptured; staring, staring at the pallid presence.

Then enough day-consciousness returned, and he sort of realised that it was dawn at the window. A strange, seething blister upon the darkness. Dawn at the window. A big, white, horrible, intensifying blotch on the darkness. Dawn at the window. Dawn at the window. Seething, seething—he could almost hear it!—seething with a pale, maleficent, leprous sound. But dawn! Dawn at the window. Could he make out the window-frame? Could he distinguish the centre-bar? Light seething like some fatal steam on the black solidity of the darkness: seething, seething its way in, like a disease.

Thus within him the normal day-consciousness fought with the awful night consciousness, which *sees* the invisible forces. He watched as from the depths of a cavern the light gather at the window. But himself he lay far back, still night-logged, and his heart seemed ruptured. He had once had a bad rheumatic fever, and his heart was not so strong.*

Gradually, gradually day came. And with it the night consciousness faded. With day, a certain normality re-established itself again. But he did not forget. He never forgot again. It was as if this night a breach was made in the walls of his house of life, so that he looked out on the prowling winds of chaos and horror. And somehow, Johanna had done

it. But probably it was his own fault. Johanna could be horrible like some were-wolf that ate men's hearts: only their hearts. His heart still pained him in his left breast.—But probably, probably he had brought it to pass upon himself. There can be no were-wolf unless men loose it
5   upon themselves. He must have wanted it.

It was full daylight. He saw Johanna sleeping, curled on her pillow. Everything seemed natural. His torn, ruptured consciousness relaxed. And soon he went to sleep, and slept deeply. And when he awoke, he had forgotten.

10 He had forgotten, she had forgotten. They had breakfast out of doors under the big trees. The table-cloth was of yellow and white checks. Chaffinches came hopping on the table, almost on to their plates.

"Aren't they awfully nice!" said Johanna. "You know that when the
15 Lord was painting the birds, He had no colour left for the chaffinch. So He just wiped his brushes on him."

Chaffinches! Flutter and dabs of yellow and red! And a yellow and white table-cloth! And a sumptuous morning, with the last white clouds walking slowly out of a superb sky, as if loath to go. Gilbert never forgot
20 it.

And a little later, as they sat on one of their favorite benches, on a hill under a wood, beside a white shrine, looking at the perfect heaven-array of mountains drawn up in the morning sunshine, far off, while myriads and myriads of dandelion seed-heads stood in the grass that
25 sloped down from their feet, round globes of mist resting in their myriads, big, fairy worlds of mist in a congregation, his heart reminded him of the night. He and she were hand in hand, in peace.

"The night was a failure," he said.

"It was, wasn't it?"
30 "Well, why not?"

"Ha—I suppose one can't always be happy," she sighed. And she sighed rather bitterly, as if against fate.

So there you are, gentle reader. It isn't my fault if I can't give you an idyll of coos. It would be a good deal easier for me too. I feel, with
35 Johanna, as if I could sigh against fate.

Not that fate would care. And that's where it is, gentle reader. It's no good sighing against the bull Typhon.* You've got to take him by the horns.

And so, gentle reader—! But why the devil should I always *gentle-*
40 *reader* you. You've been *gentle reader* for this last two hundred years.

Time you too had a change. Time you became rampageous reader,
ferocious reader, surly, rabid reader, hell-cat of a reader, a tartar, a
termagant, a tanger.*—And so, hell-cat of a reader, let me tell you,
with a flea in your ear, that all the ring-dove sonata you'll get out of me
you've got already, and for the rest you've got to hear the howl of tom-   5
cats like myself and she-cats like yourself, going it tooth and nail.

I sometimes wish it weren't so. I wish we could sing the old, old song.

"List to the sound of coo-oo-oo, of coo-oo-oo, of coooo
Sounding for me and you-ou-ou, for me-ee-ee and you-ouu——
Whether in storm or cloud you go, or under skies of blueoo   10
Nothing can sever, I will be ever, true to my coo-oo-oooooo!"

But, my dear reader, you've sung that song to rags, till there isn't a coo
left in the universe. So now you've got to listen to the fire-works, and the
fire-and-water fizzing and cat-fight of my precious protagonists.

And remember, gent—damn it all. I'll begin again. Remember, you   15
girning, snarl-voiced hell-bird of a detestable reader that you are,
remember that the fight doesn't take place because Little Jack Horner
ate all the pie, or because Little Bo-peep didn't mend Jack's socks, or
didn't cook his dinner. Remember, you bitch, that the fight is over
nothing at all, if it isn't everything. Remember that Jack and Jill* are   20
both decent people, not particularly bad-tempered, and not mean at all.

Therefore you sniffing mongrel bitch of a reader, you can't sniff out
any specific why or any specific wherefore, with your carrion-smelling
psycho-analysing nose, because there *is** no why and wherefore. If
fire meets water there's sure to be a dust. That's the why and wherefore.   25

Of course, as I've said before, fire and water may meet in sweet lovey-
doveyness, as rain and sun in spring meet with a kiss, as earth-water trips
forward in a growing plant to embrace the alighting sun-heat in a fecund
embrace. But that is only half the show. And unfortunately this half is
over, for the moment.   30

Our fathers and christian forbears have done us in. They have kept the
lovey-dovey show going so strong for such a long time, that, like summer
in September, it is temporarily played out. Hiss, bang, fizz, the fire and
water are having a spell of hard fight, before they can settle down to the
next bout of lovey-dovey. All right then, fiery one, spit on your hands and   35
go for him. It will clear the air, consume the flabby masses of humanity,
and make way for a splendider time. Make a ring then, readers, round
Gilbert and Johanna.

Chapter XIX.*

Louise, like a goddess in the machine, appears and disappears. She appeared at Schaeftlarn after our hero and heroine had been there for six days, and said that there was a flat, a country flat, belonging to one of her friends,* in the village of Ommerbach, five miles the other side of Schloss Wolfratsberg. This flat Johanna and Gilbert might inhabit, free, gratis and for nothing, until August and the summer holidays. It would be much cheaper.

Off set our friends again. They paid their bill and departed from Kloster Schaeftlarn with regret. They had loved it.

Back they went down the railway, to Ommerbach. Ommerbach was the least of villages. It contained exactly seven houses: three farms, the station house, two smaller houses, and then Frau Breitgau's. It lay in a knot on the high-road that came trailing nakedly, through open spaces, along the valley-side from Munich towards the mountains.

Frau Breitgau's house was the first in the village—and it was a shop. It was new. On the ground floor was Frau Breitgau's shop, and Frau Breitgau, like a round, shiny, rosy sausage that has been dipped in hot water, and Herr Breitgau, with a long grey brown-fringed moustache which looked as if it had grown into a long grey weed hanging over the rim of a beer-pot. The second floor we have nothing to do with. The top floor was the flat destined for our pair of finches. It was perched high up. From the sitting-room and from the adjacent bedroom opened the wooden balcony, which looked down over the lost high-road, past the big, broad-spread farm, over the rye-fields and fir-woods down to the river, then at the far-off up-slope. There was besides a little kitchen that looked over the station at the flashing Alps: a spare bedroom, and a water-closet. It was small, rather bare, but complete. There was one big deep sofa, splendid, in the sitting-room: a white bed in the bedroom: copper pots in the kitchen. The two finches whistled with pleasure.

Here they installed themselves, and blessed Louise for a fairy god-mother. And they proceeded to live for nothing. A huge loaf of black bread, almost enough for a week, cost sixpence: and this, eaten with thick firm Alp-grass butter was food for the gods. Ah, how good that black rye-bread is, when it is pure and well-made. The best of bread. A great pound of fresh butter, just made, cost ninepence. For a shilling they had fifteen or eighteen eggs. For threepence a vast jug of milk. For ninepence a pot of farm honey. For sixpence sweet honey-cakes.

Behold then Frau Breitgau beaming in the door with the milk, and Gilbert in pyjamas and Johanna in her blue silk dressing-gown. Behold Gilbert running down to Frau Breitgau's shop, for liver-sausage, or a cutlet of Ripperle,* or Schnapps, or whatever it was, and struggling with a conversation in strong Bayrisch,* with the happy Frau or the beer-dim Herr. Behold our couple living in a land of milk and honey and joyful abundance, for fifteen shillings a week for the two of them. Oh wonderful days of smiling, careless plenty. Oh days gone by! Oh bitter regret. Why are eggs a shilling each? Why can't one have honey any more? What has happened to God's tall rye, that the black bread should taste of the dust-bin?

Lovely material plenty! If one can live for fifteen shillings a week,* then one can live for three months on ten pounds. And with a hundred pounds a year one is a lord. Ah days gone by!

The storm was brewing in the soul of man, nevertheless. Johanna and Gilbert perched in their nest and surveyed the long white high-road come winding through the rye, between blasted fruit-trees. Bullock wagons slowly approached—or a great motor van charged out from the city—or peasants passed on foot. And sometimes, in the sweltering days, it was soldiers.

They would hear a far-off jingle and clatter and a fine threshing sound. A cloud of dust far off. And then soldiers on horseback galloping importantly forward, three, two young ones and an old one. The old one trotted up the little bank to Frau Breitgau's shop-door, until his horse almost had its nose on the counter. Then there was a loud shouting of commands. Meanwhile a blue lieutenant had reined up under the trees by the farm-door, and was shouting commands also. Then the three fore-runners rode on.

Immediately there was a struggle below: Frau Breitgau and Herr Breitgau tussling with a tub, a wide open tub, which they deposited just by the post where they might one day have a gate. Under the lilac bushes at the farm other great tubs rolled out. Then there was a trotting of farm-hands and of Breitgaus with pails of water, which they poured splashing into the tubs.

Meanwhile the column of dust grew higher, more silvery, between the tall green rye: the sound of innumerable feet filled the valley. So,

they hove in sight round the bend. Horsemen—blue horsemen—and then long trains of grey artillery winding round the corner of the tall rye, with a flash of accoutrements and a strange muffled trotting noise that made the heart beat. In the sunshine of the balcony above, Gilbert
5   and Johanna watched in silence.

Back the out-riders went galloping—nearer and nearer came the strange, slow-hasty cavalcade. They were level with the house. There was a wheeling of officers, a flashing of shouts and commands. The artillery had half drawn rein—but forward it went again. Endless
10 threaded the horsemen, and the grey gun-carriages drawn by four or six horses, and the strange, sinister grey wagons. What is more horrible than the neutral grey of war-implements. Ach, for the days of scarlet and silver and black plumes! No more! This hideous neuter, grey neuter of machine mouths.

15 The fearful ruffling noise went on. Bright horses, brown and chestnut and black—thank god they too are not painted neuter grey—streamed loosely on, their ruddy-faced riders sweating in their dark blue uniforms. Dust rose, wheels rattled, hoofs chattered and chuffled.*

20 Then came a shout, and at last all came to a standstill. In front of the house was a gun with six horses, and a young, strong, handsome fellow riding one of the leaders. He had a spur on one heel, and he rode a bright bay horse. And Gilbert noticed with a start that the belly of the bright bay was wounded with the spur, bloody.

25 Another shout, and down swung the riders, rushing to the water-tubs. They took off their caps, and their hair was wet with sweat. Gilbert watched his young rider crouch over the tub and put his face in the water and drink. He had a strong body, under the blue cloth, and the back of his neck was ruddy and handsome. He drank, then rose up
30 with his mouth and chin dripping. He wiped himself on his white, blue-bordered handkerchief, rubbed his hair and breathed deep, looking round.

Then he looked at his horse. And suddenly, furtively he ran with water in a dipper, and furtively washed the red wound on the belly,
35 washed it carefully. And he kicked white dust over the blood spots on the road. And he glanced round apprehensively. And the bay horse twitched.

There was a tossing of horses' heads, a springy, gingerly trotting of officers on horseback, a rubbing of sweat-moist hair, a strange scent of
40 soldiers and horses, a jingle and shuffle and a low run of voices, varied

by shouts. And then a wait: a long wait in the hot sun. Three elegant officers were gathered, their horses' heads together, under a deep green tree by the green farm-railing. Why were they waiting? Why were they waiting? It seemed an eternity before they would ride on and leave the road empty.   5

But at last came the order. The riders with their strong, heavy-muscled legs swung into the saddle. There was a hitch and strain of harness. Then forward again, with that strange pace of artillery, straining forward, as if with haste, and yet without swiftness. Grey gun-carriages—sweating horses, blue horse-riders, and lastly curious grey   10 wagons rolled on. Rolled on, and left the empty country behind, the rye gleaming in the sun, the road white, the tubs empty, water splashed around them—and a wet mark in the road where the youth had washed his scored horse.*

Gilbert watched the last horse-flanks disappear round the corner of   15 the white, low-roofed farm—and then he stared in silence across the shallow, sun-shimmering valley. And stared with regret—a deep regret. He forgot the woman at his side—and love, and happiness. And his heart burned to be with the men, the strange, dark, heavy soldiery, so young and strong with life, reckless and sensual. He wanted it—he   20 wanted it—and not only life with a woman. The thrill of soldiery went heavily through his blood: the glamour of the dark, positive fighting spirit.

So he and Johanna cooked their eggs and their asparagus and ate their Swiss cheese in the clear light in silence. A great silence seemed   25 to have come over him; the deep longing, and the far off desire to be with men, with men alone, active, reckless, dangerous, on the brink of death: to be away from woman, beyond her, on the borders.

But the longing was so deep, it was all indefinite and as yet unconscious, or semi-conscious. Brought up in the great tradition of   30 love and peace, how could he even recognise his own desire for death-struggles and the womanless life? Yet the desire lay at the bottom of it, as of every man.

"They enjoy their soldiering," he said to Johanna.

"Oh, they hate it. They hate it," she cried. "*How* many of them go   35 away because of it!"

"They love it, all the same."

"How can you say so. Ha, I know what it means!—that horrible, vile discipline, and the agonies they suffer. They used to talk to me when I was a child. Papa used to have soldiers to work in the garden, and they   40

always scolded me for talking to them. And I used to throw fruit to
them into the barracks ground from our high wall at the end of the
garden, and the officers were furious with me.—And then, when I was
a child, I knew. I knew *how* they suffered under it, what *agony* it was to
5   their pride."

"They must want it. They must want even the vile discipline and the
humiliation. They must, or they wouldn't have it. People don't have
things they don't want."

"Not at all! Not at all! How can they alter it? How can you say they
10 like it? How do *you* know. *You* don't know."

"I know what I know."

"You know what you think you know—rubbish! You talk rubbish
sometimes.—You ask them if they like it, and see. They're all dying to
be out of it."

15   "They think they are."

"They *are*!" she cried. "Why are you such a fool!—Why look—when
they meet one another, you can hear them—they say fifty-five! or a
hundred and eighty!—or five hundred!—And that means how many
day's service they still have. You can often hear it, in Bavaria."

20   "I don't believe it, for all that," he said.

"Ah, because you are a conceited ass," she said angrily, whisking
away the plates.

They set off walking in the country. They were out of doors all day,
in sunny weather. Sometimes they went through the woods, sometimes
25 they walked to Schloss Wolfratsberg, sometimes they went into the
deep tangle of the river-bed. And by the water they would sit and watch
the timber rafts come down the pale-green, fizzy river—rafts woven
together, floating from the mountains, and steered by two raftsmen
with long poles or oars. And again the nostalgia for the man's life would
30 come over Gilbert—life apart from the woman—life without domes-
ticity or marital implication—the single life of men active together. The
raftsmen were blonde, ruddy men with hard muscles, not like the
peasants. The peasants were full, muscular men, often handsome too.
But the mountain woodsmen were like hawks, with their keen,
35 unseeing faces and their bare, fierce knees under the little, wide leather
breeches, like football-breeches.

By the Isar the roses were out, wild roses, but red, almost scarlet red.
And columbines and the last lilies still lurked on the steep, moist,
hidden banks. The river made many twists—there were many shoals of
40 pink sand and gravel—the stream broke up into various arms. And

sometimes the rafts coming sailing down would get caught, and in spite of all efforts the raftsmen would be fast.

In one deep little corner, in an arm of the stream, Gilbert and Johanna would sometimes bathe. The water was cold, but wonderful once one was in. Johanna was a better swimmer than Gilbert—he was no water fowl. But she rocked on the water like a full water lily, her white and gold breasts of a deep-bosomed woman of thirty-two swaying slightly to the stream, her white knees coming up like buds, her face flushed and laughing.

"How lovely! How lovely!" she cried, in the water-ecstasy.

But he was lean and dry-souled, he never could know the water-ecstasy. And as she rolled over in the pallid, pure, bluey-effervescent stream, and he saw her magnificent broad white shoulders and her knot of hair, envy, and an almost hostile desire filled him. She came from the water full-blown like a water-flower, naked and delighted with her element. And she lay spread in the sun on the clean shingle. And he sat in his lean, unyielding nudity upon a great pinkish boulder, and he looked at her, still with the dark eyes of a half-hostile desire and envy. Strange enemies they were, as a white seagull and a gold land-hawk are enemies. And he brooded, looking at her as her strong bosom rose and fell, and the full breasts lay sideways. And with a sort of inward rage he wished he could see her without any darkness of desire disturbing his soul.

Fool that he was. As if there were not sufficient dead eyes of insentience in the world, without his wishing to escape from the sacred magnetism of desire. But it was a chain that held this land-hawk by the leg: as it held that white seagull by the wing. And in their hour they both struggled against the bond.

Ah the history of man and woman: it is a long history of their struggles to be free of one another. Egyptian king-gods, and christian crucifixion, they are only dodges to escape the fatal bond that binds man to woman and woman to man, and makes each the limit of the other. Oh what a limitation is this woman to me! And oh what a limitation am I to her almighty womanliness.

And so it is, the two raging at one another. And sometimes one wins, and the other goes under. And then the battle is reversed. And sometimes the two fly asunder, and men are all soldiers and women all weavers. And sometimes all women become as men, as in England, so that the men need no longer be manly. And sometimes all men become as women,* so the women need no longer be womanly. And sometimes—but oh so rarely—man remains man, and woman woman, and in their difference they meet and are very happy.

But man must remain man, and woman woman. There is something manly in the soul of a man which is beyond woman, and in which she 5 has no part. And there is something in woman, particularly in motherhood, in which man has no part, and can have no part. For a woman to trespass into man's extremity is poison, and for a man to trespass into woman's final remoteness is misery.

So there we are—the old, the eternal game of man and woman: the 10 time-balancing oscillation of eternity. In this we live, and from this our lives are made. There is a duality in opposition, between man and woman. There is a dual life-polarity. And the one half can never usurp the other half—the one pole can never replace the other. It is the basis of the life-mystery.

15 The universe swings in a same dual polarity. Let scientists say what they will, the sun is but one pole of our gravitation. There is another: perhaps the moon: perhaps the invisible. But between a dual polarity our round earth swings on her course. If there were but one pole, and that the sun, then she would fall into the sun. Which she does not.

20 Many times, perhaps most times, Gilbert and Johanna were completely happy. But again, each tugged the leash. He wanted life to be all his life, male; she wanted life to be all her life, female. And sometimes he fell under her tugging, and sometimes she fell under his. And then there was war.

25 For a woman doesn't want a man she can conquer: no, though she fight like hell for conquest. And the same with a man. Oh horrible submission, especially in marriage are you the foulest of treacheries! Never submit, never abandon yourself completely. This is the last word to every man and woman.

30 Ultimately, a woman wants a man who, by entering into complete relationship with her, will keep her in her own polarity and equipoise, true to herself. The man wants the same of a woman. It is the eternal oscillating balance of the universe. It is the timeless inter-related duality of fire and water. Let life overbalance in either direction, and 35 there is a fight, a terrific struggle to get back the balance. And let the mechanistic intervention of some fixed ideal neutralise the incalculable ebb-and-flow of the two principles, and a raging madness will supervene in the world. A madness which is pleasantly accumulating in mankind today.

40 Gilbert and Johanna were mostly very happy. She was wild with

pleasure at release from conventional life. She would dance in her glowing, full bodied nudity round and round the flat, and she made him dance also, in his more intense, white and ruddy-haired nudity. He was stiff and constrained. There was an intense fierce reserve and stiffness in him. His whiteness was very white and hard, his hair was black, but his body hair ruddy-brown. She was full and soft and gold-white, with delicate soft hair.

"Dance," she said to him. "Dance!"

And with her arms spread on the air, she floated round in triumph. And he, ashamed to be ashamed, danced in correspondence, with a jerky, male stiffness that seemed to her odd and strange. Woosh she went, veering as on a current of water down the passage, looping her soft nudity and her soft, soft-stemmed hands in a loop round the little kitchen, and floating back into the sitting-room, where he was dancing with odd, jerky, nigger-like motions which seemed to her so comical and curious. Why on earth dance like that, when one could swim deliciously on the air! And him, he wondered how one could abandon oneself to swim on the air, when one was sharp and intensely local. So she swam around him, and drooped her soft-stemmed hand over his hard, naked shoulder. And he came with his comical quick motions, and put his thin, hard naked arm round her full soft waist. And she shouted with pleasure and triumph, and his eyes twinkled sardonically.

To be free! To be free, Great God! Not furtive and orgiastic at night, and stiff in a linen collar of correctitude during the day. Whether Gilbert liked it or not, she insisted on floating round in her soft, ambient nudity in the morning or the afternoon, if she felt like it. And she made him float, or paddle likewise. And he, as we said before, was ashamed to be ashamed.

Likewise she insisted on going barefoot, though the roads were stony and painful. So off they trudged, both barefoot, on the roads through the forest, and they got sole-sore and he became cross. And at evening a doe ran across the sky-line, so fleet. And as they came home, the fire-flies were threading in and out of the tall, tall dark rye, carrying their little explosive lanterns in their tails.

"I love you! I love you, you dears, you dears!" she cried to the fire-flies. "I *wish* I was a fire-fly."

"Don't gush," said he.

"You—who are you?" she cried at him.

"And what are you, for a fire-fly?" he said.

"Go away, you spoil everything.—You dear, you dear fire-flies, I

love you. I wish I was one of you, to swim through the tops of the rye.
Oh, I do! I should love it. I should love to be a fire-fly, and not bother
with tiresome men and their pettiness any more."

"You might be less of a fool, if you were a fire-fly," he said to her.
5   "You're too big a fool to be a human being."

"Oh God! Oh God!" she cried, lifting her hands to the deity. "Why
am I persecuted by this person at my side."

"Because you ask for it," said he.

"Go away! Go away! I want to be happy. I want to be happy with the
10   lovely fire-flies."

"Yes, you might ask *them* first, before you go butting in."

"*They'll* be glad of me," she said.

"By God, then they're welcome."

"Go away! Go home, you hateful thing."

15   "Come away, you ass. Don't slobber any more."

"Slobber! If you weren't a dried English stick, you'd know it wasn't
slobber."

"And being a dried English stick, I just know it is."

"You would. There isn't a drop of sap in you."

20   "And you're going squashy and over-ripe."

"Oh, but isn't he a *devil*! Now he's spoiled my fire-flies."

And she went home in a dudgeon, and spent the rest of the evening
making a marvellous painting on brown paper, of fire-flies in the corn.
And he stood on the balcony, and looked at the fire-flies drifting in and
25   out of the darkness, weaving and waving in the dark air beneath him.
And the night was a great concave of darkness. And the river sounded
as in a sea-shell. And an owl flew hooting with a little sob. And the
great concave of darkness in front seemed vast, and bristling with fir-
trees and mysterious northern, eastern lands.

30   Again they walked the miles across to the Lake of Starnberg. Ah,
how Gilbert loved to emerge from the forests into the wide, half-
marshy corn-lands. There lay the broad-roofed farms: there rose a tall
white church, black-capped. A hare rushed along the road-side: a deer
flashed across out of the tall rye, and ran again into the deep corn.
35   Then she turned, and spread her wide ears, up to the chin in corn, and
watched our pair of finches. And her fawn, lost in the high corn of the
opposite side of the way, made a great rustling, and whimpered and
cried like a child for its mother. The doe flashed back at a tangent, and
called to her fawn from the hill crest. Then off they trotted, into the
40   forest edge.

Gilbert and Johanna walked through the shallow lands. A peasant, and his wife in the great blue-cotton trousers of the marsh-women were carrying their hay off the hay-sticks in their arms, and loading it on the cart, where their little boy trod it down.

Coming to the village with the trees and the tall black and white church, on the opposite crest, Johanna and Gilbert arrived at an inn, and went into the inn-garden for dinner. They were eating their soup when in chattered a class of school-boys, two by two, with their teacher in attendance. He had the self-important self-conscious look of a teacher. The boys seemed happy, carrying their jackets. After a delay and a flutter and a few reprimands, they were arranged at a long table for dinner, a chattering pleased little crowd.

Gilbert watched them ominously. A sort of horror overcame him. He could not think of his own teaching days now, without horror. To be a school-teacher: he looked at the quite pleasant German specimen.—But the ignominy of it! The horror of the hideous tangled captivity.

Ah liberty, liberty, the sweetest of all things: freedom to possess one's body and soul, to be master of one's own days. Not many souls are fit for freedom. Most get bored, or nervous, or foolish. Let them have jobs, let such have their time allotted to them. But for the free soul liberty is essential, and a job is a thing to be contemplated with horror and hatred.

It was full summer-time, and wild strawberries were ripe along the forest hedges. Gilbert and Johanna gathered them in big leaves, and tasted all the fragrance of the wild native world in them, the fierceness of the lost winter.

And again the post arrived from America, and more torrents of abuse, rage, grief, despair and self-pity. Everard wrote also to the Baron, and the family clock began to whirr again. The Baron wrote to Johanna, and added his praise to that of the injured husband. His daughter was ruining the family honor. Marriage was a social institution, and whoever attacked the social fabric deserved to be treated as a criminal and coerced into submission. A private excursion in the fields of adultery was perhaps to be condoned.

The Baron knew he was on thin ice, on the marriage question. Had he not his own illegitimate ménage, under the rose? But he kept his position. The institution was to be supported, the individual might do as he liked—under the rose. "Ach yea!" said Lotte. "If the bed isn't roses the bedcover is." So she went in and out among the rose-bushes, and hid, not behind the fig-leaf, but behind this same immortal rose.

Johanna was not hiding: and here came the difficulty. The Baron stormed against the paltry and mischievous Alfred, the intriguing Louise, and the gullible fool of a Johanna. "Do you think any man will marry you again after you have made such an exposure of yourself?" he
5 wrote. And getting hotter, he continued: "But if ever you bring this ill-bred, common, penniless lout to my house, I shall kick him down the stairs."

"Ach Papa," wrote Johanna. "Don't you talk of kicking, with so much gout in your feet."

10 Long, sombre, semi-mystical poems arrived from Rudolf. The raven of woe had made off with the pearl of the north, and hidden it in some unclean cranny. But was no falcon on the wing?

No, dear Rudolf, no falcon was on the wing. He sat with his posterior on his chair in his study and wrote inky poems.

15 And then the Baroness, Johanna's mother, fluttered near. She arrived in Munich, and descended for the moment on Alfred. Alfred and Louise meanwhile sardonically pulled both ways.

Arrived the Baroness' letter from Munich, to Gilbert in German. "Think what you do. Think what position you can give my daughter.
20 She has been used to a comfortable and honorable life, and she must not be brought down to degradation. Her father was a cultured nobleman of high family, and how could he bear to think of his daughter going about the country homeless, living on charity, with a strange man, like a tramp. Yes, like a tramp trailing across the country."

25 The Baroness had a real style of her own. Gilbert spit on his hands, and tackled the German language. He would answer Dutch with Dutch. "Your daughter wishes to stay with me, I do not detain her against her will. So long as she wishes to stay, I shall never ask her to go away. I am no more master of her actions than is anyone else. I shall
30 stand by her as long as ever she asks for it, or wishes it, or will have it. Her marriage in America is a disaster for her. I want her to stay with me. We are not tramps nor living on charity, since nobody gives us anything. I do what I can do—and it can't be otherwise."

And then, lo and behold, Johanna, happening to go into the kitchen
35 one rainy morning just after midday, just after the midday train had gone down the line, saw a figure which surely was familiar coming down the path from the station: a sturdy, even burly figure in a black coat and skirt, and a white chiffon scarf, and an insecure boat-shaped hat, bobbing along under an umbrella.

40 The Baroness, by all the powers. Johanna rushed into the bedroom,

where Gilbert was sitting stark naked, his feet under him, musing on the bed.

"Mama!" said Johanna, flinging off her blue silk wrap and appearing like a Rubens' Venus.*

"What?" said Gilbert.   5

"Quick! There's Mama! Coming from the station. Thank the Lord I saw her."

And Johanna flew into her chemise, whilst Gilbert got into his shirt.

By the time the Baroness had had a word with Frau Breitgau, and had struggled up the stairs, two correct young people were standing on   10
their feet, dressed and ready. But alas, they both, and he in particular, had that soft, vague, warm look in their eyes and in their faces, that tender after-glow of a fierce round of love and passion.

Into this mild, dawn-tender, rosy half-awakenedness came the Baroness, like the black and ponderous blast of Boreas. Gilbert was   15
bewildered at being honored so unexpectedly, but as yet he was unsuspicious. He took the umbrella of the visitor, and gave her a seat on the honorable and comfortable deep sofa. Then he took a chair at the desk, where he had the evening before been working at music.

There was a lull. And then suddenly, like a bomb which has been   20
quietly steaming and then goes off, the Baroness went off. She planted her knees square, she pushed the hat off her forehead, she let her white chiffon scarf hang loose. And then, in a child's high, strange lament voice, she turned to Gilbert and began.

It would be useless to repeat what she said. Poor Gilbert, the dawn-   25
rose going more and more bewildered in his eyes, his mouth coming apart, his face growing pale, seemed to shrink in his chair—and shrank and shrank, as if he would get down between the two legs of the pedestal desk, and there, like an abashed dog retreated in its kennel, bark uncertainly at the intruder.   30

On and on went the Baroness. It was not abuse—not at all. It was like a child in a dream going on and on, in a high, plaintive, half-distracted voice. She said everything she had said before, and everything that she would inevitably say. She said all the things that had come into her mind, all the things she had put into her letter. She   35
reminded him of poor Johanna's unhappy future—and of the children.—"Ja, und Sie wissen nicht was eine Mutter von zwei Kindern ist. Das wissen Sie nicht.—Ja, und ich meine, ihr Vater ist ein adlicher, hochgebildeter Mann—Ja, und wenn Sie Geld hätten—Ja, und ihr Mann ist doch so gut, so gelernt, und so berühmt dort in Amerika—Ja   40

und was für ein Leben ist es dann für Sie. Oh jeh, noch so jung und
unerfahren sind Sie—"

"—Yes, and you don't know what a Mother of two children is—Yes,
and I must say, her father is a cultured nobleman—Yes, and if you had
5 any money even—Yes, and her husband is really so good,* so
kind, so learned, and so famous there in America.—Yes, and what kind
of life is it for you? Oh dear, you are so young and inexperienced—oh
dear, what a sad and heavy fate you take on your young shoulders—Oh,
what a sad and heavy fate. Oh dear, it is good you have no mother, for
10 what should she say.—But why will you do this thing? Why will you do
it.—And yes, even if Johanna says she is happy now, think in six
months! In six months! Oh poor Johanna, my poor Hannele. And her
two children. Ach, and she a mother with two children. That you don't
understand. You are young, you don't understand. No, what a sad life
15 you make for yourself—ah, I cannot think of it—such a sad life for
you.—And yes, what will you do when the Herr Doktor wants this
house? Oh yea, then you have no roof to your heads! Homeless, like a
pair of tramps—like a pair of tramps—and her father is really such a
cultured nobleman———"

20   On and on went the Baroness' voice. She seemed to think of
everything, and like a bird flying high against a wind, she rose and sank,
rose and sank, and began again, almost breathless, with her—Und
ja—Und ja—Und ja!

Our young male finch shrank and shrank behind the pedestal desk,
25 and said never a word, not one single word. When the Baroness
said—Do you understand?—he only gazed at her in silence. And
Johanna, much more on the spot, gazed on the pair of them in a kind of
indignation. She could not forget, not for a second, how the dawn-rose
on her morning's bout of passionate connection was being blotted out,
30 blotted out under the Baronessial Boreas.

"Aber nein Mama! Aber das ist dumm! Aber was meinst du,
Mama!"* she shouted from time to time. But the Baroness, like a
dog that is howling at the moon, only cast a glance at her unheeding out
of the farthest corner of her eye, cast an unheeding corner of a glance
35 at the interruption, and went on with her long, long howl at the moon.
Which moon was friend Gilbert, who gazed and gaped moon-white and
moon-silent, and seemed as if shortly he would sink behind the horizon
of the pedestal desk. There was a dark, unseeing, obstinate look in his
eye. Johanna would not have been at all surprised if he had started to
40 bark.

And then, almost suddenly, like a sudden wind that drops, the Baroness was silent. There was a painful lull in the room.

"But Mama!" said Johanna. "Why didn't you *say* you were coming?"

The question was pointed.

"Ach, I am not staying. I am going to Louise's," said the Baroness, catching her chiffon scarf and grasping for her umbrella.

"But won't you have some lunch?" said Johanna.

"No! No! Thank you! Thank you! I am going."

And the elderly lady rose to her feet, sturdily.

"But you will eat something?" said Johanna.

"Nein! Nein!"

"Goodbye Mama!" called Johanna cheerfully.

"Ja, goodbye Johanna.—Goodbye Mr Noon. I mean not to be unkind, you know—" this bit in English.

That long, eternal "you kno-ow" of foreigners. The Baroness wrinkled a distressed face at him, shook hands, and left, obdurately refusing to stay another minute, although her train was not till a quarter to two.

Johanna closed the door behind her mother, and did not go downstairs with her.

"Well, I call that an irruption!" she said.

"So do I," said Gilbert vaguely.

"Just in our lovely morning——" There was a pause: "But I call it mean. I call it mean to burst on us like that! What right has she?"

And Johanna flounced into the bedroom. Then she flounced back.

"But what do you let it upset you for?" she said. "You look so ridiculous! You shrank and shrank till I thought you'd disappear between the legs of the desk.—And not a word. Not a word did you say! But not a word! Pouf! I think it's so ridiculous—"

She went out to the kitchen with a poof! of laughter. Then she called:

"Come and look."

Gilbert went. Away below they saw the Baroness going sturdily up the incline to the railway, in the rain.

"Look at her! Look at her! How long has she got to wait?"

"An hour," said Gilbert. "Ought I to go to her?"

"Go to her? What for? She doesn't want you."

"She's had no lunch."

"Oh well, she's had her satisfaction schimpfing.* I don't forgive it her. Look at her now! Doesn't she look a sight in the rain! What right

had she to spring on us like that! I call it mean of them—mean!—Now
let her stand in the station—And now she'll go to Louise's and make
more mischief. But I'm on my guard against them in the future.—
Mean! And our lovely morning. And you—*you*. What do you look such
a muff for? Why do you look as if you were going to hide in the desk
hole? A rare fool *you* looked too."

Gilbert did not answer, but his eyes were dark and full of remem-
brance.

"Ach Mama!" said Johanna, addressing the figure in the rain. "You
always were clumsy and ungraceful. And a sight you look, standing on
the station. You've made a rare angel of yourself *this* day. And I don't
forgive it you!—And *you*—" she turned on Gilbert. "You are worse
than she is—shrinking and being such a muff.—Bah, a man! You
never said *one word*!"

"Why should I?"

"Why not? Pouf!"—and again Johanna broke into a mocking laugh.
"But I'm going to eat, anyhow. And I'm going to have eggs and bacon.
Are you?"

"Yes," said Gilbert, eyeing with the greatest discomfort the stout
black figure on the little railway station. And he had no peace till the
train came—when they both ran to the kitchen and watched the
Baroness climb in—and watched the train steam off.

"We'll be on our guards, after this," said Johanna.

"How?" said Gilbert.

"Yes, that's just it. Springing upon one—!!—Yah, fools always do
rush in!*—What does she care, really, about me? Not a rap! She's
only frightened of the world. That's all she cares. I shan't forgive it
her.—And you're a fool, I don't forgive you for taking it so tragically—"

Johanna was mistaken, however. Gilbert was only deeply bewildered
by this *bruit pour une omelette*.* But she was deeply offended that he
had cut such a poor figure. In her own mind, she felt he ought to have
risen and said: "Madame la Baronne, this is not to the point. Allow me
to offer you a little refreshment." Instead of which he had sat with a
pale face and round eyes and shrinking body. For in Gilbert's world
people did not make speeches. At the bottom of his soul he too was
profoundly angry. Johanna was furious because she was humiliated by
her own family, and because he allowed her to be humiliated. He was
furious because he had, he felt, been wantonly trespassed upon. But
this was his private affair.

The next day they went to Schloss Wolfratsberg, to see Louise.

Wolfratsberg was a big village, a township. And here the soldiers were
quartered. Crossing the wide bridge over the river, he saw the soldiers
washing their clothes in the stream, ruddy and laughing. In the town
soldiers stood, dark blue, at every corner: the place seemed coloured
with them. Even in Louise's villa two privates were quartered—she   5
would not be bothered with an officer. Gilbert saw them loitering,
smoking their pipes, their tunics unbuttoned, in the little plantation
behind the house. And he heard them chaffing Marta, and singing risky
love-songs to her.

Marta appeared, her round head braided with her black plait, her grey 10
eyes full of light, her face warm and dusky with that mediaeval reserve.
She glanced a strange flash at Gilbert. And for the moment he wished
with all his soul that he was back again among the common people: that
he was lounging with his pipe in the plantation with the two privates, and
making love to the dark, proud, promising Marta. He felt sick of women 15
who talked and discussed and had privileges, of a theoretic life. Oh if
only he was with the common soldiers!—the man's reckless, manly life
of indifference and blood-satisfaction and mental stupidity.

But alas, some invisible pale intervened between him and the
lounging, unbuttoned soldiers. He had to go upstairs, to Louise's room 20
with its grey linen walls and its yellow silk curtains and dark furniture.
And he had to listen to these two ladies, Johanna and Louise, in their
endless talking-it-out: the reckless voice of Johanna beginning—"Aber
Louise—" and the musical, sardonic voice of Louise responding: "Ja,
Johanna, Ja. Das mein ich auch. *Aber*——"   25

That terrible *aber*—that eternal *but*. Hamlet would really have had
some occasion to say *Aber mich kein Abern.**

Of course nothing important eventuated at Wolfratsberg. Next
morning Gilbert worked at his music. He had found various old books
of songs at Louise's house, and these songs he set about transcribing, 30
translating, and preparing for schools. A certain rather facile inspiration, a little fever of work was upon him, and he got on quite well, and
forgot the various other matters. Johanna curled up on the sofa and
read book after book, scattering the volumes round her on the floor like
bones round the door of a dog's kennel.   35

In the afternoon they walked out towards the river woods. They went
through the tall, ripening rye. Poppies were out, and magenta corn-
cockles, and bits of blue chicory. But Johanna, instead of walking along
with him, walked behind, with a curious trailing motion of her feet. At
first he did not notice. And then his spine began to creep. He glanced 40

round irritably. And again his spine began to creep, he felt as if someone were going to stick him in the neck. So he waited for her to come up, and passed some casual remark as she joined him.

But when he went forward, he again felt her behind him—she would
5 not keep up. And again the vile feeling went up and down his spine. He felt he would hutch* his shoulders, as if really expecting a stab in the neck.

"Why do you walk behind?" he said.

"Why shouldn't I? I can walk where I like."

10 He looked at her. She had an irritating way of trailing one foot out, having her feet wide apart, and one foot on one side. A white anger began to mount his cheek.

"You won't walk after me like that," he said. "I won't have it."

"Why not? The road is not yours. I can go where I like."

15 "Not behind me."

"Why not!"

And she stood at a distance, eyeing him. He turned on his way. And she followed trailing after him. And rage ran up and down his spine, feeling her as it were jeering and destroying him from behind.

20 Again he waited.

"Go in front," he said.

"Why should I?"

"Go in front.* Or keep level," he said.

"No. Why should I? I can go where I like."

25 She stood at a little distance, eyeing him. And he hated her. So they both stood on the path, waiting. Still they waited.

After a while he shrugged his shoulders, and walked forward, determined to take no notice. But when he came to the woods, and still she dogged him, at a dozen paces behind, jeering at him malevolently,
30 he felt, then he could stand it no more.

He turned suddenly and went back towards her.

"I'm going home," he said, striding savagely.

"Goodbye. Enjoy yourself!" she cried jeeringly. And he felt her watching him, jeering, as he went through the rye.

35 However, he hurried forward towards the house, indifferent to her now. He took a book and sat down at the desk. And after a short time he heard her coming up the stairs. She was always afraid to be alone in the lonely country.

She went straight into the bedroom, without speaking. He glanced
40 from under his brows, hoping she would be softened.

He was terrified lest love should cease to be love. She came back out of the bedroom.

"Shall we have some tea?" she said.

"Yes. Shall I make some?"

"Do."

He went into the kitchen and made tea. She curled up on the sofa with another book. He hoped it was all going to be cosy again.

They had tea. Evening came—and they talked desultorily. He hoped everything was all right. But she took her book, and he went to his songs. As he was working he suddenly heard her Pouf! of laughter, and glanced up. She was curled on the sofa, her face and eyes were shining curiously, and her head was pressed back as a cobra presses back its head, flattening its neck.

"I must think of you and Mama," she said. "You looked such a fool."

He moved the green-shaded reading lamp to one side.

"Why?" he said.

"Shrinking in your chair. Why were you so frightened?"

"Frightened? When was I frightened?"

"You were terrified—of Mama."

"That's a lie."

"No, not at all. I could see you. You looked terrified—and you *were*."

"I was not terrified. It's ridiculous."

"But why did you go so little? You went so small in your chair, I thought you were going to vanish altogether."

"What should I do?"

"But why were you so overwhelmed? Why did you shrink so small? I was simply astonished."

"I didn't shrink at all. What could I say to a woman with white hair—what could I say? What was the good of saying anything?"

"Yes, but why should you go pale and shrink six sizes smaller than before. It was a sight to see you."

"You shouldn't have looked then. You shouldn't have let me in for it. She's your damned mother."

"*I* let you in for it! I! You let yourself in for it. And then you shrivel up—" she poufed with laughter.

"Have you said about enough?" he said, leaning forward over the desk, and his eyes beginning to burn.

"What am I saying? I'm just telling you."

"Have you about finished?"

"No. Not at all. I want to know why you look such a fool."

A blacker shadow went over his face.

"Because you, blast you, make a fool of me," he said sullenly.

"You must be a poor creature," she said, "if an old woman's schimpfing makes you want to crawl under the desk." And she laughed
5 unpleasantly. "I thought you were going to bark at her—" she laughed more—"bark at her like a dog."

But he, looking daggers, rose and went to the open door, to look at the night from the balcony. She got down from the sofa and confronted him.

"I thought you were going to crawl under here like a dog in a
10 kennel—" her head dropped loose with laughter—"and bark—bark at Mama!" She laughed till she was weak. And he only stood and looked at her with black eyes of fury. Because he was sore with many unalleved* humiliations, a little blinded by his own sore head.

"Look!" she cried. "Look!"—and she moved the paper-basket, and
15 crept into the space between the two sides of the desk. He stood stock still, and his cheek went yellow with fury and humiliation. She was so weak with laughter, that her forehead sank to the floor, as she kneeled bunched up under the desk. Then she looked up and barked at him.*

20 "Wuff! Wuff-wuff-wuff! Wuff!"

After which she collapsed with another little shriek of laughter.

He could see it was funny. But like a bear with a sore nose, his soreness was too big for him. He went livid with anger.

"Now stop!" he said. And the sound of his voice startled her. She
25 looked up at him.

"Now stop!" he said.

And his face was transfigured. She did not know it. It was a mask of strange, impersonal, blind fury. She crawled out from under the desk, and rose to her feet.

30 "Can't you stand a joke?" she said.

"I've had enough!" he answered, and his eyes came upon her with a black leap.

"But why? Are you such a poor thing you can't stand being laughed at sometimes? You *looked* a big enough fool!"

35 But his eyes only watched her from the white blotch of his face. And she winced. It wasn't a human being looking at her. Out of a ghastly mask a black, horrible force seemed to be streaming. She winced, and was frightened. Oh God, these Englishmen, what depths of horrors had they at the bottom of their souls! She was rather frightened of him, as of a mad
40 thing.

"Can I never laugh at you?" she said.

"Not more than enough," he said.

She could see his heart beating in his throat. And still the black, impersonal, horrible look lingered on his brow and in his eyes, his face was void.

"And must *you* say when it's enough?" she asked, almost submissively. She was afraid of him as she might be of a rock which was just going to fall.

"Yes," he said. And he looked full into her again. And she was frightened—not of him, personally—but of some powerful impersonal force of which he was only the vehicle: a force which he hardly could contain, and which seemed ready to break horribly out of him.

She became quite still, went and curled up with her book again. He sat motionless at the desk, his heart plunging violently, a sort of semi-conscious swoon drowsing his brain. He had almost forgotten, forgotten these horrible rages. When he was a boy of thirteen his sister could taunt them up in him. And he knew he could have murdered her. But that was long ago, and he had forgotten. Now suddenly the black storm had broken out again. And he was no longer a boy. He was a man now.

He sat with his head dropped—brooding, oblivious in a kind of dark, intense inwardness. There was an unspeakable silence in the room. She glanced at him from time to time. But he was motionless and as if invisible to her.

Rather nervously she slipped from her sofa and came and crouched at his side, and very timidly put her hand on his knee. He did not move. But awful fire of desire went through him at once, so that his limbs felt like molten iron. He could not move.

"Are you cross with me?" she said wistfully. And her hand sank closer on his knee.

He turned and looked down at her. A strange, almost unseeing expansion was in his eyes, as he looked on her. And he saw her face luminous, clear, frail, like a sky after a thunder-rain, shining with tender frail light. And in his breast and in his heart the great throbs of love-passion struck and struck again, till he felt he would die if he did not have her. And yet he did not move.

"Say you're not cross! Say it!" she murmured. And she put her arms round his hips, as he sat in the chair and she crouched before him. And he took her in his arms—her soft, deep breasts, her soft sides—!

Ah God, the terrible agony and bliss of sheer passion, sheer, surpassing desire. The agony and bliss of such an embrace, the very brink of death, and yet the sheer overwhelming wave of life itself. Ach, how awful and utterly unexpected it is, before it happens: like drowning, or like birth. How fearful, how causeless, how forever voiceless.

5   Gilbert afterwards lay shattered, his old soul, his old mind and psyche shattered and gone. And he lay prostrate, a new thing, a new creature: a prostrate, naked, new thing.

And he and Johanna slept, with his arm round her, and her breast, one breast, in his hand: the perfect, consummating sleep of true, terrible marriage. As a new-born child sleeps at the breast, so the newly-naked, shattered, new-born couple sleep together upon the heaving wave of the invisible creative life, side by side, two together, enveloped in fruition.

Ah gentle reader, what have we done! What have we done, that sex, and the sacred, awful communion should have become degraded into a thing of shame, excused only by the accident of procreation, or the perversion of spiritual union. It is no spiritual union. It is the living blood-soul in each being palpitating from the shock of a new metamorphosis. What have we done, that men and women should have so far lost themselves, and lost one another, that marriage has become a mere affair of comradeship, "pals," or brother-and-sister business, or spiritual unison, or prostitution? Ah God, God, why do we always try to run away from our own splendour. Why are we all such Jonahs? And why must I be the whale to swim back to the right shore* with you, gentle reader.

Marriage, gentle reader, rests upon the root-quivering of the awful, surpassing sex embrace, full and unspeakable. It is a terrible adjustment of two fearful opposites, their approach to a final crisis of contact, and then the flash and explosion, as when lightning is released. And then, the two, the man and the woman, quiver in a newness. This is the real creation: not the accident of childbirth, but the miracle of man-birth and woman-birth. No matter how many children are born, each one of them has still to be man-born, or woman-born, later on. And failing this second birth, there is no life but bread and butter and machine toys: no living life.

And the man-birth and the woman-birth lasts a life long, and is never finished. Spasm after spasm we are born into manhood and womanhood, and there is no end to the pure creative process. Man is born into further manhood, forever: and woman into further womanhood.

And it is no good trying to force it. It must come of itself. It is no use having ideals—they only hinder. One must have the pride and dignity of one's own naked, unabateable soul: no more.

Don't strive after finality. Nothing is final except an idea, or an ideal. That can never grow. But eternity is, livingly, the unceasing creation 5 after creation after creation, and heaven is to live onwards, and hell is to hold back. Ah, how many times have I, myself, been shattered and born again, how many times still do I hope to be shattered and born again, still, while I live. In death I do not know, do not ask. Life is my affair.

> "And oh that a man would arise in me   10
> That the man I am might cease to be."*

Which is putting it backwards. The shattering comes before the arising. So let us pray for our shattering, gentle reader, if we pray at all. And we, who have paid such exaggerated respect for the Gethsemanes* and Whitsuntides of renunciation, let us now proceed to 15 pay a deeper, and at last real respect for the Gethsemanes and Whitsuntides of the life-passion itself, the surging life-passion which we will never, never deny, however many ideal gods may ask it.

The year was passing on. The rye was ripe, and the farm-hands were out in a line, mowing with the scythe. The corn was tall, taller than the 20 men who stooped and swayed in a slanting line, downhill towards the wood's edge. Gilbert would stand a long time on his high balcony, watching them work in the misty morning, watching them come in at noon-day, when the farm-bell rang, watching the dusk gather over them. And always, he wished he were one with them—even with the 25 laborers who worked and whetted their scythes and sat down to rest under the shade of the standing corn. To be at one with men in a physical activity. Why could he not? He had only his life with Johanna, and the bit of work he was doing.

The life with Johanna was his all-in-all: the work was secondary. 30 Work was always a solitary, private business with him. It did not unite him with mankind.

Why could he not really mix and mingle with men? For he could not. He could be free and easy and familiar—but from any sort of actual intimacy or commingling, or even unison, something in his heart held 35 back, tugged him back as by a string round his heart. He had no comrade, no actual friend. Casual friends he had in plenty—and he was quite popular. He had even friends who wrote and said they loved him. But the moment he read the words his heart shut like a trap, and would not open.—As far as men were concerned he was cut off—and more or less he knew it. He could share their company and their casual activities, their evenings and their debates and their excursions, but one 5 with them he was not, ever, and he really knew it. As far as men went, he was a separate, unmixing specimen.

Yet he wanted, wanted to have friends and a common activity. At the bottom of his heart he set an immense value on friendship—eternal, manly friendship. And even he longed for association with other men, 10 in some activity. He had almost envied the soldiers—now he almost envied the mowers. Not quite. Not altogether.

Because, of course, he had mixed hard enough with men all his life. He knew what they were. He knew that they had no wonderful secret—none: rather a wonderful lack of secret. He knew they were 15 like ants, that toil automatically in concert because they have no meaning, singly. Singly, men had no meaning. In their concerted activities, soldier or labor, they had all their significance.

And so Gilbert felt himself cut off from one half of man's life. With a curious, blank certainty he knew it, as he leaned on the balcony, high 20 up, and watched the men at work. Because he could never be an ant in the colony, or a soldier in the hive, he must stand outside of life, outside the man's life, the world activity, in a way, divorced.

He must make all his life with Johanna, and with his work. He would finish his book of songs before August. And he had written down a 25 sketch of a symphony* which he knew in his heart was genuine from him. So much for that.

And he clung with intensity to Johanna. Since he had been with her, and his old closed heart had broken open, he knew that she and he were fate and life to one another. She was his one connection in the 30 universe. And because he had no other connection, and could have no other, apparently; and also because, since his old, closed, more-or-less self-sufficient heart had been broken open, and set in a pulsing correspondence with the soul of the woman, he could no longer live alone; therefore he grasped at Johanna with a kind of frenzy.

35 The family was working once more for a reunion with Everard. Everard had written saying that he would allow Johanna to have a flat in New York, with her boys, if she would live there in complete honor, as his wife; personally, he could never return to her, as a husband.

This seemed a very fine offer, and a very satisfactory capitulation, in 40 the eyes of the Baron and family. All pressure was to be brought to bear. Johanna was invited again by Louise to Wolfratsberg. Gilbert accompanied her: and was rather coldly received, and made to feel an interloper.

"Tonight," said the officious Louise, "Johanna will stay here. Because there is much to talk about, which we must say ALONE." 5

Whereupon, it being evening, Gilbert said Goodnight to Johanna, and Johanna said Goodnight to him. She half expected, and wished, that he would command, or at least request her to refuse Louise, and to return to Ommerbach with him. He did neither. It was part of his nature, that, cost what it might, everyone must make his own, or her own decision for 10 herself. So he said Goodnight, and Johanna rather mockingly called Goodnight back again.

"You will come tomorrow?" he said, looking at her.

She always quailed when he looked direct at her, and asked her a stripped question. 15

"Yes," she said, a little grudgingly. "I'll come."

"In the morning?"

"In the morning or in the afternoon."

"Yes—yes—she shall come. Do not fear," laughed Louise rather jeeringly. 20

Gilbert looked at them both with black eyes, and took his leave. He walked back, up the steep hill through the wood, and along the high Landstrasse* by the railway and the rye. Night fell, and a moon hung low down. The road was silent, and strangely foreign to him in the night. It seemed to him that it ran towards Russia—he could feel Russia at the 25 end of the road—and that the century was not his own century. England was all switched off, gone out of connection. One might imagine wolves.

He looked round at the bristling shadows. He saw the white, foreign road. And something in his wrists, and in his heart, seemed to be swollen turgid almost to bursting. In his wrists particularly. He veered slowly 30 right round, in a circle, and felt Europe, strange lands, wheeling slowly round him. And he felt he was mad: like a hub of a wheeling continent. And it seemed the skies would break. And his wrists felt turgid, swollen. And very dim in his consciousness was a thought of Johanna in Wolfratsberg being talked to by that infernal Louise: infernal, that was 35 what she was.

At last he came to the house, and entered the silent, empty, dark flat. He went out on to the balcony and hung over the night, hearing the distant hoarseness of the river, seeing the bristling of fir-trees in the dark, and remaining himself suspended. 40

When a man's life has been broken open, and its single flow definitely connected with the life-flow in another being, so that some invisible pulsing life-blood flows between their two selves all the time, some current of invisible vital flow, then it is a horror and a madness to
5   derange this flow. And strange, very strange Gilbert felt that night on the balcony: untellable: deranged in soul, in life-self, not in mind. He knew, with stark, deranged inevitability, that Johanna was his fate, he was to be balanced in changeless vital correspondence with her: or else there was before him a wandering incompleteness like idiocy.

10   However, he went to bed: and awoke after a short time with agony: and looked at the empty pillow at his side: and for a moment it was as if she was dead.

After which he lay watching for the dawn, and the sound of the farm-bells. And never, in all his life, was he more grateful for any
15   sound than for the sound of the jangle-jangling farm-bell in the whitish dawn. He went out at once on to the road. And there, strange enough, was a hunter or forester, in the first dawn-light, walking with a dead deer slung over his shoulder. It was tied by its four little feet, in a bunch, and its head hung back. It was hard to forget.

20   Soon the laborers came out of the farm, into the morning-chill, dew-drenched world. And he watched them go down the slope with their scythes. And the sun came up. And he thanked God there was sun, and sweet day, and that his soul's insanity was soothed.

He hung on during the day. Johanna did not come till four o'clock:
25   and then, with Louise and Professor Sartorius. Gilbert made the tea. The conversation was German and critical—and it turned on Goethe. Gilbert said Goethe was cold, less than human, nasty and functional, scientific in the worst sense: that where man should have a reverent soul, Goethe had only a nasty scientific inspiration. He talked, saying
30   what he really felt. It all arose out of a volume of Goethe's lyrics which Louise had bestowed on him. He talked as one is used to talk, openly.

He was therefore startled when Professor Sartorius bounced up as if a cracker had gone off in his trouser-seat, said he could hear no more of this from one who knew nothing about the great Goethe, ganz und
35   gar nichts, gabbled *Danke schön** for the tea, seized his hat and made for the door. There he looked round.

"You are coming?" he said to Louise.

"Ja—Ja—!—*Goodbye*—" said Louise to Gilbert, pursing her mouth. "You see we think very much of Goethe—and perhaps you
40   speak without understanding him at all. Yes?—don't you think?"

Gilbert did not answer, and they went.

"I said what I think, and I believe it's true," he said, looking at Johanna with hot, angry eyes.

"I shouldn't wonder," she said.

And she liked him for raising the professorial dust.

They were silent for some moments.

"Are you glad I've come?" she said.

"I knew you'd come," he answered, speaking more jauntily now she was actually here.

"But did you want me?"

He looked at her, a dark look. He could not bear such questions. He was queer to her—incomprehensible. He did not seem a bit glad. Yet she was awfully glad to be with him again—inexpressibly. Why wasn't he festive too? Oh she was so glad. She had escaped again. Queer and sombre and inscrutable he was. Why didn't he say anything.

"You are glad, aren't you, that I've come back to you?" she said, looking round the room with pleasure.

"Why should you ever stay away!" he replied, with a good deal of resentment showing.

"Oh, I should think I can stay away one night," she replied lightly, flattered.

"But Louise is a treacherous creature, really," she said.

"Why?"

He still did not believe in the tricks of the other woman.

Johanna was rather piqued that he did not make a fuss of her: did not make love to her. But he didn't. He was silent, and rather withheld. Inside him his soul was gripped and tense, as from the shock, and from a certain desperate clutching at certainty. He had had a shock: and his soul was desperate. It is a horrible thing for a man to realise, not so much in his mind as in his soul, that his very life, his very being depends upon his connection with another being. It is a terrible thing to realise that our soul's sanity and integrity depends upon the adjustment of another individual to ourself: that if this individual, wantonly or by urgency break the adjustment and depart, the soul must bleed to death, not whole, and not quite sane.

This pretty piece of knowledge Gilbert realised in his clairvoyant depths. And it shook him profoundly at the time, so that he could not gather himself together, or come forth, or be free. He could not finally *trust* Johanna: there was some strain of volition in his heart. So his love-making was gripped and intense and almost cruel.

Two nights after this he awoke again with a start. He felt at once that Johanna was not at his side. In the same instant he heard a low, muffled sound that seemed to shatter his heart.

He sat up. There was a white blotch beneath the low window. It was
5 Johanna crouching there, sobbing.

"What is it? Why are you there?"

"Nothing," she sobbed.

"Why have you got up? You'll be cold."

"Oh no—oh no—" she sobbed.
10 "But what's the matter? Come back to bed."

"No—No—no-o!" she sobbed madly.

The night and the dark room seemed to bristle with the sound.

"What is the matter? Is anything wrong?" he said. At last he was perhaps full awake: if man is ever full awake in the middle of the
15 sleep-night.

"No—no! Leave me alone! Leave me alone!" she sobbed in a wild despair.

He rose in pure bewilderment, and went to her.

"But what is it," he said, taking her gently in his arms as he crouched
20 beside her. "Tell me what it is."

"Oh, you are cruel to me, you are cruel to me, you are—" she sobbed, with the strange, irrational continuance of a child.

"I? Why? How? How am I cruel to you?"

"You are! You torture me. You torture me—yes—you do!"
25 "But how? How? I don't torture you.—You are cold. You are quite cold. Come to bed. You are cold."

"No. No. You don't love me. You are cruel to me. Oh, you are cruel to me, you are."

"But come to bed—you are so cold—come to bed and tell me how.
30 Come to bed and tell me how—come and be warm."

"You'll torture me. You'll torture me."

"No no! I'll only make you warm. Come. Come."

At last, still sobbing in the curious abandon, she let herself be led back to the bed. He took her in his arms, and wrapped the bedclothes
35 round her closely, and wrapped her with himself drawing her in to his breast, and putting his cheek down upon her round, soft head, so that he seemed to have folded her all together.

"You are cruel! You are cruel to me," she sobbed, sobbing more violently, but with the curious heavy remoteness departing from the
40 sound.

"But I'm not!" he said. "I'm not. How am I? I love you. I love you. I only love you. And I love nothing but you in all the world—nothing in all the world. How am I?"

"You are. You don't really love me."

"I do. I do nothing else. What have you got in this state for? It's ridiculous. And you are cold through."

He gathered her closer and closer. Her sobbing was subsiding.

"Because you don't love me," she sobbed, "and it makes you cruel to me. You torture me."

"I don't," he said, clutching her nearer. "Tell me how.—Are you getting warm now?"

"Yes," she piped faintly.

"And it's nonsense," he said. "I do love you, my love. If only I didn't love you so much.—You're so cold still. Why are you so silly? Why are you so silly. You startled me horribly."

"But you don't know."

"Yes I do! My love! My pigeon.* Be warm, be warm, my love—be warm with me."

She wriggled and nestled nearer, and gave a little shuddering sound.

"Now you're getting warm," he sang softly, in a monotone. "Now you're getting warm with me. Aren't you, my love. We're getting warm, so warm, aren't we."

She nestled nearer and nearer in his arms, seeming to get smaller, whilst he seemed to grow bigger in the darkness.

"To say I don't love you! To say such things!" he whispered into her hair. "To say I don't love you—! when—oh God!" And he clung to her and enfolded her as a tree enfolds a great stone with its roots. And she nestled in silence enveloped by him.*

So they were happy again, and restored—but a little more frightened than before. They had both had a lesson—and each began to fear the other, and to fear the inter-relation: perhaps a wholesome fear.

As Johanna sat in bed having her coffee she brooded as her plaits dangled. He sat on a chair by the bed, where he had carried the little table and the tray. He too was quiet. His heart was still again.

"Oh but Louise is wicked!" said Johanna, between the sips of her coffee. "She's wicked."

"Why?" he asked. When he was quiet and happy in his heart he did not pay much attention.

"She's wicked. She'd like to injure us. She'd like to damage our love, now she thinks it is really there. Oh, she's a wicked one. I shall beware of her in the future."

"Yes," he said.

5　　"I shan't let her play her tricks with me again. She thinks me a fool. But I've found her out."

It was an unwelcome letter which arrived from Everard that morning. This time it was abuse—and warning. "And what kind of life do you hope to have with that lout?" wrote the husband. "He will not
10　treat you as I have done. He will not give you what I have given you. Take care, or before you have finished he will beat you. Men of that sort are not to be trusted."

Johanna threw these letters aside rather easily. But for Gilbert they were a sore trial. They seemed to insult him in his soul. And he felt in
15　the wrong, confronted with them. For which, once more, he was a fool. But centuries of insistence have contrived to put him in the wrong —and he was a child of the old culture. It took some time for him to roll the centuries and their tablets of stone out of his spirit.

They walked in the woods, where the shade was grateful. The little
20　birds, tree-creepers, ran up and down the trunks of the beeches like odd flies, and squirrels came, with their snaky, undulating leap running from tree to tree, darting up a round trunk, and peeping from the edge at our friends. Gilbert nodded at them, and they chatter-chatter-chattered at him.

25　Gilbert finished his book of songs, and posted it off to London. The correspondence with Everard continued. August was drawing near—and then Ommerbach was no longer a place of refuge. After two more weeks, what were they to do, he and Johanna? They did not know.

As they were walking homewards in the lovely warm July evening,
30　they heard a motor-car behind them, running out from Munich. They stood aside on the grass to let it pass, when, to their surprise, the face of Louise appeared in the window. She waved to them, and immediately called to the driver to stop.

"Yes," she said, "from here I will walk on." She paid the driver, and
35　turned to Gilbert.

"I want," she said, "to have a talk with you. You will walk with me?—yes?"

She was in her dark-green silk town dress, and was looking very beautiful and rich.

40　"No," said Johanna. "He has a cold, and is tired."

"You are too tired? Yes? Oh, I can walk alone."

"No, I am not tired," he said.

"Are you sure?" said Louise.

"He *is* tired, and he's got a cold," said Johanna.

"Oh, Johanna—er ist doch ein Mann—he really is a man, and can speak for himself," said Louise.

"Will you go?" said Johanna.

"Yes, I will walk along. I shan't be very long," he said.

"Goodbye," cried Johanna. And she went into the house in a fury. Gilbert wondered at her unkindness.

He and Louise continued along the evening road together. And she had a heart to heart with him. She was very nice—very sweet—very kind: and so thoughtful for him, so thoughtful for him. He expanded and opened to her, and spread out his soul for her and his thoughts like a dish of *hors d'œuvres* for her. And she tasted these *hors d'œuvres* of him, and found them rather piquant, although he was a naive youngling, of course, compared to the all-knowing professors of Germany.

And so she talked seriously to him—about Johanna and his future and her future. And she said she believed that Johanna loved him, but oh, oh it would be so hard, and did he really think love was so important.

And, yes he did, said naive Gilbert. What else mattered. And "Yes. Yes. I know," replied Louise—but what of all the other difficulties. And Gilbert said they couldn't be helped. And Louise asked did he want to marry Johanna, if the divorce could be brought about. And he said he did. And she asked him, ah, life was so complicated—might he not change: he was young, he was fresh to life: might he not love some other woman? Johanna was older than he, and mother of two children. Would he not find it a burden, later, and wish to love some young girl, some young creature fresh to life—whom he could make all his own: a little like Marta—came the wicked suggestion. Johanna could never be all his, for had not twelve years of her life belonged to another man!—etc. etc.

To all of which our hero, strutting very heroic and confidential and like a warbling Minnesinger beside the beautiful, expensive woman, along the twilight road, replied *in extenso*, giving his reasons and his ideas and his deductions, and all he thought upon the matter, all he had thought in the past, all he would think in the future, and he sounded very sweet, a soul of honey and fine steel, of course. And Louise sipped it all, and estimated the honey for what it was worth, and the steel for what it also was worth, and found him a naive babbler, of course, compared to a German professor, but none the less, not unsympathetic to herself.

So they parted at last, at the entrance to Wolfratsberg, both in a 5 whoosh of wonderful sympathetic understanding, after their Rausch* of soul-communion. And he walked back the long five miles with a prancing step, fancying himself somewhat, and intensely flattered by the attentive Louise: and she went on to her house, brooding and feeling triumphant that she had still got her finger in 10 Johanna's pie.

Meanwhile Johanna sat at home gnawing her wrath, her anxiety, and her fingers. When our bright-eyed Gilbert landed back at last, she broke out on him.

"You must have been all the way."

15 "To the beginning of the village."

"The more fool you. You know you are dead tired."

"No I'm not. And how could I refuse to go with her?"

"Easily enough. She could have gone on in the taxi. But you are a simple fool. Any woman who likes to give you a flattering look, or ask 20 you for something, can dangle you after her at the end of a piece of string. Interfering minx that she is! And you to be taken in, after the other day. I bet you poured yourself out to her."

"No I didn't. We only talked."

"What else should you do! I know what talk means, with folks like 25 you and her. Nasty soul messing, that's what! What did she want? What had she got up her sleeve?"

"Nothing. She only talked about how we should manage—and what there was to consider."

"You are a fool—I hate you. Talking it over with 30 her—everything—everything—I know. How much you love me and are ready to sacrifice for me. I hate you. I hate you. You are always ready for a soul mess with one of her sort. Don't come near me."

"But it wasn't a soul mess."

"It was. I can see it in your face. I hate you when you look like that. 35 And after the other day too. You know what she wants. You know what she's after. She wants to make mischief between us."

Gilbert didn't feel guilty of the mischief part of it—perhaps a little ashamed of the deep, soulful confidence—his dish of *hors d'œuvres*. But in one respect he was not like Johanna. Talk, sympathy, soul-truck had 40 very little influence on his actions. He did not act from the same centres as he talked from, and sympathised from, and soul-communed from.—Whereas Johanna was very risky to meddle with. Set a cycle of ideas and emotions going in her, and heaven knows how fatally logical she might be in her resultant action. Hence his unreasoning horror of her loss the other day. And hence her not unwarranted anxiety this 5 evening. But the same logic did not apply to him as to her.

However, this storm blew over also, though not without a certain damage done.

It was necessary to decide what move to make. Louise had become suddenly quite friendly. She came to tea. 10

"Have you never been to Italy? Oh but it is lovely! Why not go there? Why not go, and walk some of the distance!"

"But money?" said Gilbert.

"Ach money! Money will come."

Again she said it. And he was all his life grateful to her for the laconic 15 indifference with which she said it. For some reason, he believed her. "Money will come."

Then why not go to Italy? Why not act on Louise's suggestion?

Our pair of finches grew wildly excited, ready for flight.

Money would come. It didn't mean that Louise, or anyone else, was 20 ready to give it, for all that. However, Gilbert had nine pounds, and Johanna six.*

To Italy, then. Why not?

To Italy!

Chapter XX.

Over the Hills.*

Johanna's rather ricketty trunk and Gilbert's rather flimsy bags were put on the railway to travel by themselves to Kufstein, on the Austrian frontier. Peace go with them.

5   Our hero and heroine arose at dawn one morning in early August, a little nervous and feeling very strange at setting off on foot to cross the Alps and conquer the south. They had about thirteen pounds between them, and heaven knows what in front of them.

10   It was nearly seven when they set out. Gilbert called at the little station to see if the bags had gone. They had gone. Then goodbye, Ommerbach! Goodbye little flat, and balcony over the wild road! Goodbye farm-bells that had jangled in so many of the crises of our couple! Goodbye little village of seven houses.

15   The morning was dewy but sunny, and the pale blue chicory had opened its sky-sparkles by the road. Gilbert put a sprig in his coat. He had his brown knapsack on his back, his old brown hat on his head. Johanna had her lighter grey knapsack on her back, her old panama with a cherry ribbon on her head—and she wore her dark cotton voile

20 dress. So they took to the road—feeling rather unsure, but in a mood for going on and on, inevitably.

    By eight o'clock they were on the hill above Schloss Wolfratsberg, looking down on that ancient townlet, whose chimneys smoked blue, whose two tall-necked churches lifted their bird-head cupolas,*

25 whose river ran hastily under two bridges, whose water-poplar trees were tall and plumy, whose saw-mill made a just audible sound. Touching sight, an ancient, remote little town sending up its morning woodsmoke, down below beside its river.

    So they descended, and bought a spirit-machine and a saucepan,

30 methylated spirit, bread, butter and sausage. Then they crept through the long, attractive old street on tip-toe, for fear that Louise should spy them from her villa above, or that Louise's servants or children should pounce on them.

    But heaven be praised, they passed unchallenged, and merged into

35 the water-meadows beyond the town. There they sat down a minute on

238

a bench, and heard the church bells, and watched the women washing linen in the river. Well Goodbye Wolfratsberg! There is a long road ahead, over the mountains and into the unknown.

In the middle of the morning they sat in a pine-wood a little way back from the road and ate bread and sausage and drank Frau Breitgau's Schnapps from a little bottle. A peasant with his dog, passing along the high-road through the trees, shouted a greeting and wished a pleasant wedding. Whereupon they both felt uneasy, as if he knew their involved circumstances.

They took to the road again. The sky was cloudy, and looked like rain. So when they came to a station on the little railway, they waited for a train, and rode ten miles to the terminus. There they descended, and took the high-road towards Austria. It wound at the very toes of the mountains. The steep slopes and cliffs came down on the right. On the left was a deep wood—and sometimes a marsh flat.

Darker grew the sky—down came the rain, the uncompromising mountain rain. In the grey, disconsolate, Alpine downpour they trudged on, Johanna in her burberry,* he in his shower-coat. The cherry ribbon began to run streaks into Johanna's panama, whose brim drooped into her neck. Drops of water trickled down her back. Gilbert's trouser-bottoms flapped his wet ankles. The black pine-trees over the road drooped grimly, as if promising rain for ever. And this was the first afternoon.

"Bad luck!" said Gilbert.

"Isn't it," she cried.

"But I don't mind," said he.

"I rather like it, really," said she.

"So do I," he chimed.

In which frame of mind they trudged on to a village. They entered the inn. Farmers and wagoners had been driven in by the rain, and sat with their beer and pipes. Johanna ordered scrambled eggs with ham, and wrung out her skirt-bottoms. Then the two wet ones sat on a bench and waited for their eggs.

One lonely man sat near—one of the odd, rather woe-begone figures that always appear in an inn, no matter where. He bowed to the wet finches, and asked them if they came far. Johanna told him. And of course she said, in German:

"We want to walk to Italy."

"You and your husband?"

"Yes."

"Ja—that's famous, now! That is remarkable!"

The other peasants were listening—a handsome, black-eyed man, a large, blond, taciturn Bavarian farmer, and two others.

Then the little unfortunate told his tale of woe. He was a shoemaker
5 and—But there is not space for his tale. Suffice that Johanna gave him a shilling—and he peered at it as if it were the egg of a bird of Paradise in his palm—and suddenly he spat on it, reverently—and tears came to his eyes, and he bowed three times, to Johanna, and once to Gilbert—and disappeared into the rain. And of course Johanna cried—and wiped her
10 eyes and laughed—and the dish of orange-golden eggs appeared smoking. With black beer, thin raw ham, butter, and black bread, scrambled eggs are royal. Johanna and Gilbert ate in wistful sentimental emotion, heartily.

The men at the opposite table, under the picture of Franz
15 Joseph,* watched with all their eyes. Then the black-eyed one called the usual question:

"But you are not German, lady?"

And she gave the inevitable answer:

"Yes—and my man is English."
20 Followed a lively little dialogue in Tyrolese and high German, which Gilbert could not understand. But the men were flirting with all their might with Johanna. Even the taciturn farmer of fifty put up his moustaches and flushed and became handsome. Johanna liked him better than the black-eyed one.
25 They asked if Gilbert could understand—and when Johanna said, not the dialect, then they began to make rather broad jokes about him, in the dialect. About his not understanding—about his silence and his youth.

"You don't like a German husband, then, gracious lady?"

"Ja! Ja! Auch!" laughed Johanna. "Also! Also!"
30 After which there was such a flame of male ardour around in the room, that she was frightened, and rose to go. It had almost ceased raining.

Gilbert watched the men with dark, watchful eyes.

"There are good beds here, good, warm German beds, and everything that such a fine Frauenzimmer* can wish. Will you go, then?" cried
35 the farmer.

"Yes, yes! We must go," cried Johanna, rather scared.

The two swung into their knapsacks. The men got up and shouted *Good journey*! and various other things, and bade goodbye rather jeeringly to Gilbert. He knew they jeered at him, but he did not care.
40 So they went in their damp clothes down the wet road to Bad

Tollingen. They arrived at this little summer-resort at about half-past six—and wandered looking for a room. They found one in a small house for four shillings. It was quite comfortable, but Johanna declared she smelled stables and a slaughter-house. Gilbert smelled something, but nothing so lurid.

So they changed what they could, ate some food out of their knapsack in their room, to save expense. Then they sallied out. There was a small summer-theatre, so they paid their shilling and listened to a Vienna comedy.

The next day was sunny again. As soon as possible they were out of the house where they had slept and where Johanna had smelled so acutely. Oh the joy of getting out of an hotel, or a lodging-house, in the morning, of clearing out for good! Never to see it again!

They bought food and set out again. Johanna had a pound of peaches—rather hard. They drifted on all day—camping at intervals to make food. In the afternoon they were in the high, wild rocky valley of the young Isar. Woodsmen, like wild, sharp men from the Sagas, were busy with the rafts. At five o'clock Johanna and Gilbert decided to climb over the neck of a pass between two valleys, by a footpath.* It would save ten miles of road.

So they sat by a waterfall and made tea from the ringing water, under a birch-tree. A grasshopper, a wonderful green war-horse of some tiny mediaeval knight sprang on to Gilbert's knee, and he watched it with wonder. He felt it musically—it had a certain magic, which he felt as music. Johanna gathered tall, black-blue gentians that stood in the shadow.

Then they started up the path. It was supposed to be eight miles—two hours and a half. They climbed up through the alp-meadows and entered the higher woods, where the whortleberries were bushy. And all at once the path became indefinite. However, they followed a track along the saddle of a hill, among trees and whortle-berries.

Then the track fizzled out. What to do? Gilbert thought he saw a path on the opposite hill, in among scattered trees and rocks. So down they went, down to the stream-bed. And Gilbert clambered up the opposite slope. Johanna behind saw him, with his shower-coat dangling, his knapsack a great hump on his back, as he scrambled earnestly up the steep slope, clinging to rocks.

"The camel! The camel!" she screamed from her opposite bank. "You look such a sight! You look such a sight—like a camel with a *hump*!!" So she screamed from the distance, and she laughed with derision. Perhaps his earnest, anxious haste for a path drove her to ridicule.

However, he got to the top—and found a proper track.

5   "Come on! Come on!" he called. "It's getting late."

She came reluctantly, being in one of her perverse moods. In the thin wood-spaces as she came along she found wild strawberries. "Such lovely ones!" she shouted from the distance.

    "Come on!"

10   "So good!"

    "Come on!"

They were on the high saddle of a hill, among trees and rocks. And the dusk was falling—and already it was cold, sharp cold. Yet in the distance he could see her panama hat stooping and stooping.

15   "It's getting dark," he shouted.

    "Lovely big strawberries!" she screamed in reply.

    "I'm going ahead."

    "Wait! Wait! I've found a patch."

There she was stooping. But he strode ahead. It was getting dark.

20 And he did not want to sleep on damp ground in the extreme mountain cold. So he went on without her. And she was frightened, and came half running, calling to him to wait.

    "You see the night," he said angrily.

    "But such heavenly strawberries you never did taste."

25   "Sleep with them then," he said angrily, striding on. He was anxious for some sort of shelter.

They were on a rough, rocky track among trees. It was almost night, and ice-scent strong in the air. He was silent, and she was now frightened.

30   "We shall find a hay-hut on one of the Alps," she said.

    "Let us then," he replied.

On they went in the next-to-darkness. And suddenly, at a bend of the road among thick trees, a little hut. They opened the door. It was a tiny chapel,* with two benches that would seat four persons each,

35 and a tiny altar. He struck a match and lighted the altar candles. The floor was boarded, and quite dry. If one moved the benches, two people could just lie there: it was just big enough.

All his anxiety disappeared. He looked at the doll which represented the virgin, at the hideous paper and rag flowers of the altar, and at the

40 innumerable little *ex voto* pictures that hung on the walls.

"We can sleep here," he said. "We are all right."

"Where?" she said.

"On the floor."

"I'm *sure* we could find a hay-hut if we went on."

"I'm not going on."   5

"Do think! It's so uncomfortable here."

"It's dry and weather-tight. What more do you want."

He took a candle from the altar and climbed on a bench, looking at the *ex voto* pictures. They were excellent naive little paintings on wood: a woman in a huge bed, and a man and his five children kneeling in a   10
queue across the bedroom, with joined hands, and the virgin in a cloud coming through the ceiling: a field of cattle just like a Noah's ark set out: a man with a huge rock falling on his bent leg, and blood squashing out sky-high: a woman falling downstairs into her kitchen, and Mary, in a blue cloak, looking down in mild amazement from the ceiling beams: 15
a man up to his waist in water, his arms thrown up, drowning, and Mary in a blue cloak on a white cloud high above: and so on and so on, a whole gallery. Gilbert was fascinated.

"Do come! Do let us find a hay-hut," cried Johanna.

For some reason she was mad to sleep in one of the Alpine log hay-   20
houses.

"We are well here," he replied, standing on the bench with the candle. He glanced at her who stood outside by the bushes.

"No! No!" she said. "The hard floor."

"But dry and warm. What more do you want."   25

He had found a picture which fascinated him: a prison cell, with chains and fetters hanging on the wall, and Mary in a blue cloak prison-breaking through the roof. Then the verse.

> "Du heilige Mutter von Rerelmos
> Ich bitte mach mir mein Sohn von Gefangenschaft los.   30
> Mach ihn von Eisen und Banden frei
> Wenn es dein Heilige Wille sei.*
> > Anna Eichberg. 1775."

Poor Anna Eichberg, with her son in prison in 1775, praying for him to the virgin. Why was he in prison?* And whose prison. Gilbert   35
felt he must know.

Johanna, returning from her excursion, saw through the open door of the wooden shrine how he stood on a seat with the candle and peered at this picture, and gaped and mused.

"I've found one," she cried in triumph.

"Come and look," he said.

"No. Come quick. I've found a lovely hay-hut."

"I'm sure we're better here."

5   "No. No. Come."

Reluctantly he obeyed. He blew out the candles and followed up the dark path. After a hundred yards it suddenly emerged in a great open darkness—the saddle of the pass—and twenty yards further on was the dark hay-house, built of logs, and roofed, but with a space of two yards 10 between the roof and the top of the low log walls.

Gilbert climbed in and explored. In the higher, rear half the hay went practically to the roof. In the lower half it was a little less than the log walls.

"Isn't it lovely! Isn't it perfect," cried Johanna.

15   They decided to eat. There were two bits of meat, and four little breads: all the rest eaten. An icy wind was blowing through the *col.* They went to the back of the hay-hut, and with difficulty got more or less out of the icy draught, so that they could fry the meat in the little saucepan over the spirit-flame. The night had become very dark. They crouched round 20 the blue, restless flame of the spirit-machine, and heard the wind, and heard the meat faintly frizzle. Then they ate in the darkness, feeling the cold almost resound in the upper air.

They clambered up the ill-joining logs into the hut or barn. Gentle reader, never spend the night in an Alpine hay-hut if you have a chapel 25 handy.

"Isn't it lovely! Isn't it perfect!" cried Johanna.

"Yes," said Gilbert, who was growing colder each moment.

He carefully hung the knapsacks where he could lay hands on them: carefully placed the hats: then carefully buried his boots and Johanna's 30 shoes in the deep hay, in the faint hopes that the hay might dry them, for they were sodden. Then he took off his waistcoat and spread it for a sort of pillow for the two of them.

All this was done in pitch darkness, for how shall one strike matches in a barn of loose hay. Then the two buried themselves in a deep hole in the 35 hay, and piled the hay above themselves, and thought they were all right. Johanna was in ecstasies. At last she had got away from her Marvell villa, Boston, and all civilisation, and was sleeping like a tramp. She wanted to be made love to there in the darkness of the hay: so she was made love to: and at length the two disposed themselves for sleep. They clung close 40 together, and put the coats over them, and piled the hay above the coats.

"It's lovely, *lovely!*" said Johanna.

But alas, gentle reader. Worse than fleas, worse even than mosquitoes on a sultry night is hay. It trickles insidiously in. It trickles and tickles your face, it goes in your ears and down your neck and is round your waist. The tickling becomes an intolerable irritation, then an inflammation.

Also a waistcoat is a bad pillowslip. You find your face in the arm-holes every other minute, in all the horror of hay in the night.

And then, gentle reader, there were chinks in the log walls, and there was the space above. So on top swept the ice wind. And below, through the chinks and through all the hay the icy point of the draught was slowly but surely and deadlily inserted.

Our tired pair of finches slept—but slept in the slowly trickling irritation of hay, and the slowly encroaching blade of ice-cold wind. Then they heard it rain—but for a mercy the roof was tight. They woke and woke and woke, and every time colder and colder and colder, and more and more irritated into frenzy by the filtering-in of the hay, on their faces, in their nostrils and ears, and under their clothing. To be cold, and galled with irritation. Oh gentle reader.

At last there was a sort of false dawn. And they got up. Gilbert put on his waistcoat and soddened boots—ice cold, ice cold. In the ghastly corpse-light of the dawn they looked out. They were at the top of a pass, in a sort of kettle among the mountains, peaks rising round. The rain, just a bit higher, was snow.

He hunted for sticks to make a fire for tea—all the spirit gone—and she went for water. Her shoes were so sodden she went barefoot—over the icy, piercing points of the mown Alp. A good penance for romance. At last she found water oozing up through the grass in a sort of marsh.

He coaxed a wretched fire between stones behind the log-house, as much out of the wind as possible. Then they drank tea and ate the last stale little breads—about two ounces each. That was the end of it.

Dawn among the peaks around their Alp was ghastly grey. And in this ice-cold greyness, in sodden boots and skirt-bottoms, they set off, like two ghosts. And they had not gone a hundred yards before they saw a light—and someone with a lantern—and heard a cow moo.

It was a forlorn, dismal little summer farm, inhabited only for some months in the year. Drawing nearer, they saw in the dismal light of the increasing dawn a thin, stooping man moving with a lantern in the cow-house—then another man came out of the house, on the stone track through the filth. No, the second man was a woman—a thin,

gaunt, extinguished looking woman, fairly young. She wore the big
canvas trousers, tighter at the ankles, which the peasant women wear in
the marshes. She was a rather weak man, save for her knob of dun-
coloured hair screwed up behind.

5   Johanna and Gilbert went forward, in the morning-pallor. The man
and the woman stood suspiciously. The farm was hardly more than a
hovel—squalid. And the two figures seemed silence-extinguished.
They made a great impression on Gilbert: like two wasted, stupefied,
dreary birds, immured in that kettle of the pass in the cold.

10   Johanna asked the way. And the woman answered in a high,
screaming voice, again like a desert bird. She pointed to a curving
track. It was two hours. Evidently it was almost a violation to the woman
to have to speak—the noise was a violation of the intolerable overshad-
owed, upper silence.

15   Gilbert was glad to drop on to the rock path, downwards, down a
gorge, out of that moist Alp. Water roared and roared below. The
black-blue greater gentian stood very tall, and the starry-white Grass of
Parnassus opened its watery flowers.*

       Down the gorge they went. It was steep, and they moved fast, and at
20   last grew quite hot. At about eight o'clock they came to a village of
about four houses.* At the first house—it was fairly large, and all
lined with wood—they asked for coffee. Yes, they could have it. The
woman was fresh-faced and pleasant. A boy was crying by the big green
stove. Outside rain, mountain rain was falling.

25   At length came good hot milk and coffee. Then the man came in. He
was a strapping, hard-looking mountaineer. He said he was a
forester—the region was famous for chamois. The Crown Prince came
every summer to shoot chamois. He brought photographs of the royal
highness—and a letter which the prince had written him: Dear Karl. It
30   was a simple, natural little letter.

       "My sister knows the Kronprinz—she had dancing lessons with
him," said Johanna. So Karl, the forester was suitably impressed. And
our pair of finches decided to go to bed. It was pouring with rain: that
awful Alpine rain which comes straight down and seems like the wet
35   creation of the world.

       Oh a good, deep down bed, with down bolsters deep above one!
Tired, inflamed with hay and cold, they slept in their separate beds,
glad to be apart. In extremity, one is alone. We are born single and we
die singly. All the better for all of us.

40   They got up at about two o'clock. The rain was falling like

doomsday. At four there was a post-omnibus which ran to the Achen lake, to Scholastika. They decided to take it.

At least they had dry clothes. So they sat in the bumping omnibus with two other people, on clammy wash-leather seats, and they charged through deep valleys of everlasting rain.

It was a surprise to come to Scholastika—a dark, deep lake—and find summer visitors in the hotel*—a small hotel, rough and countrified. But there was no bed. They were directed to a big farm-house, across a long flagged track through the marshy flat water-meadows heading the lake. Yes, and they got a room. Upstairs was an enormous wide corridor from which the doors opened. At one end was a broad balcony—at the other end a great barn full of hay and corn. So that as one came out of one's bedroom door one turned towards the great cavern of hay. And if one went to the edge, one saw the horns of cattle below.

The bedroom was large, with old painted Tyrolese furniture, and great blue-and-white check overbolsters. Johanna insisted on going to bed at once. So there she lay, with her fine nose just emerging from under the great bolster.

Gilbert must go and forage for food. Again, in the yellowish evening he went across the meadow at the head of the gloomy lake. And at the hotel place he was given bread, eggs, cheese, and butter—and it all cost so little. He was in Austria, for the woman asked him for Krones and Hellers. She took German money just the same. Different the people seemed here—soft, vague, easy-going, not so fierce and hostile as the Bavarian highlanders. He was in Austria, in easy Austria. And the slight fear that hung over one in Germany—an instinctive uneasy resentment of all the officialdom—did not exist any more. Pleasant, easy, happy-go-lucky Austria!

He went home pleased. People had been nice with him. The things cost nothing. He had got methylated spirit. So there in the bedroom, whilst Johanna lay in bed, he made tea, and fried eggs in butter, and they had their meal. How pleasant it was—with the wettish gold evening fading over the narrow-ended lake and the black mountains, and in the bedroom a smell of tea and fried eggs, and Johanna sitting up in bed and eating her food with joy, and more eggs spitting away in the little saucepan on the floor. Food, delicious food—how good it is when it comes haphazard, round the frail camp-fire of a little spirit-machine, in a safe bedroom far from everywhere, with yellow, wet evening falling over a rather sinister lake, and painted Tyrolese furniture, with roses and peasant tulips, looking on indoors.

Next morning they were off again, on foot. The lake was a very dark blue, ink blue, the trees tall, and some already turning gold. On the elevated road they went above the lake, right from one end to the other. And then the road plunged down-hill, towards the open.

5   They came in the afternoon to the wide, open place, where the railway went to Italy, and the imperial road.* Here again it was warm and sweet and summery. Grapes and peaches were abundant in the shops. There was a strange touch of the south.

But now the luggage remained to be fetched from the frontier. Back
10 along the line they travelled by the evening train, and they slept that night in steep, famous Kufstein, under its dark castle.* Gilbert loved the mediaeval imperial feeling of these places. Old emperors of the Holy Roman Empire had left their mark. All seemed still feudal, feudal on an imperial scale.

15 At the station they hunted for their boxes. Johanna extracted her necessities, there in the vast shed of the customs deposit. And then they gave up their goods once more to the railway. Amazing reliable days of speed and easy management. Everything happened so easily, and yet so well. Wonderful lost world!

20 They went over the bridge, and Gilbert walked across, past the blue post, to the blue letter box just inside the German frontier. And there he posted his letters. Then they took the train back to their breaking-off point.

They decided to stay at Eckershofen,* in the heart of the Tyrol.
25 It was a village at the head of a long, big valley. Arrived finally, they looked for a room, and found one in a farm-house at the end of the village, for about one-and-twopence a day. The house stood beside a rushing, deafening stream that roared beneath a bridge under the village street. At first Johanna and Gilbert heard nothing but the roar
30 of rock-torn waters. But soon they began to be unaware of the noise.

In Eckershofen they decided to camp and rest for a time. They could still live for about fifteen shillings a week each. In their bedroom they made coffee in the morning. Sometimes they picnicked out for the day meals, sometimes they cooked little roasts of veal, or beef, or kidneys,
35 over the spirit in the bedroom.

Gilbert was happy here. Three streams, and three valleys converged and met near the house. The great flat-sided slope came down from a great height across the valley, streaked with snow. The village with its low-roofed houses, seeming only just to have shaken the snow off itself
40 and taken to the sun, was pleasant, congenial. There was a strange,

mediaeval Catholicism everywhere. To see the peasants take off their
hats and sink their heads as they passed the shrines and crucifixes was
to be switched back into a dark, violent age. It was no lip-service, no
formula. Nor was it the fetish-worship of the south. It was an almost
Russian, dark mysticism, a worship of cruelty and pain and torture and   5
death: a dark death worship. And startlingly frequent in the gloomy
valleys and on the steep path-slopes were the Christs, old and young.
Some were ancient Christs, of grey-silvery aged wood. Some were new,
and terrible: life-sized, realistic, powerful young men, on the cross, in a
death agony: white and distorted.   10

For the first time in his life a certain ancient root-fear awoke in
Gilbert's heart, or even deeper, in his bowels, as he came across these
terrible crucifixes in the shadow and the roar of water by the roadside.
He knew then, he knew once more the ancient Roman terror of the
northern, tree-dark gods. He felt his breast bristle with the curious   15
primeval horror of the great Hercynian wood, of the tree-worship of
the Celts and the pristine, awful blond races. Here it lurked, as a sort of
Satanism, in these valleys.

The high-road ended at Eckershofen. Beyond, only mule-tracks.
And the muleteers with their strings of mules, fierce, bygone looking   20
men, hueing and slashing up the hills, would suddenly change as they
drew near a shrine or a crucifix. Suddenly a silence, a darkness, a
shadow came over them. They advanced insidiously, taking off their
hats to the great Christ. And then Gilbert's heart stood still. He knew it
was not Christ. It was an older, more fearful god, tree-terrible.   25

Even in the peasant greetings—*Servus*! or *Grüss-Gott**—he
seemed to hear something—something pre-Roman, northern, frightening: the bristling of wolves in the darkness of the north night, the
flash of the aurora borealis, the mystery of blond forgotten gods.
Overhead always the looming of great heights. And mankind creeping   30
furtive in the valleys, as if by some dread permission.

Once Gilbert and Johanna went into the common inn, at evening,
where zithers were twanging and men were dancing the Schuhplattler* in their heavy mountain shoes. There was a violent commo-
tion, a violent noise, and a sense of violent animal spirits. Gilbert, with   35
his fatal reserve, hung back from mingling. Besides he could not dance
the dance. But Johanna, watching with bright excited face, was invited
and accepted. In all the fume and dust she was carried into the dance
by a lusty villager with long moustaches and a little Tyrolese hat. How
powerful and muscular he was, the coarse male animal with his large,   40

curious blue eyes! He caught her beneath the breasts with his big hands
and threw her into the air, at the moment of dance crisis, and stamped his
great shod feet like a bull. And Johanna gave a cry of unconsciousness,
such as a woman gives in her crisis of embrace. And the peasant flashed
5   his big blue eyes on her, and caught her again.

Gilbert, watching, saw the flame of anticipation over the man. Johanna
was in a Bavarian peasant-dress, tight at the breasts, full-skirted, with a
rose silk apron. And the peasant desired her, with his powerful mountain
loins and broad shoulders. And Gilbert sympathised with him. But also
10 he was unhappy. He saw that legitimately Johanna was the bride of the
mountaineer that night. He saw also that she would never submit. She
would not have love without some sort of spiritual recognition. Given the
spiritual recognition, she was a queen, more a queen the more men loved
her. But the peasant's was the other kind of desire: the male desire for
15 possession of the female, not the spiritual man offering himself up
sexually. She would get no worship from the mountaineer: only lusty
mating and possession. And she would never capitulate her female castle
of pre-eminence. She would go down before no male. The male must go
down before her. "On your knees, oh man!" was her command in love.
20 Useless to command this all-muscular peasant. So she withdrew. She
said *Danke-schön*, and withdrew. And Gilbert saw the animal chagrin in
the other man. The lady had let him down. The lady would let him down
as long as time lasted. He would have to forfeit his male lustihood, she
would yield only to worship, not to the male overweening possession.
25 And he did not yet understand how to forfeit his hardy male lustihood.

Gilbert was in a bad mood. He knew that at the bottom Johanna *hated*
the peasant. How she would hate him if she were given into his
possession! And yet how excited she was. And he, Gilbert, must be the
instrument to satisfy her roused excitement. It by no means flattered or
30 pleased him. He sympathised with the peasant. Johanna was a fraud.

Sentimentally his mind reverted to Emmie. He had written her an
occasional letter, in answer to little letters from her. So now in the farm-
house by the rushing stream he remembered her again: and remembered
his sister Violet:* and wrote picture-postcards to both of them. And
35 out of the few words breathed a touch of yearning we're-so-fond-of-
one-another sentiment.

Johanna, a lynx without scruples, read everything he wrote. He rather
liked this trespass upon his privacy. For, not being at all sure about his
own emotions, it rather pleased him to see Johanna play skittles with
40 them.

Johanna read the two postcards, and her colour rose. She knew all about Emmie. Gilbert, a real son of his times, had told Johanna everything: particularly everything he should not have told her.

"You're writing again to that impossible little Emmie!" she cried.

"Why shouldn't I?" 5

"But I thought you'd finished with her."

"I can send her a postcard," he declared.

"I call it filthy, messing on with her."

"Not at all."

"Messing. Just messing.—Talking to *her* about mountains!— 10
Pah!—Oh well—" and she flung the cards aside. "Write your messy postcards if you want to. But it's an unclean carrying-on for a man in your position."

"Not at all. I do remember her."

"*Remember*! You and your remembering! Slopping to your sister, and 15
that impossible little Emmie! How manly you are!"

"And will be," said he.

"But you're not going to send her this card—you're not." And Johanna snatched it up and tore it in four pieces. "There!" And she threw the pieces down. She was a bit scared now. 20

He looked at her, and his face was dark. He looked at the torn card. And he said nothing. Amid his anger, he admired Johanna. Mistrusting his own emotions, and fearing his own sentiment, he was glad of a decided action on her part. Yet he was angry with her for her insolence.

However, he said nothing. But he gathered up the torn pieces, and 25
put on his hat to go and post the card to his sister Violet. His thoughts and emotions were bubbling. And the bottommost thought and emotion was *Damn Emmie*! He stood on the bridge and pulled off the Austrian stamp. Then he threw the torn bits into the stream. And he never wrote to the damsel again. But he posted his card to Violet. 30

The valley began to depress him. The great slopes shelving upwards, far overhead: the sudden dark, hairy ravines in which he was trapped: all made him feel he was caught, shut in down below there. He felt tiny, like a dwarf among the great thighs and ravines of the mountains. There is a Baudelaire poem which tells of Nature, like a vast woman 35
lying spread, and man, a tiny insect, creeping between her knees and under her thighs, fascinated.* Gilbert felt a powerful revulsion against the great slopes and particularly against the tree-dark, hairy ravines in which he was caught.

Bilberries were ripe, and cranberries. Sometimes he and Johanna 40 would lunch in a dark wood, and blacken their mouths with bilberries. Sometimes they would eat in a sunny place, where cranberries like tiny apples, like coral, in clusters shone rosy. There were many butterflies in these open sunny places.

5   Came letters again from Everard—and a tiny note from one of the boys, the elder. Johanna cried and looked queer. The little scrap of a note from her son upset her far more than all the ravings of her husband. But she backed away—she fought off her realisation.

To Gilbert, Everard was much more real than the children. He read
10 the other man's letters: "I have been mad, but for my children's sake I try to keep my sanity. But when I look at the future before me, it is all I can do to prevent myself from beating out my brains against the wall—I cannot stay here in Boston, where everything is leaking out. The looks of sympathy are too much for me, and the knowledge that they all
15 condemn you and look on you as a fallen woman, a pariah in society, makes me lose my reason. Think, woman, think what you have done. Think of the lives you have wrecked. Think of the simple pride and happiness of my aged parents, who loved you, who are loving you even now, in their ignorance—you will send my old father to the grave,
20 killed by his son's dishonor, and you will poison the innocent belief of my faithful mother. You have darkened forever the lives of your children, and branded their foreheads with their mother's shame. As for me, I do not live any longer, except as a broken, meaningless automaton, which works for the sake of my children, whom I must save
25 out of the inferno of their mother's infamy, though every act I make is a new death to me————"

"Ah me—!" sighed Johanna as she read. It was very upsetting. But after all, there are so many other things than the things people choose to write or think. Johanna knew well enough that at the bottom Everard
30 was infinitely relieved—that he raved the harder in order not to know his own relief. The almost diabolical connubial tension that had existed between him and Johanna was breaking him far more inevitably than this shock of her departure would break him. This shock was like an operation which removes the fatal malady: critical, but a salvation in the
35 end.

Gilbert however had not been through the marriage school, so he took Everard almost at face value. He imagined a dark-eyed, aristocratic-looking, handsome man with grey temples and greying moustache tortured under the stars, away there in Boston, tortured with tortures
40 more than man can bear. And the crucifixes hanging over the Alpine

paths, over the little, wistful summer flowers: the strange, deathly, veined pallor of the Grass of Parnassus flowers, in dark, marshy places; the intense gloom of the ravines, with rushing water; and the strange dark eyes of some of the lean peasant men who came over the slopes with their oxen filled our young hero with an almost preternatural apprehension.   5

Once at twilight he was watching again a dead Christ on a Cross: a dead, naked man dropping forward realistically on the nails, above the darkening highway. And at that moment a bullock-wagon was heard slowly descending from above. Gilbert turned and watched in silence. 10
Slowly, strangely the foreheads of the cattle swayed nearer, with the soft, static step of oxen placing their feet. And when they were abreast the driver, crouched between the shafts, looked up at Gilbert. And from the dark eyes, from the aloof, handsome face seemed to come such a strange look, that Gilbert winced and turned instinctively away, 15
to the dead, dropping burden of the Christ.

It was a dark look, torture, and hate: so it seemed to our friend. A dark look from a passionate face—from the face of a man dying on the cross of passion—tortured to death—having chosen the death—yet at the last moment black with hate and accusation. It is no joke being 20
crucified on the cross of sex-passion and love. And at the last moment—at the last moment breaks out the black hate against the death-dealers, against the death itself.

The bullock-wagon clattered on. Johanna had drifted down the road. At Gilbert's feet the mountain pansies still pricked their little 25
ears, in the underlight. Above, the Christ dropped slack on his nails. And Gilbert remembered Everard's letter: "I gave you everything. I would have been cut to pieces for you."* And he shivered.

For the first time in his life, he knew what it was to be hated. He had seen clearly Everard's black, helpless eyes of hate, bottomless hate. 30
The dark mountains seemed to reverberate with it.

"*So* he hates me," thought Gilbert to himself.

And he shrank from the knowledge—it was a piece of pure knowledge, and it seemed to project his soul naked out of his body, among the darkening hills.   35

To be hated—fathomlessly hated. He knew it among the terrible, black-gulfed mountains.

And he tried to shrink away: to shrink far away. "I would have been cut to pieces for you." The words made him sick. Fancy wanting to be cut to pieces for somebody—nay, by somebody one loves! How 40 fearful—how foul! "I gave you everything, body and soul." Perhaps it was not true. But in so far as it was true, why this horrible sexual self-sacrifice in marriage? Surely it was obscene.

Supposing Pontius Pilate had come at the last hour to Calvary, and said "No more of this unclean business!" Suppose he had ordered Jesus to be taken down, restored, healed, and sent home to live. Would the world have been worse? Would it?

The position was, in a degree, Everard's. His marriage was an awful torture to him. Yet he wanted to die of it. And now Johanna had left him, so that he must live. The terrible sexual-passional crucifixion was interrupted—and the crucified husband taken down, told to live.

And on Master Gilbert devolved the responsibility for the interruption. He knew it. And at the bottom of his soul he believed that Everard should be grateful. Should be. Perhaps even was—or would be in the end. Grateful that another man had taken this wife away from him—this Gethsemane cup. Gilbert would have to swallow the same cup: but with a different stomach, surely.

At the bottom of his soul he firmly believed that Everard should be grateful to him. But the bottom of one's soul is rather a remote region. And for the present he had to realise the blind, black hate that was surging against him. To be hated—to be blackly, blindly, fathomlessly hated!

He shrank, and there came on his face the wistful, wondering look of an animal shot in mid-flight—a look which Johanna detested. She had been sufficiently cursed by the wounded-animal look. She preferred the light of battle. But as yet Gilbert was down and wincing.*

Chapter XXI.

Over the Gemserjoch.

Arrived a friend—a botanising youth of twenty-one, a Londoner whom Gilbert had known in England and again in Munich. He was called Terry*—an ardent youth of Fabian parents, who had been given a rare good time all his life, and who expected the jolly game to continue. He was of that ephemeral school of young people who were to be quite quite natural, impulsive and charming, in touch with the most advanced literature. He wore a homespun jacket and flannel trousers and an old hat and a rag of a tie, and was a nice, quaint youth, ten times more sophisticated than our pair of finches, but quite amiable, sophisticated. He swam in a fierce river, he clambered over mountains, he collected flowers and pressed them in a blotting-paper book, and he talked mysteriously and sententiously, in a hushed, cultured voice, and was never offensive.

He was a great camper-out. If they had been in the wilds of Australia it could not have been more thorough. Down they clambered to black depths between the cliffs—they got on to a bushy island in mid-stream—they roasted pieces of veal on sticks before a fire, far away down there in the gloom. Then Terry flung himself into a water-fall pool.

At night—he had a room in the same farm-house—they improvised ballets. The Russian Ballet with Anna Pavlova and Nijinsky had just come to London.* Neither Gilbert nor Johanna knew it. But Terry drilled them. He was a brawny fellow. He stripped himself naked save for a pair of drawers and a great scarlet turban and sat in a corner intensely playing knuckle-stones.* Gilbert, feeling rather a fool, sat on the bed in Johanna's dressing-gown, turned the scarlet side outwards, and with a great orange and lemon scarf round his head, and being Holofernes. Johanna, handsomely rigged in shawls, was to be Judith charming the captain.*

So Terry, as a slave, squatted in his corner and buried himself in his knuckle-stone business. Gilbert and Johanna were deeply impressed. Johanna began to swim forward like a houri or a Wagner heroine, to Gilbert, who was perched cross-legged, in the scarlet-silk wadded

dressing-gown, upon the large bed. But Gilbert looked so uneasy and
Johanna herself felt such a fool she fell to laughing, and laughed till her
shawl arrangements fell away. Then the slave in the corner grew really
angry, and it was all a fiasco. But both of them wondered at Terry: he
5 was really angry.

Next day arrived a second young man,* an American, acquaintance of Johanna. He came from Odessa, where he had been vowing
eternal love to a Russian girl whom he had known as a political refugee
in London. This young man's name was Stanley. He was handsome
10 and American-aristocratic, with large dark eyes and attractive lean face
and American dégagé elegance. He was twenty-two years old. There
was something very American about his slender silk ankles and doe-
skin shoes. But he had been educated in England and spoke English
without trace.

15 Of course he was dead with fatigue after the journey. He made those
dark, arch, American eyes at Johanna, rather yearning you know, and in
a whimsical fashion told all about his love affair: all about it, don't you
know: rather humorously. And he wasn't sure now whether his heart's
compass hadn't shifted a few points. No—oh no—he was less bowled
20 of a heap than he thought he would be.

Oh dear, that Russian life—what *would* his own dear mother say to
it! What would his mother say when she knew he was with the errant
Mrs Everard. Oh dear oh dear, he was always tipping a little fat in his
dear mother's steady if neurotic American fire. But there you
25 are—men shouldn't have mothers.

Stanley, however, had a mother. Gentle reader—which reminds me,
I've not spoken to you for at least twenty pages, gentle reader. I hope
you're not sulking, and on the brink of closing this friendly book for
ever. Gentle reader, we're going from bad to worse. Never say you
30 weren't warned. Stanley had a nervous, cultured, dear mother away in
America.

> —The roses round the door
> Make me love mother more
> But when they're in the bud
35 > She scarcely stirs my blood—

Even that bit of poetry I stole.

Stanley was always talking about his mother. But though he was
quite a well-bred young man, even I daren't transcribe his language
faithfully.

"Oh, my mother!" he moaned. "She *is* a bitch."

"But you love her," said Johanna.

"Me! Love her! Not at any price. I'm her only son. She knows what I think of her."

"I'm sure she does," said Johanna. "She knows you can't do without her."

"Me do without her? Her and her nerves. Why if it's a south wind she hates me and if it's an east wind she prays for me. Oh dear oh Lor! And nobody loves me."

"Ah, you! Too many people love you," said Johanna.

"None! None!"

"What about Katinka?"

"She's a little bitch. What's the good of *her* loving me? Besides, she doesn't really.—Nobody loves me! Nobody loves me!" And he ran out and leapt on to the parapet of the bridge, and ran there riskily and funnily, like a boy, or like a dog. His black hair was brushed straight back, he had a beautiful profile, pale, with an arched nose and a well-shaped brow. His delicate ankles in their purple socks showed as he ran backwards and forwards there in the air, to the amazement of the villagers. He was looking for the postman. His letters having been forwarded to Terry's care, he was nervously wanting some communication, something to come and reassure him.

The postman came and brought him one letter. He read it unheeding and rushed again into the house.

"Nobody loves me! Nobody's ever going to love me," he wailed.*

Terry understood and was amused. Gilbert looked on in wonder. He did not know the spoiled, well-to-do sons of a Fabian sort of middle-class, whose parents had given them such a happy picknicky childhood and youth that manhood was simply in the way. Yet there was a charm, a wilful, spoilt charm about Stanley. He had a shrewd petulant humour, and was no fool. An engineer by training, he went into the little electric works by the stream, and examined the machinery and the dynamos. How quiet his touch was then. And what a still concentration there was in his interest. But the moment he had seen everything, and was through with it, he broke into his wails about being loved.

He liked to walk with Johanna and be half mothered by her, completely admired by her. He could be so charming in his winsome fretfulness. And, like a queer mother's child, he understood so much of a woman's feelings, particularly of her nerves. He discussed Everard

and the children with much length and earnestness, in private with
Johanna. And she unbosomed herself to him as she never could to
Gilbert. About Gilbert there was something resistant, just resistant.
But Stanley could be a pure sympathetic, nerve-corresponding crea-
5   ture. She thought any woman might love him. And besides, she knew
he was rather brilliant as an engineer. Terry said so. And she had
seen his quiet, potent touch on the machinery.

Like Gilbert, he was very sensitive to the crucifixes with which the
valleys abounded. Either at the foot or at the head of the cross were
10 usually the sacred initials, INRI,* on a scroll.

"Inry!" said Stanley. "*Another* Inry! Have they none of them got any
homes to go to and any mothers? Lor lummy, Hinry! Woman, what
have I to do with thee?" He strayed on inconsequently, singing:

"Henery the eighth I am I am
15   Henery the eighth I am."*

"We have a friend," said Johanna, "a Baron Potowski. And he was
an only son, and his mother adored him. But when he was a student
he was very wild. So one day his mother came to Bonn to see him,
and she met him in the street, and he was very drunk. 'Ach Heinrich!
20 Heinrich!'—'Weib, ich kenne dich nicht!' he said to her solemnly,
and he marched on. Poor Frau von Potowski. It nearly broke her
heart."

"Weib, ich kenne dich nicht!" repeated Stanley with joy. "Woman,
I know thee not. I'll cable it to my mother if she doesn't send me
25 something tomorrow."

"But it isn't that in the English bible,"* said Johanna.

"Woman, what have I to do with thee?—But I like Weib, ich kenne
dich nicht. I shall cable that to my mother."

"You won't be so horrid to her," said Johanna.

30 "Isn't she horrid to *me*? Doesn't she pray for me, and have another
bout of nerves? Doesn't she make the house smell of valerian? Isn't
she a bitch? Has she written to me since I'm back from Odessa?
Weib, ich kenne dich nicht."

"Jawohl!"* said Johanna.

35 Stanley's mother was to come to London, and he was to meet her
there.

"Oh my poor father, won't he be glad to be rid of her for a bit. But
fancy a woman who swallows valerian! He bears with her, he bears

with her. I tell her, she's like a sick persian cat. Oh my poor father! And
he's stood it for nearly thirty years. Of course she'll never die."

"No, you're too bad. You don't want her to die."

"I do! I do! I'm going to tell her I'm pining for her death."

"She'll only laugh."

"No she won't. She'll swallow valerian, like a bewitched cat, and
threaten to pray for me. Let her if she dares! I've promised her, if she
prays for me again what'll happen to her.—Hello Inry! You're there
again, are you? My compliments to Maria. Lord what a lot of Inrys she
brought forth at a shot.

> 'Ennery the eighth I am.
> I got married to the woman next door
> She'd been married seven times before
> And every time 'twas an Ennery,
> She never had a Willie nor a Sam;
> I'm the eighth old man called Ennery,
> Ennery the Eighth I am.'"

"Aren't you wicked!" said Johanna.

"Me? I'm mother's little pet lamb. I'm Ennery the eighty-eighth I am
I am. And you're an adulteress you are. You're a Scarlet Letter.*
So don't you go saying nothing to me, so there."

"I'm glad I'm a red letter. Most folks are dead letters," said Johanna.

"*Poste restantes*, like my mother. She's a blooming belated *poste
restante*. She's a *fermo in posta* she is."

"And you love her."

"Lor' golly, I don't and never did. I hate and abominate her for a
bitch. I'm *always* telling her. But it doesn't seem to do her much good."

The party decided to move on.* Johanna and Gilbert had been a
fortnight in one place. Time to go. So they packed up once more and
put their goods on the railway. Then, four together, they prepared to
set off into the mountains, to cross the Gemserjoch and descend to the
Imperial Road again well below the Brenner, on the southern slope.

At the last moment arrived a postcard from Stanley's mother. She
was in London—"and have had so many headaches since I am here
that I have had several *nuits blanches*—"

"Lor-lummy!"* cried Stanley, "hark at her! Writes a post-card
to say she's had several *nuits blanches*. Oh, why has nobody ever
smacked it out of her. *Nuits blanches*! My poor father. He married her
for her beauty, and wasn't he taken in! Got a *nuit blanche* instead—a

damn blanched bad egg. Golly, I can't stand that woman any longer.
Here, take her post-card."

And he tore it in bits and flung it into the stream, which now had a
second set of fragments to carry towards the Danube.

5   So they set off, Stanley fuming about *nuits blanches*—his mother's
white nights of sleeplessness—Terry murmuring esoterically about the
marvels of eurythmics*—Johanna shocked and a little bewildered,
but withal charmed by the graceless son, and Gilbert silently wondering. Of course there were all kinds of worlds besides his own.
10 Meanwhile the stream ran hastily on below, in the opposite direction.

They took the high-road inwards, into the knot of the valley. The
high-road ended, they followed the bridle-path in the ravine. Here, in
the gloom, stood one of the largest crucifixes.

"Goodbye Inry," said Stanley to the figure. "See you later, old boy.
15 Best wishes to Maria."

"I do wish you wouldn't," said Johanna. "It really makes me
unhappy."

"There y'are, Inry!" said Stanley, turning round to the figure.
"Here's another of 'em. Another nuit-blancher. Another Blanche
20 newter. Lor-lummy, Blanche neuter. We've struck it Inry. Shake hands
on it, old sport. So long. See you later, as the hymn says.

> 'We're marching to Zion
> Beautiful beautiful Zion——'"*

They crossed the covered bridge, which always appealed to Gilbert's
25 fancy, and proceeded along the other side of the ravine. From time to
time Terry, whose knapsack was enormous because of his blotting-
paper book and press-covers, went scrambling up or scrambling down
the ravine, for a yellow violet or a bit of butterwort or some other
flower. Sometimes they met a couple of pack mules, sometimes a
30 priest. Servus! Servus! came the greeting. On straggled the four. Each
one had a rucksack. It was a fine day, so Johanna's was bulky with her
burberry. She had her old panama hat.

At noon they made a fire, grilled bits of meat and made scrambled
eggs. Terry had a famous receipt for scrambled eggs, so he took off his
35 coat and rolled up his sleeves and altogether was as portentous as an
alchemist concocting the elixir of life. Stanley did nothing, but
complained and wailed whimsically. They went on to the next village
where they bought food—then on till dusk, which found them in a

high, shallow open valley, grassy, rather forlorn, high up under heaven. They had been climbing all the time. Behind them, about three miles back, was the village where they had bought food—the last village till they came once more to the world's roads, over the southern slope. In front, nothing they could be sure of. But in the meadow, a block-house for hay—another hay-hut.

So they all voted for it. It was of two storeys, with a platform round the upper storey. Up they climbed, and Terry, who always had the scientific and alchemistic theories, decided where it would be safe to cook the food, so as not to burn the place down.

Dusk had well fallen. It was cold—very cold. Part of a moon was low in the sky, and a smell of snow. There were no high peaks near—only upper, roundish rock-slopes on which lay slashes of snow. In the darkening twilight they crouched over the spirit lamps on the platform of the hay-hut, trying to keep off the cold draughts from the flame. No living creatures were in sight—nor cows nor human habitation. Only the slopes beyond, the shallow, shorn meadow near, the rocky bridle-path and a little stream between rocks and marshy places.

Terry in triumph, always more like an occult alchemist than a mere cook, mysteriously brought off the ham and eggs. They ate rapidly and rather silently, inside the hay-loft in the almost-darkness. Stanley complained because he lost his slice of sausage. Then mysteriously they packed up and prepared for sleep. Terry of course gave a brief exhibition of how to sleep in a hay-hut, in deep hay. One made a hole as deep as possible, and etc. etc. etc. and finally one was buried completely under three feet of hay.

"You don't need any breathing hole," said Terry in answer to Gilbert's expostulation. "The atmosphere travels quite freely through hay, and the small amount of retardation is only just enough to ensure warmth."

This being so, Johanna and Gilbert prepared a large matrimonial burrow for the two of them, whilst at brief distances the two men burrowed in separate holes. It was quite dark. The faintness of the moon was gone again under clouds, there was wind hissing. But heaven be praised, this hay-house was solider than that other, warmer. Gilbert, staring through his hay, could not make out the cracks in the door—it was so dark altogether.

Johanna drew him into an embrace. The other men were so near—yet it was so dark. She seemed so fierce. And he let himself go, buried there in darkness and in hay. Buried—fiercely active, but buried. Buried alive. He felt as the creatures must do, which live in lairs deep under the earth, and know their passions there. Deep under hay and darkness.

The night passed fairly well. It was warm, and therefore the irritation of hay was not intolerable. Yet by the first greyings of dawn all were up, and Terry had discovered how to make the tea safely inside the hut, among the hay near the door. It was cold and rather blowy outside. And they did not want some farmer to come and abuse them before they had had their tea and were ready to go. So they moved rather stealthily.

The dawn came grey outside. It had snowed in the night—heavy snow—but not quite down to their level. The road and the grass-alp were still free. But on the slope just above—it seemed only a few yards above—there was snow, and great snow-slopes of deep, new white snow just beyond them. Strange it was to see it, when the August morning began to be blue and the sunlight clear. It was a lovely morning after all. When they came to a stream—their own was but a trickle—they washed and were refreshed. But not *inwardly* warmed. So they were glad when they came to a single wooden house which provided refreshments for mountain excursionists. There they could have hot coffee and milk, plenty, and fried eggs and ham. It was good—especially the hot, rich milk: so restoring.

Other excursionists came, footing the same way.

The four went on, Gilbert and Terry usually botanising together, Johanna and Stanley talking. The sun came suddenly quite fierce, quite fiercely hot. There were little fir-trees, little woods of fir, and many cranberries, many clusters of scarlet and coral cranberries in tufts everywhere, on the rocks overhead and the rocks beneath, as they climbed the winding mule-path upwards. They ate cranberries all the afternoon, after having had a jolly lunch near another small hut for travellers, which sold some food and sweet fruit syrups.

It was about five o'clock when they came at last to the top of the climb—into a shallow last valley, where stood a house of brown wood, the accommodation for travellers* this side the pass. Other walkers, mountaineers, excursionists, four or five, were here for the night. Our pedestrians got their rooms, had coffee and cake, and went out to look at the world, as the night fell.

It was a wonderful place—the last upland cradle where the summer grass grew. At the end, about a mile off, was a vast precipice, like a wall, and beyond that a cluster of mountain peaks, in heaven alone, snow and sky-rock. That was the end.

But nearer, on the flanks, were the last fir-trees, rather wispy and cold-shrivelled, growing in patches. Between these, and around them, the rock avalanches, like terrific arrested floods of rock and stones. Then smoothish rocky-grassy slopes. While in the valley bed itself, great rocks cropped out naked, there was the inevitable hay-house like another rock all alone, there were strange marshes with vegetation, that curious cold-bitten, cold-shrunk vegetation.

Gilbert went botanising with Terry up one of the rock rivers round the corner of the trees. And what looked like a slope of stones, when they clambered up amongst it was a jagged mass of great broken rocks that had wedged and ceased to slip. It was rather terrifying, as the silent, icy twilight drew on, to be jumping one's way across these jagged massive avalanches. Even the fir-trees and some of the green growth that Terry was exploring grew out of the hollows between the blocks of avalanche rock. And the tiny stream-bed was so deep and difficult in the side of the great slope, once one was in it.

Gilbert was really rather frightened. There was something terrific about this upper world. Things which looked small and near were rather far, and when one reached them, they were big, great masses where one expected stones, jagged valley where one saw just a hollow groove. He had climbed alone rather high—and he suddenly realised how tiny he was—no bigger than a fly. Such terrible, such raw, such stupendous masses of the rock-element heaved and confused. Such terrible order in it all. He looked at the inaccessible, dread-holy peaks of snow and black rock beyond the precipice—and the vast slopes opposite, the vast slope on which he was overwhelmed, the fir-trees just below like a hairy fringe. It all looked of a comfortable human size. And now that he was scrambling between fierce rocks which had looked to him like stones, now he felt all the suspended mass of unutterably fierce rocks round him, he knew it was not human, not life-size. It was all bigger than life-size, much bigger, and fearful.

He clambered and jumped down again, hastening to get back. He wanted to get back, back to the level of the cranberries and the grass, back to the path, to the house. He had lost Terry, and was alone.

It did not take him very long to get down. He seemed to be climbing down out of the light into a trough of substantial shadow. He threaded his way through the marshy place, where some hay was still hung out like washing to dry, upon the cross-sticks. As he got near the house he heard the tong-tong of the cow-bells, and saw the cows being driven into their house. At the front door of the accommodation

house stood a mule whose packs were being unladen. Somebody was
playing a zither.

He went upstairs, but Johanna was not there. Stooping to look out of
the window, he saw the flush of evening on the peaks. Strange and icy
5   the heart became—without human emotion—up here: abstracted, in
the eternal loneliness. The eternal and everlasting loneliness. And the
beauty of it, and the richness of it. The everlasting isolation in
loneliness, while the sun comes and goes, and night falls and rises.
The heart in its magnificent isolation like a peak in heaven, forever.
10 The beauty, the beauty of fate, which decrees that in our supremacy we
are single and alone, like peaks that finish off in their perfect isolation
in the ether. The ultimate perfection of being quite alone.

It seemed to be getting dark. Yellow lamp-light streamed out below,
from the doorway. Where was Johanna? He went downstairs to look.
15 She was not in the one public-room—where was a bar and the tables at
which one ate. Terry was there with his almighty blotting-paper book.
Gilbert went to the door. There was Johanna sauntering up with
Stanley.

"Where have you been?" said Gilbert.

20   "We went a walk—that way—" and she pointed across the grass to
the left, through rocks, towards the hay-house in the darkening
distance. "Where did you go?"

"I climbed to get up."

"Isn't it wonderful!"

25   "Yes. Do you like it here, Stanley?" asked Gilbert.

"Marvellous!" said Stanley. "Marvellous."

"Can we eat soon?" asked Johanna.

"I don't know," said Gilbert.

Before long they were eating hot broth, and lumps of boiled
30 beef—and after that an omelette with jam—at one of the little tables in
the public-room that was just the bar-room of a public-house, quite
bare of ornament, but warmed by a big glazed stove. It was warm, and
they ate and were happy.

After supper Johanna walked for a few minutes with Gilbert, holding
35 his arm. Stars were in the sky, big, bright, splendid.

"It's so marvellous," she said, "it frightens me."

"So it does me."

They went soon indoors, and to bed. Somebody, somewhere at the
back, was playing a zither—and making love. The sound was unmis-
40 takeable. Everybody went to bed by nine o'clock. The upstairs was icy

cold: the bedrooms just bare cells, two single beds in the finches' room. Gilbert felt he had never got into such a thoroughly cold bed. Johanna cried to him to come and help her to get warm. But it was impossible to sleep two in one small bed. So after a while he hopped back. And once one was warm one was very warm under the huge down bolster, which seemed to rise like a balloon above the sleepers' noses.

The morning came clear and sunny. Our four were rather excited at the thought of crossing the Gemserjoch, over the ridge to the south slope. This side still was Germany, with the north behind it. The other side was the southern Tyrol, all Italy in front. Even geographically, one can pass so definite a turning-point.

There were various other pedestrians, tourists, setting off from the wooden rest-house to cross the pass. They had guides too. The guides said there was much snow: that the boots and shoes of the four were too thin. But if people walked over a pass quite easily in thick boots they could walk in thinner ones. Our four would not saddle themselves with a guide: they had no belief in any difficulties.

So, in the first sunshine, they set off, climbing gently the rocky, roundish slope. Flat iron peaks, slashed fierce with snow, stood away to the right. There was a thin but a very cold wind under a sharp sun.

It was a long, high-up, naked slope, not very steep. There were no more trees, the Alp-roses were tiny shrubs—then they left off. The road was almost pure rock, with pockets and patches of snow here and there. The first great pads of snow, silvery edged. And still the road wound, dipped into a scooped hollow, and inclined up again, naked among the great harsh rocks, over tracts of snow, over iron-bare rock surfaces, always aloft under a clear blue heaven. It was cold in the wind, hot in the sun. But they all felt light and excited. Every little crest ahead seemed the summit.

In a hollow of rock was a last little crucifix—the small wooden Christ all silvery-naked, a bit of old oak, under his hood. And neither Stanley nor Gilbert made any jokes. He was so old and rudimentary.

So they walked and climbed and crossed slanting slopes for two or three hours. The road was quite easy to follow—no difficulty of any sort. At length they came to a last strange and desolate hollow, a sort of pot with precipice walls on the right. Over the ridge they came, and down the long, slanting track between huge boulders and masses of rock, down into the shallow prison. How was one to get out? They scanned and scanned ahead: but only precipices, and impassable

rock-masses, and a thin water-fall. The water fell into the wide, shallow
summit-valley. How did it get out again. They could not see.

The sun fell into this shallow, rocky, desolate place as into a rugged
bowl. There was no snow, save in patches where there was shadow,
5 under some rocks and in some stony pits. Our four slanted still on, into
the prison. It seemed impossible there was a way out. A sort of summit
rock-trap.

And yet, when they got almost to the face of the precipice on the far
side, suddenly the path turned to the left, and there, almost like a
10 ladder sideways against the steep face went a slanting, stony ledge, and
the road up it. They climbed, and sweated, and were excited. This
must be the top.

They emerged between rocks and pools and hillocks of rock—and
then, it *was* the top. Smooth as plates of iron, a flat summit, with great
15 films of snow like silver plating on the black bronze-iron. And a wind, a
painful cold wind. And low in the near-distance a brown shelter-hut
with people there. And beyond the brow, a great peak, a magnificent
wedge of iron thrust into the upper air, and slashed with snow-slashes
as if it were dazzlingly alive, so brilliant and living the snow-stripes
20 on its aloof dark body. For Gilbert, it was one of the perfect things of all
his life, that peak, that single great sky-living blade of rock. He tramped
across the snow-slush, he tramped across the slanting, difficult slope of
deep snow, over the bare, iron and snow-bound flattish top. He felt the
awful wind, so slow yet so killing. He saw the people, guides and
25 tourists at the hut—he passed the house itself and smelled wood-
smoke. But he wanted only one thing—to come to the further,
southern brink of the summit, and look across, across clear space, at
that marvellous god-proud aloof pyramid of a peak, flashing its snow-
stripes like some snow-beast, and bluing the clear air beyond.

30 They came to the rounded curve of the down-slope. Beyond,
mountain tops. They went on, till they could see beneath the whole
slope—where vegetation began, and shrubs, and trees, and the dense
greenery.—It was a deep valley, narrow, and full of trees and verdure,
far away below sinking to a still visible high-road. And it was so sunny,
35 so sunny and warm.

So they sat in a shelter of rocks in the full sun, no wind, no wind at
all. It was about midday. Gilbert had to go to a brow to look clear at his
queen. She was beyond this valley—and beyond other valleys. Other,
blunter peaks rose about her. Yet she lifted her marvellous dark slopes
40 clear, a marvellous prism of substance in the ether, rayed with her snow

as with lightning-strokes. Beyond—and crystal—and almost mathematically pure.

And he was satisfied—one of the eternal satisfactions that man can find on his life-way. He felt a pure, immortal satisfaction—a perfected aloneness.

So he was glad to be back in the nook of sun, eating with the others. There was not much food either. They promised themselves a meal when they were down.

They began quickly to descend into the steep narrow valley. Far below, their track could be glimpsed, going down to the pale thread of a high-road that lay between black pine-trees in the profundity. And they counted their progress: there they entered the zone of scrubby vegetation—there the first hairy little trees—there was alp-meadow—there were oak-trees, far down.

It was already another world. Sun and profusion already. One must change one's heart as one crosses that rock-plated, snow-sloped flat top.

Down and down, down a rocky, curving path. How tiring it is, descending. How quick one is—and yet the desired zones of the meadow alp and the oak-trees, how far still. They passed the fir-scrubs. They wound across the grassy dip, over a stream. There were alpine roses in flower still—as there had been on the other side, coming up. They went between rocks and big fir-trees. There were yellow rock-roses in flower, and comfrey. They came to the oaks. And the road broadened now into a proper bridle-path. In the warm shadow they descended. But tired—almost too tired to notice.

In the middle afternoon they emerged, over the last bank, over a stream, and on to the white wide high-road. Ah, how different it seemed. They were hot. There seemed a heat, a relaxation already in the air. And a darkness. It seemed very dark down there in the valley, in the deep cleft between the pine-trees.

So they found the inn, and drank beer and ate good food, and discussed the next day. Stanley and Terry, the moment they were down on the high-road, feeling themselves beyond the Brenner, wanted to get back. They wanted to get back at once to Munich, where their goods were. They asked how far the nearest station was—twelve miles. Quite easy to do it that evening. And they looked up trains. They could catch the express from Italy. It stopped at Sterzing at ten o'clock at night.

So on the road again. There were some beautiful tufts of flowers in

the shade by the stream, in that deep valley: cranesbill, and dark gentian, and yellow flowers. They went into a shrine. It was all hung with *ex voto* arms and legs and bits of people, in wax. And in the back sat a ghastly life-size Christ, streaked livid with blood, and with an awful,
5 dying, almost murderous-looking face. He was so powerful too—and like a man in the flush of life who realises he has just been murdered.*

"There's Inry selling joints," said Stanley sardonically. But Gilbert was startled, shocked, and he could not forget. Why? Why this awful
10 thing in a fine, big new shrine? Why this.

They walked on—and Johanna complained she was tired. They lingered hap-hazard in a saw-mill by the road: watching the saw-threads eat across the sweet wood, the saw-dust fall like meal: watching the great long planks move slowly: watching the oil-sticky cog-wheels
15 slowly turn, and the great centre beam turn from the outer wheel: watching the water in the black sluice drop on the creaking wheel: and hearing all the noises, smelling the sweet scents and the dank scents: watching the men, who were quite friendly. They seemed happy, the men in the saw-mill. They had dark eyes, and looked well. They
20 smiled.

But yet, there was something in reserve—something at the back of their eyes. Gilbert tried to connect it with the ghastly Christ on the road behind. But it was too difficult, and he was tired.

They crossed the log bridge over the stream. It was falling dusk.
25 They were still in the narrow valley. Johanna complained bitterly of being tired. But Gilbert had one of his nervous fevers. He felt they must reach Pfitzen that night. They must reach Pfitzen. And Johanna would not hurry. She would not walk on.

"We *must* get to Pfitzen, and it's getting dark. Why do you stand
30 there staring at the water. You *must* come on."

"I won't come on. Why should I? I won't come on. Don't bully."

"We *must* get to Pfitzen," persisted he.

"Leave me alone. Go yourself to Pfitzen. Leave me alone."

She loitered, she lingered, and he chafed like a mad-man at the bit.
35 Stanley said nothing, but meandered rather stupidly at the side of the road. It was Terry who took up the cudgels.

"Why should Johanna hurry if she's tired? Why should she go to Pfitzen tonight if she doesn't want to? She's not going to Pfitzen tonight."
40 "No, I don't want to," she said.

Gilbert was silent. The moment Terry turned on him, he realised that there was absolutely no need to get to Pfitzen. He realised that his fever, his frenzy was something unnatural. He realised that Johanna might actually be too tired. So he was silent, and wondered at himself. Yet he was angry at Terry's interference. And from straining, urging, tugging at Johanna he became suddenly released, separate.

At nightfall they came to an inn by the road-side: quite a large inn, but no sign of any village. It was quite alone in the still narrow valley. And Gilbert felt afraid. A distinct sense of fear possessed him.

Yet the landlord, a burly, handsome man was pleasant, even attractive. He lighted the lamp that hung from the ceiling, and promised food. He gave Johanna and Gilbert an enormous bedroom on the ground floor—a vast dark place, quite comfortable and nice: and the two young men a room above.

So the four tired ones sat round a little table in the public bar-room. No one came to the inn. They saw only the burly, genial host. And they waited and waited, and studied the map that hung on the wall. It seemed very dark outside.

There were still seven miles to the nearest station. The two youths seemed determined to leave that night.* Johanna begged them to stay just one day—one day together at Sterzing. Gilbert also begged them. But no. They must go. They must go. There was a fast train stopped at Sterzing at a quarter to five in the morning. They would rise at three, and walk on. It was decided.

So the four friends sat round the table in the public-house, and talked it all out. Terry and Stanley were quite determined: they would rise at three and make good speed to the station: and by tomorrow afternoon they would be in Munich—Johanna and Gilbert would sleep on—and then take their vague way southwards. It was all settled.

Dinner came, good soup and boiled meat and cabbage. The two young men settled with the host: he gave them an alarm clock. The four friends made plans for meeting again. Under the hanging lamp in the inn-bar they talked of the future.

"It's been so lovely knowing you both," said Johanna. "I feel it can't come to an end."

"We won't let it," said Gilbert. "I believe one should keep one's friendships forever: even put a bit of eternal feeling into them."

"There is that feeling in me," murmured Terry rather impressively.

"Oh yes. I'm game," said Stanley.

And so—they would all go to bed.

"Goodbye!" said Johanna to Stanley. "You'll come and see us wherever we are, won't you?"

"I will," said Stanley.

"Goodbye Terry. I am so glad of you in the world," she said to the other.

"Not as glad as I am of you," murmured Terry, and he kissed her fingers.

"Goodbye," said Gilbert to Stanley. "You will come and see us."

"Yes thanks—I should like it awfully."

"Goodbye Terry—remember me to your mother and father. Tell them what a good time we've had. I shall see you all again—and we'll have a longer holiday together another time, shall we?"

"Yes. We will. Goodbye Noon. Remember I love you," and Terry looked at Gilbert protectively. Gilbert laughed—it seemed so comic.

So, in the inn passage, they parted, and Johanna and Gilbert went with their candle into their vast bedroom, to sleep.

Chapter XXII.

A Setback.

When Gilbert and Johanna woke it was a lovely sunny morning.

"Have they gone, I wonder," said Gilbert.

"Yes," said Johanna. "I heard them."

"Did you? Did you hear them go out?"

"Yes. I heard the alarum, and I heard them go past our door: ever so quietly."

"Isn't it queer to be without them!" said he.

"Quite.—Yes, it's awfully queer. I miss them, don't you? I like them awfully. Do you? Do you like Stanley?" asked Johanna.

"I like him even better than Terry. He's more real."

"Yes, that's what I feel. I think he's amazingly attractive. Now why doesn't a young man like that *do* something with his life—something that matters—I'm sure he could," said she.

"Oh yes," he answered. "I believe he could too—if he ever got started."

"Of course!" she cried. "What he wants is a woman behind him. What good are his silly little Katinkas to him? And really, his mother must be awful for him."

"Yes," said Gilbert.

It was true, he missed the two young men, particularly Stanley. He missed him almost acutely—missed the sort of heightening of life that the American youth had brought, the thrill, the excitation. It was as if Stanley's presence sent little thrills through the air, as electricity thrills through water. And this acted as a stimulant, almost like a drug on the nerves of the pair of finches. And now it was taken away, they felt an emptiness, a wanting.

But the morning was lovely. They had coffee in the little arbour of the small garden of the inn, just across the road from the house itself. Roses were blooming on the lattice, and deep purple and crimson convolvulus, like wine-stains. Lovely to sit in the sun in the stillness. They both felt tired. The excitement gone, their energy seemed to collapse.

So they walked rather slowly, rather with difficulty, to the old town of

271

Sterzing, where they arrived in the afternoon. The old, picturesque street, the handsome old tower,* the mediaeval houses made Gilbert think again of the emperors of the Middle Ages. Sterzing is on the old imperial road. And in the sunshine, with people going lazily, and women sitting in the street under their green umbrellas selling black grapes and white grapes, and pears and peaches, and the old pointed houses rearing above the narrow, sunny flagged street, and the great tower rearing up to look, like some burly but competent feudal baron, and the shadows falling so dark and the sun so very bright— why, it all had that unspeakable charm of the real old Germany, before science came, and the horrible German theorising. The lovely old Germany that roamed along, so individualistic and vigorous under its lords, but so careless, so deep with life force. Alas and alas for Prussian officialdom—horrible scientific rectitude.

Gilbert felt rather in an alas-and-alas mood. His spirits had all gone flat. And Johanna complained of being tired—she was tired, she wanted to rest. They bought grapes in the street, and looked for a house. They soon found one: an old house in the High Street, with a thin, peeping old woman. Yes, she had a room: it cost two and six a day. Yes, they could have it for a day or two.

So they installed themselves, and Johanna lay on the bed, and he sat and looked out of the window. Then he walked again in the town, to buy food. There was such a charm about the High Street itself—the meandering, magical charm of the Middle Ages, when the world was still full of unknown potencies and undiscovered worlds and undefined deities. But alas—Gilbert looked at it all through the greenish glass of spirits gone flat and meagre.—Also here was the first ripening touch of the south—Italy, the warring Italy of Popes and Emperors. He felt how glamorous, how blood-rich it had been.—But alas, walk towards the station you saw the new, thin-spirited scientific world: the big new tenement buildings, the gasometers, the factory. You felt the North German with his inhuman cold-blooded theorising and mechanising.

They stayed their few days in Sterzing: never very happy. Johanna was disinclined to move—and Gilbert went mad if he had to sit long in the bedroom. It was clean and pleasant. But the sense of the dark, unknown house all around him, with its lurking inmates of whom he saw nothing, its unrevealing silence and its truly mediaeval gloom, its passages, its formlessness, all this he could not bear. At least he could not bear to be shut up in it.

Most typical was the privy: one could not call it a W.C. This was a

little cupboard on the same floor as the bedrooms, right in the centre of
the house. It had absolutely no communication with the air outside, and
at midday was completely dark, so that one must take a candle. It was
very like those stair-cupboards on the landing under the stairs of the
upper floor, where the dirty linen basket stands: so dark, so shut in. But   5
it was not under any stairs. Heaven knows how it was let in between the
bedroom walls. But there it was. It had no water—nothing: but
consisted simply of a long shaft which descended into unknown and
unknowable depths. And most peculiar was the smell. It was not so
ordinarily offensive. It was rather such an acute ammonia as to make   10
one catch the breath—like breathing smelling-salts. Gilbert always felt
that it really might explode if one went in with a light: and how go in
without a light.

This privy was typical of the Tyrol, in so far as it consisted of a long
dark pit-shaft from the upper floor down to unknown depths. But its   15
absolute buried darkness in the core of the house was a more city-like,
and perhaps mediaeval feature. Anyhow our friends never forgot it.

Do not grumble, gentle reader, at this description. Don't talk to me
about bad taste. You will only reveal your own. Strange are the ways of
men. And since these are the ways we have to follow, why make any   20
pretence.

As much as possible Gilbert and Johanna went out into the country.
It was queer, rather formless country, among mountains that seemed
suddenly to have become low. And there were one or two factor-
ies—and great new macadamised roads—and further out, a big   25
sanatorium among woods and among giant rhododendron bushes.
Sterzing too seemed to lie in a wide, shallow round pot. Far off, one
could see pine-forests on the up-slope, and white roads, far off, trailing
upwards and into the unknown.

After a few days they set off again with their knapsacks on their   30
backs. They were recovering, and instead of half-faint reelings of spirit,
backward towards Munich and Stanley and England, they set their
breasts forward towards the unknown.

Gilbert did not want to follow the modern road to Bozen. Neither
did he want to take the great high-road to Meran. He made out a path   35
up a long valley, and decided that in one long day's walk they could do
the twenty-five miles to the rest-house on top of the Neering
pass.* Then from the summit of the pass down to Meran.

It was Sunday, and the bells were ringing for Mass in the fresh
morning when they set out. They took a path across the water-   40

meadows, past a strange old ruined church—then the high-road by the river, on till they came to a Sunday-morning village. The women were at the water-fountain with their brass pails, the men were in their black Sunday clothes. Men were out with guns and dogs.

5   Then they left the high-road and took the bridle-path. It climbed under trees from one side to the other of the valley. By midday they found themselves fairly high up. Shy, wildish, wondering mountain peasants went along the road, queer thin men. High up on the opposite mountain flank, beyond the trees, they could see a little village

10   clustered like stones, with broad roofs on which large stones rested. So they continued, always following the same stream, apparently, through the afternoon. The air became wilder, the mountain hamlets more desolate: just little bunches of houses set down among manure heaps and grassy springs and stones, without any semblance of street, any

15   unity. And the peasants up here—always tall, thin, somewhat bird-like, inhuman creatures, stared hard at our two travellers, and gave no greeting. Johanna felt rather frightened. Nobody wore Sunday clothes. It was like a week-day, save for a certain Sabbath emptiness of feeling—work being half-gripped.

20   By five o'clock they had passed the last hamlet, and seemed to be nearing the end of the valley. The stream had petered out into thin channels among marsh and stones. The path had become almost indistinct. The valley had widened into a desolate sort of bay. In the bed of this bay went the path, between huge rolled-down rocks, and

25   over the stream again and again, and beside the last marsh. There a youth and a ragged girl were driving home two cows: the tong-tong of the melancholy cow-bells. Away in front could be seen the cliffs and inaccessible slopes that closed in the valley. Shadows seemed to be gathering. Johanna was frightened.

30   She asked the youth if this was the path up to the Neering hut. With great difficulty she got an answer. Which way did the path go up?—At last he waved his hand vaguely to the right. How far was the hut from the top of the path?—Perhaps an hour.

"An hour from the top!" cried Johanna. "I am dead already."

35   "Probably it isn't," said Gilbert. "The map gives it about a quarter of a mile."

They went on—the youth and the cows clambered up the slope towards the last hamlet: five forlorn, squalid houses which Gilbert and Johanna had seen above them perched on a little table, half an hour

40   ago.

So they plunged on and on, across the desolate, end-of-the-world valley-head, towards the cliffs and the shutting-in slopes. It was evening, and the air was thin and cold, making the heart beat. The track, instead of swerving to the right, swerved to the left, and over a water-fall. There was the hoarse noise of water among vast, loose stones, in the pale, colourless evening. Gilbert pressed forward, Johanna began to lose her nerve.

"I shall never get up there," she said, eyeing the rock-slopes. "How do we get out?"

"The path will take us."

The path veered to the right, and began to climb with a vengeance. It was as Johanna had said—this was no mule-track. One had to clamber in foot-holes up rocks like the side of a house. And Johanna kept repeating:

"I shall never get up here. I tell you I'm too tired. I can't do it. I can't do it."

Gilbert took her knapsack and clambered up the next piece.

"Come. You must come," he said, standing there and looking at her.

"I can't."

"Very well then, I shall just go on without you."

For as a matter of fact it was not at all dangerous or even difficult. Only, with the high thin air, and the fatigue, it was terribly strenuous, the heart beat wildly, and the cold made them feel faint. Gilbert stood half-way up the slope—they had perhaps climbed the most jagged piece. The path looked plainer above.

But the moonless night was really falling. It was already dusk. And the world was desert, a cold desert of rock. He looked back, from the cliff-face on which he stood, over the stony bay of the valley-head just beneath, on towards the dim bush-scrub, into the dark valley mouth. Not a sound save water. Not a sign of life. Nothing, but the bareness of rock masses, and a sort of savage world away below. Above, the slope going up like a great bastion, a sky-line dark against a darkening sky, with the first stars.

"I can't come. Oh I can't come any further. I can't come any further!" she cried like a child below, bursting into tears.

"You can come perfectly easily. Good God, what a mardy baby. I'm going now without you."

And he turned to clamber still up.

"Wait! Wait for me!" she wailed. And up she came, regaining her composure as she did so.

As she drew nearer, he moved on ahead.

"Wait for me. Wait for me!" she cried imperiously. "Wait! I want to tell you something."

He stood on the stony-rocky little path on the slope-face, with the black mass of the valley-head curving round, and the gulf of the darkening valley away below. Already stars were out. But he thought he could see on the sky-line the depression where the path would emerge, over a sort of rock-studded shoulder. So he waited for her, wondering what would be over the top.

"Listen," she said. "I want to tell you something. I want to tell you."

"What?" said he.

"I want to tell you. Stanley had me the night before last."*

Everything went vague around them.

"Where?"

"The evening when we slept at the Gemserjoch hut."

The vagueness deepened. Night, loneliness, danger, all merged.

"But when?"

"When we went for a walk—and you went with Terry. He had me in the hay-hut—he told me he wanted me so badly—."

He looked at her as she stood a little below him in the dusk of that Sunday evening, there in the coldness on the face of the valley-head. She was vague in the darkening twilight. And it was such a surprise to him, that he did not know what to feel, or if he felt anything at all. It was such a complete and unexpected statement that it had not really any meaning for him. He turned vaguely and went clambering up the path, while she followed in silence behind. And so they climbed for some time.

Suddenly he turned to her—she was close behind him. He dropped her knapsack and threw his arms around her.

"Never mind, my love," he said. "Never mind. Never mind. We do things we don't know we're doing."

And he kissed her and clung to her passionately in a sudden passion of self-annihilation. His soul opened, and he gave himself up. He rose above the new thrust on wings of death. He kissed her and kissed her, and kept on saying:

"We do things we don't know we are doing. And they don't signify. They don't signify really, do they? They don't really mean anything, do they? I love you—and so what does it matter!"

"No, it doesn't matter," said Johanna a little testily. She was quite mute and unresponsive under his kisses, and quite unyielding under his embrace as he clasped her to his bosom.

Johanna did not at all care for the conclusion "that it did not matter." Those marvellous pearls of spiritual love. "I love you—and so what does it matter!" fell on completely stony ground. She felt rather caught-out by his passionate spiritual forgiveness: put in a false position than ever. So she took up her own knapsack, and they resumed their scramble up the hill-face. It really was not very far now. In about ten minutes they wound their way out on to the shoulder, between wild rocks. It was quite dark, save for the stars. And perfectly silent and summit-stern. And very cold, extremely cold.

But he could still make out the path. So he pushed on, and in a few minutes, to his great relief, saw a yellow light shining in the darkness ahead.

"There—that's it," he said.

And his chief anxiety fell away from him.

"Thank God," said Johanna.

It was nearly nine o'clock when they reached the wooden rest-house. They ate and went to bed in the ice-cold bedroom. And there he loved her with a wild self-abandon. But she kept something hard against him in the middle of her heart. She could not forgive him for his forgiveness of her. After all, forgiveness is a humiliating thing to the one forgiven. And she did not choose such humiliation. Moreover she did not like his convulsion of selflessness by means of which he soared above a fact which she faced him with: thereby leaving her still saddled with the self-same burdening fact. He seemed to have put her more in the wrong, and assumed a further innocent glory himself. She could not sleep, because her brain was hard.

He however slept the sleep of the innocent and the exalted. He woke rather late, feeling still exalted. It was another sunny morning. He thought of Johanna's piece of news, but still did not have any clear feelings about it. He did not attempt to realise it imaginatively. On the contrary, he left it as a mere statement, without real emotional force. And he liked Stanley—he had liked him all along: so why pretend to hate him now? And he believed people must do what they want to do. And he knew that Johanna believed in much love, à la Magdalen. "For she hath loved much." And he himself, Gilbert, he could stand aside for a moment.

"Didn't you *know*? Didn't you suspect anything?" said Johanna, rather gloomy.

"No," he answered, with his strange clear face of innocence. "No—never. It wouldn't have occurred to me."

And half she felt enmeshed, even a little fascinated by his clear, strange, beautiful look of innocent exaltation. And half she hated him for it. It seemed so false and unmanly. Hateful unmanly unsubstantial look of beauty!

5   "Well," she said. "It wasn't much, anyhow. It meant nothing to me. I believe he was impotent."

Gilbert looked at her. This brought him to earth a little. And for the first time he felt a pang of hate and contempt for Stanley.

"It meant nothing to me," she said gloomily.

10   He did not answer. The words fell into the deep geysers of his soul, leaving it apparently untroubled. But in the end the irritable waters would boil up over this same business.

They decided to take the high-road to Meran. There it ran, the looping white mountain high-road, in a loop past the hut. It was the
15   Meran road. Gilbert looked back over the path they had come last night. It was a sort of moor-track between low heath and great standing boulders. It came from over the brow of nowhere.

So they took the high-road in the opposite direction. It looped and looped across the broad slope of the pass-head. And in one place there
20   was a little, wind-withered crucifix.* And one leg of the grey old wood had broken at the knee, and hung swinging in the wind from its nail. Funny the Christ looked, like a one-legged soldier: but pitiful, forlorn, the ancient, snow-harried little crucifix, all falling to bits, standing back among moor-like heath from the road.

25   As the day went on, as they wound and wound round the long, many loops of the road, seeing the sun-dim country away below, with its valley and other hills, a certain heaviness, darkness came over Gilbert. As a heaviness and an inert darkness follows most exaltations. He felt he could not see the world. His soul was rather dreary and hard. And
30   he wished he could get back his own real, genuine self.

So they tramped on the whole day. He watched for newnesses in the landscape. The one pleasure still was the new world ahead. He liked the southern plumage of the trees, the feeling of sun and luxuriance.

But about four in the afternoon he suddenly stopped. They had
35   come to a river side—and in front was a forge where a cart was standing. The river was pale-green and full.

"Why!" he said, and his heart fell bang down into his boots. She looked at him.

"Haven't we come back to Sterzing?"* he said.

40   "No! How can we! How can we!"

But they had. They walked along the road—and they were made certain. They reached the woods, and the place where yesterday's bridle-path branched off. They had come back to Sterzing.

In the overclouded evening, grey and dismal, they trudged back the long familiar mile-and-a-half into the familiar town. It was really a bitter blow—really a bitter blow. With shame and ignominy Gilbert crept along the High Street, and past their lodging-house. He had a horror lest the landlady should see them.

"Well," said Johanna. "We'd better go back to our old room."

"I couldn't stop in Sterzing," he said, with that peculiar pallid finality there was no answering.

"What will you do then?"

"Take the train to Bozen."

So they passed through the town and along the embankment to the station. There was a train at half-past six. He bought second class tickets, because they were both so tired. And soon they sat in the warm, brilliant, beautifully-appointed train—it was the Rome express, running swiftly and smoothly south.

But Gilbert's soul was full of bitterness. Not the news of Johanna, but the taking the wrong road, the finding himself back on his own traces was bitter to him. He felt, somehow, foiled, cast back, thrown down again. He would never walk from the Neering pass to Meran—he would never see Meran—there was some part of his life lost to him. There was some part of his life lost to him. There was some part of his life lost to him. He felt it with hateful fatality. Because he had taken the wrong road. He had made a mistake. He hated now, with deep, acid hatred, to think of the scene on the path of the pass-head: Johanna's confession and his passionate getting over it. He hated to think of it. His soul was all gone acid and hard.

Johanna was hungry, and insisted on having dinner on the train. So they sat amid smart people, who eyed them in their shabbiness. And they ate their swaying soup on the luxurious train. And Gilbert paid, and begrudged the money, and begrudged the tip he had to leave for the superior waiter.

For the joint stock of money was getting low—it was getting seriously low. And here was another thing that tightened his nerves and irritated his spirit. They had hardly any money—and yet they were spinning south in a luxurious dining car—whither—and why, God alone knew.

Bozen* was quite dark. They found themselves walking under

huge high walls—railway embankment walls, or something like that. But enormous, stupendous walls in the darkness, under which they crept.

They came into the streets. Question of finding a room. This, in a 5 town, was always a great bugbear to both of them. Each hated asking: simply hated it. And yet they *had* to look for a room in a house. If they went to hotels, their money would fizzle into nothing.

This night Gilbert had one of his paralysed stupid fits. He would not, could not ask. Behold then Johanna going into a sort of public-house, 10 and asking the old harridan. Four shillings.—"But that is too much," said Johanna.

"Go and find something cheaper," yelled the old harridan, while the drinking men laughed.

Nice recollections of Bozen.

15 However, after three shots they found a room—more or less all right—for three shillings. How much better and cleaner, besides infinitely cheaper, rooms were before the war!

Chapter XXIII.

They arrived in Trento*—by train—to find all at once that no one understood them. It was really the southern slope now. From the train they had watched the grapes hanging so black under the leaves, and women and men among the vines looking up. Vintage had begun. The world had changed.

One felt it immediately. The station at Trento was still Austrian—there one was still on Germanic ground. But the moment one was outside, in the piazza with its gaudy flowers, and in the streets of the town, one knew one had passed the mysterious dividing line. It was a sunny afternoon. But the streets had that dark, furtive air, as if everybody were watching like suspicious animals from the depths of cavernous houses. The shops indeed were open: but seemed to be abandoned, neglected. That secret, forlorn, suspicious atmosphere that pervades all southern towns the moment one leaves the main street was very evident in Trento. Gilbert and Johanna both felt it for the first time. And Gilbert was thrilled, and Johanna all at once felt homeless, like a waif.

They had not much money, and they wanted to eat, having had no midday meal. So they entered a small, simple-looking café, and asked for eggs and milk. The man looked at them with a negative look and answered:

"Non parliamo tedesco."

Johanna repeated her question in German.

"Non si capisce. Non facciamo mangiare."*

The man shook his head, and stood there blank, neuter, negative: a hostile cypher in the atmosphere.

Neither Gilbert nor Johanna understood one single word of Italian. The waiter made not the faintest attempt to understand or to cope with them. He just presented a dead negation of anything they might be or request. Which so bewildered them that they sat at a little table.

"Che cosa desidera?" said the neutral native, in a way that would put you off desiring anything.

Johanna tried French, and asked for milk. Was there milk? And since

281

no Italian could be considered anything but a perfect Frenchman as far
as the sister language is concerned, the native replied:
"Oui, il y est du lait."*
Whereupon Johanna ordered two glasses of milk—which came.
5 Then she proceeded to eggs—there were no eggs:—bread—there was
no bread. The waiter brought two biscuits each. So the pair of finches
sat in perfect bewilderment and ate this most unsatisfactory lunch.
"What do they mean by it?" cried Johanna. "It's an Austrian town."
"They don't want to understand," said Gilbert, who remembered the
10 black, big-nosed French inn-keeper at the village outside Detsch.
"But how monstrous!" cried Johanna. "One must eat."
They set out to try again: a rather superior café this time, with a clean
German fresh-air look about it. Here there must be something. In they
went.
15 The first waiter, a boy, mumbled something in Italian: the marble-
topped tables looked arid: was the scene going to repeat itself. But no: a
clean little man in a white jacket, and what did they want? To eat. He
was sorry, but there was nothing to eat. Not even eggs and bread? He
was sorry, but they didn't have eggs, and the morning bread was
20 finished, and the afternoon bread had not come yet.—Could one then
get nothing to eat in this holy town of Trento?—Yes, one must go to
the large restaurant there—there—he pointed to the corner. Danke
schön! and Bitte!*—and they departed again.
"Anyhow he was nice," said Johanna.
25 "Oh yes!" said Gilbert.
Strange and silent and empty the town seemed in the sunny
afternoon—a new, strange, dead-seeming atmosphere. Rather
panic-stricken at having to go to the huge-looking restaurant—which
for sure would cost huge sums—and yet of necessity driven to
30 eat,—they entered the place. Innumerable void tables—everybody had
eaten long ago. But a grubby waiter in a grubby evening suit that
bagged greenly wherever it could bag. A German–Austrian, however.
Quite plain sailing.
And at last the food came—rather cold. Johanna ate eagerly, and
35 they drank beer with relish.
"So this is Trento!" said she. "I'd heard of it—but I never thought I
should find it like this."
"No—" he said. "I rather like it."
"Ye-es—" she said, very doubtfully.
40 To tell the truth, the warm, half-desolate, half-furtive indifference of

the first southern town he had ever known appealed to him. The indefinable slackness, the sense that nobody is on the spot, and nobody cares, and life trails on, nobody ever taking it in hand, was rather fascinating to him. He could feel the curious half-listless indifference of the south—and through it all something pagan, only half moral, not alert. To Johanna it was a new experience: but she recoiled.

It was three o'clock by the time they had eaten. They went out and rather aimlessly trailed the streets of the town. There seemed to be absolutely nothing to look at—except a few shops. A few quite good, modern shops—and the rest the repelling-looking Italian frowstiness. The only thing they bought was a German–Italian dictionary: one of those little red objects. They sat among the trees and shrubs of the public gardens to study this awhile. Then they set off once more to look round.

"We'll see if we can find a furnished apartment—either today or tomorrow," he said.

"We will," replied Johanna, with a sinking heart.

They climbed up the narrow, steep streets, upwards, till they could emerge and look out. This was what Gilbert wanted. And when they emerged, they were more or less above the town, which lay on the side of a hill like an amphitheatre—or a section of an amphitheatre. Beyond was the country—rather like a low, stony, dreary amphitheatre. It was autumnal, buff-coloured, and looked dry, with that curious ancient dryness of bygone civilisations.

"The Romans! Doesn't one feel the Romans!" said Gilbert, spellbound.

"One does!" said Johanna, grimly. To her fresh, northern, forest-leaved soul it was indescribably hideous, the dry vineyards on their terraced hills, the low, bare, treeless slopes.

"We'll look for rooms in the morning," he said.

She did not answer for a moment.

"Where are we going to sleep tonight?" she said.

It was the old problem. So they went down and wandered the terribly unpromising streets of Trento. There was nothing they dare tackle—not even the large hotel with innumerable pale-blue, elegant, plump, femalish Austrian officers. So they went back to the restaurant—and could they have a room.* Yes, certainly.

They followed the green-mossed waiter through endless passages and stairs, of an evidently huge house. And they came to a large, very lofty bedroom with two beds and monumental furniture which looked as if it had stood there and never been looked at for centuries, and wall-paper with nasty smears on it, and a rather sticky tiled floor. Very well—that would do—repugnant though it was.

They went to the station where they had deposited their knapsacks, 5 and felt relieved that there was a place where they might sit alone. Night came—and they hung in the windows, looking into the street far below. There were innumerable soldiers: German–Austrians, friendly, lively, and noisy in an alien land. They all seemed to appear towards nightfall. In the day they must have been out marching or 10 exercising.

The barracks* was across the road, a little further down the street. Johanna and Gilbert watched the soldiers at the windows. They shouted and sang. And somebody on a cornet played *yip-i-addy!* * with terrible éclat. Strange the American noise sounded, ripping out 15 like bright brass on the darkness of this far-off, world-lost, meaningless barren town. Then at nine o'clock came the imperious bugle-call to turn in. The whole town seemed to ring with military bugles.

In the morning Gilbert and Johanna woke at five, to another bugle-call. They lay and dozed uneasily, aware of the great noise of soldiers. 20 Then more bugles, and more noise of soldiers. And the sun coming up warm. They got up and looked out at the soldiers.

It was decided that after breakfast they would go out and look for an apartment: look for an apartment in Trento! First, however, look for the privy. Gilbert was sent to scout. He found a large, high 25 apartment—a long room. It had a stone floor, that was most unsavourily wet—and along the wall ran a low stone trough, about a foot high. Whoever liked used this trough—who didn't, used the floor. Do not, gentle reader, attempt to imagine this privy. Gilbert reported it to Johanna as impossible. And as he took a handkerchief out of his 30 knapsack he saw a bug slowly walking up the wall of their bedroom. So they put their knapsacks on their backs, went downstairs and paid the bill: not very dear.

The first thing was to deposit their knapsacks at the station once more. For sanitary arrangements the station was just a horror. Then 35 into the town to look for rooms. They had learnt two words of Italian for the purpose: *camera*, a room, and *affitare*, to let. And so they hunted up the chaos of streets jammed dark and unsavoury on the hill side. They saw a notice—and they climbed a dark stair. But evidently lots of people lived up this stair, in the ancient warren of a narrow house.

40 Gilbert, as usual, flatly refused to commit himself to the act of

asking. Johanna took her courage, and knocked at one of the old doors: and knocked again. From the inner darkness appeared a yellow, evil old crone.

"Er—er—camera—affitare—affitarsi—" stammered poor Johanna.

The old crone mumbled something vindictive and completely unintelligible, and shut the door in Johanna's face with a clap. Our pair of finches slunk down that vile stair. They had not imagined they could feel so diminished. Still they persisted for some time in the jumbled, gutter-like streets. And then they descended into the more wholesome town, into the open.

They sat in the Piazza di Dante and surveyed the new statue* of that uncongenial poet, and the trees and plots of grass. And Johanna in her old panama that was hopelessly and forever streaked with dye that had run out of the cherry ribbon; in a burberry that sagged at the sides like a tramp-woman's; and in a weary battered frock of dark cotton voile; poor Johanna sat on a seat in the Piazza di Dante, in that ghastly town of Trento, and sobbed bitterly.*

"There's nothing to cry for!" said Gilbert. "You needn't cry. There's no harm done. We'll go somewhere else."

But to his bewilderment, she just sat and sobbed. He thought she would ride cheerfully over everything, and was quite bewildered and infinitely troubled to see her sobbing and saying nothing there on the bench in the Piazza di Dante, in the sunshine, where women and soldiers and officers were passing between the grass-plots, and two workmen, gardeners, were busy near some shrubs.

"Let us go to the station and look," he said. "Don't cry. It's no use crying. Why do you cry? There's nothing to cry for. It's all right. Everything is all right."

But sanitary arrangements and one thing and another had unnerved her. However, at length she blew her nose and wiped her eyes and accompanied him rather disconsolately to the station—to look.

Looking, they saw a poster showing the Lake of Garda, with Riva, at the head of the lake, described as a glowing autumn resort.

"Shall we go to Riva?" said Gilbert.

"Yes!" said Johanna, once more joyfully. "There will be a lake, and lovely water. I think it's so horrible and waterless here. It will be lovely, lovely, lovely! I *adored* Lake Maggiore.* I know I shall *love* it."

When was there a train? There was a train then due: and a crowd of peasants, thick, solid, round the ticket office. Gilbert got the knapsacks from the deposit, and entered the fringe of the crowd. The crowd of

peasants—all men—pressed tighter, more madly on the ticket office. Many were workmen going down the line—who the others were, heaven knows. The bell rang—the train was coming—and still that mad wedge of angry peasants and laborers at the ticket office. More
5 bells rang—somebody shouted that the train was in sight. Somebody went into the ticket office. A clerk appeared in the doorway, and beckoned Gilbert in. Like a lord, Gilbert followed into the privacy of the ticket office. The train thundered in meanwhile. Our hero asked for two third-class to Riva. The great train stood hissing in the station,
10 Johanna stood frenzied by the footboard. Then up dashed Gilbert, with his tickets and his change and his knapsack, and they climbed into their carriage. And the great train rolled on*—towards Verona, which was not far off.

Ah, it seemed so pleasant in that airy third-class carriage, with the
15 yellow wooden seats and the open space all down. The sun was shining brightly outside, from a blue sky. Innumerable clusters of black grapes—miles and miles—dangled under leaves of the vines, and men in broad straw hats, and women with their heads bound in coloured kerchiefs looked up at the train. The other passengers were poor
20 people—pleasant, simple, and excited at being in the express train. Ah it was all so nice, so pleasant! The two knapsacks sat on the rack, next to the big, blue-check peasant bundles. What an escape from hell into a sort of sweet, sunny, roaming heaven.

They changed from the big train before reaching the frontier, and
25 got into a side train. Strange the scenery was. There were vineyards—and then patches of tall maize, very tall, and sere yellow—and then groves of mulberry trees—and then water, and tall high reeds, like bamboo, tall canes leaning in dishevel—and odd pink villages, all sunny—and odd clusters of cypress trees—and then craggy
30 rocks and juniper slopes—and then dark rocks and a water-fall—and a few bunches of dark orange trees.

It all seemed so luxuriant, almost tropical—and all so sun-tissued. The leaves, the earth, the plant-stems, all seemed rather like heat-fabrications: whereas in England and Germany all nature is built of
35 water, transfigured water. But no—here already Gilbert saw, as by an inspiration, the magic of tigerish heat-substance, sharp leaves and blades built of heat, and black, black, impenetrably dark grapes, and pale grapes like drops of slow, stealthy light dripping. He loved it, and they were both inordinately happy. He imagined rice-fields on a flat
40 piece of plain.

So Riva:* and there the lake-head glittering in the sun. They left their knapsacks at the station and set off along the white, hot, dusty road to the little town, which was near. Carriages were rolling along, containing, like flowers in a flower-bowl, an inevitable plump sky-blue officer with a rose-red sash and white cap, and a lady* with an 5 enormous enormous hat with feathers, and a decolleté bosom with necklaces. Under the trees of the avenue other little officers were strolling alert, all beautiful and sky-blue, with sashes and glitter, all plump, and with very tight military trousers of thin fine cloth, making the virility of the plump, brisk captains almost unnecessarily conspicuous. 10

Poor Johanna—forced to keep on that hideous dark green burberry with its drooping sides, because her dress beneath was not much better than a tatter: forced to wear that drooping, drip-stained, weather-battered panama: and accompanied perforce by Gilbert, whose travel-worn trousers had frayed at the heel, and whose hat was all that 15 remained of it. Poor Johanna! Those were the days of huge huge hats and satin walking-out dresses. It was a hot September afternoon—officers were strolling or more often driving out with these gorgeous ladies. And poor Johanna trailed round the length of the avenue from the station, to the quay of the lake, and into the town for food. In a thick, heavy dark 20 burberry all fallen out of shape, and a panama hat likewise.

Gilbert was fortunately oblivious of her distress. To him Riva was lovely. In the first place, near the quay of the lake rose the wide ancient tower with its great blue clock-face that showed the hours up to twenty-four. There was the rippling, living lake, with its darkish, black-blue 25 pellucid water, so alive. And there were boats with vivid yellow sails,* and red-and-orange sails, and boats with two white sails crossed like sharp white wings. And there was a friendliness, a glitter, an easiness that was delightful beyond words, southern in its easiness, and northern in its alert charm. 30

Ah charming plump officers of the Austrian army, whoever found fault with you, with your uniforms of exquisite fine blue cloth, fitting like a skin, and your virility so amiably in evidence, and your peacocking so inoffensive and good-humoured. What a genial, cosy, elegant holiday-feeling you created, you and your cocottes!—So different from those 35 Prussian wasps of Detsch.

If Johanna had not been extinguished in that burberry she would have been blissfully happy. Gilbert *was* blissfully happy. They ate in a lovely inn-garden, and it did not seem expensive.

When Gilbert had paid for the dinner he had left one English 40 sovereign and a few Austrian Heller. Just a little over a pound, in all the world.

"We can always pawn my watch or your rings," he said, "if nothing comes."

5 "Of course we can," she said easily.

"But something will come."

Remained, however, the eternal problem: to find a room in which they could live, and where they could make their own meals. They set out on the vague search, wandering on a wide road out of the little
10 town. And fortune led them, as fortune always led them when they were happy. They came, after five minutes, to a nice-looking square villa behind a high garden-wall. The villa had blue decorations inserted over the windows. It was called Villa Florian. And it said, in French, Apartment to Let.

15 Would it be too expensive! Heaven save it would not. In trepidation they rang. Johanna was thinking of their appearance—with horror! and he was thinking, with fear, of the scornful people turning them away because the price was too much for them.

A gentle little Italian old maid, so fluttered that she spoke only
20 Italian. And she would bring her sister. An inevitable old-maid sister who has importantly to be "fetched." The important sister of the two. But a lady, and still gentle, with Venetian delicate breeding. And yes—there was a room: such a sunny room with three windows: and when Johanna asked, trembling, how much, it was only three and
25 sixpence a day. Johanna looked at Gilbert.

"Alors—" the conversation had lapsed from the little lady's excruciated German.

"Combien?"* said Gilbert—oh vile word.

And with joy they stayed. And Johanna explained to the two little
30 elderly sisters—the Miss Florians. And they were grave and delightful, and treated Johanna like the baroness she had been brought up as, so she was mollified and happy.

When the little ladies had left them, they looked round their room with perfect joy. So clean, so fresh, so airy and sweet, so nórthern in all
35 this. And then a lovely medallion of flowers on the ceiling just over the beds. This was the real Italy. To be sure, the political border was about five miles off, down the lake. Nevertheless, they had reached the land of painted ceilings, and they hailed it with joy, little knowing the horrors that would accumulate overhead, thicker and thicker, as they went
40 further south. This painted ceiling was nothing but charming. It had

only a band and lines of delicate colour round the edges, and this medallion of flowers, a pink rose and blue plumbago flowers and white jasmine packed together, just over Gilbert's bed. He lay and looked at it and felt very happy indeed, that first sunny morning.

Outside in the garden were fig-trees and vines and dark, shady trees. 5 And before Johanna was dressed, the maid had tapped, and would they care for figs. And there was a beautiful plate of golden figs, those little, soft, deep-yellow figs that burst and have a pellucid gold twilight inside. All nicely piled on vine-leaves. A gift from the little ladies. What could be more charming, to our doubtful and impoverished finches. 10

They were really happy in Riva: rather guilty feeling in the bedroom when they made their own tea and boiled their own egg for breakfast. For surely the little ladies might expect to send in coffee and milk. But no—oh precious economy. The fugitives could make tea and buy their own food for a mere trifle. And when you haven't more than twenty- 15 five shillings in the world! Gilbert had written to England.

Carefully they cleared up their crumbs and tidied the bedroom. And the little ladies didn't mind in the least, though Gilbert always felt sure they did.

Johanna's one grief was that she had no clothes. The luggage had 20 been left at Bozen, and would take a couple of days. However, she got her frock ironed, and she bought a new ribbon for that hat, and some of the fringe was clipped from Gilbert's frayed trouser-bottoms. Moreover everybody treated them with respect, everybody was char- ming in Riva. Perhaps it was because they were happy, but at any rate 25 things seemed to go well.

They loved the place: the old clock-tower, the massive dark waters of the lake, the gorgeous sails that were bright as flowers, the hot September sun, and the profusion of fruit. Black grapes, white grapes, muscatel grapes, black figs, yellow figs, pears, apples, 30 pomegranates—an overwhelming abundance of fruit everywhere, for twopence or threepence a pound. Gilbert and Johanna would buy lunch, and go into the old grove of olives above the shore, and there they would boil their eggs and make their tea and eat their fruit, and sit in the hot September afternoon watching the lake glitter, and feeling the 35 mellowness of the world, the rich, ripe beauty of this Italian, sub-Alpine world, its remoteness and its big indifference. Why have problems!

And for some time there was no problem: except that poor Johanna, suddenly, had a touch of autumn colic. And she who had a passion for figs, and adored muscatel grapes, must see all Pomona's profusion 40

around her yet not dare to taste. Gilbert selfishly bought his basketfuls,
and ate them alone. Judge that this was a grief to Madame Johanna. It
was her only real grief in Riva.

In Riva too something seemed to come loose in Gilbert's soul, quite
5   suddenly. Quite suddenly, in the night one night he touched Johanna as
she lay asleep with her back to him, touching him, and something broke
alive in his soul that had been dead before. A sudden shock of new
experience. Ach sweetness, the intolerable sensual sweetness, the
silken, fruitlike sweetness of her loins that touched him, as she lay with
10 her back to him—his soul broke like a dry rock that breaks and gushes
into life.* Ach richness—unspeakable and untellable richness.
Ach bliss—deep, sensual, silken bliss! It was as if the old sky cracked,
curled, and peeled away, leaving a great new sky, a great new pellucid
empyrean that had never been breathed before. Exquisite deep possibi-
15 lities of life, magnificent life which had not been life before. Loveliness
which made his arms live with delight, and made his knees seem to
blossom with unfolded delight. Now all his life he had been accustomed to know his arms and knees as mere limbs and joints for use.
Now suddenly like bare branches that burst into blossom they seemed
20 to be quivering with flowers of exquisite appreciation, exquisite,
exquisite appreciation of her. He had never known that one could enjoy
the most exquisite appreciation of the warm, silken woman, not in one's
mind or breast, but deep in one's limbs and loins.

Behold a new Gilbert. Once the old skies have shrivelled, useless to
25 try and retain their ancient, withered significance. Useless to try and
have the old values. They have gone.

So it is with man, gentle reader. There are worlds within worlds
within worlds of unknown life and joy inside him. But every time, it
needs a sort of cataclysm to get out of the old world into the new. It
30 needs a very painful shedding of an old skin. It needs a fight with the
matrix of the old era, a bitter struggle to the death with the old, warm,
well-known mother of our days. Fight the old, enclosing mother of our
days—fight her to the death—and defeat her—and then we shall burst
out into a new heaven and a new earth, delicious. But it won't come out
35 of lovey-doveyness. It will come out of the sheer, pure, consummated
fight, where the soul fights blindly for air, for life, a new space. The
matrix of the old mother-days and mother-idea is hell beyond hell at
last: that which nourished us and our race becomes the intolerable dry
prison of our death. Which is the history of man.
40 And once it has become an intolerable prison, it is no use presuming

what is outside. We don't know what is outside—we can never know
till we get out. We have therefore got to fight and fight and fight
ourselves sick, to get out. Hence the Germans really made a right
move, when they made the war.* Death to the old enshrouding
body politic, the old womb-idea of our era! 5

Master Gilbert could never have known what lay outside his rather
dry, restless life-mode. From his Emmies and so on he could never
have deduced it. If he had married some *really* nice woman: for of
course, gentle reader, we have decided long ago that none of my
heroines are *really* nice women; then he would never have broken out of 10
the dry integument that enclosed him. He would have withered with
the really nice woman inside the enclosure. For the act of birth, dear
reader, really is not and cannot be a really nice business. It is a bloody
and horrid and gruesome affair. And that is what we must face.

Whatever Master Gilbert had set himself to postulate, as the new 15
world he was seeking, he would never have been able to hit upon this
new, profound bliss in a dawning sensual soul. He would not have
conceived, as you cannot conceive, gentle reader, that a man should
possibly have a sensual *soul*. A *sensual soul*! Are not the two words just
contradictory? 20

Ah no, gentle reader, once your ideal sky has withered and shown
you a much vaster universe, a much wider world, a wonderful,
unbreathed firmament. When that has happened you will realise that
the ideal sky of our day is a horrible low ceiling under which we stifle to
death. To you it is the sky, the infinite, the all-beautiful, the *ne plus* 25
ultra. To Master Gilbert, after his sudden seeing-forth, it was a painted
ceiling of the most detestable stifling plaster-and-distemper stuff. To
be sure the painted ceiling of the old ideal doesn't fall all in one smash.
It first gives a little crack, yielding to pressure. And through that little
crack one has one's first glimpse, as Gilbert had his first sudden 30
newness of experience and life-comprehension in Riva. Afterwards one
loses the crack, and sits just as tight under the painted ceiling. Even one
chants the praise of the ideal, the infinite, the spiritual. But one will
come to the crack again, and madly fight to get a further glimpse, madly
and frenziedly struggle with the dear old infinite. And thus rip just a 35
little wider gap in it, just a little wider: after tearing oneself consider-
ably.

Do not imagine, ungentle reader, that by just chasing women you
will ever get anywhere. Gilbert might have had a thousand Emmies,
and even a thousand really nice women, and yet never have cracked the 40

womb. It needed the incalculable fight such as he fought, unconscious
and willy-nilly, with his German Johanna: and such as I fight with you,
oh gentle but rather cowardly and imbecile reader: for such, really, I
find you.

5   For the time, in Riva, he was not only happy but he was a new
creature in a new world. And at such times, as usual, nice things
happened. The first was that one morning, again before they were up, a
knock and the maid with a large hat-box* for the Signora:
addressed to Frau Johanna Noon, from Vienna. Johanna was nowadays
10 Mrs Noon by name if not by nature.

"My sister Lotte!" cried Johanna in excitement, leaping out of bed to
undo the hat-box.

Behold then—an enormous black hat of chiffon velvet and black
plumes—huge: a smaller hat of silky woven straw, very soft: a
15 complicated Paquin dress of frail, dark-blue, stone-blue silky velvet
and purplish heavy embroidery, for evening wear: a complicated
whitey-blue petticoat of very soft silk: a voluminous dressing-gown
wrap of thin silk and endless lace: a chemise of more lace than linen:
two pairs of high laced shoes, of greeny grey thin kid with black patent
20 golosh:

[end of manuscript]

EXPLANATORY NOTES

EXPLANATORY NOTES

1:1 **Part I.** Neither the MS nor the typescripts are divided into parts; but DHL decided to divide them when he hoped to publish the first part separately, and later he included this division in his plan for the novel; see Introduction, pp. xxix–xxx.

3:4 **He** Lewie Goddard is modelled on William ('Willie') Edward Hopkin (1862–1951). An active socialist, who started as a colliery and then a post office clerk, he was a leading member of the Congregational Literary Society (cf. 9:21). See *Letters*, i. 176n. At 9:1 DHL wrote and then deleted 'Will' in MS (p. 12). Hopkin is also portrayed as Willie Houghton in *Touch and Go* (1920) and contributes to the characters of Mr Saxton and Hudson in *The White Peacock* (1911), ed. Andrew Robertson (Cambridge, 1983); see also note on 4:5. See Roy Spencer, *D. H. Lawrence Country* (1979), pp. 37–8.

3:6 *New Age* ... **Mr Orage nor Miss Tina** *New Age*, a radical socialist weekly, was edited by Orage from 1907 to 1922. Subtitled 'An Independent Review of Politics, Literature and Art', it was a lively, iconoclastic paper; contributors included George Bernard Shaw, H. G. Wells, Arnold Bennett and G. K. Chesterton.

Alfred Richard Orage (1873–1934), journalist and editor, contributed 'Notes of the Week' and other pieces.

'Miss Tina' was Emily Alice Haigh (1879–1943); she contributed polemical commentary, fiction and verse. Her pseudonyms included 'B.L.H.', 'Ninon de Longclothes' and 'Robert à Field'.

3:19 **his own pet devils.** Mrs Enid Hilton (see next note) confirmed the accuracy of DHL's description: 'one point [DHL] remarks – the DEVILS my father collected. There were a number of them, he found them amusing ... The devils were a *protest* against the falseness of so many of the pious folk around him' (letter to the editor, 14 March 1983).

3:26 **She** Patty Goddard is modelled on Sarah Annie ('Sallie') Hopkin (1867–1922), wife of Willie Hopkin, good friend of DHL in his youth and strong feminist. (The Hopkins had a daughter Enid, b. 1896; now Enid Hilton.) In MS (pp. 10–12) DHL wrote 'Pattie' nine times before reverting to 'Patty' and at 7:16 started with an 'S' (p. 9) before writing the fictional name. See Spencer, *Lawrence Country*, pp. 38–9.

4:5 **homespun clothes.** Implying 'advanced' intellectual inclinations, stemming from the taste for the hand-made, the authentic and the simple fostered by the Arts and Crafts movement. Cf. Will Renshaw in 'The Overtone', probably written in 1924 (*The Lovely Lady*, 1933), in his 'homespun suit' (included in *St. Mawr and Other Stories*, ed. Brian Finney, Cambridge, 1983, p. 6). Renshaw and his wife Edith may be based on the Hopkins; see also note on 66:9.

4:24 **as sound** As sound asleep.

4:34 *New Statesman.* Weekly journal (1913–) of politics, art, letters and science, originally an organ for the Fabian movement (founded 1884, to work for the introduction of socialism); propounded socialism independent of a party. First editor was Clifford Sharp; George Bernard Shaw and Beatrice and Sidney Webb were regular contributors.

5:24 **she heard her husband so plainly.** Cf. Mrs. Enid Hilton on her father Willie Hopkin: 'Father's whistling was peculiar – an announcement. In the early morning he took a cold bath . . . and there he whistled, rather in the manner of Chanticleer announcing his presence and the new day. Occasionally it could be irritating, as suggested by Lawrence. Again, it offered security, certainly to me and probably to mother most of the time, unless she was annoyed with him' (letter to the editor, 14 March 1983).

5:29 **Unco Guid . . . just umbrellas** Used ironically of persons who make a great show of piety and straitlacedness (Joseph Wright, *The English Dialect Dictionary*, 6 vols., 1898–1905); cf. Robert Burns, 'Address to the Unco Guid, or the Rigidly Righteous' (1786) . . . 'just umbrellas': see Matthew v. 45 (God 'sendeth rain on the just and on the unjust', AV).

6:5 **The wiles . . . ten birth-rights** Genesis xxv. 27–34 and xxvii. 1–33.

6:33 **scawd-rags!'** 'Scaw'd' is faded, discoloured; worthless (Wright, *English Dialect Dictionary*).

7:5 **Nankin cups,** Chinese underglazed blue and white ware, known as 'Nanking', made in large quantities for export to Europe in the eighteenth and nineteenth centuries.

7:18 **Mr Noon,** Gilbert Noon in Part I is modelled on George Henry Neville (1886–1959), a close friend of DHL's youth; they attended Nottingham High School and went on holidays together; both became teachers. Neville's amatory adventures culminated in 1911–12 in a hasty marriage, a child born less than three months later and resignation from his teaching post at Amblecote, Stourbridge; see *Letters*, i. 373–4. Neville is also portrayed as Dr George Grainger in DHL's play, *The Married Man* (1940) and was a partial model for Leslie Tempest in *The White Peacock*; see *Letters*, i. 68. See also *A Memoir of D. H. Lawrence* by G. H. Neville, ed. Carl Baron (Cambridge, 1982) and Spencer, *Lawrence Country*, p. 53.

In Part II Noon's character and experiences become those of DHL himself thinly disguised; see Introduction, pp. xxxiii, xl–xli.

F. B. Pinion notes that a student contemporary with DHL at the Ilkeston Pupil–Teacher Centre was named Gilbert Noon (*A D. H. Lawrence Companion*, 1978, p. 249). George Henry Noon (1863–1945), son of James, farmer, was a butcher in Church Street (*Kelly's Directory of Nottinghamshire*, 1895). From at least 1903 to 1913 he was a Foundation Manager for New Eastwood School (Nottinghamshire Education Committee records).

7:31 **twenty-five or twenty-six,** Neville would have been 26 in 1912; see also note above. DHL's own elopement and 'flight' took place in 1912 when he too was 26.

8:1 **Woodhouse** DHL's recreation of his home town Eastwood. He used the same name in *The Lost Girl*, ed. John Worthen (Cambridge, 1981); see Introduction to this volume, p. xxi. Woodhouse is a common place name in the area, e.g. Annesley Woodhouse and Kirkby Woodhouse, about 4 miles n. of Eastwood.

8:31 **"Many waters . . . love,** Song of Solomon viii. 7.

9:4 **His father owned a woodyard** James Neville (d. 1939?) was a miner and later a dairyman (*Memoir of D. H. Lawrence*, by Neville, ed. Baron, p. 3); Sarah Ellen Neville died in 1918.

9:16 **Whetstone [9:5] . . . Haysfall Technical School,** Name of a hamlet in Derbyshire (but 25 miles n.w. of Eastwood) . . . Haysfall, apparently not a place name, may be based on Mansfield, the only town within the specified distance *and* in Nottinghamshire that had a secondary school (and a grammar school; MS (p. 107) originally read 'Haysfall Grammar School' at 57:17).

9:21 **Woodhouse Literary Society,** Cf. the Congregational Literary Society in Eastwood which DHL attended. Papers were given on varied topics: literary persons and works, biography, biology and geography and travel illustrated by magic lantern (see *Letters*, i. 3–4 and David Newmarch, 'D. H. Lawrence's Chapel: Aspects of a Cultural Tradition', unpublished Ph.D. thesis, University of Nepal, 1979, pp. 79–89).

9:24 **and so entertaining.** DHL wrote 'yet so magical' in MS (p. 13), and altered the last word to 'revealing'; he then revised the phrase identically in TSI and TCCI.

10:8 **"Better the . . . the deed."** *Michaelmas Term* (1607) by Thomas Middleton (1580–1627), III. i. 14–15 ['the better day the better deede'].

10:19 **stinks** School slang for chemistry lessons; also for trouble with authority.

15:2 **Spoon.** 'To make love, especially in a sentimental or silly fashion', colloquial from 1831 (*OED*). In *The White Peacock* DHL's definition may be deduced from his revision of 'spoony' to 'sentimental' in 'The irruption of Alice into the quiet, sentimental party was like taking a bright light into a sleeping hen-roost' (ed. Robertson, p. 119). Cf. *The Trespasser* (1912), ed. Elizabeth Mansfield (Cambridge, 1982), p. 123; *The Lost Girl*, ed. Worthen, p. 270; and *D. H. Lawrence: A Composite Biography*, ed. Edward Nehls (Madison, 1959), iii. 584.

However, spooning as Noon and Emmie practise it and as Patty Goddard defines it (16:10–15) would be more accurately described as amorous kissing and caressing – which is not intended to lead to marriage (86:24–5). (See also note on 21:5.) Emmie differentiates between a 'nice innocent lovely spoon' and 'the last step which *may* cost' (26:30–2), but Noon fears that Emmie's 'neuralgia of the stomach' may be pregnancy (62:34; 64:11–14).

DHL made many revisions in this and the next chapter: the final MS readings and deletions in MS, TSI and TCCI are given below (for final TSI readings, see textual apparatus). DHL also revised Alf Bostock's and Emmie's reactions against spooning; see notes on 68:38 and 69:3 and 23 below.

15:8 **A yellow dog** DHL wrote 'A wastrel dog' in MS (p. 22); see also textual apparatus.

15:25 **"Don't get your hair off [15:10] . . . hard lines** Keep your hair on, i.e. don't lose your temper . . . bad luck; originally a nautical term (slang).

16:20 **Last Day** See John xii. 48.

16:27   **an intense gossip** In MS, the women went for 'a talk' (p. 24).

17:13   **cap over . . . and they** MS (p. 26) read 'cap over his nose and his coat-collar turned up, and his cigarette under his nose, and they'. In TCCI DHL marked the second and third phrases for transposition, deleted the 'and' between them and underlined two words; the typist of TCCII muddled the 'and's, and missed the underlinings.

17:18   **loitered like a pale ghost** Cf. the knight 'Alone and palely loitering' in Keats's 'La Belle Dame Sans Merci' (written 1819).

17:23   **needle's eye** See Matthew xix. 24.

17:28   **Agatha,** Agatha Sharp (45:1) may be based on Agatha M. Kirk, (b. 1885) as identified by Mr Steve Bircumshaw, her husband. She taught at New Eastwood School in 1905.

17:33   **Emmie's voice.** Emma Grace ('Emmie') Bostock (54:30–1) may be based on Sarah Ethel Giddens (b. 1888) who taught at Eastwood British School from 1903 and then Eastwood Church Walk School until at least 1912. Ethel married Arthur Robert Smith (b. 1881), colliery agent's traveller and sapper in the Royal Engineers, 1914 (Spencer, *Lawrence Country*, p. 36 and S. Bircumshaw; Nottinghamshire Education Committee records). See also note on 28:6.

17:36   **swimming . . . on the shelf . . . oven shelf** Going swimmingly, and very wet . . . an old maid . . . pregnant (cf. 'expecting' in line 38).

18:1   **tad-poles,"** DHL first wrote 'water-hens' in MS (p. 27); he added 'saying in a guarded voice:' (line 4) to TSI and TCCI.

18:11   **to Hackett's** Cf. Alvina Houghton in *The Lost Girl* going 'down to Hallam's' after chapel (ed. Worthen, p. 68).

18:23   **Co-operative Stores.** The co-operative movement, springing originally from the ideas of Robert Owen (1771–1858), took its present form of shops returning profits to customers in the 1840s. Cf. Langley Mill and Aldecar Co-operative Society Ltd, 14 Nottingham Road, Eastwood (*Bennett's Business Directory*, 1914) and Eastwood Co-op, in 'Return to Bestwood', *Phoenix II* 257.

19:20   **Pupil Teacher's Centre.** Pupil–Teacher Centre, Ilkeston, which Neville, DHL (1904–5) and Ethel Giddens attended.

19:30   **Shelley's early portraits,** Probably a reference to the 1819 oil portrait by Amelia Curran (d. 1847); it was frequently reproduced and copied, and is in the National Portrait Gallery.

19:36   **mo,"** Moment.

20:7   **modern love . . . grail-like effulgence.** The Holy Grail was the legendary vessel used by Christ at the Last Supper and in which Joseph of Arimathea is said to have caught his blood. According to Malory and Alfred, Lord Tennyson, it was the object of quests by King Arthur's knights. In Wagner's *Parsifal* the Grail sheds a light when raised in blessing.

MS read 'the English people, let us trace its course softly' (p. 32), and 'metallic object' (line 9) read 'concrete utensil'.

20:9 **classes; and … classes; will** The TCCII typist erased the semi-colon in the first instance and substituted a dash; the typist typed the second as 'classes?', and then added a dash.

20:26 *con molto espressione?* With great expression? (Italian) ['con molta …'].

20:27 **old-beaniness!** From the middle-class slang 'old bean', said to good friends.

20:30 **spades being spades** Proverbial: calling a spade a spade (cf. line 32).

20:32 **Adam no … tout cela.** 'Adam no … spins': 'When Adam delved and Eve span / Who was then the gentleman?' (Morris Palmer Tilley, *A Dictionary of the Proverbs in England in the Sixteenth and Seventeenth Centuries*, Ann Arbor, 1950, A30). 'Nous avons … cela': 'We have changed all that'; the 'doctor's' response when questioned about his statement that the heart is on the right side and the liver on the left in Molière's *Le Médecin malgré lui* (1666), II. iv.

21:5 **the mystic business** [20:11] … **between us.** DHL revised the MS version of this passage twice: in TSI *and* TCCI. The original MS reading was
the affair. We hear of black silk bed-sheets, the nude lady on the fish-salver, with a half lemon in her mouth, at a sub-royal banquet; we know all about champagne suppers, aigrettes, diamonds, debts, and the whole Balzackian Maupassantian show; we have read of Oxfordly young men and Chorus girls; tarts, bits of fluff, and so on. Now the lower classes spoon in semi-public privacy, in shop-doors, entries, and at field stiles⟨.⟩ ⌐, on the sands and in the parks.⌐ The middle-classes languish in first-class railway carriages, at the theatre, on the river etc. The upper classes are said to go in for wickedness, black silk bed-sheets, and other Frenchiness. But on the whole, they are barely distinguishable from the middle classes in their tactics.
One and all, however, they spoon: from princes downward. The English race is a spoony race. Let us not be ashamed of our national qualities.
For we can say of the spoon, if we like, that there is no harm in it. It is all above-board. There is a sound social principle involved, for every kind of spooning is semi-public, and the ⌐thrill of it⌐ bounces back and forth from the spooner to the passer-by elastic as a tennis-ball. The public participates, as it should in everything English. There is no mean hiding the light under a bushel. Then again, it is a highly spiritualised process, a sort of swoon in mid-air. If, unfortunately, it leads on nowadays to real ⟨"wickedness,"⟩ ⌐slips,⌐ this is the fault of the defiant quality in modern youth, which cannot be content to call a spoon a spoon, but must start ⟨talking about spades and such-like unnameable implements.⟩ ⌐walking down the slippery slope where late it spun in a trance.⌐ (pp. 32–3)
Transcription practice: ⟨ ⟩ indicates a deletion; ⟨⟨ ⟩⟩, a second deletion, etc.; ⌐ ⌐, an addition.
When pp. 30–1 containing the revised passage in TSI were retyped, the unidentified typist must have had difficulty reading the last line and 'never?' was added in an unknown hand; see textual apparatus entry on 21:1. Cf. in Frieda's fictionalised memoirs a story she overheard in her childhood: 'The prince gave a party to his friends. For the fish course, carried in on a silver platter, carried by six footmen, lay a nude damsel trimmed with parsley and lemon' (Tedlock 67).

21:17 modern daughter of Venus . . . affectionate comradeship of a dear girl MS (p. 33) readings were 'sport' and 'downyness of a bit of fluff'. See textual apparatus for TSI.

22:2 some iridescent sphere . . . Watts picture. Perhaps the later version of *Endymion* (exhibited 1904) by George Frederic Watts (1817–1904); Watts described it as 'Endymion loved the moon, who is here represented under the form of Diana, in pale blue robes, descending from heaven, and embracing him as he sleeps on the ground' (*G. F. Watts: A Nineteenth Century Phenomenon*, ed. John Gage, 1974, no. 49).

22:13 bit of . . . warm amber. MS reading was 'piece of warm amber lifts up a bit of paper' (p. 35).

22:14 rising up . . . Simon Magus. A sorcerer who attempted to fly to prove his supernatural powers in the presence of the emperor Nero and Peter; Peter prayed, and the magician fell, and either died or broke some bones.

23:12 from his, aside. Cf. the descriptions in *The Trespasser*, ed. Mansfield, p. 64; '[Burns Novel]', written December 1912, *A Composite Biography*, ed. Nehls (Madison, 1957), i. 192–3; and *The Rainbow* (1915), chap. viii.

23:23 a secondary mundane consciousness. MS reading was 'an arrière-pensée' (p. 37).

23:32 —We have risen . . . Emmie? Practise . . . swing suspended MS reading was 'Nevertheless, and notwithstanding, all extravagancies I have portrayed realised themselves between the two. What was Mr Noon and what was Emmie Bostock swung-suspended' (pp. 37–8). 'They were . . . of faculties' at the end of the preceding paragraph was added to TSI and TCCI. MS read 'oblivion' which was revised to 'infinity' (line 32) in these typescripts. (The punctuation after 'Emmie' did not print clearly in either copy of TCCII, and the E1 printer interpreted it as an exclamation mark.)

23:36 Ah, we . . . goings on. The paragraph in MS was shorter, ending with 'blue ether'. DHL first added in TSI: 'Only practice, and never be gross. ⟨And⟩ Learn from the lower classes' (p. 35), and see also textual apparatus.

24:8 Whitman's Songs of Himself and Other People 'Song of Myself' and other poems, or 'songs', in *Leaves of Grass* (1855–92) by Walt Whitman. See also 99:15.

24:10 —Ah, the spoon [24:4] . . . hollow spoon. This paragraph was added to TSI and TCCI. TSI, the earlier version, was squeezed between two lines of type; in TCCI DHL crossed out the whole paragraph, wrote the new material between the lines and then rewrote the crossed-out paragraph (with a few variations from MS and TSI). See textual apparatus for the complete passage; the deletions and additions in TSI with the corresponding final readings are the following:

⟨men are all one,⟩ ⌐all men are ⟨mud [*or*] mind⟩ ⌐⌐one,⌐⌐ and so are ⌐⌐all⌐⌐ women.⌐ . . . ⟨meeting place⟩ ⌐Infinite and Nirvana⌐ . . . ⟨hope, not fear,⟩ ⌐abstraction, not uplift,⌐ . . . but ⟨in⟩ the . . . spoon-⟨equals.⟩ ⌐perfected.⌐ (p. 36)

24:27 scarlet MS originally read 'yellow' (p. 39).

24:30 brolly . . . gamp Clipped form of 'umbrella' (slang) . . . from Mrs Sarah

Gamp who had a large cotton umbrella in *Martin Chuzzlewit* (1843–4) by Charles Dickens.

24:39 Ah, dear [24:29] . . . poor pair. This paragraph was added to both copies of the typescript; see Introduction p. xxxviii. TSI includes the following deletions with the corresponding final readings (see textual apparatus):

⟨know you are⟩ ⌐hope you are not⌐ . . . umbrella ⟨even⟩ a . . . ⟨So you can rightly⟩ ⌐But don't therefore⌐ . . . ⟨But,⟩ ⌐No,⌐ . . . ⟨far famed⟩ ⌐notorious⌐ . . . the same⌐.⌐ ⟨old spoon thing.⟩ (p. 37)

25:4 Let none complain . . . public concern. The original MS reading with deletions and additions was

Let no one take it amiss that I describe the spoon in all ⟨too great⟩ ⌐its⌐ detail. ⟨⟨I ⟨cannot⟩ ⌐am not allowed to⌐ walk a hundred yards ⟨in any direction⟩ ⌐on any public road or path⌐ on a Sunday night in England, without being ⟨party to⟩ ⌐involved in⌐ an affair of this kind. And I insist that ⟨we should all know what it is exactly that we are made parties to—⟩ ⌐I may make a public statement of what I am publicly involved in—⌐ I insist⟨, moreover, that I encroach on no privacy.⟩ ⌐that this is no privacy breaking.⌐⟩⟩ (p. 40)

TSI has one deletion: 'presume' was revised to 'complain' (p. 37). 'Open mirror . . . public road': Stendhal said that 'a novel is a mirror carried along a main road' (*Le Rouge et le Noir*, 1830, chap. lxix).

25:10 and since . . . the innocence. MS read: 'and feel myself called upon to set forth their innocence before all eyes' (p. 40). For 'bare outline' in line 12, MS read 'botched beginnings' (p. 40).

25:11 raffinés Refined, sophisticated persons (French).

25:13 above-board This is the MS and TCCI reading; TSI was revised to 'true' (p. 37).

25:17 There are . . . even of MS reading was 'There is a spooning which is not above-board. There is Frenchy, and there is even' (p. 40). (DHL revised only the first sentence in TSI, p. 37.)

25:23 Every nation . . . in short, MS reading was 'But I am ⟨British, and feel myself involved in⟩ ⌐what I am, and feel myself competent to speak of⌐ the genuine English above-board spoon, ⟨in⟩ ⌐of⌐ that and no other. And on this occasion, ⟨on⟩ ⌐of⌐ (p. 40). See textual apparatus for TSI.

25:25 and shoulders, nor yet . . . fard Deleted MS reading was 'nor shoulders, nor even' (p. 41) . . . white cosmetics for the face (French).

25:26 no dealer . . . from it. MS reading was 'sure I am a fairly just recorder' (p. 41).

25:29 as one should . . . love's . . . dear spoon-memories! Deleted MS reading for 'as one should' was 'as I ought, and so you ought' (p. 41). The next sentence was added in TSI and TCCI. TSI originally read for 'the spoon from . . . infinite moments': 'which spoon which contains the essence of all modern love-making, high and low alike' (p. 38); see also textual apparatus. In TCCI DHL wrote 'life's' and revised this to 'love's'.

26:3   **turning traitor . . . his dose.** MS reading was 'too conscious of the technical innocence of the kiss' (p. 41).

26:5   **quarter to ten,** In MS Emmie originally had to be in by ten (p. 41).

26:11 **bally** Euphemism for 'bloody', but almost meaningless (slang).

26:18 **A black . . . over him.** Added in TSI and TCCI (p. 39).

26:25 **"Go on!"** Deleted MS reading was ' "What for?" ' (p. 42).

26:37 **persistence in [26:31] . . . dear reader?** MS reading was 'insistence on going further. But in herself was also a fund of rebellious defiance of fathers and stone tablets. And she was a sport. She had her reputation as a sport' (p. 42). Deletions and additions in TSI are 'Emmie ⟨was⟩ ⌐is⌐ a . . . tablets ⟨also⟩ there is ⌐also⌐ bliss . . . ⟨lovely⟩ ⌐final⌐' (p. 39); see also textual apparatus.

In the Old Testament God inscribed his commandments on 'tables of stone' for Moses to give to the Jews (Exodus xxiv. 12).

'The last step which *may* cost' (line 32): variation of 'il n'y a que le premier pas qui coûte' ('It is only the first step that counts'; French), comment by Madame du Deffand (1697–1780) on St Denis walking after decapitation.

27:4   **came suggestive and rather pleading** Deleted MS reading was 'seemed suggestive and rather nice' (p. 43).

27:9   **Galahad . . . Minnesinger** The perfect knight of King Arthur's Round Table . . . a medieval German troubadour; cf. 235:35. See also *Letters*, i. 411. (DHL had reviewed a book of translations, *The Minnesingers*, ed. by Jethro Bithell, in *English Review*, x, January 1912, 373–6; reprinted in *Phoenix II* 271-2.)

27:17 **and she [27:5] . . . the grass.** MS reading was
and so was he. They had licked the cream: they might as well finish the milk: especially as it was forbidden, and she had a Dad whom she hated and called Wire-whiskers.

So he took it for granted that she would come out again. But she was mistaken about his pleasant, ⟨insidious⟩ ⌐pleading, sinful⌐ suggestivity and ⟨naughtiness⟩ ⌐wickedness⌐ of mood. He wasn't that at all, tonight. (p. 43)
DHL added the comments in TSI and TCCI following 'state of feeling' (line 20).

27:26 **twitchel,** A narrow passage or alley (between gardens) (*OED*).

27:33 **circumstances.** This word occurs at the end of the line in MS (p. 44) and does not have a loop for the final 's', but the downward continuation after 'e' suggests another letter was meant (the full stop is present below the line).

27:40 **Black devils . . . the spoon.** These lines were added to TSI and TCCI. MS (p. 44) read 'any further' which was revised to 'very far' (28:5) in both copies.

28:6   **Her father,** Alfred Wright ('Alf') Bostock (54:35) may be based on John Giddens, a signalman for the Great Northern Railway. He and his wife Annie, née Buckley, and three daughters (Ethel, Cissie and Mabel) and one son (George, a joiner) lived in one of a row of three cottages, which belonged to the railway, at the bottom of Church Street, New Eastwood. Ethel and Cissie (see note on 46:2) were schoolteachers (S. Bircumshaw).

Thomas Henry Bostock was a chemist in Market Place, and Thomas Bostock ran a public house, 'Thorn Tree'; cf. in a fragment (p. 34) of an early version of 'Paul Morel' (*Sons and Lovers*, 1913) where men are leaving the pubs at eleven o'clock: 'And far-off shouts from the Mansfield high-road, as the men came out of "Bostock's" . . .' in *Sons and Lovers: A Facsimile of the Manuscript*, ed. Mark Schorer (Berkeley, 1977).

28:16 **of warmth about them . . . human** MS read 'or imagination . . . gallant' (p. 45). See textual apparatus for TSI.

28:25 **"Down Among . . . crew———"** Drinking song with words by John Dyer (1699–1758); DHL quotes stanza 2, lines 3–4, which continues 'And they that woman's health deny, / Down among the dead men let them lie' (*The Oxford Song Book*, ed. Sir Percy C. Buck, 1916, i. 56–7). 'Dead men' are also empty bottles.

28:27 **Alas, he . . . in oil.** Added to TSI and TCCI. 'Kicked with fury against . . . spoon': variation of Acts ix. 5: '*It is* hard for thee to kick against the pricks.'

28:29 **her father,** Emmie originally lied to 'wire-whiskers' in MS (p. 45).

28:36 **narrow-pathdom.** See Matthew vii. 13, 14 (AV): 'Because strait *is* the gate, and narrow *is* the way, which leadeth unto life' while 'wide *is* the gate, and broad is the way, that leadeth to destruction'.

30:15 **the sleep of the nagged** 'Of the just' is the usual phrase.

30:37 **Like the wicked . . . said Ha—Ha!** Cf. Psalms xxxv. 19, 21; xl. 15.

31:34 **Till nowadays . . .. had triumphed.** These comments were added to TSI and TCCI. TSI originally had 'better nature' for 'higher nature' (p. 47); see also textual apparatus.

31:37 **her.** The question mark in TCCI is added in pencil in an unknown hand) (possibly that of Ruth Wheelock); cf. other minor corrections (also not in DHL's hand which were made in pencil, e.g. amiably (29:26), greenhouse (31:23) and woodyard (34:9; 35:27) in textual apparatus.

32:7 **Whore of Babylon** See Revelation xvii. 4–5.

34:2 **Aphrodite and the Cow.** In Greek mythology Aphrodite was the goddess of beauty and love who sprang from the foam of the sea (in Roman, Venus). Enid Hilton has reported that this incident happened to her parents and herself, and that her father distracted the cow while she and her mother escaped across the stream (letter to the editor, 14 March 1983).

34:35 **Could they [34:30] . . . odd aloneness** MS reading (p. 57) was 'The one little element of *self*, not derivable from' which was revised to 'Could they? . . . attributable to' in TCCI (lines 30–3); 'hear the equivalent in music' to 'make quite . . . it musically'; 'satisfactory' to 'suggestive'; 'apartness' to 'aloneness'. See textual apparatus for TSI.

35:6 *Lloyd's Weekly*, *Lloyd's Weekly News*, from 1842 under varying names until it was incorporated with the *Sunday Graphic* in 1931.

35:17 **domineering gratified** MS reading was 'very glad' (p. 58); TSI was revised to 'conceitedly gratified' and then to match the TCCI reading (p. 52). In line 17 'the lad' originally read 'his son' in MS (p. 58).

36:11 **felt** Deleted MS reading was 'thought he caught', and 'spite' (line 18) originally read in MS 'significance' (p. 60).

36:15 **I. L. P.** International Labour Party.

36:32 **the park,"** Eastwood Hall park; the Walker family of Barber Walker and Co. lived in the house until just before the First World War.

37:27 **franchised woman,** Some women were enfranchised in 1918 under the Representation of the People Act: those who were married, householders and university graduates of 30 and over (the age was lowered to 21 in 1928).

39:3 **heels** DHL wrote 'heels' in MS (p. 66), which Ruth Wheelock typed as 'feels' (p. 58); DHL altered this to 'feet' in both TSI and TCCI. The MS reading has been restored; see also 55:40 and 62:5 and notes.

40:10 **this Balaam's ass . . . opposing angel.** Numbers xxii. 21–31.

40:20 **modern,** MS readings were '⟨reckless⟩ ⟨⟨⌐fearless,⟩⟩ modern,⌐' (p. 70).

40:33 **strange** Deleted MS reading was 'dark' (p. 71).

43:16 **an abstract,** Deleted MS reading was 'an old,' (p. 77).

44:2 **Choir Correspondence.** Cf. the choir episode in 'Fanny and Annie', written in May 1919, published in *Hutchinson's Magazine* (21 November 1921) and collected in *England, My England* (1922).

44:12 **wistful** Alf's look was 'seraphic' in MS (p. 79).

45:2 **Alvina Houghton.** Heroine of *The Lost Girl* (see Introduction, p. xxi); modelled on Florence ('Flossie') Cullen (1879–1924); see note on 2:20 in *The Lost Girl* (ed. Worthen).

45:37 **snappily [45:30] . . . awfully bad** Snappishly (*OED*) . . . very ill.

46:2 **Cissie Gittens** May be modelled on Cissie Giddens (S. Bircumshaw).

46:8 **catamaran.** A contrary, difficult person (slang).

46:24 **Great Northern's** Cf. the Great Northern railway line (Pinxton branch), which ran just s. and w. of Eastwood.

46:34 **with a shudder as if someone had** Deleted MS reading was 'as if an alarm clock' (pp. 84–5).

47:7 **endurance. I** DHL wrote 'endurance. And I' in MS (p. 85); he then deleted 'And', but the typist included it.

48:10 **mutiny on the upper deck.** Deleted MS reading had the choir behaving like a 'meeting among the Valkyries' (p. 88); the choir was first described as a 'highly democratic' body given to 'insurrection' (p. 86), but this was revised to 'highly oligarchic' and 'insubordination' (47:26–7). Also DHL corrected 'members of society' to 'members of the christian community' (47:28).

48:36 **stumbled, it . . . the stones.** Cf. Romans xiv. 13.

49:9 **"Lord keep . . . light appears."** Hymn (1792) by John Leland (1754–1841), American Baptist minister.

49:30 Parkers Probably Dixon and Parker, Ltd, clothiers, with three shops in Nottingham.

50:16 packet Noon's original offering in MS was a 'box' (p. 93). 'Ah spoony . . . no more.' (lines 17–18) was added to TSI and TCCI.

51:19 "While from . . . Hood line 'A Nocturnal Sketch' (1839) by Thomas Hood (1799–1845), line 1 ['Even is come; and from the dark Park, hark']; the poem continues: 'The signal of the setting sun – one gun! / And six is sounding from the chime, prime time . . .'

51:25 on Thursday . . . in the evening This is inconsistent with 57:5 where the next day is Saturday.

52:22 Dea ex machina. Goddess from the machine (Latin); cf. 92:34–6. In Greek and Roman theatre, a god descended from heaven onto the stage by a mechanical device; now a contrived solution to a difficulty in a plot.

53:32 a baby . . . of the sea Allusion to *The Water Babies* (1863) by Charles Kingsley (1819–75).

54:20 French poet . . . don't bark." Gérard de Nerval (pseudonym of Gérard Labrunie, 1808–55), in defence of walking a lobster on a blue silk ribbon in the gardens of the Palais Royal, said: 'Why should a lobster be any more ridiculous than a dog . . . or any other animal one chooses to take for a walk? I have a liking for lobsters. They are peaceful, serious creatures. They know the secrets of the sea, they don't bark . . .' (Théophile Gautier, *My Phantoms*, tr. Richard Holmes, 1976, pp. 149–50).

54:31 criminal commerce 'Commerce' and 'correspondence' (57:26; *OED*) mean intercourse in archaic or legal usage; and 'criminal conversation' is adultery.

54:40 find DHL revised two words in Mrs Britten's speech in TSI and TCCI: 'feel' became 'find' and at 55:14 'trouble' became 'annoyance' (TCCI pp. 83, 84).

55:40 Gilbert The typist typed 'Gilbert' at the end of a line and repeated it at the beginning of the next; DHL responded to the error with different punctuation in TSI and TCCI, but did not remove the duplicated word. The MS reading has been restored.

57:14 Lachesis shears . . . of fate, In Greek mythology one of the three Fates or Moirai who determined the length of life: Clotho spun the thread of life, Lachesis measured its length and Atropos cut it short with her shears.

57:22 to Germany . . . to study for his doctorate. After recovering from a serious illness in late 1911 and resigning his teaching post, DHL planned to go to Germany in April or May 1912; he gave various reasons, but plainly was restless and wanted to 'clear out' (see *Letters*, i. 350ff. and Frieda Lawrence 22). But cf. DHL's fellow- student at University College, Nottingham, Tom Smith who, in 1913, was awarded a scholarship for research at Göttingen University towards a Ph.D. in science; see *Letters*, i. 142 n. 7.

58:13 Sufficient unto the day etc. Matthew vi. 34 ['. . . day *is* the evil thereof.']

59:12 What'st [59:6] . . . t'art . . . Tha What do you (What does ter) . . . you (i.e. thou) are . . . You (dialect).

59:36 **"Save thy wind [59:20] ... t'same ... ha'e ...wi' ... Tha'lt ... me an'
all.** Save your breath ... the same ... have ... with ... You shall (Thou shalt) ...
truly, indeed (Wright, *English Dialect Dictionary*).

61:2 **Chapter VIII ... Mother-in-law.** This chapter division and title were added
by DHL when he revised TSI and TCCI (p. 91); see also textual apparatus for TSI
variants. From this point on, MS chapter numbering is incorrect; new chapter
divisions (and titles) were added to the typescripts at 71:2 and 88:2; the chapter
number was altered and title added at 81:2 (pp. 116, 133, 122).

62:1 **Trinity College** Neville's education ended with his training in a Pupil–
Teacher Centre in 1905, while DHL won a scholarship which enabled him to
continue at University College, Nottingham. (The headmaster at Nottingham High
School was Dr James Gow (1854–1923), a former fellow of Trinity College,
Cambridge.)

62:5 **said it so** Ruth Wheelock omitted 'it'; DHL did not notice this in TCCI, but
altered TSI to read 'said so so'. The MS reading has been restored.

63:3 **keep your smiles ... going out.** I.e. like gloves. 'The crown of your hat':
DHL had problems with this phrase in MS (pp. 117–18): '⟨⟨your ⟨top-coat⟩ ⌐jacket⌐
pocket⟩⟩ ⌐⌐the crown of your hat⌐⌐'.

63:36 **I'll back** I'll bet (Wright, *English Dialect Dictionary*).

64:2 **Mrs Harold [63:36] ... of company."** The Wagstaffes are characters in local
gossip in *The White Peacock*, ed. Robertson, p. 81, and a Henry Wagstaff is a
Woodhouse town councillor in *The Lost Girl*, ed. Worthen, p. 240. (It was a local name,
e.g. an Arthur Wagstaff was a grocer in Princes Street in the 1890s.)
   DHL's friend Edith ('Kitty') Holderness and her father George were from at least
1911 infants' mistress and headmaster respectively of Eakring Public Elementary
School (mixed) ('Eakrast'). When DHL visited them in August 1911, he noted that the
school house was attached to the school (63:40), and planned to go again in March
1912, probably both times by bicycle; see *Letters*, i. 295, 369. DHL is misleading here:
the Wagstaffs lived in School House (see 69:30–2).
   DHL revised this passage in MS (pp. 119–20):
   Mrs ⟨Ephraim⟩ ⌐Harold⌐ ... ⟨Church Cottages,⟩ ⌐School House,⌐ ... ⟨Duke's
   keepers,⟩ ⌐schoolmasters,⌐ ... ⟨A fine big chap he is. Was a soldier. It's the third
   cottage from the church—you can't miss it.—Quiet little place, but very nice, you
   know. The Dukeries. Yes, you know it.'⟩ ⌐A clever young ... of company.'⌐
(The Dukeries: an area which includes seven large country houses in Sherwood
forest.)

66:9 **State Endowment of Motherhood,** State welfare for mothers was demanded
by the Women's Suffrage movement and supported by the Fabian society from the
early 1900s; maternity allowances were not introduced until 1945. This topic
interested DHL; he mentioned it in *The White Peacock*, ed. Robertson, p. 296 and 'The
Overtone', *St. Mawr*, ed. Finney, p. 5.

67:24 **scalp-fringe** Her trophy string, from an American-Indian practice of taking
the scalp of a victim and sewing it onto a garment.

67:32 **Warsop.** Deleted MS reading was 'Southwell' (p. 127).

68:8 The honey ... And therefore, so The deleted MS reading was more complimentary to Walter George Whiffen: 'In fact he is the wisest young person we have met with. So' (p. 128). He originally 'said No' instead of 'wip[ing] his ears' (lines 2–3) when he heard rumours about Emmie, and she had 'the decency not to mollify him' instead of 'not to offend' (lines 9–10). 'Golden syrup' is a syrup of a bright golden-yellow colour, drained off in the process of obtaining refined crystallised sugar (*OED*).

There was an Alfred Wiffen, pastry cook and confectioner, 34 Nottingham Road in 1908.

68:12 allotment gardens A small portion of land let out for cultivation under a public scheme.

68:16 *chacun à son goût*. Everyone to his own taste (French).

68:23 Roses and rapture From Swinburne's *Dolores* (1866): 'Change in a trice / The lilies and langours of virtue / For the raptures and roses of vice' (ix).

68:24 cauliflower ... abiding blossom. Cf. the joke about the '*Colly posy*' in *St. Mawr*, ed. Finney, p. 113.

68:30 *au fond* At bottom, basically (French).

68:34 purge off ... pink roses. Red roses are the symbol of passion (and the flower of Venus); pink roses of something less.

68:38 he reacted ... realise this. Deleted MS reading was 'the reaction within him against his own past, of whose lurking potentialities he was not yet sure, revived to such a pitch that he became unseemly' (pp. 129–30).

69:3 demonstrated that ... society rests; 'Domestic arch ... society rests': mocking reference to the symbolism of *The Rainbow*; e.g., see the end of chapters iii. and vi.

Deleted MS readings were '⟨proved⟩ ⌐demonstrated⌐ ... ⟨that they know⟩ ⌐having ⟨shown⟩ revealed their acquaintance with the fact⌐ ... ⟨pinnacle⟩ ⌐keystone⌐ ... ⟨connubial felicity,⟩ ⌐domestic arch ... society rests;⌐ (p. 130).

69:23 except she would [69:17] ... her life. The MS reading with deletions and additions was

⟨frosted over⟩ ⌐but crisp⌐ with a little flirtiness as ⟨like castor sugar and sweetened⟩ ⌐⟨with⟩ a well-baked loaf, and lightened⌐ inside with lovey-dovey mixture; ⟨still it would remain⟩ ⌐still it would come out⌐ of the oven as the bread of her future ⌐passional⌐ existence, this hatred of rose-leaves, this deliberate affection for the cauliflower. (p. 131)

See textual apparatus at 69:17: in TSI 'also' (p. 104) was revised to 'mark you'.

69:40 on the sofa ... then she In MS Fanny perceived Emmie's condition as more serious: 'to bed, gave her a hot bran-bag, and' (p. 132). For bran-bag see note on 72:15.

70:5 Witham Welland ... its savour? 'Witham ... Great Ouse': the four major rivers, from n. to s., which formed the fens of s. Lincolnshire and w. Norfolk, and which drain into the Wash. 'And if the Salt ... its savour?': Matthew v. 13 ['Ye are the salt of the earth: but if the salt have lost his savour, wherewith shall it be salted? ...']

70:21   **mardy,** Petted, spoiled (dialect). See also 275:36.

71:5   **Spanish juice.** Extract of liquorice-root.

72:15   **bran-bag,** A flat flannel bag filled with bran and warmed on the oven shelf; of supposedly medicinal value.

72:24   **chuck,"** Chick, chicken; a term of endearment (*OED*).

73:27   **his own ... of course."** DHL toned down Emmie's description of the scuffle in MS: '⟨Gilbert knocked his cap off ⟩ ⌐his own cap knocked off⌐ ... ⟨our Dad scratched his face."⟩ ⌐all the blame laid on me, of course."⌐ (pp. 140–1).

77:22   **cant though correct** Deleted MS reading was 'vulgar' (p. 147).

79:15   **she's a king to** 'To be a king to' is 'to be superior to'; 'a king better' is 'a great deal, much better'; so 'much better than' (Wright, *English Dialect Dictionary*).

79:27   **Roland,** Perhaps an allusion to Edgar's song in *King Lear* III. iv. 182 or 'Childe Roland to the Dark Tower Came' (1855) by Robert Browning (1812–89); see also 84:21–2.

80:21   **young Tristan** Ironic allusion to the tragic romance of Tristan and Isolde.

81:30   **Man proposes, God disposes** Proverb (Tilley, *Dictionary of the Proverbs in England*, M298).

82:27   **at seven ... the world.** *'The year's at the spring / And day's at the morn; Morning's at seven / ... God's in his heaven – / All's right with the world!'*, *Pippa Passes* (1841) by Browning, lines 221–3, 227–8.

82:31   **enrich the dip of her bacon ... Hood's pun.** Possibly from 'Literary and Literal', lines 106–9, 111–12 (*Hood's Own*, 1839, reprinted 1855, p. 180) by Hood: 'What author for a lecture was the richer, / Bacon or Hogg? there were no votes for Beaumont, / But some for *Flitcher*; / While others ... / ... thought their pork / Would prove more relishing from Thomson's Season-ing!'
In TCCII, after 'Browning' a comma is typed over a question mark, and is followed by a dash; this became 'Browning?—' in E1.
DHL revised 'egg' in MS to read 'bacon' (line 24), and 'dip of her bacon' originally read 'grating[?] of her emotion' (p. 157).

83:11   **take the biscuit!"** Surpass all others (ironically).

83:27   **old Lad."** The devil (Wright, *English Dialect Dictionary*).

84:17   ***Girl of the Limberlost*** *A Girl of the Limberlost* (1909) by Gene Stratton-Porter (1863–1924), American author of books for girls.

85:2   **Sandow exercises** Eugene Sandow (1867–1925), pseudonym of Karl Frederick Mueller; German wrestler and advocate of physical culture. See *Letters*, i. 76.

85:19   **intrude in the sacred scene,** The deleted MS reading had Harold not wishing to 'intrude ⟨on⟩ the ⟨union of two hearts,⟩ ⟨⟨moment⟩⟩ ⟨⟨⟨scene⟩⟩⟩ ⟨⟨⟨⟨issue⟩⟩⟩⟩' (p. 162). The lovers first felt 'awfully moved' instead of 'superlative' (p. 163) at 86:4. DHL changed 'gazed' and 'gazes' to 'looked' and 'looks' in TSI and TCCI (p. 128) at 84:35.

85:20 when fate caused a rift in the lute. Vivien sings Lancelot's song to Merlin: that unfaith will be 'the little rift within the lute' in 'Merlin and Vivien', *Idylls of the King* (1859–85) by Tennyson.

86:23 as Napoleon . . . un homme." After giving Goethe the cross of the Legion of Honour at Erfurt in 1808 Napoleon said 'Vous êtes un homme', and Goethe turned away with 'Voilà un homme'. See also note on 117:9.

87:5 "The cottage homes . . . a dream." Adapted from 'The Homes of England' (*Blackwood's Magazine*, xxi, April 1827, 392) by Felicia Dorothea Hemans (1793–1835): 'The stately Homes of England, / How beautiful they stand! . . . / O'er all the pleasant land, . . . / The Cottage-Homes of England! / By thousands on her plains' (lines 1–2, 4, 25–6).

87:9 "There's a little . . . the west." 'Little Grey Home in the West' (1911), music by Hermann Löhr (1871–1943) and words by D. Eardley-Wilmot (b. 1883), lines 3–5: 'But with love brooding there, / Why no place can compare / With my little . . .' This line is also quoted in Frieda Lawrence 52 and *Women in Love* (Seltzer, 1920), chap. xxvii.

88:30 ormin'. Listless hovering, lounging; also clumsy (Richard Scollins and John Titford, *Ey Up, Mi Duck!*, Ilkeston, 1976, ii. 57).

90:15 owl, Deleted MS reading was 'duck' (p. 168) and 'monument' (line 19) originally read 'stuffed duck'.

90:20 Harold Hardraade The Viking warrior-king, Harald Hardrada (or Haardraade), invaded England in 1066 and was defeated and slain at the battle of Stamford Bridge.

90:34 Thoresby, Possibly Bilsthorpe (see map). Thoresby (Earl Manvers) is one of the large country houses in the Dukeries.

92:22 glotzing, Staring, adapted from 'glotzen' (German).

93:1 into deleted MS reading was 'its holy' (p. 172).

93:14 The cow . . . spoon. From the nursery rhyme 'Hey diddle diddle' (*The Oxford Dictionary of Nursery Rhymes*, ed. Iona and Peter Opie, Oxford, 1952, no. 213).

93:15 Gentle reader [93:6] . . . forward to. This passage was added to TSI and TCCI when DHL decided to publish Part I separately; see Introduction, p. xxvii. See textual apparatus for the final version of TSI; the deleted and added readings are ⟨they lived⟩ ⌐all went⌐ . . . But ⟨there is a ⟩ ⌐the⌐ second volume⟨, no getting away from it.⟩ ⌐is in pickle.⌐ . . . ⟨A S⟩ ⌐s⌐candalous ⌐the⌐ elopement, ⟨occasioning a divorce from⟩ ⌐and a decree nisi for⌐ the fork. ⟨⟨Doesn't that ⟨sound [two words illegible]⟩ titillate your curiosity?⟩⟩ ⌐Which is something to look forward to.⌐ (p. 141A).

97:7 the Marienkirche . . . palaces Frauen-Kirche, or the Cathedral and Parish Church of Our Lady, the cathedral of the Archbishopric of Munich and Freising; s.w. of the Residenz. The most prominent landmark in the city, late-Gothic style (1466–88) with its two uncompleted towers, 318 feet high, covered in 1625 with helmet-shaped cupolas. It overlooks within a 400 m. radius more than a dozen palaces or major buildings, including the Alter Hof (the first Wittelsbach castle), Residenz (the Royal Palace) encompassing several buildings and some on Ludwig-Strasse.

97:11 **the time ... birds has almost come ... flaming swords** Song of Solomon ii. 12 ['the time ... *of birds* is come']. Cherubim and a flaming sword were placed at the e. of the garden of Eden to keep Adam and Eve and their descendants out (Genesis iii. 24).

97:21 **islands of the west ... Cerberus,** In Greek and Roman mythology, the souls of the virtuous dead were in the Fortunatae Insulae ('Blessed Islands') located in the far w.... The sop for Cerberus is proverbial from *Aeneid* vi: in classical mythology the three-headed dog who guards the entrance to Hades, and who had to be pacified by passers-through.

98:4 **King George** George V, reigned 1910-36.

98:28 **Biedermeier furniture** A style of furnishing and interior decoration, which originated in Germany during the 1820s; the name comes from the fictitious author of poems, published 1855 and after, to satirise German bourgeois taste.

98:33 **overbolster.** Or 'bolster' (246:36); not a long pillow, but a thick quilt (duvet) for the bed.

99:6 **"Let your light so shine—"** Matthew v. 16 ['... shine before men, that they may see your good works ...'].

99:9 **lost a leg in Badajos's breaches,** 'Faithless Nelly Gray: A Pathetic Ballad' (1826) by Hood, lines 35–6 ['At duty's call, I left my legs / In Badajos's *breaches!*']. Wellington besieged and took the fortified city of Badajos, Spain from the French in 1812 during the Peninsular War.

99:13 **Mount Batten ... Windsorial ... but soap.** Family name of the Battenbergs, changed in 1917 ... family name of the British royal family, changed in 1917 from Saxe-Coburg-Gotha ... Windsor soap is a kind of perfumed toilet-soap (usually brown).

99:19 **What is man ... next summer,** 'What is man ... grass': Psalms ciii. 15 ['As *for* man ...'], and verse 16 ('The wind ... next summer') ['For the wind ... gone; and the place thereof shall know it no more.']. See also the funeral service in the *Book of Common Prayer*, Psalms xc., especially verses 5–6.

99:26 **Te Deum laudamus.** Hymn ('We praise thee, O Lord'; Latin).

99:29 **Noon is *now*.** 'Nun' means 'now', with pronunciation suggesting 'Noon'.

99:37 **Bayern** German for the state of Bavaria, a kingdom ruled by the Wittelsbach family until 1919. When it became part of the new German Empire in 1871, it retained its own postal service.

100:2 **Kammerjunker** Gentleman-in-waiting (German).

100:10 **Herr Professor,** Alfred Kramer (lines 17–18) is a recreation of Edgar Jaffe (1866–1921), teacher of Political Economy at Heidelberg University and from 1910 at Munich Academy of Commerce; his speciality was banking and finance. Jaffe was one of fourteen children of a wealthy Jewish merchant family centred in Hamburg; he had represented the family textile export firm abroad, spending over ten years (from 1888) in Manchester. m. 1902, Else von Richthofen, Frieda's sister (see note on 111:25). See Martin Green, *The von Richthofen Sisters* (New York, 1974), p. 24. DHL wrote 'Edg' at 102:5 before realising his mistake.

101:31   **found a von.** 'Von' before a name indicates nobility.

102:14   **"Na!"** 'Now then!' (German).

102:19   **Court Brewery ... Pinakotheks or Glyptotheks** Hofbräuhaus, or 'Court Brewery', s.e. of the Residenz, 'famous among Bavarian beer-houses, and one of the sights of Munich, occupies a building decorated with frescoes by Ferd. Wagner' (Baedeker, *Southern Germany*, Leipzig, 1907, p. 192) ... Old Pinakothek (picture gallery), n.w. of the Residenz, classical paintings, including southern German artists, also Dürer and Rubens; New Pinakothek, immediately opposite, modern pictures; and Glyptothek (sculpture gallery), just s.w., chiefly Greek and Roman works.

102:37   **the word is God ... not with God,** John i. 1 ['In the beginning was the Word, and the Word was with God, and the Word was God.'] See also 193:38ff. ('Logos' is 'word'; Greek.)

103:9   **niemand and nichts,** Nobody and nothing (German).

103:20   **Ach Gott ... Ach jeh! Wo ist——?"** Ah God ... Ah yea! Where is – (German). Cf. 'Oh yea' and 'Oh jeh' (112:38; 218:1); the latter is more commonly spelled 'oje', which is short for 'ojemine' (abbreviation of 'O Jesus Domine') and usually suggests sympathy ('oh dear'; 218:7).

104:22   **weiss' du—?"** Do you know – ? (German). Alfred uses the second person singular, the familiar form of 'you'; 'weiss' should be 'weißt'.

104:25   **Theorie des Unbewussten.** Theory of the Unconscious. ('Unbewussten' means unconscious as the result of a physical blow; German.)

105:4   **Schmerzen** Pains (German).

105:9   **Ludwigshöhe** Alfred Kramer may be looking down on the Ludwig-Strasse, which runs n. from the centre, a wide boulevard with many historic buildings; the Frauen-Kirche and the palaces are visible from it.

105:28   **Sonntag—Isartalbahn ... halb-neun** Sunday – Isar-valley railway ... half-past eight (German).

105:38   **Off to ... mo-orning."** From the refrain of an Irish song titled 'My name is Paddy Leary' or 'Off to Philadelphia in the Morning'.

108:36   **a summer-house** DHL and Frieda stayed at 'Villa Jaffe, Irschenhausen, post *Ebenhausen*, bei München, Isartal' April–June 1913:

> We are in a lovely little wooden house in a corner of a pine or rather fir forest, looking over to the Alps, which are white with snow ... The house belongs to Frieda's brother in law. It is quite new – a lovely little place ... The meadow has blue patches of gentian ... [and] ... The place is a little summer house ... The deer feed sometimes in the corner among the flowers. But they fly with great bounds when I go out. (*Letters*, i. 541, 543)

The house was completed by early August 1912 (*Letters*, i. 431); cf. line 33. 'Genbach' (106:35): cf. Jenbach in note on 248:6.

109:12   **Marianne."** The Jaffes' daughter was named Marianne (b. 1905).

109:21   **Rehbock!"** Roebuck (German).

110:4   **walk to the Starnberg lake** A marked path led from Ebenhausen to Schloss Berg, a royal chateau with a large park, and the first station on the e. bank for the steamboat. There were a number of villas and chateaux (also an old castle) on the n. end of the lake (line 20).

110:14 **Hercynian forest,** The Roman name for an ill-defined forest-covered mountain region in s. and central Germany. Cf. chap. iv, *Movements in European History*, begun in 1918 and corrected in proofs in November 1920, and chap. iv, *Fantasia of the Unconscious*, first drafted in June 1921 (Seltzer, 1922).

111:8 **pantoffles.** Slippers; 'Pantoffeln' in German, and 'pantoufles' in French.

111:25 **a woman** Frau Professor Louise Kramer is a recreation of Elisabeth Frieda Amalie Sophie ('Else') von Richthofen (1874–1973), elder sister of Frieda Lawrence (see note on 119:1) and wife of Edgar Jaffe. Pupil of Max Weber at Heidelberg University; later professor of social economics there. She had four children. See *Letters*, i. 395, 409; see also note on 113:10. Although Louise is Johanna's (Frieda's) 'school-sister' in the novel (145:23), DHL slipped and first wrote 'my father' at 171:35–6.

112:14 **"Aber—**! But! (German).

112:35 **A handsome white-haired lady** Modelled on Baroness Anna von Richthofen, née Marquier (1851–1930), mother of Else, Frieda and Nusch (see note on 154:35). DHL apparently does not distinguish between this Baroness and Baroness von Hebenitz (143:14–15), Johanna's (Frieda's) mother; cf. this character's 'high, lament-voice' (117:33) with Baroness von Hebenitz's 'a quaint, plangent, lamentoso voice' and 'a child's high, strange lament voice' (177:39–40; 217:23–4). See also note on 219:39.

113:10 **Professor Ludwig Sartorius,** Modelled on Alfred Weber (1868–1958), professor of sociology and political science at Heidelberg University. He had been a student in Bonn, Berlin and Göttingen. He was Else Jaffe's lover: Else 'left her husband, gone with two other men (in succession)' and 'has a lover – a professor Weber of Heidelberg, such a jolly fellow. Her husband, also a professor, but at Munich, doesn't mind' (*Letters*, i. 395, 413; see also p. 415). See also note on 206:5.

113:28 **Wendolf."** Perhaps Friedrich Gundolf (1880–1931), pseudonym of Friedrich Gundelfinger, disciple of the Stefan George circle; literary critic and translator; professor of German literature at Heidelberg University, 1920.

114:23 **Maulberg,** Probably Heidelberg ('Maul' means mouth).

115:20 **said in German ... found it?"** In MS (p. 200), Professor Sartorius repeated the two song lines and then continued ' "But where have you found it?" '; DHL deleted the set-off lines and rewrote them so that he would have room for his additional material.

116:5 **'Jost like [115:29] ... to you.'"** 'Just like the Ivy', popular song by A. J. Mills, music by H. Castling; Gilbert corrects the seventh line at 116:24 ('constant and true'). Louise's French translation (115:15–16) is more provocative: 'And like the ivy / I shall climb up you – '.

116:8 **du Papagei,** You parrot (German).

117:4 **Athena ... professorial scales** In Greek mythology the goddess of wisdom, industry and war (the equivalent of the Roman Minerva, 52:40); she is sometimes portrayed in statues carrying a scale (of justice).

117:9 **the immature manuscript ... had not burnt,** Johann Wolfgang von Goethe (1749–1832) wrote an early draft of scenes of his *Faust* in 1772–5; he probably destroyed this manuscript sometime after 1816. But Luise von Göchhausen, a Weimar court lady-in-waiting, had made a copy of the manuscript about 1776; it was discovered and published as the *Urfaust* (1887) by Erich Schmidt (1853–1913), then Director of the Goethe-Schiller-Archiv. See *Goethe's Faust: Its Genesis and Purport* by Eudo C. Mason (Berkeley, 1967), pp. 39–92.

117:38 **sartor stick to his patching ... Schneider—*Sartorius*."** 'Sartor' (Latin) and 'Schneider' (German) both mean 'tailor'; 'sartorius' is the tailor's sitting position (*OED*). DHL is also alluding to *Sartor Resartus* (the tailor re-patched) (1833–4) by Thomas Carlyle (1795–1881). E. Sartorius was the pseudonym of Emil Schneider (b. 1839), German poet and man of letters.

118:13 ***fleur du mal ... outre-tombe* Monsieur Beardsley.** Flower of evil (see also note on 251:37) ... beyond the grave (cf. the title of Chateaubriand's autobiographical *Mémoires d'Outretombe*, 1849–50). Aubrey Beardsley (1872–98), illustrator with fantastic, mannered style (see also note on 152:35), and (line 13) Jonathan Swift (1667–1745), author of *Gulliver's Travels* (1726), etc. and dean of St Patrick's Cathedral, Dublin, from 1713, are both mentioned in the *Observer* review of *The Lost Girl* (5 December 1920), p. 5:

> It is easy to forget that Mr. Lawrence's chief preoccupation is beauty; yet it is as true of him as it was of Beardsley, another artist whose search led into byways rarely explored without danger to the explorer and disgust [to the observer] ... [Lawrence's] obsession is quite different from that of such an author as Swift, whose real preoccupation was truth, and who was also led to handle things generally left untouched ... Mr. Lawrence never gives us the whole of anyone; for he who is preoccupied with beauty is doomed not to find truth ...

118:15 **Yahoo ... spangled lily** Man-shaped creature in *Gulliver's Travels*, iv ... There is a story that Oscar Wilde (1854–1900) carried a lily down Piccadilly as a declaration of his cult of beauty and of his adoration of Lily Langtry.

118:27 ***let-down*,** *OED* gives this as a slang usage, with examples 1768–1894.

118:31 **How a *Times* critic ... word *toney*!** Also in the *Observer* review (see note on 118:13): 'His style in this book is still unformed. It has brilliant passages, but continuously it is tiring. He uses ungraceful words like "toney" – "the toney, intellectual élite," a deplorable phrase.' The *Westminster Gazette* reviewer commented on the 'dreadful colloquialisms, the loose journalism' (11 December 1920), p. 9. See note on 273:23 in *The Lost Girl*, ed. Worthen.

Toney (or tony), meaning 'having a high or fashionable tone, stylish', was colloquial USA usage, 1886 (*OED*).

119:1 **Morgenland** Orient (German)

119:1 **a lady** Mrs Johanna Keighley (122:4–5) is based on Emma Maria Frieda Johanna von Richthofen (1879–1956), born in Metz. m. (1) Ernest Weekley, 1899–1914 (see note on 122:5), (2) DHL, 1914 and (3) Angelo Ravagli (1891–1975), 1950. She bore three children (one boy and two girls) to Weekley; they lived in Nottingham. For Frieda's accounts of her early life and first marriage (in fictionalised form) see

Frieda Lawrence: The Memoirs and Correspondence, ed. E. W. Tedlock (1961) and of her life with DHL see *"Not I, But the Wind . . ."* See also *Letters*, i. 404.

120:30 **like a Wagner Goddess** In *Der Ring des Nibelungen* the goddess Erda appears in this way to warn Wotan of ultimate consequences (e.g. in Act IV of *Das Rheingold* she rises to half her height).

120:34 **danke . . . Gott sei dank!** Thanks . . . thank God! (German).

121:28 **what am I for a stupid ass!** Literal translation of the German phrase meaning 'what kind of stupid donkey am I!'

121:40 **'When the cat . . . mouse will play.** Proverb ['. . .mice will . . .'] (Tilley, *Dictionary of the Proverbs in England*, C175).

122:5 **My husband** Dr Everard Keighley is based on Ernest Weekley (1865–1954), Frieda's first husband. Professor of French, University College, Nottingham; from a lower middle-class family, he financed his own education including his studies at the Universities of Berne, Cambridge (Trinity College, *Letters*, ii. 281), Paris and Freiburg (where he met Frieda). Well-known etymologist; author of *Romance of Words* (1912), *Romance of Names* (1914), etc. DHL, who had attended lectures in French by Weekley, went to lunch at the Weekleys' house in March 1912 (and first saw Frieda) to discuss his plans for Germany.

On Weekley as a husband see *Letters*, i. 388 and Tedlock 72–4, 423–4.

122:21 **Frau Doktor—!"** A German wife is given her husband's title.

123:6 **the Hebers and the Wolfstangels** Perhaps Alfred and Max Weber (1864–1920): see also note on 111:25; and Karl Wolfskehl (1869–1948), a poet and professor of German literature at the University of Munich; associated with the Stefan George circle.

124:21 **swallow their . . . the man?** Pelops was butchered by his father Tantalus and served to the gods (they recognised the flesh as human and restored him). Pelop's son Atreus, to revenge himself on his brother Thyestes for seducing his wife, served Thyestes the flesh of his children to eat. On mother–son love see *Letters*, i. 477 and Frieda Lawrence 22, 74.

125:4 **kiss my feet . . . snowflower,** Frieda recorded in her memoir 'Gisla', 73pp. (University of New Mexico), that Weekley kissed her feet and called her 'My snowflower' (Tedlock 70–1). For a full transcription see 'Gisla', ed. Albert James Diaz, *Manuscripts*, x (Winter 1958), 11–29, 59. Cf. the play *The Fight for Barbara*, written August–October 1912 (*Argosy*, December 1933, 68–90 as 'Keeping Barbara'; collected in *The Complete Plays of D. H. Lawrence*, 1965) in which Frieda ('Barbara') tells Weekley: 'You went on worshipping me instead of loving me – kissing my feet instead of helping me. You put me on a pedestal . . .' (III. ii).

125:39 **horizontale.** Prostitute (French).

126:21 **a wonderful lover** Eberhard is a recreation of Dr Otto Gross (1877–1919), Austrian specialist in neurology and psychiatry; one time disciple of Freud; believer in total freedom from social rules and sexual libertarianism; drug addict. Gross moved in 1906 to Heidelberg with his wife (Frieda, née Schloffer) and child; he had numerous mistresses, including Else Jaffe, 1906–7, and Frieda Weekley,

1907–8. See *Letters*, i. 424 and Green, *The von Richthofen Sisters*, pp. 32–73. See also Frieda's account of their affair in Tedlock 82–91, 351 and Frieda Lawrence 21–2.

126:30 **Utrecht.** It is possible that Frieda met Gross at a conference in the Netherlands (possibly at Amsterdam or Leyden) in 1907; he vividly describes the boat trip back to England (letters at the Humanities Research Center, University of Texas at Austin).

127:3 **a white Dionysos.** Greek god, identified with Bacchus; god of the fertility of nature, a suffering god who dies and is resurrected, god of wine. DHL was influenced by Gilbert Murray's 1904 translation of *The Bacchae* by Euripides (480–406 B.C.) in which Dionysos is described as 'white'; see *Letters*, i. 261 and n., 525.

127:13 **Freud.** DHL was introduced to the work of Sigmund Freud in psychoanalysis by Frieda (and her family and friends): 'I never did read Freud,' DHL wrote in October 1913, 'but I have heard about him since I was in Germany' (*Letters*, ii. 80; see also pp. 218, 655). 'These theories' (line 28): Frieda Lawrence 21–2, 23 echoes the novel. See also *Letters*, i. 424.

129:2 **Berry.** See note on 145:1.

131:2 **Jupiter Tonans.** See 137:22: Jupiter the Thunderer was the chief god in Roman mythology, and like his Greek counterpart Zeus, was god of the sky and weather (including thunderbolts).

134:35 **As the afternoon** [132:39] **. . . I be drowned?"** If the account in *Letters*, i. 413 is added to that in Frieda Lawrence 60, they relate a similar incident at Kochelsee (131:20), which took place when DHL and Frieda were staying in Beuerberg (see note on 197:33).

135:39 *du guter Alfred* You good Alfred (German). 'Armer' (136:20) is 'poor'.

136:15 **"Green grapes . . . the grapes,"** From the fable of 'Le Renard et les raisins' by Jean de la Fontaine (1621–95): the fox says the grapes are green when he discovers he cannot reach them (*Fables choisies mises en vers*, 1668, book iii, fable 11).

137:15 **into a new dynamic reaction,** MS reads 'into a new dynamic reactions,'.

137:27 **gentilissimo,** Most kind (Italian).

137:37 **Essénnn! Kòmmmm!'** 'Essen' is food; 'komm' is come (German).

139:2 **Detsch.** Based on Metz which was French before the Franco-Prussian war of July 1870–February 1871; ceded to Germany by the Treaty of Frankfurt (1871); then administrative and garrison town for the Prussian army, strongly fortified (16,000 men), until 1918. See note on line 5 below. Cf. the description in 'The Thorn in the Flesh', *The Prussian Officer*, ed. John Worthen (Cambridge, 1983), pp. 22–7. ('Deutsch' means German.)

139:5 **Wilhelm Freiherr von Hebenitz,** A recreation of Baron Friedrich Carl Louis Ernst Emil von Richthofen (1845–1915), father of Frieda. He entered the Prussian army in 1862; was wounded in the Franco-Prussian war and removed from active duty; in 1912 he was garrison administrative officer in Metz. The von Richthofens and relations were assembling at the Baron's home in Montigny in May

1912 to celebrate his fiftieth anniversary of being in the army. Partial portraits of him are found in *The Fight for Barbara* and also in 'The Thorn in the Flesh', *The Prussian Officer*, ed. Worthen, pp. 1–21, 36–9; see also note on 180:35.

139:11 **name was legion** Mark v. 9 ['name is Legion'].

139:13 **Rudolf von Daumling**, Based on Udo von Henning, who was killed at Charleroi, 7 September 1914 (*Letters*, ii. 221). On 16 and 17 May 1912 DHL wrote to Frieda: 'If you want Henning, or anybody, have him. But I don't want anybody . . . But I don't believe even *you* are your best, when you are using Henning as a dose of morphia – he's not much else to you' and 'I think you're rather horrid to Henning. You make him more babified – baby-fied. Or shall you leave him more manly?' (*Letters*, i. 404, 406). DHL originally gave Daumling's name as Menner (here and line 34); he also referred to the Baroness von Hebenitz as Menner at 143:15; see textual apparatus.

140:6 **Tolstoi and chastity,** Cf. DHL's comment in the 'Study of Thomas Hardy', written September–December 1914 (published in *Phoenix* 398–516): 'Probably because of profligacy in his [Tolstoi's] youth, because he had disgusted himself in his own flesh, by excess or by prostitution, therefore Tolstoi, in his metaphysic, renounced the flesh altogether . . .' (p. 479). See 'Epilogue to The Kreutzer Sonata' (1890): 'Chastity is not a rule or a precept, but an ideal . . . The whole meaning of human life consists in a motion toward this ideal . . . [in] the striving after the Christian ideal, in all its entirety, and after chastity . . .', *The Complete Works of Count Tolstoy*, tr. Leo Wiener (1904), xviii. 425.

140:26 *Unglücksrabe*, A person who often draws bad luck on himself (literally, unlucky crow) (German).

140:30 **Speriamo.** Let's hope so (Italian).

141:3 **empyrean . . . winds of hell?** The highest heaven in Dante's *Paradiso* in the *Divina Commedia* . . . Francesca da Rimini, married to Giovanni Malatesta, fell in love with his younger brother Pàolo; the lovers were caught and killed by her husband, and Dante places them in the second circle of the Inferno, for great sinners of the flesh, where they are tossed and beaten continuusly by furious winds.

141:14 **gentille lecteuse, gentilissima lettrice,** Gentle (female) readers (French, Italian).

141:19 **Magdalen had . . . own feet.** There are three accounts of the incident – Mark xiv. 3–9, Luke vii. 36–50 and John xii. 2–8 – where Mary Magdalene, 'a sinner', anointed Christ's feet (or his head) with oil of spikenard and wiped his feet with her hair. See also 129:24. Christ said her many sins were forgiven 'for she loved much' (Luke vii. 47); cf. 277:34–5. DHL also alludes here to the popular saying about not crying over spilt milk.

141:21 **Hauptmann** Captain (German).

142:10 **Wolkenhof?** DHL (and Frieda) stayed at the Hotel Deutscher Hof, 3 rue des Clercs, now 'Grand Hôtel de Metz' (*Letters*, i. 390–1, 393–4 and Frieda Lawrence 25); there were (and are) many barracks in Metz, although some of the old town has been rebuilt.

143:14 **cathedral square ... Wilhelmgarten,** The Cathedral square (Parade-Platz, or Place d'Armes) is on the w. side of the old town, which is moated between the Moselle and the Seille. The Cathedral is Gothic and is highly visible in the town and the surrounding countryside: the 'hedgehog pricking its ears' (lines 20–1) and the 'brown rat humped up' of 'German Impressions: I. French Sons of Germany', *Westminster Gazette*, 3 August 1912 (reprinted in *Phoenix* 73). See also Tedlock 43, 58.

The Wilhelmgarten, or Esplanade, is directly s. of the Cathedral; the Jardin Boufflers (147:18) is at a right angle to the Esplanade. Cf. the description in 'The Thorn in the Flesh' (*The Prussian Officer*, ed. Worthen, p. 26). The river to the 'left', i.e. west (143:21), is the Moselle which runs just below the gardens.

143:31 **pale blue and silver and scarlet.** The uniform of the Bavarian Infantry regiments, which DHL would have seen in Bavaria in May–August 1912 and April–June 1913: he may also have seen them in Metz, but see note on 139:2. Cf. 'The Thorn in the Flesh', *The Prussian Officer*, ed. Worthen, p. 24 and note on 24: 2 and first two notes to the 'The Prussian Officer', p. 249.

144:19 **at ten [144:9] ... till after lunch.** There is a discrepancy between these two passages; cf. 145:33–4.

144:34 **would smell no sweeter.** Allusion to *Romeo and Juliet* II. ii. 43–4: 'What's in a name? That which we call a rose / By any other word would smell as sweet.'

145:1 **Berry:** Based on Will Dowson, a lace manufacturer in Nottingham; see *Letters*, i. 409 and n. 2. In her fictionalised account Frieda recalled: '[Frieda] had one great friend who had one of the first automobiles in England. He would drive into the forests with her, where the great hoary oaks stood apart from each other. There were pools of bluebells ... and the primroses ... Then she felt alive again; there weren't only dull teas and servants and grimy towns. But she always longed to go home' (Tedlock 82). DHL first called Berry 'Behn' (129:2, 26).

145:9 **Daphne.** In Greek mythology she ran naked through the trees (in a forest) to escape from Apollo (she was changed into a tree).

146:19 *n'ont pas de quoi.* Don't have the means (French).

146:25 **for the wings ... a dove,** From 'Oh for the wings of a dove' (1844), words by William Bartholomew (1793–1867) from 'O könnt' ich fliegen wie tauben dahin' by German composer Jacob Ludwig Felix Mendelssohn-Bartholdy (1809–47); lines 1–2 are 'Oh for the wings, for the wings of a dove! / Far away, far away would I rove!'

147:4 **to meet Louise** Cf. Else Jaffe's recollection of this meeting in *A Composite Biography*, ed. Nehls, i. 165.

147:16 **Kein chocolat,** No chocolate (German, French).

148:16 **das ist wirklich so ... Eben!"** That is really so ... Exactly! (German).

149:28 **du bist so dumm!"** You are so stupid! (German).

150:24 **The barber was French, and talked anti-German.** Cf. 'German Impressions: I. French Sons of Germany' (*Phoenix* 71).

150:40 **post office.** DHL's contemporary account of this incident (144:31–40 and 147:19 to here) was that Frieda 'told him [Weekley, before they left England] about two *other, earlier* men, but not about me. He however suspected. He said "if it is true, wire to me 'Ganz recent' (quite recent)." I saw the letter – we were sitting under the lilacs in the garden at Trier. Oh Lord – tragedy! I took F. straight to the post-office, and she wired "ganz recent"' (*Letters*, i. 409). (Weekley responded: ' "kein moeglich-keit" – (no possibility – i.e. all is over)'.)

152:13 **The course . . . run true.** *A Midsummer Night's Dream* I. i. 134 ['. . . love never did run smooth'].

152:35 **Salome . . . her chemise!"** Beardsley illustrated *Salomé* (1894), a play by Wilde. (DHL uses the same phrase in *The White Peacock*, ed. Robertson, p. 159.) . . . ' "Quick, sharp . . . her chemise!" ' is also quoted in '. . . . . . Love Was Once a Little Boy', written in 1925 (*Reflections on the Death of a Porcupine*, 1925; *Phoenix II* 458).

153:10 *in puris naturalibus,* Quite naked (Latin).

153:36 **"Die gnädige . . . Madame here?"** DHL originally wrote only the German and French phrases; he then crossed out the closing quotation marks and added the dashes and English translations. 'Frau': the accent recorded in textual apparatus was sometimes used to differentiate between 'u' and 'n'. 'Non, elle . . . ici.' (line 38): 'No, she isn't here' (French).

154:6 **"pipe of half awakened bird."** From a song ('Tears, idle tears . . .') in 'The Princess' (1847) by Tennyson, iv. 50 ['. . . half-awakened birds'].

154:35 **a handsome, ultra-fashionable woman** Lotte is a recreation of Helene Johanna Mathilde ('Nusch') von Richthofen (1882–1971), younger sister of Frieda. m. (1) Max von Schreibershofen, 1900–23 and (2) Emil Krug, 1923. DHL described Nusch as 'very beautiful . . . and, in a large, splendid way – cocotte' and 'rather splendid in her deliberate worldliness' (*Letters*, i. 395, 409); she lived in Berlin. See also Tedlock 80 and Frieda Lawrence 25.

155:4 **"Ja Lotte [154:37] . . . Mille pardons!** 'Yes Lotte – here he is – not the real Mr Berry.' 'Good day sir, . . . So you are not Berry!' . . . I gave you a nasty turn, did I? A thousand pardons! 'Ai-dà' (and 'hein') is a characteristic French interjection with no real meaning.

156:11 **nothingness, put** In MS DHL wrote 'nothingness. And', and when he inserted 'put it in your pocket', he neglected to change the full stop to a comma; see textual apparatus.

156:27 **the world is void and dark.** Cf. Genesis i. 2.

157:6 **in kingdom come** Matthew vi. 10 ['Thy Kingdom . . .'].

157:18 **uplift-wooshers,** DHL coinage, the second part presumably a variant of 'whooshers' (cf. 140:40).

157:19 **Pluto-drizzle of charity** Pluto ('wealth-giver') was the Greek god of the underworld (and indirectly, of the earth, the source of wealth).

158:2 **the wind . . . shorn lamb.** God tempers the wind . . . to the shorn lamb: from a French proverb, but best-known from Sterne's *A Sentimental Journey through France and Italy* (1768).

158:4 **the May fair** Cf. Frieda Lawrence 25.

158:39 **"Allez! Allez ... Mauvaise occasion!"** 'Go! Go then! ... And goodbye. Inopportune moment!' (French).

159:33 **a village [159:8] ... and maliciously.** Gilbert walked up the hill to the village of Scy (now Scy-Chazelles); in German, Sigach. Metz can be viewed from the natural platform with its several rows of horsechestnut trees, where Gilbert watched the soldier exercise his horse (line 14). Cf. 'German Impressions: I. French Sons of Germany' (*Phoenix* 72–5) in which the narrator recorded similar experiences and an anti-German café owner (in the *Westminster Gazette* text, 3 August 1912) gave the French name of the village as 'Sey'.

159:36 **forcé,** Forced, compulsory (French).

160:24 **"Dear Doctor X [160:16] ... than this———"** Cf. DHL's letter to Weekley, *Letters*, i. 392.

161:2 **St. George ... Sabra,** Sabra, the daughter of an Egyptian king, was rescued from the dragon by St George whom she married, in *The Seven Champions of Christendom* (1596) by Richard Johnson (1573–1659?). The cross (line 7) of St George, the patron saint of England, is a red upright cross with arms of equal length on a white background.

163:12 **Marvell.** The Weekleys lived at 9 Goldswong Terrace, 8 Vickers Road and Cowley, later renamed Hillcrest, 32 Victoria Crescent, Mapperley, all in Nottingham. Abraham Cowley (1618–67) and Andrew Marvell (1621–78) both attended Trinity College, Cambridge, and were metaphysical poets.

165:4 **Panacea—,"** 'All-Healing'; in Greek mythology the daughter of Asclepius, honoured as the god of medicine.

165:38 **take all men ... Watts picture.** Probably G. F. Watts's *Hope* (1885–6), which portrays a young woman in light draperies sitting on a large globe. For DHL's opinion of his paintings see *Letters*, i. 107–8, 530.

167:24 **some of her fury.** This phrase came at the end of the third MS notebook; hence, the confusion recorded in textual apparatus.

168:9 **"Shall we [161:22] ... the little path.** DHL wrote on 9 May:
> I had to quit Metz because the damn fools wanted to arrest me as a spy. Mrs Weekley and I were lying on the grass near some water – talking – and I was moving round an old emerald ring on her finger, when we heard a faint murmur in the rear – a German policeman. There was such a to-do. It needed all the fiery little Baron von Richthofen's influence – and he is rather influential in Metz – to rescue me. They vow I am an English officer – *I* – *I*!! The damn fools. So behold me, fleeing eighty miles away, to Trier. (*Letters*, i. 394–5)

See also *Letters*, i. 395, 397. Frieda records her father's assistance and his meeting with DHL (168:34ff.) in Frieda Lawrence 26.

168:38 **"Sie sprechen ... parlez français?"** 'Do you speak German – or French? Do you speak French?' (German, French).

169:13 **"Vous fumez [169:8] ... en Allemagne?"** 'Do you smoke?' ... 'Yes, thank you,' ... 'Have you been in Germany for long?' (French).

169:28 **"Vous êtes ... intéressante."** 'You have been in Munich, my daughter tells me. You like Bavaria?' 'Yes! Yes! A lot! And the people are very interesting.' (French) (The Baron then corrects Noon's grammar: 'peuple' is a masculine noun.)

170:31 Guten Abend [170:23] ... **oder Käse?**" Good evening (German) ... Fruit or cheese? (French and German).

171:16 Darunten—links ... **Danke sehr,**" 'Down that way – to the left' ... 'Many thanks' (German).

172:40 *verbotens.* Forbidden things or activities (German adjective given the English plural 's').

173:5 Trier, The town lies in a narrow valley, bounded by steep hills ('hills like Matlock', *Letters*, i. 397) on the e. and w.: 'The vines are all new young slips, climbing up their sticks. The whole hillside bristles with sticks, like an angry hedgehog ... The Mosel winds below. The vine sticks bristle against the sky' actually describes Trier (not Metz) in 'German Impressions: I. French Sons of Germany' (*Phoenix* 72–3) which DHL wrote after arriving in Trier; see *Letters*, i. 393–7.

The railway station is on the e. side of Trier and has been rebuilt since the Second World War; Hotel Rheinischer Hof ('Grünwald Gasthaus', 175:7), once on Nord Allee, is no longer in existence as a hotel; see *Letters*, i. 393–4. M. Hermesdorf ('Fritz', 175:15) was the proprietor; see *Letters*, i. 393, 396.

174:14 a massive, heavy round-bowed Dom, The Cathedral, e. of the central market place, is one of the oldest churches in Germany, dating from the mid-fourth century. The exterior is of local red sandstone (with no steps at the main entrance); the baroque interior is varicoloured stone, and the half dome in the back, which is reached by two sets of stairs, has white figures in relief on a blue background. See also *Letters*, i. 396–7.

175:10 Nord-Deutscher-Lloyd boats. Shipping company, mainly to the Americas and Asia.

176:8 a barracks, and a drill-ground, The Archbishops' Palace, just s. of the Dom, was used as a barracks, and the Exercier-Platz is further s.

176:21 God Save the King! [176:6] ... **Sieger Kranz—**" Gilbert thinks they are singing the British national anthem, 'God Save our gracious King!', and then realises they are singing German words ('Hail to thee in the victor's wreath') to almost the same tune.

177:9 *Jugend Die Jugend,* German satirical weekly, founded in 1896 in Munich as a national liberal competitor of *Simplicissimus.*

177:19 "Moi, je ... trouver, Mère." 'I'm not part of the embassy. I'm off. I'll come back for you, Mother.' (French).

177:39 Wissen Sie—" You see (literally, you know) (German).

178:15 hier in ... drei Jahrelang. Here in Germany divorce requires three years ... over a period of three years (German).

179:33 es ist zuviel. It is too much (German).

180:4 **"Gleich! Fünf Minuten!"** 'Right away! Five minutes!' (German).

180:25 **Vier Uhr,** Four o'clock (German).

180:35 **"Poor Papa ... Poor Papa!"** Cf. Frieda Lawrence 25: 'My father, who loved me, said to me in great distress: "My child, what are you doing? I always thought you had so much sense. I know the world." I answered: "Yes, that may be, but you never knew the best." I meant to know the best.'

180:40 **his Elena ... his illegitimate son!** In *The Fight for Barbara* Sir William Charlcote has a mistress Selma and an illegitimate son (Act I). For the Baron as an 'unfaithful, gambling husband' (179:11) see Tedlock 389–90 and Green, *The von Richthofen Sisters,* p. 14.

182:6 **all along the Moselle valley ... for Cologne.** DHL's train trip took a long day: nine hours according to *Letters,* i. 398 (fourteen according to a deletion in MS; see textual apparatus). He went via Coblenz (w. bank of the Rhine), Ehrenbreitstein (immediately opposite on the e. bank), Niederlahnstein, Cologne, Troisdorf and Hennef to Waldbröl; see *Letters,* i. 398. See also notes on 184:28 and 187:11.

183:15 *fünf Mark fünfzig.* Five Marks fifty (Pfennige) (German).

183:23 **"Zuschlagen ... Was meint zuschlagen?"** 'Additional charge – ' ... 'What does additional charge mean?' The noun form (Zuschlag) would be correct German; also Gilbert's question is stated in a very English way ('Was heißt . . .' would be correct).

184:3 **a Wotan God** Wotan is the leader of the gods in the *Ring* cycle. He sires a human champion whose son Siegfried (200:21) succeeds in returning the Rhine-gold to its rightful owners.

184:6 **Germanic Over-Allness.** Allusion to the German national anthem, 'Deutschland über Alles' ('Germany beyond, or before everything'); see also 187:22. Written in 1841 by August Heinrich Hoffman, generally called Hoffman von Fallersleben (1798–1874).

184:17 **godlifying ... olympising ...** *dieu gratuite!,* DHL's coinages ... here's a gratuitous God! (French).

184:28 **at Hennef ... by the stream** Cf. *Letters,* i. 398 and 'Bei Hennef', *The Complete Poems of D. H. Lawrence,* ed. Vivian de Sola Pinto and Warren Roberts (1964), i. 203: 'The little river twittering in the twilight, / ... All the troubles and anxieties and pain / Gone under the twilight' (lines 1, 5–6). (The river is the Sieg.) When compiling *Collected Poems* (1928) DHL added this poem to the *Look! We Have Come Through!* (1917) section: he stated in the introductory note that '"Bei Hennef", written in May, 1912, by a river in the Rhineland, starts the new cycle' (*Complete Poems,* i. 28); see also *Letters,* i. 462.

The events and feelings of DHL's early relationship with Frieda which are included in *Mr Noon* were recorded in the *Look!* poems, e.g. 'On the Balcony', 'Frohnleichnam', 'Mutilation', 'Quite Forsaken', 'Fireflies in the Corn' (especially the early version, ii. 944–5) and 'A Doe at Evening' (i. 208–10, 212–13, 220–2): and see notes on 233:29 and 254:26.

'Peace like a full river' (line 34): cf. Isaiah xlviii. 18, lxvi. 12.

184:39 **Bummelzug** Slow train; a Bummelzug is a Personenzug which stops at *every* station (German).

185:6 **Dilly-Dilly-Dilly ... be killed.** From the nursery rhyme which begins: 'Oh, what have you got for dinner, Mrs Bond? / There's beef in the larder, and ducks in the pond; / Dilly, dilly, dilly, dilly, come to be killed / For you must be stuffed and my customers filled!' (*Oxford Dictionary of Nursery Rhymes*, ed. Opie, no. 62).

185:29 **elective affinities** English title of *Die Wahlverwandtschaften* (1808) by Goethe; the German is a technical term for a chemical process, which Goethe extended to human relationships: a person would be attracted to another to whom he had an 'affinity' and would thus prefer that person over another (established) relationship.

187:11 **Wensdorf** Recreation of Waldbröl: see *Letters*, i. 399, 409–10. The Lutheran church (lines 16–17) is on higher land and has a taller steeple than the Catholic church (St Michael); they face each other about a block apart between the parallel old east–west main streets.

187:12 **by his friend and his friend's wife Ulma.** Joseph Heyser (181:7) and his wife are recreations of Karl Albert Bernhard Krenkow (1871–1943), a civil servant, who married his cousin Johanna Gertrud Maria ('Hannah') (1874–1945); DHL was related by marriage to Hannah Krenkow: she was the sister of DHL's uncle by marriage, Fritz Krenkow. For DHL's reactions to Hannah and Karl see *Letters*, i. 399, 406, 409. (DHL originally called Marta, Louise's servant, Hannah, 110:28 and 111:1) Heyser is probably Gilbert's friend 'in the Rhine province' (167:10); DHL referred to the Krenkows as 'friends' *Letters*, i. 352 and gave 'Rheinprovinz' as part of their address (*Letters*, i. 394ff.). For a portrayal of Hannah Krenkow (as 'Johanna') see 'German Impressions: II. Hail in the Rhineland', *Westminster Gazette*, 9 August 1912 (reprinted in *Phoenix* 75–81).

187:27 **Pommeland bread ... Kringeln:** Pommerland bread (from Pommern; then one of the Prussian provinces, now part of Poland), darkish rye bread ... a sweet or salted pretzel (German).

187:30 **long walks ... to villages** For a description of one such walk to Nümbrecht, see 'German Impressions: II. Hail in the Rhineland' (*Phoenix* 75–81).

187:40 **They went to a fair ... some high, famous castle.** DHL went to the Kermesse with the Krenkows; see *Letters*, i. 399. They made the trip from Bonn down the Rhine to the Drachenfels, a high peak (327 m.) with a castle ruin at the top (Königswinter castle can be seen on a neighbouring mountain); *Letters* i. 407–8, 410.

188:2 **rather lofty and sweet letters,** Cf. *Letters*, i. 400–4, 406–7.

188:14 **cris de cœur,** Cries from the heart (French).

189:34 **secret of tree worship** See the opening of section i 'Tree-spirits', chap. ix of *The Golden Bough* (1890–1915) by James Frazer (1854–1941), ii. 7ff.

189:39 **tree of life ... was crucified.** Christ is sometimes depicted as dying on a cross made from the Tree of Knowledge (of Good and Evil), but at other times it is the Tree of Life.

190:5 **immortels.** DHL's error for 'immortelles', an everlasting flower, usually artificial, placed on graves (French).

190:16 **Basta! Revenons ... deux moutons.** Enough! Let us return to our two sheep, i.e. our subject (Italian, French). The latter from the mediaeval farce, *L'Avocat Pathelin* ['... nos moutons'] occurs in several of DHL's works.

190:23 **"Man survives ... the bedroom."** From Maxim Gorky's *Reminiscences of Leo Nicolayevitch Tolstoi*, trans. by S. S. Koteliansky and Leonard Woolf (July 1920), p. 19 ['... but for all time his most tormenting tragedy has been, is, and will ...']; see also note on 251:37.

191:8 **seven dark hills ... sensual fulfilment.** Glancing references to the ideas that man goes through seven levels of spiritual development (from James Pryse's *The Apocalypse Unsealed*, 1910) and that there are seven heavens based on the cosmology of the Ptolemaic system. See also *Apocalypse and the Writings on Revelation*, ed. Mara Kalnins (Cambridge, 1980), pp. 4–5, 101 and note on 101:17.

192:17 **Rabelais ... Maupassant** François Rabelais (1494?–1553), French humanist, satirist and physician; author of *Pantagruel* (1532 or 1533) and *Gargantua* (1534), often thought of as coarse and obscene ... Guy de Maupassant (1850–93), French novelist of the naturalist school and master of the short story, whose cynical frankness about sexual relationships disturbed the young DHL (see *Letters*, i. 29, 91–2).

192:22 **OO.** Some German toilets have 'OO' (said 'Null-Null') on the door; in hotels this distinguishes them from the numbered bedrooms. There are various explanations of its origin.

193:31 **the hopeless tragic, like Hardy ... Conrad passes.** Chap. iii of the 'Study of Thomas Hardy' is entitled 'Containing Six Novels and the Real Tragedy' ... DHL was not in general impressed with Joseph Conrad's writings (see *Letters*, i. 456, 465), but liked a few of them (see E. T. [Jessie Wood], *D. H. Lawrence: A Personal Record*, 1935, reprinted Cambridge, 1980, p. 121; *A Composite Biography*, ed. Nehls, Madison, 1958, ii. 291; and *Letters*, i. 118).

On some of these poets see 'Study of Thomas Hardy', pp. 459–60, 513 and *Letters*, ii. 101–2.

194:23 **Schloss Wolfratsberg.** Else Jaffe lived at Haus Vogelnest, Wolfratshausen (*Letters*, i. 412–13). Louise's house is on the steep, forested hill w. of and parallel with the main street and the Loisach river.

194:32 **Lady of Shalott ... sat weaving** Cf. Tennyson's 'The Lady of Shalott' (1852) who weaves 'the mirror's magic sights' (i.e. the 'shadows of the world'); her web breaks, and the mirror cracks when she does look out of the window (II. 29, 12).

195:35 **Er ist doch so schwer."** But he is so difficult (German).

195:40 **to write so *plainly!*"** See Ernest Weekley's letters in Tedlock 178–81 and *Letters*, i. 430, 440–1, 457 and 485.

196:8 **"When I am a prostitute—"** Cf. DHL's report of Weekley's comment to Frieda in December 1914: 'Isn't the commonest prostitute better than you?' (*Letters*, ii. 245). See also *The Lost Girl*, ed. Worthen, p. 328.

196:9 **Das ist Frechheit.** That is impudence (German).

196:37 **saudumm.** Awfully stupid (German).

197:33 **Kloster Schaeftlarn,** 'Beuerberg is about 40 kilometres from Munich, up the Isar, near the Alps. This is the Bavarian Tyrol. We stayed in the Gasthaus zur Post" (*Letters*, i. 413). See DHL's description of the Alps, the river (Loisach) and the flowers, and also 'my week's honeymoon', in *Letters*, i. 411–15, 417–18. The railway now stops at Wolfratshausen. (There is a Kloster ('cloister') Schäftlarn where DHL wrote 'River Roses', collected in *Look! We Have Come Through!*) See also note on 238:24.

200:30 **brand** Archaic meaning was 'a sword', from its glitter.

200:36 **MacWhirter's picture** ... *the Tyrol, June in the Austrian Tyrol* (exhibited 1892) by John A. MacWhirter (1839–1911), in the Tate Gallery: there is a profusion of the flowers DHL mentions in the foreground (with a girl picking some), and the Alps in the background are darkened by approaching storm clouds. The same misremembered title is given in 'The Crucifix Across the Mountains', *Twilight in Italy* (1916) (first appeared as 'Christs in the Tirol', *Westminster Gazette*, 22 March 1913; reprinted *Phoenix* 82–6).

202:7 **Dunkels** A dark one, i.e. a dark beer (German).

202:20 **"Think of my little boys!"** The 'trouble about the children' lasted for years: first Frieda's grief over losing them and then her struggles to see them; see *Letters*, i. 421–2, 430 *passim* and *Letters*, ii. 21, 46, 51 *passim*; Frieda Lawrence 52, 58, 78; and Tedlock 96–8.

203:35 **once had ... so strong.** DHL was seriously ill with pneumonia in 1901 and 1911; he was convinced the first permanently damaged his health.

204:37 **the bull Typhon.** In Greek mythology a monster with a hundred heads of dragon-shape and whose voices could sound like a lion, bull or dog; overthrown by Zeus with his thunderbolts.

205:3 **a tanger.** Literally, something which stings (dialect): hence, a sharp, stinging person (Wright, *English Dialect Dictionary*).

205:20 **Little Jack Horner ... Little Bo-peep ... Jack and Jill** From three separate nursery rhymes: 'Little Jack Horner', 'Little Bo-peep' and 'Jack and Jill' (*Oxford Dictionary of Nursery Rhymes*, ed. Opie, nos. 262, 66, 254).

205:24 *is* DHL underlined this twice in MS (p. 329).

206:1 **Chapter XIX.** This chapter and the final one do not have titles; DHL several times added the title after starting a chapter.

206:5 **a country flat, belonging to one of her friends,** The flat in Icking belonged to Alfred Weber (218:16). See *Letters*, i. 413–15 and Frieda Lawrence 52–3. Frau Leitner, the 'Frau Breitgau' of line 16, had the shop underneath (Frieda Lawrence 54).

207:8 **a cutlet of Ripperle,** A pork rib (also 'ripple'; see note on 207:17) (German).

207:9 **strong Bayrisch,** The Bavarian dialect is *very* hard to understand, even for Germans from another part of Germany.

207:17 **live for fifteen shillings a week,** Cf. Frieda's account: 'We had very little money, about fifteen shillings a week. We lived on black bread that Lawrence loved, fresh eggs, and "ripple"; later we found strawberries, raspberries and "heidelbeeren"' (Frieda Lawrence 53). ('Heidelbeeren' are bilberries).

208:19 **chuffled.** DHL's coinage, perhaps onomatopoetic.

209:14 **They would hear** [207:25] ... **scored horse.** Cf. a similar incident in 'The Young Soldier with Bloody Spurs', *Complete Poems*, ed. Pinto and Roberts, ii. 732–5. Cf. Johanna's reaction at 209:35–210:19 with Frieda Lawrence 55–6. (The dark blue uniforms, 208:18, were worn by the Prussian army; cf. note on 143:31).

211:40 **all women become as men ... all men become as women,** A topic in DHL's late essays and poems, e.g. 'Master in His Own House' (originally titled 'Men Must Rule'), 'Cocksure Women and Hensure Men', 'Is England Still a Man's Country?' (collected in *Assorted Articles*, 1930), and 'Women Want Fighters for Their Lovers', 'Don'ts' and 'Energetic Women' (*Complete Poems*, ed. Pinto and Roberts, i. 457–9, 537).

217:4 **a Rubens' Venus.** Rubens portrayed Venus as a voluptuous, naked woman several times. Cf. *Letters*, i. 415.

218:5 **"—Yes, and ... so good,** DHL's translation is substantially correct, except for the omission of 'You don't know it' (for 'Das wissen Sie nicht') and the addition of 'even' and 'so good' which are not present in the German. DHL's German is rather odd, i.e. 'adlicher' for 'adliger' and 'gelernt' for 'gelehrt'.

218:32 **Aber was meinst du, Mama!"** But what do you mean, Mama! (German).

219:39 **schimpfing.** 'Scolding, abusing' from 'Schimpfen' (German). DHL wrote on 4 August 1912 of this encounter (*Letters*, i. 429–30):

> Oh, I must tell you how the Baroness von Richthofen 'schimpfed' me on Friday night. She suddenly whirled in here on her way from The Tyrol to Constance, stayed an hour, and spent that hour abusing me like a washerwoman – in German, of course. I sat and gasped. 'Who was I, did I think, that a Baronesse should clean my boots and empty my slops: she, the daughter of a high-born and highly-cultured gentleman' – at the highly-cultured, I wanted to say 'I don't think!' – 'No decent man, no man with common sense of decency, could expect to have a woman, the wife of a clever professor, living with him like a barmaid, and he not even able to keep her in shoes.' – So she went on. – Then in München, to Else, her eldest daughter, says I am a lovable and trustworthy person. – You see I saw her off gracefully from the station.

DHL first used this encounter in Act II of *The Fight for Barbara*, where Lady Charlcote visits Barbara and Jimmy Wesson in Italy.

220:26 **fools always do rush in!** From 'For Fools rush in where Angels fear to tread' in Pope's *Essay on Criticism* (1711), line 625.

220:30 **bruit pour une omelette.** Fuss about nothing; literally, 'row about an omelette' (French).

221:27 **Das mein ... kein Abern.** I think so too. but – ... *But me no buts* (German). The phrase was popularised by Sir Walter Scott in *The Antiquary* (1816). (Correct German would be 'Abere mir keine Abers'.)

222:6 hutch Huddle together, i.e. hunch (Wright, *English Dialect Dictionary*).

222:23 front. MS reads 'front?', but DHL's eye may have been caught by the question mark immediately above ('I?').

224:13 unalleved Unrelieved, unalleviated (*OED*).

224:19 barked at him. Cf. the description of this scene in *The Fight for Barbara*, Act II.

226:24 such Jonahs ... right shore See Jonah i–ii. For his disobedience Jonah was swallowed by 'a great fish', but was 'vomited out' when he repented.

227:11 "And oh ... to be." *Maud* (1835) by Tennyson, X vi. 1–2 ['And ah for a man to arise in me, ... am may cease to be!'].

227:15 Gethsemanes. Mark xiv. 32–6; see also 254:16.

228:25 finish his book of songs ... had written down a sketch of a symphony The references here and elsewhere to Gilbert's creative activity are too nebulous to correlate with DHL's writing. By late July 1912 he said he had planned some German sketches (five completed) for a possible book and six short stories (*Letters*, i. 430–1), sketched out *The Fight for Barbara* ('I am amusing myself writing a comedy', *Letters*, i. 427), started the fourth revision of 'Paul Morel' and composed more than a dozen of the *Look! We Have Come Through!* poems. As for 'a sketch of a symphony' DHL mentioned 'I've thought of a new novel – purely of the common people – fearfully interesting' on 4 August (*Letters*, i, 431) which may be the one he intended to call 'Scargill Street' (*Letters*, i. 466); nothing is known about it. See also David Garnett, *The Golden Echo* (1953), p. 245; for Garnett see note on 255:5.

229:23 Landstrasse High-road (German).

230:35 ganz und gar nichts ... Danke schön Nothing at all ... thank you very much (German).

233:17 My pigeon. One of Paul Morel's pet names for his mother in *Sons and Lovers*.

233:29 Two nights after [232:1] **... by him.** Cf. another treatment of this incident in 'In the Dark', *Complete Poems*, ed. Pinto and Roberts, i. 210–12.

236:6 Rausch Intoxication, frenzy (German).

237:22 nine pounds, and Johanna six. DHL and Frieda each had about £12 (*Letters*, i. 424, 430), which Garnett confirms (*Golden Echo*, p. 247).

238:2 Over the Hills. Cf. the route and the sights in 'A Chapel Among the Mountains' written in August 1912, as was 'A Hay-Hut Among the Mountains' (see below); both were published posthumously in *Love Among the Haystacks and Other Pieces* (1930) and reprinted in *Phoenix II*. 'A Chapel' parallels pp. 238:3–244:3, e.g. tea by a waterfall and the grasshopper, Johanna ('Anita' in 'A Chapel') laughing at Noon's (the narrator's) 'camel hump' rucksack, Noon looking at the *ex voto* pictures in the chapel and Johanna's preference for sleeping in the hay hut (*Phoenix II* 29–36).

238:24 two tall-necked churches ... cupolas, The Catholic church in Wolfratshausen has a tall slender cupola, but Beuerberg has two, which are visible from some distance: the convent (see 200:2) and the parish church.

239:18 burberry, Trade name for cloth or clothing made by Burberrys Ltd; here, a raincoat (*OED*).

240:15 Franz Joseph, Emperor of Austria, 1848–1916.

240:34 Frauenzimmer An old usage meaning 'woman' (German).

241:19 by a footpath. Gilbert and Johanna follow the Isar (Frieda Lawrence 66) from Bad Tölz until they reach Fleck and then take the path over the pass.

242:34 a tiny chapel, Röhrlmoos; cf. the chapel at 'Rerelmos' in 'A Chapel Among the Mountains'. See also Frieda Lawrence 66 and *Letters*, i. 441: 'Crossing the mountains, we got stranded one night. I found a lovely little wooden chapel, quite forsaken, and lit the candles, and looked at the hundreds of Ex Voto pictures – so strange.' Many of the *ex voto* pictures (presented in recognition of answered prayers) match those given in 'A Chapel'; see next note. (The chapel has been rebuilt closer to the hay hut, 244:7.)

243:32 "Du heilige . . . Wille sei. 'You holy mother of Rerelmos [Röhrlmoos] / I pray you free my son from imprisonment. / Free him from iron and bondage / If it is your holy will' (German). Cf. the verse in 'A Chapel Among the Mountains' (*Phoenix II* 34):
   'Oh Mutter Gottes von Rerelmos, Ich bitte mach mir mein Kind von Gefangenschaft los mach im von Eissen [Eisen] und bandten frey wansz des Gottliche [Göttliche] willen sey

Susanna Grillen 1783.'
DHL undoubtedly had trouble reading the Gothic script; see F. I. Owen, 'Lawrentian Places: I. A Chapel and a Hay-Hut Among the Mountains: 1971', *Human World* (May 1973), 46. Owen's article has descriptions of some of the *ex voto* pictures which remain in the new chapel.

243:35 Why was he in prison? In 'A Chapel Among the Mountains' DHL speculated that it was for political reasons. Bavaria had been disputed territory between Prussia and Austria for many years.

246:18 After a hundred [244:7] . . . watery flowers. Cf. 'A Hay-Hut Among the Mountains' (*Phoenix II* 37–43) in which Anita and the narrator sleep in a hay hut situated in a 'kettle' between the mountains, discover the disadvantages of using a waistcoat for a pillow and the irritation of hay, etc. See also Frieda Lawrence 66.

246:21 a village of about four houses. Glashütte, a hamlet with an inn: see *Letters*, i. 432 and 'A Hay-Hut Among the Mountains' (*Phoenix II* 43); both refer also to the forester's story (lines 27–30) about Archduke Franz Ferdinand (assassinated at Sarajevo on 28 June 1914).

247:7 Achen lake . . . the hotel 'A dark-blue lake . . . the finest in N[orthern] Tyrol' . . . Hotel Scholastika (Baedeker, *Southern Germany*, p. 281).

248:6 the wide, open place . . . the imperial road. Jenbach is a junction of railroads (and roads) . . . DHL also mentioned the imperial road at the opening of 'The Crucifix Across the Mountains', *Twilight in Italy*.

248:11 dark castle. The ancient fortress (before 1205) of Geroldseck, which dominates Kufstein, the scene of many battles. It was abandoned in 1872 and then served as a barracks. (DHL posted two cards written at Glashütte in Kufstein on 8 August; see *Letters*, i. 432).

248:24   Eckershofen, DHL wrote on 19 August about Mayrhofen: 'Here we are lodging awhile in a farmhouse [bei Fräulein Schneeberger]. A mountain stream rushes by just outside. It is icy and clear. We go out all day with our Rucksacks . . . We go quite long ways up the valleys. The peaks of the mountains are covered with eternal snow' (*Letters*, i. 441; see also p. 443). The valley divides into four branches, not three (line 36).

249:26   *Servus!* or *Grüss-Gott* Austrian and Bavarian colloquial greetings; the second is an abbreviation of Grüss Sie / dich Gott (God greet you). See *Letters*, i. 544.

249:34   men were dancing the Schuhplattler Tyrolese clog-dance. Cf. in *Women in Love* 'the Tyrolese dance of the clapping hands and tossing the partner in the air at the crisis' (chap. xxix). (DHL wrote the verb form; see textual apparatus.)

250:34   to Emmie . . . his sister Violet: Probably a reference to Louisa ('Louie') Burrows (1888–1962), to whom DHL was engaged December 1910–February 1912; see *Letters*, i. 29 n. 3. 'Violet' would be Lettice Ada Lawrence (1887–1942), his younger sister.

251:37   a Baudelaire poem . . . thighs, fascinated. 'La Géante' ('Giantess') in *Les Fleurs du Mal* (1857) by Charles Baudelaire (1821–67): 'To see her body flower with her desire / And freely spread out in its dreadful play, / . . . To feel at leisure her stupendous shapes, / Crawl on the cliffs of her enormous knees, / And, when in summer the unhealthy suns / Have stretched her out across the plains, fatigued, / Sleep in the shadows of her breasts at ease / Like a small hamlet at a mountain's base' (lines 5–6, 9–14), tr. Karl Shapiro in *The Flowers of Evil*, ed. Marthiel and Jackson Matthews, rev. edn (New York, 1962), p. 26. But cf. Tolstoi's description of a landowner's dream: 'On the steppe he saw two hills, which suddenly turned into a woman's breasts, and between them rose up a black face which, instead of eyes, had two moons like white spots. The old man dreamt that he was standing between the woman's legs, in front of him a deep, dark ravine, which sucked him in . . .' (*Reminiscences of Tolstoi*, by Gorky, p. 31).

253:28   cut to pieces for you." Cf. Frieda's report of Weekley saying: 'No man can do more than give his life, but I would have gladly been tortured for you and laughed . . .' (*Letters*, i. 475).

254:26   Once at twilight [253:7] . . . and wincing. Cf. 'Meeting Among the Mountains', written at 'Tuxtal' (Tuxertal) (*Complete Poems*, ed. Pinto and Roberts, i. 224–6); DHL confirmed that he identified the oxen driver in the poem with Weekley (*Letters*, ii. 154). (Chatto and Windus insisted that this poem be omitted from *Look! We Have Come Through!*)

255:5   Terry A recreation of David Garnett (1892–1981), trained as a botanist, Royal College of Science; later novelist and autobiographer. See *Letters*, i. 429, 526–7. His father Edward Garnett (1868–1937) had been one of DHL's earliest and most sympathetic literary advisors; DHL (and Frieda) had visited Edward Garnett and Constance (1861–1946), celebrated translator of Russian literature, at their home, The Cearne, near Edenbridge, Kent. David met DHL and Frieda at Icking in mid-July 1912; for his account of the journey over the Alps see *Golden Echo*, pp. 240–8.

255:24   The Russian Ballet . . . to London. Diaghilev's company, the Ballets-Russes, appeared in London 12 June–1 August 1912; Anna Pavlova (1885–1931) did not perform with them then. (Pavlova and Vaslav Nijinsky (1890–1950) danced together in the 1911 autumn tour.)

DHL may have based Terry's costume (lines 25–6) on Nijinsky in *Cléopâtre*, *Schéhérazade* or *Le Pavillon d'Armide* in all of which he played a slave and wore exotic Oriental costumes. (Leonide Massine, b. 1895, in *Cléopâtre*, 1918, wore a loin-cloth.) But cf. the description in *Letters*, i. 429 where Mikhail Mordkin (1882–1944) is the dancer.

255:27 knuckle-stones. DHL's variation on knucklebones (also known as huckle-bones, dib-stones, five-stones, etc.) a game in which the knucklebones of a sheep, usually five (see textual apparatus entry), are tossed and caught. (There is a slight precedent for DHL's name, but the prevailing term in the Midlands is 'snobs'; letter to the editor from Mrs Iona Opie, 23 April 1983.) Presumably Terry is making 'music' in a similar way.

255:31 charming the captain. See Judith viii-xiii. Frieda wrote to David Garnett in November 1912: 'I never look at my scarves without thinking of you and our acting and what a God forsaken idiot [you] looked as Holofernes!' (*Letters*, i. 476); see also Garnett, *Golden Echo*, p. 246.

This story was not performed as a ballet by the Ballets-Russes, but the opera *Judith* (produced 1863) by Aleksandr Nikolayevich Serov (1821–71) was included in their first season. Cf. the description of the dancing of the story of Ruth 'in the style of the Russian Ballet of Pavlova and Nijinsky' in chap. viii of *Women in Love*.

256:6 a second young man, Stanley is a recreation of Harold Hobson (1891–1974), a close friend of David Garnett. Consulting engineer and manager with several companies, 1912–28; and finally Chairman of Central Electricity Board. Hobson was returning from following his Russian love Lola Ertel (b. 1890?) to Moscow when he joined DHL, Frieda and David in Mayrhofen. DHL described Hobson as a 'ripping fellow' (*Letters*, i. 443 and n.) See also *Letters*, i. 446, 521, 533; and Garnett, *Golden Echo*, pp. 240, 246–7 (pp. 209–10 include a description of Hobson's mother). At 271:25 DHL wrote 'Harold's'.

257:26 The postman ... he wailed. Cf. Frieda's comment when Hobson visited them at Gargnano in December 1912: 'Every day an hour before the postman comes, Harold goes about crying, nobody loves me, nobody loves me, if there is no letter, you should just hear him ...' (*Letters*, i. 497).

258:10 INRI, Iesus Nazarenus Rex Iudaeorum ('Jesus of Nazareth King of the Jews'; Latin).

258:15 "Henery the ... I am." From the refrain of 'I'm Henery the Eighth', music-hall song by Robert P. Weston (1878–1936) with music by Fred Murray (d. 1922), which was popular in the 1910s; see also 259:11–17 ['I'm Henery the Eighth, I am! Henery the Eighth I am! I am! I got ... widow next door, She's been ... before. Ev'ry one was a Henery She wouldn't have a Willie or a Sam. I'm her Eighth old man named Henery, I'm Henery the Eighth, I am!'] © 1910 Francis Day & Hunter Ltd, Reproduced by permission of EMI Music Publishing Ltd.

258:26 "But it isn't ... English bible," Johanna is confused by the similarity of two denials: Heinrich and Stanley repeat Peter's denial of Christ during the crucifixion ('Woman, I know him not'; Luke xxii. 57), but Stanley twice quotes Christ's rebuke to his mother ('Woman, what have I to do with thee?'; John ii. 4).

Cf. Frieda's account in a fragment from her memoirs: 'When Baron P[odewils] was a wild young student he met his mother one morning in the street when he was not quite sober and she said to him: "O my son, my son"! And he answered: "Woman, what have I got to do with thee?"' ('Xmas at home.', 22pp., Frieda Lawrence collection, Humanities Research Center, University of Texas at Austin. (The name is given in full in notebooks 12 and 27.)

258:34 "Jawohl!" 'Yes, indeed!' (German).

259:20 a Scarlet Letter. Allusion to *The Scarlet Letter* (1850) by Nathaniel Hawthorne, in which the heroine wears the red letter A, signifying adultery, on her breast.

259:24 *Poste restantes . . . fermo in posta* To be kept until called for (French, Italian); these phrases should be 'poste restante' and 'fermo posta'.

259:28 to move on. The party follow the Zemm Tal over the Pfitscher Joch (2251 m.); cf. the route in Baedeker, *Austria–Hungary* (Leipzig, 1905), p. 135. The Brenner is the lowest pass over this part of the Alps and was used by the Romans.

259:36 "Lor-lummy!" 'Lord love me!' (slang).

260:7 eurythmics The system of musical training through physical movement expounded by Emile Jaques-Dalcroze (1865–1950), Swiss composer and teacher.

260:23 "We're marching . . . Zion———'" Beginning of the refrain of a hymn (*Hymns and Spiritual Songs*, 1707) by Isaac Watts (1674–1748) which opens 'Come, ye that love the Lord' ['. . . Zion, / Beautiful, beautiful . . .'].

262:33 the accommodation for travellers Dominicus Hütte (now rebuilt); see *Letters*, i. 443 and Garnett, *Golden Echo*, p. 247. Cf. this description with the mountains near 'Hohenhausen' (Mayrhofen) in chap. xxix and the end of chap. xxx in *Women in Love*.

268:7 a shrine . . . been murdered. Cf. the seated 'most ghastly Christus' in a 'chapel near St. Jakob' (at Larch) in 'Christs in the Tirol' (*Phoenix* 85) and 'The Crucifix Across the Mountains', *Twilight in Italy*. For other crucifixes see both versions of the essay, e.g. the large crucifix at 260:13 is the one 'deep in the Klamm' (p. 83).

269:20 youths seemed determined to leave that night. Cf. Garnett, *Golden Echo*, pp. 247–8 and *Letters*, i. 444. The hut at the summit (266:25) would be Rainer's Inn (Baedeker, *The Eastern Alps*, Leipzig, 1911, p. 246).

272:2 Sterzing . . . old tower, 'A charming place – already quite Italian in feeling' (*Letters*, i. 444). Cf. Baedeker: 'Clean little town (1700 inhab[itants]), with its picturesque old buildings, arcades, balconies, and turrets . . . on the right bank of the Eisak, which is confined between strong embankments'; mining town in the fifteenth and sixteenth centuries (*Austria–Hungary*, pp. 145–6) . . . Zwölferturm, built 1468, is the n. boundary of the late-Gothic city centre (Baedeker, *Tyrol and the Dolomites*, Leipzig, 1927, p. 251).

273:38 Meran . . . the Neering pass. The ancient capital of the Tyrol with a castle, Gothic church, etc. . . . . Baedeker gives two routes (through the Ratschinges Tal and the Jaufen Tal – both are 'long valley's (line 36) to Jaufenpass (2099 m.), and then the descent through the Walten Tal to St Leonhard and the Passeier Tal to Meran; the walk should take about seven hours, and a guide is 'useful' (Baedeker, *Eastern Alps*, p. 265).

276:12 Stanley had me ... before last." Cf. *Letters*, i. 489; Garnett, *Golden Echo*, p. 247; and Paul Delany, *D. H. Lawrence's Nightmare* (New York, 1978), p. 395. Hobson visited DHL and Frieda for three weeks during Christmas 1912; see *Letters*, i. 483, 500.

278:20 a little, wind-withered crucifix. Cf. the 'fallen Christus' on 'a small mountain track on the Jaufen, not far from Meran' in 'Christs in the Tirol' and 'The Crucifix Among the Mountains', *Twilight in Italy*.

278:39 "Haven't we come back to Sterzing?" 'And last night again we slept in a hut 2000-some odd hundred metres high. It was damnably cold ... And I nearly got lost', but to David Garnett: 'Then we set off to walk to Meran, and got stranded in a wild place, worse than Pfitscher Joch, Frieda dead with weariness, I furious for having come the wrong way, the night rolling up filthy and black from out of a Hell of a gulf below us, a wind like a razor, cold as ice ... scrambled over the ridge into the Jaufen House ...' (*Letters*, i. 445, 450). The 'rest-house' (277:16) could have been the Sterzinger Jaufenhaus or the Passeirer Jaufenhaus (on the Meran side of the pass); Gilbert and Johanna must have mistakenly taken the main road n.

279:40 Bozen A commercial town since the Middle Ages. DHL wrote to David Garnett of Bozen (Bolzano in Italian): 'beautiful, but beastly, and [we] slept in a room over a pig sty' (*Letters*, i. 450).

281:2 Trento 'Once the wealthiest town in the Tyrol, founded according to tradition by the Etruscans, possesses numerous towers, marble palaces, and broad streets, and still presents all the characteristics of an important Italian town' (Baedeker, *Austria–Hungary*, p. 162). The town may be viewed from the terrace of the Capuchin monastery looking w. or Doss Trento (307 m.) looking e. (Also Trent; Trient in German). On the lack of a chapter title see note on 206:1.

281:25 Non parliamo ... facciamo mangiare." 'We don't speak German.' ... 'You don't understand. We don't cook' (Italian).

282:3 "Che cosa ... du lait." 'What would you like?' ... 'Yes, there is milk.' The waiter uses the polite form in Italian (third person) 'desidera'; the usual French idiom would be 'il y a du ...'.

282:23 Bitte! Don't mention it! (German).

283:37 the large hotel ... a room. Probably the Imperial Hotel Trento (now a government building), n. of the railway station (which has been rebuilt). The Isola Nuova was listed as a restaurant with rooms (now rebuilt), e. of the station (Baedeker, *Austria–Hungary*, p. 162).

284:11 The barracks The Castello del Buon Consiglio to the n.e. had been the residence of the prince-bishops and was in 1912 a barracks. Other buildings were military offices.

284:13 *yip-i-addy*! 'Yip-I-Addy-I-Ay' (1908), a nonsense song with lyrics by Will D. Cobb, and music by John H. Flynn (d. 1926), in the musical *The Merry Widow and the Devil*.

285:11 Piazza di Dante ... new statue Immediately opposite the railway station; the monument (57 feet) by Cesare Zocchi (1851–1922) was erected in 1896.

285:17 **sobbed bitterly.** Cf. Frieda Lawrence 72:

We arrived at Trento, but alas for the glamour! We could only afford a very cheap hotel and the marks on the walls, the doubtful sheets, and worst of all the W C's were too much for me.

The people were strangers, I could not speak Italian, then.

So, one morning, much to Lawrence's dismay, he found me sitting on a bench under the statue of Dante, weeping bitterly. He had seen me walk barefoot over icy stubble, laughing at wet and hunger and cold it had all seemed only fun to me, and here I was crying because of the city-uncleanness and the W C's.

See also *Letters*, i. 450: '[Trento]'s a pure Italian ancient decrepit town, where F[rieda] had blues enough [. . .] to re-pave the floor of heaven.'

285:37 **Lake Maggiore.** This was the other place DHL and Frieda considered spending the winter (*Letters*, i. 430).

286:12 **train then due [285:38] . . . rolled on** Cf. *Letters*, i. 455–6:

At Trient there was a great crowd at the ticket office – then the train came. So a man – a higher station official – sauntered up and told them to buck up . . . I, amidst a herd of soldiers and black sombrero'd Italians caught his eye. He put up his finger to me. Then he led me, and two others, into the booking-clerks office . . . Meanwhile the Italy train sat peacefully in the station, and waited for us. That's Austria I say, it waited for *me*, the train into Italy.

287:1 **Riva:** 'A busy town and harbour with 3200 inhab[itants] . . . charmingly situated at the N. end of *Lago di Garda* . . . The lake is rarely perfectly calm . . . The water . . . is of a striking azure blue' (Baedeker, *Austria–Hungary*, p. 165).

DHL and Frieda stayed at Villa Leonardi, viale Giovanni-Prati 8, *Riva*, Lago di Garda, Austria: 'I [Frieda] was grateful to the three ladies who took us into their pensione and, instead of fearing the worst for their silver, sent us yellow and blue figs and grapes to our room, where we cooked our meals on the spirit lamp for economy, in fear and trembling of the housemaid' (Frieda Lawrence 72). See also *Letters*, i. 447–56. (They moved into a flat, Villa Igéa, *Villa di Gargnano*, Lago di Garda, Italy, on 18 September; see *Letters*, i. 453, 456–8.)

287:5 **plump sky-blue officer . . . and a lady** DHL called them 'Chocolate Soldiers' after the popular comic opera, *The Chocolate Soldier*, music by Oscar Straus (1870–1953) and based on Shaw's *Arms and the Man*; see *Letters*, i. 452 and n., 455 and 'Christs in the Tirol' manuscript (Humanities Research Center, University of Texas at Austin). Frieda recalled: '[Riva] was an Austrian garrison town at that time. Elegant officers in biscuit colored trousers and pale-blue jackets walked about with equally elegant ladies. For the first time I looked at Lawrence and myself; two tramps with rucksacks! Lawrence's trousers were frayed . . . I had a reddish cotton crepe dress all uneven waves at the skirt; the color of the red velvet ribbon had run into my panama hat' (Frieda Lawrence 72).

287:27 **rippling, living lake . . . vivid yellow sails,** DHL wrote of Lago di Garda in September 1912: 'The lake is dark blue, purple, and clear as a jewel, with swarms of fishes. And the boats have lemon-coloured sails' (*Letters*, i. 456; see also pp. 447–8, 452, 457).

288:28 **"Alors— . . . Combien?"** 'Well – ' . . . 'How much?' (French).

290:11 **his soul broke ... gushes into life.** Biblical allusion; see, e.g. Exodus xvii. 6; Numbers xx. 11; Isaiah xlviii. 21.

291:4 **Hence the Germans ... the war.** Cf. DHL in a letter of 20 January 1921: 'If I knew how to, I'd really join myself to the revolutionary socialists now. I think the time has come for a real struggle. That's the only thing I care for: the death struggle. I don't care for politics. But I know there *must* and *should* be a deadly revolution very soon, and I would take part in it if I knew how' (*Letters*, iii. 649). But see also his letter to the German publisher Dr Anton Kippenberg, 4 March 1921, in which DHL declares the ideal of internationalism is dead, and nationalism prevails (which means 'war ahead: not love and peace') – and internal struggles (he no longer believes in a revolution in Italy, but foresees factional fighting) in *Letters*, iii. 679–81.

292:8 **a large hat-box** Frieda received such a present from Nusch about 7 September; see *Letters*, i. 449, 451 and Frieda Lawrence 72. Nusch had given her several years earlier 'A real Paquin, a wonderful creation of "shrimp" colour and a steely blue mixed with chiffon' ('Gisla', ed. Diaz, p. 59; Tedlock 82).

Madame Isidore Paquin (d. 1936) founded the House of Paquin (1891–1956). First woman to achieve importance in dress design; her name was synonymous with elegance in the first decades of this century. Her evening gowns were noted for the use of rich fur, braid and gold lamé trimmings.

TEXTUAL APPARATUS

7:36   oven shelf] oven-shelf *TCCII*
7:39   up.— *MS*] ~ . *TCCI*
7:39   Goodnight *MS*] goodnight *TCCI* good-night, *TCCII* good night, *A1*
7:39   Goodnight] Good-night, *TCCII* Good night, *A1*
8:1   tad-poles] tadpoles *TCCII*
8:18   are.— *MS*] ~ . *TCCI*
8:21   you!] ~ ? *TCCII*
8:21   soft?] ~ . *MS, TSI*
8:24   doorway *MS, TCCII*] door-way *TCCI*
8:25   weekdays] week-days *TCCII*
8:27   tick!] ~ , *TCCII*
8:32   And] ~ , *TCCII*
8:37   darkness,] darkness, and *TSI*
8:37   distance] ~ , *TCCII*
8:39   packing cases] packing-cases *TSI, TCCII*
8:40   dark. *P* Emmie *MS*] ~ . Emmie *TCCI*
9:4   recess, *MS*] ~ *TCCI*
9:14   packing cases] packing-cases *MS, TCCII*
9:16   brilliantly-lighted *TCCII*] brilliantly lighted *TCCI, A1*
9:20   Teacher's] Teachers' *TCCII*
9:24   wet-frizzy] wet, frizzy *A1*
9:27   kissing:] ~ ; *E1*
10:6   clasp our ... grail-like effulgence.] look at ourselves in its brightness. *TSI*
10:7   all] our *A1*
10:8   classes; and] ~ —~ *TCCII*
10:8   classes; will] ~ ?—~ *TCCII see notes*
10:11   mystic business. *P* Dear] mystic affair. Dear *TSI*
10:12   have we not all] we have all of us *TSI*
10:12   evil?] ~ . *TSI*
10:13   therefore is it not true that] so *TSI*
10:13   dead?] ~ . *TSI*
10:14   maid] maid, they *TSI*
10:14   We live in better days. *P* There] Better days are ours. There *TSI*
10:16   now, a worldful of spoons.] now: everybody spoony! *TSI*

20:17   society people] aristocrats *TSI*
20:17   fast young ... ah, how ... lust, it ... be lustful!] naughty fast young man, oh how soft and melty they are with the naughty women, in our improved epoch. *TSI* fast ... ah! how ... lust; it ... lustful? *TCCII*
20:20   men] gallants *TSI*
20:20   chorus/girls] chorus-girls *TCCII*
20:21   ah] oh *TSI* ah! *TCCII*
20:22   really!—not ... their minds.] *really!* *TSI*
20:22   look at] come to *TSI*
20:23   factory lasses] factory-lasses *TCCII*
20:23   they fairly reek] and they are reeking *TSI*
20:24   sentiment. *P* It] ~ . It *TSI*
20:24   do—] ~ : *TSI*
20:24   it.—Isn't ... maxims?—And ... do. So] it. And so, ah me, we all do it so nicely and so finickily, with so *TSI* it. Isn't ... So *TCCII* it. Isn't ... maxims? And ... So *A1*
20:26   nowadays, and so much] and such *TSI*
20:27   old-beaniness! How ... any real] old-beaniness, that, really, how can there be any *TSI*
20:28   Old wives tales!] *Om. TSI* Old wives' tales! *TCCII*
20:28   it.] it, now is there? *TSI*
20:29   perfectly sweet] moist *TSI*
20:29   it all, and] it, *TSI*
20:29   plane. *P* Why bother] plane. Why talk *TSI*
20:30   spades any more?] spades! *TSI*
20:31   than] that *E1*
20:31   spins, in ... Nous avons changé tout cela.] spins any more. We've got beyond all that. *TSI* spins, in ... *Nous avons changé tout cela.* *TCCII*
20:32   spoon if] ~ , ~ *TCCII*
20:32   But don't ... plough metaphor.] *Om. TSI*

TEXTUAL APPARATUS

The following symbols are used to distinguish states of the text:

    MS   = Autograph manuscript
    TCCI   = Corrected carbon typescript
    TSI   = Corrected ribbon copy typescript
    TCCII   = Carbon typescript (Berkeley)
    E1   = First English edition
    A1   = First American edition

All subsequent editions follow *E1*.

Whenever the *TCCI* reading is adopted for Part I, it appears within the square bracket with no symbol. The reading for *TSI* follows the square bracket immediately if it differs from *TCCI*; other variants follow in chronological order. In the absence of information to the contrary the reader should assume that a variant recurs in all subsequent states.

When a reading from a source other than *TCCI* has been preferred or coincides with the adopted reading, it appears with its source-symbol within the square bracket. If the *TCCI* reading has been rejected, it follows the bracket immediately. Further variants from later states follow in chronological order.

For Part II the entry to the left of the square bracket indicates the final *MS* reading, with the entry to the right indicating the reading of the *MS* before DHL revised it; a still earlier reading is indicated by pointed brackets. When an editorial emendation has been made, it is identified by '*Ed.*', and the final *MS* reading appears to the right of the bracket.

The following symbols are used editorially:

    Ed.   = Editor
    Om.   = Omitted
    ~   = Substitution for a word in recording a punctuation or capitalisation error
    /   = Line or page break resulting in punctuation error
    P   = New paragraph
    ⟨ ⟩   = Early deleted *MS* reading (Part II)

1:1   Part I. *Ed.*] *Om. TCCI see notes*
3:8   'cuter] ~ *TCCII*
3:8   fidgetting] fidgeting *E1*
3:9   window,] ~ *TCCII*
3:10   cosy] cozy *A1*
3:14   inspiring:] ~ ; *E1*
3:16   mantel-piece *MS*] mantel piece *TCCI* mantelpiece *TCCII*
3:17   *New Age*] New Age *MS, TSI*
3:18   response:] ~ ! *TCCII*
3:18   response.] ~ ! *TCCII*
3:19   mantel-piece] mantelpiece *TCCII*
3:21   mantel-piece] mantelpiece *TCCII*
3:25   in!] ~ ? *TCCII*
3:26   dark, *MS*] ~ *TCCII*
3:31   eye] eyes *E1*

3:34 curb] kerb *A1*

3:34 blow,] ~ ; *TCCII*

4:3 heartily. P And *MS, TCCII*] ~ . /And *TCCI*

4:5 forehead *MS, TCCII*] ~ , *TCCI*

4:6 beard,] ~ ; *TCCII*

4:6 socialist,] Socialist, *TSI* socialist; *TCCII*

4:6 Shakspeare's] Shakespeare's *TCCII*

4:18 humour.] ~ , *A1*

4:25 crouched] ~ , *TCCII*

4:26 rust-brown,] ~ *TCCII*

4:31 eyeglass] eye-glass *E1*

4:33 Ay-y-y] Ay-y-ye *A1*

4:34 *New Statesman TCCII*] New Statesman *TCCI*

4:37 chat, *MS*] chat, or *TCCI*

4:39 time *MS*] ~ , *TCCI*

5:5 treasure-day] treasure day *A1*

5:6 fine weather] ~ ~ , *TCCII*

5:19 brilliantly-lighted] brilliantly lighted *A1*

5:22 same:] ~ ; *E1*

5:25 tired:] ~ ; *E1*

5:28 Unco] ~ ' *A1*

5:32 much.— *MS*] ~ . *TCCI*

6:5 birth-rights *MS*] birth-/ rights *TCCI* birthrights *E1*

6:18 connection] connexion *A1*

6:19 connection] connexion *A1*

6:20 connection] connexion *A1*

6:33 Well] ~ , *TCCII*

6:35 said] ~ , *TCCII*

7:1 doing the] doing *TCCII*

7:5 ginger:] ~ ; *TCCII*

7:7 evening] ~ , *TCCII*

7:11 this!] ~ ? *TCCII*

7:12 pinged. P Patty *TSI, TCCII*] ~ ./ Patty *TCCI*

7:14 home—"— *MS*] ~ —" *TCCI* ~ ..." *TCCII*

7:15 in,"— *MS*] ~ ," *TCCI* ~ ." *TCCII*

7:18 Oh] ~ , *TCCII*

7:19 walked?— *MS*] ~ ? *TCCI*

7:26 ages.— *MS*] ~ . *TCCI*

7:30 The Sun *MS*] the ~ *TCCI* the "~ ." *A1*

7:34 dark blue] dark-blue *TCCII*

8:7 Ah—! *MS*] ~ -! *TCCI* ~ ! *TCCII*

8:8 course! Of] ~ , of *TCCII*

8:8 street corner] street-corner *TCCII*

8:9 public-house] public house *A1*

8:10 public-houses] public houses *A1*

8:11 start of *MS*] start on *TCCI*

8:14 once] ~ , *TCCII*

8:14 hope,] ~ ? *TCCII*

8:17 half-scornfully] half scornfully *A1*

8:17 half-bitterly] half bitterly *A1*

8:19 going] getting *TCCII*

8:20 it] ~ , *TCCII*

8:21 half an hour *TCCI, A1*] half-an-hour *TCCII*

8:35 brow *MS*] brows *TCCI*

8:37 Ah] ~ , *TCCII*

8:38 lots] a lot *TCCII*

8:39 smoke] ~ , *TCCII*

8:39 you'd *MS*] you *TCCI*

9:5 well off] well-off *E1*

9:7 music, *MS, A1*] ~ *TCCI*

9:10 university] University *E1*

9:13 public-houses *TCCII*] public houses *TCCI, A1*

9:14 dances,] ~ — *E1*

9:14 hops"] ~ ," *E1*

9:14 called,] ~ — *E1*

9:16 and] ~ , *E1*

9:24 lantern slides] lantern-slides *TCCII* lantern-/ slides *A1*

9:26 canals] ~ , *TCCII*

9:32 or] *Om. E1*

10:5 eyebrows *TCCII*] eye-brows *TCCI*

10:10 up-aloft] up aloft *E1*

10:11 Why] ~ , *TCCII*

10:12 bathing drawers] bathing-drawers *TSI, TCCII*

10:12 an immortal] a *TSI*

10:17 it,] ~ *TCCII*

10:29 M.A. *MS, TCCII*] M. A. *TCCI*

10:29 maths.—] ~ . *A1*

10:34 But] ~ , *E1*

10:35 might] ~ , *E1*

10:36 it.] ~ ! *TCCII*

11:5 thing, *MS, E1*] ~ . *TCCI* ~ *TCCII*

11:6 Besides] ~ , *TCCII*

11:13 work.— *MS*] ~ . *TCCI*

11:15 talents—] ~ ... *TCCII*

11:20 worth— *MS*] ~ . *TCCI*

11:21 Nay now—] ~ , ~ ... *TCCII*

11:27 Oh] ~ , *TCCII*

11:35 Arabian Nights.] '~ ~ '. *TCCII* '~ ~ .' *E1* Arabian Nights. *A1*

11:36 Oh *come*—] ~ , ~ ... *TCCII*

11:37 Arabian Nights,] '~ ~ ', *TCCII* '~ ~ ,' *E1* *Arabian Nights, A1*

11:38 another *TCCI, A1*] ~ , *TCCII*

11:38 some time] sometime *A1*

11:39 Oh] ~ , *TCCII*

11:39 Or *MS*] Is *TCCI*

12:2 surprising,] ~ ! *TCCII*

12:5 Well *MS*] ~ , *TCCI*

12:14 No, why] ~ . Why *TCCII*

12:21 don't] can't *TCCII*

12:22 Ay] Ay, *TCCII* Aye, *A1*

12:33 you—! *MS*] ~ ! *TCCI*

12:40 "Yes] "~ , *TCCII*

12:40 Yes] ~ , *TCCII*

13:1 Ha—] ~ !— *TCCII*

13:7 of the] of *TCCII*

13:8 difference. *MS*] ~ ? *TCCI*

13:8 girl.—] ~ .... *TCCII* ~ ... *E1*

13:9 Sunday-night *TSI, TCCII*] Sunday night *TCCI*

13:10 fun: isn't] ~ ! Isn't *TCCII*

13:10 she *MS*] ~ , *TCCI*

13:15 No] ~ , *TCCII*

13:16 cruel,] ~ *TCCII*

13:20 Yes] ~ , *TCCII*

13:29 Why, *MS, TCCII*] ~ *TCCI*

13:30 Where?] ~ ! *TCCII*

13:33 boy." P There *Ed.*] ~ ."/ There *MS* ~ ." There *TCCI*

13:39 rendez-vous] rendezvous *TCCII*

15:3 fidgetted] fidgeted *E1*

15:8 A yellow] An unowned *TSI*

15:14 hearth-rug *MS, TCCII*] hearth rug *TCCI*

15:17 *spoon*—" she] ~ !" She *TCCII* ~ !" She *A1*

15:25 Oh] ~ , *TCCII*

15:26 *you*] ~ , *TCCII*

15:28 But] ~ , *TCCII*

15:35 Goddard."— *MS*] ~ ." ~ !" *TCCII*

16:3 But] ~ , *TCCII*

16:10 awkwardly:] ~ ; *E1*

16:13 cuddle,] ~ *MS, TSI* ~ ; *A1*

16:14 merely:] ~ *A1*

16:19 oh] ~ , *TCCII*

16:19 night:] ~ ; *E1*

16:19 it.] ~ ! *TCCII*

16:20 Monday, *MS, TSI*] ~ *T...*

16:21 grip,] ~ *TCCII*

16:28 recognised *MS, TCCII*...* nized *TCCI, A1*

16:30 you] ~ , *TCCII*

16:38 vesper-verse] vesper ve...

16:39 raspberry-juice] ~ , *A1*

17:1 spiders *MS*] ~ , *TCCI*

17:3 out:] ~ ; *TCCII*

17:8 said,] ~ *TCCII*

17:8 rain:] ~ , *A1*

17:8 Well] ~ , *TCCII*

17:8 never, it's] ~ ! It's *TC...*

17:8 ever!"— *MS*] ~ !" *TC...*

17:8 called] ~ , *A1*

17:9 Goodnight *Ed.*] *TCCI* Good-night, *T...* night, *A1*

17:10 smiling!" *MS*] ~ ~ !"— *TCCI*

17:11 boy," *Ed.*] ~ ", *TCCI...*

17:12 *over* his nose and] ov... *TCCII see notes*

17:12 *under* his nose,] und... and *TCCII*

17:13 up,] ~ ; *TCCII*

17:16 gate] gates *TCCII*

17:23 out;] ~ , *TCCII*

17:26 course] ~ , *A1*

17:28 Oh] ~ , *TCCII*

17:29 short-sighted,] ~ —

17:29 boy.] ~ ! *TCCII*

17:29 Hello] ~ , *TCCII*

17:32 Hello] ~ , *TCCII*

17:32 two!] ~ . *TCCII*

17:33 Oh] ~ , *TCCII*

17:36 am:] ~ ; *E1*

20:36 to get] and get *TSI*

20:36 will be ... improved: so ... harm is there] do need me to pull down that scarecrow, that dark designing seducer, once and for all. You do need me to show that there's no harm in it really. How could there be? so refined, so spiritual even. There's no harm *TSI* will ... improved; so ... there *E1*

20:40 spoon?] ~. *TSI*

21:1 goes rather far: even ... far: well ... that! As ... it. No ... between us.] may lead to harm—why, don't you believe it. A spoon is a spoon, whatever it leads to, and there is nothing low about it, as there is about a spade. May the spoon of England [never?] grow dull! *TSI* goes ... that? As ... it! No ... us. *TCCII* goes ... far; even ... far; well ... that? As ... it! No ... us. *E1* goes ... far, even ... far—well ...that? As ... it! No ... us. *A1 see note on* 21:5

21:6 though] ~, *TCCII*

21:16 good] *Om. TSI*

21:17 dear girl] happy maiden *TSI*

21:18 enveloping] *Om. TSI*

21:19 into] in *TSI*

21:21 again:] ~; *E1*

21:27 deep, into *MS*] ~ ~ *TCCI*

21:27 vision:] ~; *E1*

21:29 delicious:] ~; *E1*

22:1 him:] ~; *E1*

22:3 pulse beat] pulse-beat *TCCII*

22:6 kiss-curls *TSI, TCCII*] kiss curls *TCCI*

22:7 neck:] ~; *E1*

22:7 nape of ... most delicate *MS*] *Om. TCCI*

22:11 central] centred *TCCII*

22:14 shoulders,] ~; *TCCII*

22:17 apart,] ~; *TCCII*

22:18 kiss,] ~; *TCCII*

22:25 senses:] ~; *E1*

22:28 oh] ~, *TCCII*

22:29 new, *MS, TCCII*] ~ *TCCI*

22:32 tinier:] ~; *E1*

23:1 mouth; *MS, E1*] ~: *TCCI*

23:5 for ever] forever *A1*

23:21 lived! *MS*] ~. *TCCI* ~? *TCCII*

23:28 —We] ~ *TCCII*

23:30 Co-op. *TCCII*] Co-op *TCCI*

23:31 Noon] Mr Noon *TSI*

23:31 Emmie?] ~! *TCCII see notes*

23:31 Practise then: and you] Practice makes perfect. You *TSI* Practise, then: and you *TCCII* Practise, then; and you *E1*

23:33 bookstalls] book-/ stalls *TCCII*

23:34 nowadays:] ~; *E1*

23:36 Nothing earthy, not ... goings on.] We're nothing if not in mid-air. *TSI* Nothing earthy; not ... goings-on. *TCCII*

23:37 away,] ~ *TCCII*

24:2 time,] ~ *TCCII*

24:2 audience. Gradually] ~. *P* Gradually *A1*

24:4 —Ah] ~ *TCCII*

24:6 sacrifice] noble toil *TSI*

24:7 fuse into perfect] melt into *TSI*

24:7 All Whitman's ... abstraction: but ... hollow spoon.] This is the perfect Infinite and Nirvana of all men: not death, not abstraction, not uplift, but the spoon. We are spoon-perfected. "Be ye also perfect" *TSI* All ... abstraction; but ... spoon. *E1*

24:11 lifted,] lifted abstracted, *TSI*

24:13 packing cases *Ed.*] packing-cases *TCCII*

24:17 Dad." *P* He] ~." He *TSI*

24:29 horribly] terribly *TSI*

24:31 so much as seen] *seen TSI*

24:31 Co-op. *TCCII*] Co-op *TCCI*

24:31 on this small account] therefore *TSI*

24:32 Emmie] Miss Emmie *TSI*

24:32 No,] ~; *TCCII*

24:32 notorious] notorious silent and secret *TSI*

24:33 really enjoying herself,] having a real good time, *TSI*

24:34 is better than] comes up to *TSI*

24:36 in communion] commune *TSI*

24:36 say whether] and tell yourself whether or no *TSI*

24:37 Emmelian] veered to Emmelian *TSI*

24:37 profundities] ~, *TSI*

24:38 kiss—] ~, *TSI*

24:38 something] something still *TSI*

24:38 even] *Om. TSI*

25:3 none] no one *TSI*

25:5 Co-op. entry] Co-op.-entry *TSI*

25:8 soul; *MS, TSI*] ~, *TCCI*

25:9 slipping] stepping *TSI*

25:9 Co-op. *TCCII*] Co-op *TCCI*

25:11 raffinés] *raffinés TCCII*

25:13 above-board] true *TSI see notes*

25:14 In the] In *TSI*

25:15 days] ~, *TCCII*

25:15 wicked black silk bed-sheets,] black silk bed-sheets for the wicked, *TSI*

25:16 interlarded] *Om. TSI*

25:16 Different seasoning ... the same.] *Om. TSI*

25:16 I have heard too of ... even of] There is Frenchy, and there is even *MS, TSI* I ... heard, too, of ... of *TCCII*

25:20 dodges] privacies *TSI*

25:21 concern myself ... essential English] myself will give you just the English essence of the *TSI*

25:22 with the ... essential: in short,] the essence of the essence, *TSI* with ... essential; in short, *EI*

25:23 Co-op. entry] Co-op.-entry *TSI*

25:24 and shoulders] nor shoulders *TCCII*

25:27 of our clean-minded age,] *Om. TSI* of ... clear-minded age, *AI*

25:28 limpidest sweets. Ah infinite spoon-moments! dear · spoon-memories!] dearest sweets, life's

most infinite moments. *TSI* limpidest ... Ah, infinite spoon moments ... spoon-memories! *TCCII*

25:30 ours.] he ought to have been. *TSI*

25:31 much,] ~; *TCCII*

26:1 Why] ~, *TCCII*

26:1 Gilbert *MS*] ~, *TCCI*

26:2 his dose] its depths *TSI*

26:5 night duty] night-duty *TCCII*

26:7 Ay, *you* ask] Ah, you *ask TCCII*

26:7 hell.—Oh!— *MS*] ~—~! *TCCI*

26:8 road—"*now MS*] ~. "*Now TCCI*

26:10 Oh] ~, *TCCII*

26:16 Noon, *MS, AI*] ~ *TCCI*

26:21 ten:] ~; *EI*

26:25 with *MS*] with a *TCCI*

26:28 "Go] '~ *MS*

26:28 on," *Ed.*] ~,' *MS* ~!" *TCCI*

26:31 going further.] ultimates. *TSI*

26:32 Half-tiresome *TSI, TCCII*] Half tiresome *TCCI*

26:32 *may*] may *TSI, TCCII*

26:32 And] ~, *AI*

26:33 Remember] Don't forget *TSI*

26:34 fathers] father *TCCII*

26:34 moreover] ~, *AI*

26:34 the man] a man *TSI*

26:35 faithful] perfect *TSI*

26:35 dear] sweet *TSI*

26:36 last clean sweep in sympathy!] final matter of sympathy. *TSI*

26:36 not] *Om. TCCII*

26:36 in this ... conjunction!] when all is spiritualised by soft and spoony sympathy! *TSI*

26:37 Don't you agree] You agree, don't you *TSI*

27:1 Cooey] *cooey TCCII* Cooey *EI* "cooey" *AI*

27:1 *Coo-ee! MS, TCCII*] Coo-ee! *TCCI Coo-ey! EI* "*Coo-ey!" AI*

27:6 could come on:] was a sport: *TSI* could come on; *EI*

27:6 pressed fearless forward] rode fearless on *TSI* pressed on *TCCII*

27:7 bitter end. Bitter! Well, bitter-sweet. Oh] last high geste. Ah *TSI* bitter . . . Bitter? Well, . . . Oh, *TCCII*

27:8 joust of ultimate] spoony joust of *TSI*

27:8 oh last] on, on to the last *TSI* oh, last *TCCII*

27:8 throw of . . . spoon-overthrown!] throw. *TSI*

27:9 Shall I . . . the spoon?] And let me be your Minnesinger. *TSI*

27:11 But] ∼, *TCCII*

27:12 Alas, poor . . . Instead of] Alas for poor Emmie! Instead of his *TSI*

27:13 melting] true and lovely melting *TSI*

27:14 melt right down] merge *TSI*

27:14 her,] her in sheer liquid union, *TSI*

27:14 he is] he was *TSI*

27:15 the last] its last *TSI*

27:15 coming on] coming-on *TCCII*

27:15 Galahad of . . . the goal!] encroaching to merge in the timeless spoon. *TSI*

27:20 feeling] feelings *TCCII*

27:20 Beware, gentle reader! For] Ah, dear reader, *TSI*

27:20 and kissy] true *TSI*

27:21 pay, both . . . for her.] pay. *TSI*

27:23 garden gate *TCCI, A1*] garden-gate *TCCII*

27:24 high-road] high road *A1*

27:28 watching.— *MS*] ∼ . *TCCII*

27:33 circumstances *MS*] circumstance *TCCI see notes*

27:37 fidgetted] fidgeted *TCCII*

27:39 barbed] pointed *TSI*

27:40 election] elation *A1*

28:2 voices; *MS*] ∼, *TCCI*

28:4 down] from *TCCII*

28:4 black, *MS*] ∼ *TCCII*

28:4 canals] canal *E1*

28:13 of warmth] or warmth *TSI*

28:20 womaniser:] ∼; *TCCII* womanizer; *A1*

28:20 it:] ∼; *TCCII*

28:23 Among] among *A1*

28:23 Fine *MS*] fine *TCCI* A fine *TCCII*

28:23 tune] ∼, *TCCII*

28:24 And may . . . woman-hating crew——— *MS*] And . . . crew— *TCCI* And . . . crew . . . *TCCII And may Confusion still pursue/ The senseless woman-hating crew . . . A1*

28:28 Meanwhile] ∼, *A1*

28:30 sulky] ∼, *TCCII*

28:32 Jinny:] ∼; *E1*

28:34 job; *TSI*] ∼, *TCCI*

28:35 an old . . . paces of] *Om. TCCII*

28:37 off-spring] offspring *TCCII*

29:9 Hey] Hoy *TCCII*

29:17 the *MS*] my *TCCI*

29:20 compulsory *TSI*] Compulsory *TCCI*

29:24 floor.] ∼? *TCCII*

29:26 amiably] aimiably *MS, TSI*

29:27 minutes *MS*] ∼, *TCCI*

29:27 on] ∼, *A1*

29:29 weakly *MS*] ∼, *TCCI*

29:32 minute] ∼, *TCCII*

29:33 stairs. Emmie *Ed.*] ∼ . / Emmie *TCCI* ∼ . P Emmie *TCCII*

30:13 No,] ∼; *TCCII*

30:20 currant bushes] currant-bushes *TCCII*

30:37 Ha—Ha! *MS*] Ha-Ha! *TCCI* Ha-ha! *TCCII* "Ha-ha!" *A1*

31:1 summer-house] summer house *E1*

31:2 nettle-stalks,] ∼ *E1*

31:3 high-road] high road *A1*

31:7 Ah-ha] ah-ha *TCCII*

31:11 low,] ∼ *TCCII*

31:23 greenhouse] green-house *MS, TSI*

31:23 glass-house. *MS*] glass-/ house. *TCCI* glass-/ house! *TCCII* glasshouse! *E1*

31:24 Well] ∼, *TCCII*

31:25 one.] ∼! *TCCII*

31:25 his own *MS*] *Om. TCCI*

31:27 a] *Om. TSI*

31:27 type,] ~ *TCCII*
31:30 was still] ~, ~, *TCCII*
31:31 spoony saying] ~, ~ *TSI*
31:32 prayers.] ~! *TSI*
31:33 Emmie for ... now that] to be reminded of it, now *TSI*
31:35 word] ~, *TCCII*
31:37 her. *MS, TSI*] ~? *TCCI see notes*
31:38 inquisitorial *MS*] inquisitional *TCCI*
31:39 her,] ~ *TCCII*
32:1 daughter] girl *TCCII*
32:3 plants. He'd show her.] ~! ~ ~ ~! *TCCII*
32:5 re-potted] repotted *A1*
32:8 lurid *MS*] livid *TCCI*
32:9 He'd show her. *MS*] *Om. TCCI*
32:13 cramped:] ~; *TCCII*
32:15 twitchel] twitchell *MS, TSI*
32:16 he just.] ~, ~! *TCCII*
32:19 hate,] ~ *TCCII*
32:21 listened:] ~; *E1*
32:22 'cute *Ed.*] ~ *TCCI*
32:23 Emmie.] ~! *TCCII*
32:23 greenhouse:] ~; *TCCII*
32:26 coming on] coming-on *TCCII*
32:32 beastly, *MS*] ~ *TCCI*
32:33 paralysed *MS, TCCII*] paralyzed *TCCI*
32:35 on,] ~; *TCCII*
33:3 with a crash down] down with a crash *TCCII*
33:6 third,] ~ *TCCII*
33:9 you] ~, *TCCII*
33:10 calling "Mother] ~: *P* "Mother *A1*
33:14 madly:] ~; *TCCII*
33:15 twitchel] twitchell *MS, TSI*
33:24 back. Gilbert] ~. / Gilbert *TCCII* ~. *P* Gilbert *E1*
34:6 Woodhouse:] ~; *E1*
34:7 again:] ~; *E1*
34:9 woodyard *MS, TSI*] wood-yard *TCCI* wood-/ yard *E1*
34:16 trunk-bottoms] trunk bottoms *A1*
34:16 plant-histology] plant histology *A1*
34:20 grandly-based] grandly based *A1*
34:22 leaf-tip:] ~; *E1*

34:24 was, that] ~ ~, *TCCII*
34:31 cause] scientific cause *TSI*
34:31 abstractedly ... piqued him.] abstractedly for a long time. *TSI*
34:32 He had almost] And something in him *TSI*
34:32 not] *not TSI*
35:6 Lloyd's Weekly *E1*] Lloyd's Weekly *TCCI*
35:7 paper] newspaper *TCCII*
35:7 apple dumpling] apple-dumpling *TCCII*
35:8 oven:] ~; *E1*
35:9 pudding-cloth] pudding cloth *A1*
35:9 vegetable steam:] vegetable-steam: *TCCII* vegetable-steam; *E1* vegetable steam; *A1*
35:11 fidgetty] fidgety *TCCII*
35:14 half-scorning] half scorning *A1*
35:15 woodyard *Ed.*] wood-yard *TCCI*
35:17 gratified] grateful *TCCII*
35:19 married] ~, *TCCII*
35:27 woodyard *MS, TSI*] wood-yard *TCCI*
35:29 room too] ~, ~, *TCCII*
35:31 violin:] ~; *TCCII*
35:32 music:] ~; *TCCII*
35:39 half an hour *TCCI, A1*] half/ an-hour *TCCII* half-an-hour *E1*
35:40 out] ~, *TCCII*
35:40 tidy] ~, *TCCII*
36:4 street:] ~; *E1*
36:4 afternoon chapel] afternoon-chapel *A1*
36:6 dark, *MS*] ~ *TCCI*
36:6 wine-coloured *MS, TCCII*] wine-colored *TCCI*
36:7 full, *MS, TCCII*] ~ *TCCI*
36:10 Oh—! *MS*] ~-! *TCCI* ~! *TCCII*
36:15 I. L. P.] I.L.P. *TCCII*
36:16 him?" *P* Again *MS*] ~?" Again *TCCI*
36:22 Oh well] ~, ~, *TCCII*
36:34 pink-coloured *MS, TCCII*] pink-colored *TCCI*
36:35 up,] ~; *TCCII*
36:38 beech-tree] beech tree *E1*
36:39 overshoes *Ed.*] over-shoes *TCCI*

37:3 hawthorn-trees] hawthorn trees *TCCII*
37:4 look,] ~; *TCCII*
37:4 haws *MS*] haw *TCCI*
37:6 ponds,] ~ *TCCII*
37:13 branches, she] ~. She *TCCII*
37:14 pungent] ~, *TCCII*
37:17 beautiful!] ~? *TCCII*
37:17 lovely!] ~? *TCCII*
37:18 white-heavy] white heavy *TCCII*
37:23 She stepped . . . ideal happiness. *MS*] *Om. TCCI*
37:26 me] ~, *TCCII*
37:30 Why] ~, *TCCII*
37:38 could] should *TCCII*
37:38 Oh, *MS, TCCII*] ~ *TCCI*
38:2 dark blue eye] dark-blue eyes *TCCII*
38:9 stopped] ~, *TCCII*
38:9 suddenly *MS*] ~, *TCCII*
38:10 ivory-coloured *MS, TCCII*] ivory-colored *TCCI*
38:19 woman:] ~; *E1*
38:26 moment] ~, *E1*
38:29 spoon spell:] spoon-spell: *TSI, TCCII* spoon-spell; *E1*
38:29 marriage, alas] marriage also *TSI*
38:36 perhaps:] ~; *TCCII*
38:37 wine-coloured *MS, TCCII*] wine-colored *TCCI*
38:40 her— *MS*] ~, *TCCI*
39:1 ivory-white:] ~; *TCCII*
39:3 heels *MS*] feet *TCCI see notes*
39:6 Ah!"— *MS*] ~!" *TCCI*
39:16 thinking-woman] thinking woman *TCCII*
39:17 No!] ~. *TCCII*
39:23 flower:] ~; *E1*
39:24 probably where . . . off! Very *MS*] *Om. TCCI*
39:25 on to] onto *A1*
39:25 ground:] ~; *E1*
39:26 it:] ~; *TCCII*
39:29 infallible. *P* She *MS*] ~. She *TCCI*
39:33 world:] ~; *E1*
40:3 you judge, now? Can] *Om. E1*
40:3 men] ~, *TCCII*

40:9 side-tracks *MS, TCCII*] side tracks *TCCI*
40:11 dark blue eye] dark-blue eyes *TCCII*
40:14 inquiry *A1*] enquiry *TCCI*
40:15 beating,] ~; *TCCII*
40:19 her:] ~; *E1*
40:21 full, *MS, TCCII*] ~ *TCCI*
40:22 the ideal] ideal *E1*
40:30 no one *TCCI, A1*] no-/ one *E1*
40:33 strange] ~, *TCCII*
40:37 ebbed,] ~; *TCCII*
40:40 automatic *MS*] automatically *TCCII*
41:5 fence. *P* Patty] ~. Patty *E1*
41:7 on to] onto *A1*
41:7 road:] ~; *E1*
41:10 them] ~, *TCCII*
41:13 Oh] ~, *TCCII*
41:24 coming.] ~! *TCCII*
41:26 And] ~, *TCCII*
41:32 forwards] forward *E1*
41:33 walking-stick *MS, TSI, TCCII*] walking stick *TCCI*
41:37 suddenly] ~, *TCCII*
41:37 swerve] ~, *TCCII*
42:23 garment] ~, *TCCII*
42:25 tree] ~, *TCCII*
42:27 heaving, she] ~. She *TCCII*
42:28 up] ~, *TCCII*
43:5 goloshes *Ed.*] galoshes *TCCI*
43:7 wet] ~, *A1*
43:9 you! Thank you!] ~. ~ ~, *TCCII*
43:11 answered kindly . . . [43:17] goes," he *MS*] *Om. TCCI*
44:3 choir-loft *MS, TSI*] choir loft *TCCI*
44:8 pew,] ~; *TCCII*
44:11 minister] ~, *E1*
44:11 gown *MS, TSI, A1*] ~, *TCCI*
44:14 demon:] ~; *E1*
44:16 rebellion level *TCCI, A1*] rebellion-level *TCCII*
44:20 weather:] ~; *E1*
44:27 felt *MS, TCCII*] fell *TCCI*
44:29 soared and *MS*] soared or *TCCI*
44:30 comic:] ~; *TCCII*

45:3 better behaved] better-behaved *TCCII*

45:5 fidgetted] fidgeted *TCCII*

45:6 chapel, *MS, A1*] ~ *TCCI*

45:7 fidgetty] fidgety *TCCII*

45:8 anthem-sheet] anthem sheet *A1*

45:9 again:] ~; *TCCII*

45:9 lap:] ~; *TCCII*

45:9 hymn book] hymn-book *TCCII*

45:10 pocket] ~, *A1*

45:10 anthem-sheet *TCCII*] anthem sheet *TCCI, A1*

45:11 back.] ~: *TCCII*

45:12 G.N.— *MS*] G. N. *TCCI*

45:12 think.] ~? *A1*

45:12 Wire-whiskers] Wire-Whiskers *A1*

45:13 Oh my] Oh ay *TCCII* Oh, aye *A1*

45:14 G.N. *MS, TCCII*] G. N. *TCCI, E1*

45:14 W-W. *MS*] W-W *TCCI* W.W. *TCCII* W. W. *E1* W.-W. *A1*

45:14 another] ~, *TCCII*

45:16 anthem-sheet] anthem sheet *A1*

45:16 consequences, reached over *MS*] consequences *TCCII*

45:19 she too] ~, ~, *E1*

45:24 half-past *MS, TCCII*] half past *TCCI*

45:30 snappily *MS*] snappishly *TCCI*

45:32 home.] ~? *TCCII*

45:32 G.N. *MS, TCCII*] G. N. *TCCI, E1*

45:32 since.] ~? *TCCII*

45:33 up] *Om. E1*

45:33 pencil] ~, *E1*

46:1 round] ~, *TCCII*

46:2 Cissie *Ed.*] Cissy *TCCI*

46:6 fidgetting] fidgeting *TCCII*

46:8 seen *MS, TCCII*] see *TCCI*

46:8 G.N. *MS, TCCII*] G. N. *TCCI, E1*

46:13 G.N.'s *MS, TCCII*] G. N.'s *TCCI, E1*

46:16 went] ~, *TCCII*

46:18 G.N.'s *MS, TCCII*] G. N.'s *TCCI, E1*

46:19 G.N.— *MS*] G. N. *TCCI* G.N.? *TCCII* G. N.? *E1*

46:19 Oh] ~, *A1*

46:21 gooseberry bush] gooseberry-bush *TCCII*

46:22 W-W's] W.-W.'s *TCCII*

46:22 pitch dark] pitch-/ dark *TCCII* pitch-dark *E1*

46:26 tonight.] ~? *TCCII, A1* to-night? *E1*

46:26 him Agatha] ~, ~ *E1*

46:32 pince-nezzed *TCCI, A1*] pince-nezed *E1*

46:38 interruptions *MS*] interruption *TCCI*

47:1 choir-gallery *Ed.*] choir gallery *TCCI*

47:2 evening— *MS*] ~. *TCCI*

47:3 readjustment *TCCI, A1*] re-adjustment *E1*

47:4 allforgiving] all-forgiving *TCCII*

47:6 endurance. I *MS*] endurance. And I *TCCI see notes*

47:8 christian *MS*] Christian *TCCI*

47:9 dockleaves] dock-leaves *TCCII*

47:9 eyeglasses] eye-/ glasses *E1* eye-glasses *A1*

47:17 X-ray *TCCI, A1*] x-ray *E1*

47:24 body politic] body-politic *TCCII*

47:25 christian *MS*] Christian *TCCI*

47:26 unpaid,] ~ *TCCII*

47:28 christian *MS*] Christian *TCCI*

47:29 christian *MS*] Christian *TCCI*

47:31 choir.] ~! *TCCII*

48:5 college. *MS*] ~? *TCCI*

48:9 music sheets *TCCI, A1*] music-sheets *TCCII*

48:13 perplexity *MS*] ~, *TCCI*

48:17 Meanwhile] ~, *A1*

48:17 pulpit] ~, *TCCII*

48:18 viscous *MS*] vicious *TCCI*

48:22 wrath, and] ~, ~, *A1*

48:25 Thee,] ~ *TCCII*

48:25 stumblings *MS*] stumbling *TCCI*

48:28 his *MS, TCCII*] *Om. TCCI*

48:30 brings *MS, TCCII*] bring *TCCI*

48:31 For] ~, *A1*

48:31 thoughtlessness—— *MS*] ~ —
   TCCI ~ . . . . *E1* ~ . . . *A1*

48:34 No *MS*] ~ , *TCCI*

48:34 stumbled,] ~ *A1*

48:37 for?— *MS*] ~? *TCCI*

49:1 agreed . . . agreed] ~ , . . . ~ ,
   TCCII

49:2 Norman *MS*] Norman Dixon
   TCCI

49:5 grittily *MS*] guiltily *TCCI*

49:5 vesper.] ~ : *TCCII*

49:6 "Lord keep . . . night / Secure
   . . . fears / May . . . sleep / Till
   . . . appears." *Ed.*] Lord . . . appears. *TCCI* Lord, keep . . .
   night, / Secure . . . fears. / May
   . . . sleep, / Till . . . appears.
   *TCCII Lord, keep us safe this night,
   / Secure from all our fears. / May
   angels guard us while we sleep, /
   Till morning light appears. A1*

49:11 breaking point] breaking-point
   TCCII

49:15 Oh] ~ , *TCCII*

49:15 say *MS*] ~ , *TCCI*

49:16 for.— *MS*] ~ . *TCCI* ~? *TCCII*

49:17 Oh] ~ , *TCCII*

49:19 Oh] ~ , *TCCII*

49:22 And] ~ , *A1*

49:23 me *MS*] ~ , *TCCI*

49:25 And] ~ , *A1*

49:26 he!] ~? *TCCII*

49:27 him.— *MS*] ~ . *TCCI*

49:30 Knarborough, *MS*] ~ *TCCI*

49:32 bother— *MS*] ~ — *TCCI* ~ .
   TCCII

49:33 needle's eye] needle's-eye *TCCII*

49:38 policeman-like *TCCII*] po-
   licemanlike *TCCI*

50:1 Yes] ~ , *TCCII*

50:1 Goodnight *MS*] Goodnight,
   TCCI Good-night, *TCCII* Good
   night, *A1*

50:6 Agatha, meanwhile] ~ , ~ , *A1*

50:7 Good-evening *MS*] Good evening, *TCCI*

50:8 you—? *MS*] ~ — *TCCI* ~ . . .
   TCCII

50:10 Chapel *MS*] chapel *TCCI*
   chapel, *TCCII*

50:12 boy!] ~ . *TCCII*

50:12 you—?] ~ . . . *TCCII*

50:17 Ah] ~ , *TCCII*

50:17 chocolates! Tis] ~ , tis *TSI*

50:18 fortunes.] ~ ! *TSI*

50:19 night,] ~ : *TCCII* ~ ; *E1*

50:20 she had *TSI*] she *TCCI*

50:21 oil] ~ , *TCCII*

50:24 course . . . course] ~ , . . . ~ ,
   A1

50:25 them.— *MS*] ~ . *TCCI*

50:27 Moreover *MS*] ~ , *TCCI*

50:27 book, *MS*] ~ *TCCI*

50:28 him, *MS*] ~ *TCCI*

50:29 smoke.— *MS*] ~ . *TCCI*

50:29 said,] ~ ; *TCCII*

51:3 Meanwhile] ~ , *A1*

51:7 unpleasant] *Om. TCCII*

51:7 skin,] ~ *TCCII*

51:10 again:] ~ ; *E1*

51:15 Goddards' *TCCII*] Goddard's
   TCCI Goddards', *A1*

51:18 hark—— "/ The *MS*] ~ —"The
   TCCI ~ . . ." The *TCCII*

51:21 circumstance] circumstances
   TCCII

51:24 in camera] *in camera TCII*

51:25 Committee, *MS*] ~ *TCCI*

51:28 *M. Britten*] "M. Britten" *A1*

51:29 above:] ~ ; *TCCII*

51:30 her:] ~ ; *E1*

52:1 half-an-hour] half an hour *A1*

52:2 eyeglass] eye-glass *A1*

52:3 county *MS*] County *TCCI*

52:3 dovecotes *E1*] dove-/ cotes *MS,
   TCCII* dove-cotes *TCCI*

52:6 Britten] ~ , *TCCII*

52:9 course] ~ , *A1*

52:10 bothers:] ~ ; *E1*

52:15 Britten] ~ , *TCCII*

52:15 then:] ~ ; *E1*

52:15 B.A. *MS, TCII*] B. A. *TCCI*

52:17 yes] ~ , *TCCII*

52:17 *head* teacher *TSI*] head teacher
   TCCI, A1 head-teacher *E1*

52:20 revolver] ~ , *TCCII*

52:22 Dea ex machina] *Dea ex machina*
 TCCII Deus ex machina Eı

52:26 fact] ~, *TCCII*

52:28 stone grey] stone-grey *TCCII*

52:29 She had lots of brains. *MS*] *Om.*
 TCCI

52:33 dust-pan *MS, TCCII*] dust pan
 TCCI

52:39 him:] ~; *TCCII*

53:1 oh] ~, *TCCII*

53:5 moral] ~, *Aı*

53:7 in camera *Ed.*] *in camera TCCI*

53:10 school,] ~ — *TCCII*

53:10 fitting up] fitting-up *TCCII*

53:18 returned, *MS*] ~ *TCCI*

52:23 good-evening *Ed.*] good evening
 MS good-evening, *TCCII* good
 evening, *Eı*

53:23 *there—!"— MS*] ~ —!" *TCCI*
 ~?"— *TCCII* ~ ?"— *Aı*

53:25 Good-evening] good-evening *Eı*

53:25 and looking] ~, ~ *TCCII*

53:29 and mutely *MS*] *Om. TCCI*

53:32 under-sea] under-/ sea *TCCII*
 undersea *Eı*

53:33 inquiring *Aı*] enquiring *TCCI*

53:39 Yesterday] ~, *TCCII*

54:3 submarine glare. *MS*] submarine. *TCCI, Aı* sub-marine. *Eı*

54:12 eye] eyes *Eı*

54:13 in camera] *in camera TCCII*

54:14 satisfactorily, *MS, TCCII*] ~ *TCCI*

54:16 Oh] ~, *TCCII*

54:20 why?, *MS*] ~? *TCCI*

54:20 see] ~, *TCCII*

54:21 under-water *MS, TCCII*] under
 water *TCCI*

54:25 going on] going-on *TCCII*

54:29 science-teacher] science teacher
 Aı

54:35 Signed] ~ — *Eı*

54:35 Bostock—] ~. *TCCII*

55:16 services:] ~; *Eı*

55:18 Answer then] ~, ~, *TCCII*

55:19 It is *MS*] Is it *TCCI*

55:20 false?—] ~? *TCCII*

55:20 yes?— *MS*] Yes?— *TCCI* Yes?
 TCCII

55:22 Britten:] ~; *Eı*

55:24 right] ~, *TCCII*

55:25 half-rising] half rising *Aı*

55:25 back:] ~; *Eı*

55:29 No] ~, *TCCII*

55:29 down! Please! *MS*] ~! ~ *TCCI*
 ~. ~! *TCCII*

55:38 Oh] ~, *TCCII*

55:39 lobster-pots] ~, *TCCII*

55:40 shouted—] ~: *TCCII* ~, *Aı*

55:40 Here] ~, *TCCII*

55:40 Gilbert *MS*] Gilbert—Gilbert
 TCCI, TCCII Gilbert, Gilbert
 TSI see notes

56:4 doors] door *Eı*

56:9 Oh] ~, *TCCII*

56:10 Oh] ~, *TCCII*

56:16 *Sine diē Ed.*] Sine diē *MS* Sine
 die *TCCI Sine die TSI, TCCII*

57:3 one:] ~; *Eı*

57:5 Saturday:] ~; *TCCII*

57:5 half-day *MS, TCCII*] half day
 TCCI

57:8 Britten-women *TSI*] Britten
 women *TCCI*

57:8 Goddard-women *TSI*] Goddard
 women *TCCI*

57:9 Emmie-women *TSI*] Emmie
 women *TCCI*

57:11 Mr *MS*] *Om. TCCI*

57:15 fountain pen] fountain-pen *TCCII*

57:21 place] ~, *TCCII*

57:24 But—] ~... *TCCII*

57:25 buts.] '~'. *TCCII* "~." *Eı*

57:34 Monday] ~, *TCCII*

58:2 at the school *MS*] *Om. TCCI*

58:5 Then] ~, *TCCII*

58:10 fifty-five *MS, TCCII*] fifty five
 TCCI

58:10 had.] ~? *TCCII*

58:13 day] ~, *Eı*

58:14 care] ~, *TCCII*

58:16 half a pint *TCCI, Aı*] half-a-pint
 Eı

58:18 house *MS*] home *TCCI*

58:20 Gilbert. *MS*] ~, *TCCII*

58:21 Oh] ~, *TCCII*

58:23 you! *MS*] ~? *TCCI*

58:25 Oh] ~, *TCCII*
58:34 first,] ~; *TCCII*
58:35 Oh] ~, *TCCII*
59:3 parts. *MS*] ~? *TCCI*
59:5 quid.] ~? *TCCII*
59:6 Geermany] Germany *TCCII*
59:6 for!] ~? *TCCII*
59:9 Nay] ~, *TCCII*
59:10 doin' *MS*] doing *TCCI*
59:11 No,] ~; *TCCII*
59:15 see *MS*] ~, *TCCII*
59:15 father] Father *A1*
59:16 'em] 'em, *TCCII*
59:19 do!] ~? *TCCII*
59:21 money? *TSI, A1*] ~. *TCCI*
59:24 th' *Ed.*] the' *TCCI* the *TCCII*
59:28 it *MS*] it to *TCCI*
59:29 niver] nivir *E1*
59:29 on to] onto *A1*
60:1 bicycle] ~, *TCCII*
60:7 his *MS*] *Om. TCCI*
61:1 VIII. *Ed.*] VIII *TCCI*
61:2 His Might-have-been Mother-in-law.] Might be a Mother-in-law. *TSI*
61:5 you] ~, *TCCII*
61:5 Then] ~, *TCCII*
61:5 lower *MS*] low *TCCI*
61:7 her? *MS*] ~. *TCCI*
61:12 hat] ~, *TCCII*
61:16 slip-shod] slipshod *A1*
61:17 amiable] aimiable *MS, TSI*
61:24 conic sections *MS*] Conic Sections *TCCI*
61:25 said, *MS*] ~. *TCCI*
61:26 Bostock,] ~ *E1*
61:26 slip-shod] slipshod *A1*
61:27 and said] ~ ~, *TCCII*
62:5 it so *MS*] so *TCCI* so so *TSI* so, *E1 see notes*
62:6 letters were *MS, TSI*] letter *TCCI* letter was *E1*
62:9 our Dad *TSI*] he *TCCI*
62:10 good] ~, *TCCII*
62:13 come] came *TCCII*
62:14 her] to her *TCCII*
62:14 said] ~, *TCCII*
62:14 silly like *MS*] silly-like *TCCI*

62:16 after:] ~, *A1*
62:16 Why you] ~, ~ *TCCII*
62:17 nothing!] ~? *TCCII*
62:21 Oh, *MS, TCCII*] ~ *TCCI*
62:22 th' *MS*] the *TCCI*
62:23 why] Why *TCCII* 'Why *E1*
62:23 don't] didn't *E1*
62:23 laugh.] ~? *TCCII* ~?' *E1*
62:26 Patty; *MS*] ~, *TCCI*
62:30 over] ~, *TCCII*
62:32 you can] You ~ *TCCII* 'You ~ *E1*
62:33 worse.] ~.' *A1*
62:33 had had *TCCI, A1*] has had *E1*
62:34 it!] ~? *TCCII*
62:35 well,] Well, *TCCII* 'Well,' *A1*
62:35 I don't] '~ ~ *A1*
62:37 anyhow."] ~.'" *A1*
62:38 young *MS*] *Om. TCCI*
63:1 you're] You're *TCCII* 'You're *A1*
63:2 Dad,] ~; *TCCII*
63:3 out.] ~.' *A1*
63:6 she's] She's *TCCII* 'She's *A1*
63:7 your *MS*] your *TCCI*
63:7 daughter,] ~; *TCCII*
63:7 moon.] ~.' *A1*
63:16 heads.— *MS*] ~. *TCCI*
63:19 Oh] ~, *TCCII*
63:20 him] ~, *TCCII*
63:28 others] ~, *TCCII*
63:29 No,] ~; *TCCII*
63:31 do] ~, *TCCII*
63:37 you know, *MS*] *Om. TCCI*
63:38 class *MS*] *Om. TCCI*
64:5 least *MS, TCCII*] ~, *TCCI*
64:5 possible] ~, *TCCII*
64:11 Moreover] ~, *A1*
64:18 time] ~, *TCCII*
64:21 Oh] ~, *TCCII*
64:21 tea,] ~? *TCCII*
64:23 half-past *MS, TCCII*] half past *TCCI*
64:24 teas] tea *TCCII*
64:25 has] have *TCCII*
64:28 Oh] ~, *TCCII*
64:34 had:] ~; *TCCII*
65:9 gastritis—] ~...*TCCII* ~....*A1*
65:10 baby— *MS*] ~. *TCCI* ~? *TCCII*

65:22　anyhow.] ~? *TCCII*
65:23　Natural—] ~?— *TCCII* ~? *A1*
65:23　yes] Yes *A1*
65:24　are—] ~?— *TCCII* ~—? *A1*
65:25　No *MS*] ~, *TCCII*
65:26　Well] ~, *TCCII*
65:26　then! *MS, TCCII*] ~. *TCCII*
65:30　did] ~, *TCCII*
65:32　then.] ~? *TCCII*
65:34　Well] ~, *TCCII*
65:36　Prince!] ~? *TCCII*
65:40　trouble— *MS*] ~. *TCCII*
66:3　yours.] ~? *TCCII*
66:4　everything.] ~? *TCCII*
66:5　is,] ~! *TCCII*
66:9　Motherhood,] ~; *TCCII*
66:16　Yes] ~, *TCCII*
66:18　No] ~, *TCCII*
66:20　on *MS*] of *TCCI*
66:20　all *MS*] Om. *TCCI*
66:24　arm-chair] ~, *TCCII*
66:26　Goodness] goodness *TCCII*
67:6　Bostock] ~, *TCCII*
67:9　ring:] ~; *E1*
67:14　engagement finger *TCCI, A1*]
　　　engagement-finger *TCCII*
67:15　re-made] remade *A1*
67:23　them,] ~; *TCCII*
67:25　£. s. d. *MS*] £.s.d. *TCCI* £.s.d. *A1*
67:26　a quite *MS*] quite a *TCCI*
67:26　boy:] ~; *E1*
67:31　newly-opened] newly opened *A1*
67:32　bank] Bank *TCCII*
68:4　easy] ~, *TCCII*
68:5　of love *MS*] Om. *TCCI*
68:8　And] ~, *A1*
68:11　allotment gardens *A1*]
　　　allotment-gardens *TCCI*
68:13　sweet-william:] ~; *E1*
68:13　rose-avenues] rose avenues *A1*
68:14　gnat-bitten:] ~; *E1*
68:15　fancy—] ~. *TCCI*
68:15　*chacun à son goût Ed.*] *Chacun à son gout MS, TCCII* chacun à son gout *TCCI* Chacun à son gout *TSI*
68:16　allotment gardens *TCCI, A1*] allotment-gardens *TCCII*

68:17　afternoons. Which *MS*] ~, which *TCCI*
68:18　bank-clerk *MS*] ~, *TCCI*
68:24　Co-op. *TCCII*] Co-op *TCCI*
68:26　life-time] lifetime *TCCII*
68:26　No,] ~; *TCCII*
68:27　own] ~, *TCCII*
68:30　*au fond MS, TSI, TCCII*] au fond *TCCI*
68:33　or] ~, *TCCII*
68:33　still *MS*] ~, *TCCI*
68:38　away] ~, *TCCII*
68:40　common-sense] common sense *A1*
69:3　arch, *MS*] ~ *TCCII*
69:5　sense;] ~, *TCCII*
69:8　fact] ~, *TCCII*
69:13　lovey-doves *TSI, TCCII*] lovey doves *TCCI*
69:15　reactionary] re-actionary *E1*
69:16　off:] ~; *TCCII*
69:17　except she . . . up: still . . . assurance too . . . her life.] except that she would retain a little crisp flirtiness as a nicely curled feather to put in her matronly tam: still, this sound and sensible emotion, this hatred of rose-leaves because she knew what roseleaves were (that being the feather in her cap, mark you); this dislike of the immortal rose, and the consequent sound predilection for cauliflower, would be the force that henceforth directed her life. *TSI* except . . . up; still . . .assurance, too . . . life. *TCCII*
69:28　common-sense] commonsense *TCCII* common sense *A1*
69:30　school-house] schoolhouse *A1*
69:31　school-room] schoolroom *A1*
69:34　good-natured *TCCII*] goodnatured *TCCII*
69:37　Emmie] ~, *TCCII*
69:39　up, and] with a shawl, *TSI*
69:40　tea; then she] tea, and *TSI*
70:2　Witham] Withan, *TCCII*
70:2　Welland] ~, *TCCII*

70:2 Nene *Ed.*] Nen *TCCI* Nen, *A1*
70:4 you.] ~? *TCCII*
70:5 Salt!] ~? *TCCII*
70:5 savour?] ~...? *TCCII*
70:5 you.] ~? *TCCII*
70:7 Geography:] ~; *TCCII*
70:11 girl,] ~ *TCCII*
70:12 school-room] schoolroom *A1*
70:13 then—." *MS, TSI*] ~—" *TCCI*
~..." *TCCII*
70:17 half-past *TCCII*] half past
TCCI
70:19 school-house] schoolhouse *A1*
70:21 perhaps—] ~... *TCCII*
70:22 Hello] ~, *TCCII*
70:22 said] ~, *TCCII*
70:25 Woodhouse] ~, *TCCII*
70:26 thought] ~, *TCCII*
70:27 No,] ~; *TCCII*
70:29 afternoon.—] ~. *TCCII*
70:29 amiss] ~, *TCCII*
70:29 then. *MS*] ~? *TCCI*
70:31 bit] ~, *TCCII*
70:34 damn *TCCII*] dam *TCCI*
70:36 you, why] ~? Why, *TCCII*
71:1 *I've MS*] I've *TCCI*
71:1 a *MS*] *Om. TCCI*
71:5 that] ~, *TCCII*
71:9 Fanny meanwhile] ~, ~, *A1*
71:9 oven] ~, *TCCII*
71:12 dear,] ~; *TCCII*
71:18 prevent *MS*] ~, *TCCI*
71:24 mute] ~, *TCCII*
71:28 good] ~, *TCCII*
71:29 shirtsleeves] shirt-sleeves *TCCII*
71:30 oven shelf] oven-shelf *TCCII*
71:34 oven shelf *Ed.*] oven-shelf *TCCI*
71:37 said] ~, *TCCII*
71:39 shirtsleeves] shirt-sleeves *TCCII*
72:1 oven shelf] oven-shelf, *TCCII*
72:4 paraffin oil-stove *MS*] paraffin
stove *TCCI* paraffin-stove *TCCII*
72:4 curious *MS*] ~, *TCCI*
72:6 slimy *MS*] *Om. TCCI*
72:9 cod-liver *MS*] cod-/ liver *TCCI*
codliver *E1*
72:15 bad.] ~? *TCCII*
72:15 bran-bag] bran bag *MS*

72:16 I?— *MS*] ~? *TCCI*
72:16 good looks] good-looks *MS*
72:16 anyhow.— *MS*] anyway. *TCCI*
72:18 Ay— *MS*] Ay, *TCCI* Aye, *A1*
72:19 on] ~, *TCCI*
72:20 some: *MS*] ~, *TCCI* ~; *E1*
72:21 bag,] ~; *E1*
72:22 piping hot] piping-hot *TCCII*
72:31 school-room] school-room, *TCCII*
schoolroom, *E1*
72:32 time he] ~, ~ *TCCII*
72:33 there] ~, *TCCII*
72:33 end!] ~. *TCCII*
72:37 school-house] school-/ house
A1
72:40 Oh] ~, *TCCII*
73:2 yet *MS*] *Om. TCCI*
73:7 man. "If] ~, "if *A1*
73:12 Oh] ~, *TCCII*
73:13 just *MS*] *Om. TCCI*
73:16 you,] ~ *TCCII*
73:19 oration *MS, A1*] ovation *TCCI*
73:26 gooseberry bush]
gooseberry-bush *TCCII*
73:29 interfering] ~, *TCCII*
73:33 burnt offering] burnt-offering
TCCII
73:35 Well] ~, *TCCII*
73:35 length. "You] ~, "you *A1*
74:6 blotting-paper *TCCII*] blotting
paper *TCCI* blotting-/ paper *E1*
74:10 you *MS*] ~, *TCCI*
74:11 motion] action *TCCII*
74:12 you] ~, *TCCII*
74:14 No] ~, *TCCII*
74:14 fat-head] fathead *TCCII*
74:16 scyllas *MS, A1*] scylla *TCCI*
74:17 snow-scape] snowscape *E1*
74:18 Well] ~, *TCCII*
74:22 you.—] ~. *A1*
74:26 christmas *MS*] Christmas *TCCI*
74:33 once,] ~: *TCCII*
74:33 she'll *MS*] She'll *TCCI*
74:36 yet—] ~... *TCCII*
74:39 make] made *TCCII*
75:3 fore-ordained] foreordained *A1*
75:17 bean-pod] ~, *TCCII*
75:18 Lo *MS, TCCII*] "~ *TCCI, A1*

75:20 bit] ~, *TCCII*
75:21 E.B. *MS*] E. B. *TCCI*
75:22 Ollivoy] '~' *TCCII* "~" *E1*
75:27 midday] mid-day *E1*
75:28 wet] ~, *TCCII*
75:28 creeper stalks] creeper-stalks *TCCII*
75:32 school-room] schoolroom *E1*
75:38 stomach. *TCCI, A1*] ~? *E1*
75:38 Nourishing] ~, *TCCII*
76:4   five past] five-past *E1*
77:2   George. *TSI*] ~ *TCCI*
77:4   lamp] ~, *E1*
77:11 twenty-one *TCCII*] twenty one *TCCI*
77:11 round] ~, *TCCII*
77:13 sideways:] ~ — *A1*
77:13 backwards:] ~ — *A1*
77:14 a High-School boy, and a High-School boy grown into] *Om. TCCII*
77:18 choir-boy *TCCII*] choir boy *TCCI*
77:22 phrase] ~, *A1*
77:22 *in love with*] *In-love-with TCCII*
77:27 Hello] ~, *TCCII*
77:27 Harold! *TSI*] ~. *TCCI*
77:29 schoolmaster *TCCII*] school-master *TCCI*
77:31 bicycle clips] bicycle-clips *TCCII*
77:32 nose.] ~? *TCCII*
78:4   Bad!] ~? *TCCII*
78:9   nights] ~, *TCCII*
78:11 She couldn't . . . that funny. *MS*] *Om. TCCI*
78:12 you and] ~, ~ *TCCII*
78:14 hot water-bottles]
       hot-water-bottles *TCCII*
       hot-water bottles *A1*
78:21 faint.—] ~. *A1*
78:31 another] ~, *TCCII*
78:34 eyes] ~, *TCCII*
78:35 contents] ~, *TCCII*
78:36 note-paper] note-/ paper *TCCII*
       notepaper *E1*
78:36 heartily,] ~ *TCCII*
79:1   *I TSI*] I *TCCII*
79:5   Had] Has *TCCII*

79:5   bank-clerk *TCCII*] bank clerk *TCCI*
79:6   Why] ~, *TCCII*
79:8   bank-clerk *MS, TCCII*] bank clerk *TCCI*
79:10 thing *MS*] ~, *TCCI*
79:11 Harold. "She] ~, "she *TCCII*
79:13 devil,] ~! *TCCII*
79:13 bank-clerk *MS, TCCII*] bank clerk *TCCI*
79:15 Oh] ~, *TCCII*
79:16 thing,] ~ — *TCCII*
79:16 bad: *MS*] ~. *TCCI*
79:21 Yes—" but] ~..." But *TCCII*
79:23 Oh] ~, *TCCII*
79:28 half way] half-way *TCCII* half-/ way *E1*
79:28 parlour *MS, TCCII*] parlor *TCCI*
79:36 No] ~, *TCCII*
79:38 Oh no] ~, ~, *TCCII*
79:39 entrance passage]
       entrance-passage *TCCII*
79:40 dining-room *TCCII*] dining room *TCCI*
80:2   down] ~, *TCCII*
80:9   also] too *TCCII*
80:10 tea-pot *MS, TCCII*] tea-/ pot *TCCI* teapot *E1*
80:15 bank-clerk *TCCII*] bank clerk *TCCI*
80:20 pins and needles] pins-and-needles *TCCII*
80:22 nervous etc. *Ed.*] ~ ~ *MS* ~, ~. *TCCI* ~, ~., *TCCII*
80:24 high-road] highroad *E1* high road *A1*
81:2   Meeting. *TSI*] ~ *TCCI*
81:3   "My *Ed.*] ~ *TCCI*
81:12 but] ~, *A1*
81:12 oh] ah *E1*
81:21 million *MS, TCCII*] ~, *TCCI*
81:35 Well goodbye] ~, ~, *TCCII* ~, good-bye, *E1*
82:2   Oh] ~, *E1*
82:6   sleep] ~, *TCCII*
82:7   ever-loving] ~, *A1*
82:8   Walter George Whiffen." *MS*] ~ ~ ~. *TCCI* WALTER

GEORGE WHIFFEN. *TCCII*
WALTER GEORGE WHIFFEN. *E1*

82:11 better, *MS*] ~ *TCCI*

82:16 baby face *MS*] baby face, *TCCI* baby-face, *TCCII*

82:16 baby face and] baby-face ~ *TCCII*

82:17 love." *MS*] ~". *TCCI*

82:18 sea-side] seaside *A1*

82:21 dust-storm] dust storm *A1*

82:30 Browning,] ~?— *TCCII* ~?— *E1*

82:34 dressing jacket] dressing-jacket *TCCII*

83:2 tittivated] titivated *A1*

83:2 and her] or her *A1*

83:11 Well] ~, *TCCII*

83:12 towel." *P* And *MS*] ~." And *TCCI*

83:21 that,] ~! *TCCII*

83:22 fact] ~, *TCCII*

83:24 Well] ~, *TCCII*

83:32 mirror. "What] ~, "what *TCCII*

83:35 Oh] ~, *TCCII*

83:38 said] ~, *TCCII*

83:40 on,] ~; *TCCII*

84:3 bed:] ~; *E1*

84:9 half an hour *TCCI, A1*] half-an-hour *TCCII*

84:14 engaged] ~, *TCCII*

84:14 prrring—pring] prrring-prrring *TCCII*

84:14 bicycle bell] bicycle-bell *TCCII*

84:17 *Girl of the Limberlost*] "The Girl of the Limberlost" *TCCII The Girl of the Limberlost A1*

84:17 hand,] ~ *TCCII*

84:21 voices,] ~ *TCCII*

84:23 as he came . . . for her] *Om. E1*

84:25 pheasant's-eye] pheasant's eye *TCCII* pheasant-eyed *A1*

84:26 mimosa:] ~; *E1*

84:27 Hello] ~, *TCCII*

84:28 Hello!"] ~!"— *TCCII*

85:1 then] ~, *TCCII*

85:3 motions.] ~? *TCCI*

85:10 another,] ~; *TCCII*

85:19 scene, *MS, TCCII*] ~ *TCCI*

85:21 bedroom *TCCI, A1*] bed-/ room *TCCII* bed-room *E1*

85:22 Rolande *MS, TCCII*] Harold *TCCI*

85:36 do] ~, *TCCI*

85:36 him. *P* And *MS*] ~. And *TCCI*

86:5 kneeling] ~, *TCCII*

86:5 curtseying-knight] curtsying-knight *A1*

86:19 Why] ~, *TCCII*

86:19 we. *MS*] ~? *TCCI*

86:23 Voilà un homme.] *Voilà un homme! TCCII*

86:26 spoony:] ~; *E1*

86:29 after days] after-days *TCCII* after-/ days *A1*

86:30 fruit.] ~! *TCCII*

86:32 true-love] true love *TCCII*

86:33 pike-staff] pike staff *A1*

86:33 allotment garden] allotment-garden *TCCII*

86:36 end:] ~; *E1*

86:39 her then] ~, ~, *TCCII*

86:40 piano.] ~: *TCCII*

87:1 "The cottage . . . England / How . . . land." *Ed.*] The . . . land. *TCCI* The . . . England, / How . . . land. *TCCII The cottage homes of England, / How thick they crowd the land. A1*

87:3 Or] ~, *TCCII*

87:4 "The stately . . . a dream." *P* Play *Ed.*] The . . . dream *P* Play *MS* The . . . dream. / Play *TCCI The stately homes of England / Are furnished like a dream. / Play A1*

87:9 "There's a . . . the west."] *There's a little grey home in the west. A1*

87:12 invitingly: *MS*] ~, *TCCI*

87:13 tin,] ~ *TCCII*

87:14 feast, if] feast when *TSI*

87:19 saying:] ~, *A1*

87:19 Oh] ~, *A1*

87:19 word,] ~! *TCCII*

88:1 XII. *Ed.*] XII *TCCI*

88:2 Interloper. *TSI*] ~ *TCCI*

88:18 me] be *A1*

88:27 Rolande *MS, TCCII*] Harold *TCCI*

88:28 right,] ~; *TCCII*
88:28 up] ~, *TCCII*
88:35 up?] ~, *MS, TSI*
89:1 moment. *MS*] ~: *TCCI*
89:2 stairfoot] stair-foot *TCCII*
89:9 Good-evening] Good evening *TCCII*
89:19 Oh, *MS, TCCII*] ~ *TCCI*
89:23 down] ~, *TCCII*
89:34 measles:] ~; *TCCII*
89:36 them] ~, *TCCII*
89:38 Because] ~, *TCCII*
90:1 Eakrast——" *P* And *Ed.*] ~——"/ And *MS* ~—" And *TCCI* ~..." *P* And *TCCII*
90:2 George, *MS, A1*] ~ *TCCI*
90:5 *fracas*] fracas *A1*
90:9 ruby,] ~ *TCCII*
90:15 died,] ~; *TCCII*
90:16 Meanwhile] ~, *A1*
90:16 bed] ~, *TCCII*
90:18 tears:] ~; *E1*
90:18 feet] ~, *TCCII*
90:20 Hardraade *TCCI, A1*] Hardraada *TCCII*
90:21 motor-bike *MS*] ~, *TCCI*
90:25 then] ~, *TCCII*
90:25 Huthwaite] ~, *TCCII*
90:29 Why] ~, *TCCII*
90:29 quarter to six] quarter-to-six *E1*
90:30 ten.] ~! *TCCII*
90:33 round-about] roundabout *A1*
90:39 mortified] mortifiedly *TCCII*
91:8 No thanks,] ~, ~; *TCCII*
91:9 Yes] ~, *TCCII*
91:9 one] ~, *TCCII*
91:9 Harold] ~, *TCCII*
91:10 cries.] ~? *TCCII*
91:13 resigned] ~, *TCCII*
91:18 baby,] ~! *TCCII*
91:26 can-opener] can opener *A1*
91:30 infant in arms *TCCI, A1*] infant-in-arms *E1*
91:37 re-composed] recomposed *A1*
91:39 Walter-George's *MS*] Walter George's *TCCI*
92:20 him:] ~; *E1*
92:23 footing,] ~; *TCCII*

92:25 Time now] ~, ~, *TCCII*
92:28 Oh] ~, *TCCII*
92:28 Deus ex machina] *Deus ex machina TCCII*
92:31 bread and butter *TCCI, A1*] bread/ and-butter *TCCII* bread-and-butter *E1*
92:32 cauliflowers] cauliflower *TCCII*
92:34 Deus ex machina] Deus exMachina *TSI Deus ex machina TCCII*
92:34 God *TCCI, A1*] god *TCCII*
92:34 Machine] machine *TCCII*
92:34 Come! *MS*] come! *TCCI* come./ *TCCII* come. *E1*
92:36 oh] O *TCCII*
92:36 Machine-God] machine-God *MS*
92:38 remain] remains *E1*
92:39 God] god *TCCII*
92:40 axle] axis *TCCII*
93:2 Rolande, *MS*] ~ TCCI
93:4 Well] ~, *TCCII*
93:7 prize] prime *TCCII*
93:7 cauliflowers,] ~ *TSI*
93:8 dear] sweet *TSI*
93:10 Noon! Ah] ~—~ *TSI* ~. ~ *TCCII*
93:11 third. *P* But] ~. But *TSI*
93:12 in this vol. having] having in this vol. *TSI*
93:13 next] ~, *TCCII*
93:14 decree nisi] *decree nisi TCCII*
95:1 Part II. *Ed.*] *Om. MS see note on* 1:1
97:1 XIII *Ed.*] VIII
97:27 someone *Ed.*] some-one
98:28 Biedermeier *Ed.*] Biedermayer
98:29 with] and
98:31 amber] gold
98:33 overbolster *Ed.*] over-bolster
98:35 Biedermeier *Ed.*] Biedermayer
99:8 Badajos's *Ed.*] Badajoz's
99:14 today] as high
99:22 Biedermeier *Ed.*] Biedermayer
99:23 doing in connection with] doing, being in
99:23 a disreputable] an impossible
99:24 Biedermeier *Ed.*] Biedermayer
99:28 Löffel *Ed.*] Loeffel

100:25 linen] heavy
100:37 soul] man
101:3 He] Therefore he
101:4 whichever *Ed.*] which-ever
101:6 in his spirit was mortified] was
    superficially cross
101:8 liked, and . . . so free] liked still,
    and if the guest was very gener-
    ous towards himself
101:10 under his *Ed.*] under this
101:11 managed to expend] could have
101:11 inside] to
101:13 meannesses] nature
101:22 every] at a meal
101:27 cause of self-satisfaction] relief
101:28 pettyfogging] bourgeois
101:30 professor] mean
101:30 free soul] nobleman
101:33 littleness,] little nature,
102:21 "I am . . . professor crossly.]
    "Would you like to come with
    me to look at the land I have
    bought for my little wooden
    house, my dog-kennel, my little
    Vow-Wow? Yes? You would?" *P*
    "Yes, I should like that." *P* "All
    right then. Very well. We'll catch
    the ten oclock train? Yes? Shall
    we do that then?" *P* "Yes, let us."
    P Already the professor's blue
    eyes were lighting up, he was as
    pleased as a child now he had
    something in front of him. His
    horror was lest he should have
    time like a blank wall before him,
    a void which confronted him. To
    be sure he might always say he
    was busy: his duties, etc. But his
    book and his theories and his
    duties were not *life* to him. He
    had reached the point where life
    meant doing things, not thinking
    or writing or reading, or even
    seeing pictures or hearing music.
    No, he was so intellectual that he
    he felt all intellectuality to be
102:29 artificial to . . . to theorise.] my
    eye to him. He didn't believe in it

one bit. He enjoyed it—or had
enjoyed it—the self-important
game of learning and theory. But
he didn't believe in it. He knew it
was all tricks.
102:35 all-too-serious] solid
102:40 after] of
103:14 Blotting paper *Ed.*] Blotting-
    paper
103:24 pens, *Ed.*] ~
103:29 imagines] finds
103:30 buffoons like himself.] life.
103:30 anxious,] ⟨isolated,⟩ ennuyé,
103:37 fingertips *Ed.*] finger tips
104:25 *Theorie*] *Die*
105:9 Ludwigshöhe *Ed.*] Ludwigshohe
105:23 Vow-Wow *Ed.*] Vow-wow
105:36 Vow-Wow *Ed.*] Vow-wow
106:1 school-boy *Ed.*] schoolboy
106:11 between] with
106:12 trousers] hose
106:18 foot-hills *Ed.*] foothills
106:26 Alfred and Gilbert] They
106:28 high] its
106:30 that the] that they
107:12 an] like
107:27 life.] life range.
108:3 manyness. His] ~, his
108:27 peaks] range
108:32 have] shall
108:35 will you] shall you
108:36 summer-house *Ed.*] summer
    house
109:21 Rehbock *Ed.*] Rheebok
110:28 Marta] Hannah
111:1 Marta,] Hannah,
111:6 and a] and with
111:8 heelless *Ed.*] heel-less
111:30 Ludwig] Friedrich
112:2 outdazzling *Ed.*] out dazzling
    ⟨more dazzling than⟩
112:5 Well,] But
112:28 peasant girl *Ed.*] peasant-girl
112:35 white-haired *Ed.*] whitehaired
112:36 under her] with
112:38 "Oh] "Oh jeh, Alfred,
113:2 old] and
113:17 settled] seated

113:21 Professor] Ludwig
113:24 spirit-flame *Ed.*] spirit flame
113:38 her face] it
114:12 me] Mama
115:5 will] may
115:11 in preference."] first."
115:13 Before this] Till then
115:15 le *Ed.*] la
115:17 German: *Ed.*] ~ .
115:18 le *Ed.*] la
115:19 to put] in vain
115:23 speaking] sparking
115:29 'Jost] 'Just
116:7 du Papagei,] leave it to the parrots,
116:15 Baroness *Ed.*] baroness
116:22 forehead *Ed.*] fore head
117:7 immature] Goethe
117:8 Goethe] poet
117:18 Let every ... own rubbish."] Don't be so clever, you people."
117:25 ·rising.] jumping up.
117:26 Alfred] the
118:1 XIV *Ed.*] IX
118:6 because] when
118:6 so] most
118:9 *Observer Ed.*] Observer
118:14 infernal] remote [?]
118:30 *Times Ed.*] Times
119:26 knees] legs
120:1 Japanese] porter
120:12 zu Hause *Ed.*] zuhaus
120:16 no one *Ed.*] no-one
120:29 night-porter *Ed.*] night porter
121:13 telegraph] telephone
121:14 telegraph] telephone
121:19 Papa *Ed.*] papa
122:33 drawing-room *Ed.*] drawing room
122:38 overcoat *Ed.*] over-coat
123:10 [in] the *Ed.*] the the
123:20 such a bother] so far away
123:23 Frauenkirche."] Eiffel Tower."
123:33 glowing with zest] gleaming with a warm radiance
123:36 glints] gold-warm
125:4 snowflower *Ed.*] snow-flower
125:28 snowflower *Ed.*] snow-flower

129:2 Berry.] Behn.
129:26 Berry *Ed.*] Behn
131:1 XV *Ed.*] X
131:3 Johanna and] either Johanna or
131:5 did not get] never got
131:5 either, *Ed.*] either, ⟨of them⟩,
131:12 half-past *Ed.*] half past
131:18 midday *Ed.*] mid-day
131:19 Kochel] the
131:25 bought] had
133:1 small] little
133:7 pleasure ground *Ed.*] pleasure-ground
133:8 boots. *P* She ... alone. She] boots. And then he rose and went after her. *P* But in that tiny little place they took opposite ways. He
133:13 look up] see her. How could it be.
133:15 birch-trees *Ed.*] birch trees
133:38 No one *Ed.*] No-one
134:16 her. *Ed.*] him.
134:21 you." *Ed.*] ~ ?"
134:24 and *Ed.*] an
136:20 *armer Ed.*] *arme*
136:23 good, *Ed.*] ~ .
136:25 brightly,] spitefully,
136:27 no one *Ed.*] no-one
137:15 reaction *Ed.*] reactions *see notes*
137:31 Tonans *Ed.*] tonans
137:31 oh] of
138:2 small,] little
138:3 Noo—oon] Noon
138:5 dining-room *Ed.*] dining room
138:8 dining-room] drawing-room
138:17 dish] plate
139:1 XVI *Ed.*] XI
139:4 Wilhelm Freiherr *Ed.*] Freiherr Wilhelm
139:5 government] the
139:11 whose] and their
139:13 Daumling] Menner
139:13 rather] poor,
139:17 *gute Ed.*] *guter*
139:21 as] with
139:24 him.] Rudolf.
139:34 Daumling *Ed.*] Menner

140:7　purity] chastity
140:19　in] with
140:32　substantial] a
140:37　Rudolf *Ed.*] Rudolph
141:14　lettrice *Ed.*] lettore
141:31　winds] wings
143:3　correct] another
143:13　cathedral *Ed.*] Cathedral
143:15　Hebenitz *Ed.*] Menner
143:16　fifty-five *Ed.*] fifty five
143:18　gardens] public
143:22　through] and
143:34　was] is
143:38　unreality:] enclosure:
144:1　German *Ed.*] german
144:11　pale-blue *Ed.*] pale blue
144:20　hard-souled,] hard-souled
　　　　⟨women⟩,
145:2　young business man,] manu-
　　　　facturer,
145:4　idealism. *Ed.*] idealism ⟨alone-
　　　　ness[?].⟩
145:6　don't] didn't
145:15　Beere] Bach[?]
145:15　Not] which is
145:22　would] could
145:27　inevitable] just
145:37　his] the
145:40　a quarter of] half
147:2　whom] to
147:2　naive *Ed.*] naïve
147:4　cathedral *Ed.*] Cathedral
147:31　cran-berry *Ed.*] cran berry
148:5　except] but
149:10　Johanna *Ed.*] Louise
150:23　Detsch *Ed.*] Detch
151:17　took a] took his
151:18　shirtsleeves *Ed.*] shirt-sleeves
152:1　him. He . . . with] him with
152:4　he] she
152:37　*Macbeth Ed.*] Macbeth
153:4　voices *Ed.*] voice
153:7　And still dead] "See who
153:32　Frau *Ed.*] Fraŭ *see note on* 153:36
154:5　"pipe . . . bird." *Ed.*] '∼ . . . ∼.'
154:9　he] at him
154:39　n'êtes] n'est
155:31　marrow] soul

156:1　candle] candle, and stuck
156:5　unison.] moment.
156:6　oh] of
156:11　nothingness, put . . . pocket and
　　　　Ed.] nothingness. ⟨And⟩ put . . .
　　　　and *see notes*
157:3　mid-heaven's *Ed.*] midheaven's
157:4　in our eye,] to us,
157:6　but we] that
157:6　it.] us.
157:23　tailors,] trousers,
157:28　a sound vacuum,] all there,
157:30　spirit] airy
157:30　most vacuous] lightest
157:30　vacuosities] the gases
157:32　Ah humanity, humanity . . . the
　　　　float-void. *Ed.*] Ah humanity hu-
　　　　manity . . . float-void ⟨If you
　　　　don't believe me—well, all I
　　　　would advise you is to put your
　　　　hand behind you and make quite
　　　　sure you are all there in that
　　　　region.⟩
157:36　lyrical] too
157:38　skin] bit of
158:6　monkeys; *Ed.*] ∼,
158:7　arm-flesh] so-called muscle
158:8　head, *Ed.*] ∼;
158:8　a sickly object; *Ed.*] a . . . object:
　　　　⟨that he made one sick;⟩
158:12　superior] shallow
158:13　ancient and coarse.] ancient,
　　　　pagan.
158:16　Since] Though
158:21　Roman] roman
158:21　brutality] brutal display
158:23　coarse old Europe.] communion
　　　　in grossness.
158:25　crudity] classic barbarism
159:13　Horse-chestnut *Ed.*] Horse
　　　　chestnut
159:17　a cavalcade.] lowdown.
159:18　vineyards *Ed.*] vine-yards
159:28　inn-keeper *Ed.*] innkeeper
159:35　was beginning to gall him:]
　　　　seemed so insulting to any stranger:
160:5　asking for it,] working their own
　　　　ruin,

160:7   natural] sacred
160:18 and] whom
160:31 nastiness] horror
160:38 his *Ed.*] him
161:5   brute. How very agreeable!]
        business half-sanctimoniously.
161:9   reptile] dragon
161:20 almost] on the
161:23 under the trees] into the wood
161:29 greensward *Ed.*] green-sward
161:31 it] the
165:25 Gilbert *Ed.*] Everard
166:15 fellow] soldier
166:16 creeping] striding
166:16 exultant] aggressiveness
166:17 police or soldier individuals] sol-
        diers
166:17 specimens] soldiers
166:21 police-soldier] soldier
167:1   solid] heavy
167:13 he said] said the soldier
167:21 creature.] soldier.
167:23 some of her fury. *Ed.*] ⟨her fu⟩
        her fury./ some of her fury. *see
        notes*
169:11 our] the
169:17 of a] which is so
169:27 à Munich *Ed.*] a Muniche
169:27 plaît *Ed.*] plait
169:28 très *Ed.*] trés
170:16 his own] this
171:10 Germans] French
171:35 her] my
172:1   you are *Ed.*] your are
172:37 keener] greater
173:1   XVII *Ed.*] XII
173:2   Valley. *Ed.*] ∼
175:7   host] Host
175:29 Grünwald *Ed.*] Grunwald
176:13 voices] men's
176:14 stroke] deep
176:36 clatter-clatter-clatter *Ed.*] clatter-
        clatter-/ -clatter
177:9   *Jugend Ed.*] Jugend
177:18 Bonjour *Ed.*] Bon jour
177:19 Je viendrai te trouver, Mère."]
        Train de quatre heures,
        Johanna."

178:15 Jahrelang *Ed.*] Jahrenlang
178:25 her husband] he
179:4   reckon the costs,] pay the cost,
179:8   Baroness *Ed.*] baroness
179:33 zuviel *Ed.*] zu viel
180:26 Baroness' *Ed.*] baroness'
180:33 'My *Ed.*] ∼
180:34 world.' *Ed.*] ∼.
181:30 Frau *Ed.*] Fraŭ
182:6   Cologne.] Cologne: and changed
        again, and took a little train that
        landed him at ten oclock at night,
        after fourteen hours travelling, at
        a little village lost far away in the
        hills of the Rhineland
183:1   XVIII *Ed.*] XIII
183:15 sixpence *Ed.*] six pence
183:18 verstehe *Ed.*] ⟨weiss⟩ versteh
183:28 when] you
184:9   Middle *Ed.*] middle
184:22 six] five
184:27 Rhineland *Ed.*] Rhine-land
185:20 blow your nose?] brush your
        teeth?
185:37 out of] into a new shape
186:39 and marriage bed *Ed.*] and mar-
        riage-bed
186:39 the marriage bed *Ed.*] the mar-
        riage-bed
187:14 over] in
187:30 to] the
188:9   well] nice
188:10 the scene of battles] everything
188:33 the station *Ed.*] a station
189:10 craft] trade
189:11 Should] Should ⟨should a trade
        be⟩
189:24 unity] mystery
190:23 bedroom *Ed.*] bed-room
190:37 there has got to be the] you have
        got to
190:38 polarised] the
190:39 profound] deep
191:21 a bit] rather pleas[ant]
191:26 it] this love
192:8   snowflower ... snowflower *Ed.*]
        snow-flower ... snow-flower
192:18 sensual] real

192:19 by] for
193:11 maddening] shameful
193:28 like Everard] or at the rom[antic]
194:27 sitting-room *Ed.*] sitting room
195:18 Johanna *Ed.*] Louise
195:22 no good *Ed.*] nogood
196:6 Piccadilly *Ed.*] Picaddilly
196:7 Piccadilly *Ed.*] ⟨Piccadilly⟩ Pi-caddilly
196:24 Johanna] Louise
196:31 Not all ... I know."] Yes, but it becomes real," said Johanna.
197:7 frenzy] fine
197:12 was] is
197:19 sufferings] own
198:30 commented.] answered.
198:31 public-room *Ed.*] public room
199:1 the handsome] with
199:28 birch-trees *Ed.*] birch trees
199:40 inn-door *Ed.*] inn door
200:32 blue bell-flowers *Ed.*] blue bell flowers
200:36 *Spring in the Tyrol Ed.*] Spring in the Tyrol
201:8 dark-brown *Ed.*] dark brown
201:8 peat] bog
201:32 How are you?] Come down a bit.
201:36 I] we
201:38 How are ... a drop."] Aren't I to have a word with you?" he conti-nued. "Why not? Come down, Mister. You've had enough. You give me the arm-ache to look at you. Come down, come down. You've kept it up long enough. Come down and be cheerful."
202:7 Dunkels *Ed.*] Dunkles
202:12 At] From
202:12 Johanna] they
203:10 currents] emissions
204:15 Lord] lord
204:15 He] he
204:18 table-cloth *Ed.*] table cloth
206:1 XIX *Ed.*] XIV
206:11 Ommerbach.] the flat.
206:21 The second] On the second
206:23 bedroom *Ed.*] bed-room
206:28 rather] but

206:28 big] great
206:29 bedroom *Ed.*] bed-room
206:30 finches whistled with pleasure.] were enraptured
207:3 threepence *Ed.*] three-pence
207:4 ninepence *Ed.*] nine-pence
207:8 Schnapps *Ed.*] schnapps
207:28 Frau *Ed.*] Fraŭ
207:29 on] in
207:34 tussling] struggling
208:10 four ... six] six ... eight
209:1 Three] Four
210:26 river-bed *Ed.*] river bed
211:11 water-ecstasy *Ed.*] water ecstasy
211:20 her as] Yet they
211:34 am I] I am
212:4 which is] to
213:30 barefoot *Ed.*] bare-foot
214:10 fire-flies *Ed.*] fireflies
214:39 fawn *Ed.*] doe
215:22 a job] the job
215:31 honor *Ed.*] honour
215:35 Baron *Ed.*] baron
216:18 Gilbert *Ed.*] ∼:
216:35 the midday *Ed.*] the mid-day
217:17 seat on the] seat. Then
217:21 Baroness *Ed.*] baroness
217:22 hat] veil
217:37 Sie wissen] sie kennen
217:37 eine] ist
217:38 Das wissen] Das kennen
218:1 Sie.] Ihren
218:2 sind] Sie
218:20 Baroness' *Ed.*] baroness'
218:30 Baronessial Boreas *Ed.*] bar-onessial boreas
218:32 Baroness *Ed.*] baroness
219:21 Well] What
220:19 stout] sturdy
220:22 Baroness *Ed.*] baroness
221:10 black] big
222:17 way.] road.
222:23 front. *Ed.*] ∼? *see notes*
222:38 country.] company.
224:13 unalleved *Ed.*] unallieved
224:24 startled] frightened
224:34 fool! *Ed.*] ∼?
224:35 white] black

226:21　pals," *Ed.*] ~ ",
226:22　Ah God, *Ed.*] ~ ~
226:33　has *Ed.*] his
227:5　But] And
227:24　farm-bell *Ed.*] farm bell
228:15　like] rather
228:17　labor *Ed.*] labour
228:37　there *Ed.*] their
228:37　honor *Ed.*] honour
229:12　back again.] after him.
229:38　on to] onto
229:39　fir-trees *Ed.*] fir trees
230:3　selves] bodies
230:30　Goethe's *Ed.*] Goethe
230:33　trouser-seat *Ed.*] trouser seat
230:39　mouth.] mouth at Gilbert.
231:28　clutching] ⟨illegible⟩ grip
232:2　low] big
234:18　roll] kick
234:38　dark-green *Ed.*] dark green
235:35　beside *Ed.*] besides
236:25　what! *Ed.*] ~ ?
236:39　Johanna] Louise
237:4　unreasoning] not
238:1　XX *Ed.*] XIV
238:7　feeling very strange] very much excited
239:4　pine-wood *Ed.*] pine wood
239:13　high-road *Ed.*] highroad
239:21　pine-trees *Ed.*] pine trees
239:32　skirt-bottoms *Ed.*] skirt bottoms
240:33　good,] gracious lady
241:1　half-past *Ed.*] half past
241:6　ate some food] went out and
241:28　alp-meadows *Ed.*] Alp-meadows
241:29　whortleberries *Ed.*] whortle berries
241:30　bushy] rather
242:2　drove] worried
242:12　on] in
242:38　which] of
243:13　out: *Ed.*] ~ ;
243:31　ihn *Ed.*] ihm
243:37　through] him staring
243:38　candle] candle, on a seat
244:3　hay-hut *Ed.*] hay hut
244:12　less] lower
244:24　hay-hut *Ed.*] hay hut

244:31　spread] folded it
245:27　Alp *Ed.*] alp
245:32　Alp] foot kettle
245:36　some] ⟨three⟩ two or three
246:8　stupefied *Ed.*] stupified
246:17　Grass *Ed.*] grass
246:34　like] to
246:40　falling like doomsday.] tumbling down.
247:16　check *Ed.*] cheque
247:37　spirit-machine *Ed.*] spirit machine
248:26　farm-house *Ed.*] farmhouse
249:32　Gilbert] or twice
249:33　Schuhplattler *Ed.*] Schuhplatteln
250:13　more a] the
250:32　farm-house *Ed.*] farm house
251:38　great] deep
252:20　dishonor *Ed.*] dishonour
252:37　dark-eyed *Ed.*] dark eyed
253:22　hate against] hate of
254:13　believed] knew
255:1　XXI *Ed.*] XV
255:2　Gemserjoch. *Ed.*] ~
255:3　friend] friend of Gilbert's
255:11　amiable *Ed.*] aimiable
255:23　Pavlova *Ed.*] Pavlovna
255:27　knuckle-stones] five-knuckle-stones
256:1　dressing-gown *Ed.*] dressing gown
256:8　whom he had known as] who had been
257:38　completely] half
259:11　'Ennery *Ed.*] ~
259:17　am.'" *Ed.*] ~ ."
259:22　red letter] Scarlet Letter
259:32　well] near
260:1　damn *Ed.*] dam
260:11　the high-road *Ed.*] the highroad
260:22　'We're *Ed.*] ~
260:23　Zion——'" *Ed.*] ~ ——"
260:32　burberry *Ed.*] Burberry
260:32　panama *Ed.*] Panama
261:18　bridle-path *Ed.*] bridle path
261:24　hay-hut *Ed.*] hay hut
262:33　pass] path
263:6　another] a naked
263:15　stream-bed *Ed.*] stream bed

263:24 peaks] rock
264:3 to look out of the window,] out,
264:15 public-room *Ed.*] public room
264:20 to the] past
264:31 public-room] public-house
264:31 public-house *Ed.*] public house
265:2 a thoroughly] an thoroughly
266:1 water-fall *Ed.*] waterfall
266:19 snow-stripes *Ed.*] snow stripes
266:37 midday *Ed.*] mid-day
267:11 high-road *Ed.*] highroad
267:16 snow-sloped *Ed.*] snow-slopped
267:20 oak-trees *Ed.*] oak trees
267:38 ten o'clock at night. *Ed.*] ⟨two in the morning—⟩ ten oclock at night
268:1 stream] sheep
268:3 *ex voto Ed.*] ex-voto
268:12 saw-threads] round
268:27 And] But
269:7 nightfall *Ed.*] night-fall
269:19 There were ... station. The] It was still seven miles to the nearest station. The
269:23 five] six
269:25 public-house *Ed.*] public house
271:1 XXII *Ed.*] XVI
271:2 Setback. *Ed.*] ~
271:25 Stanley's *Ed.*] Harold's
272:40 W.C. *Ed.*] W. C.
274:17 clothes *Ed.*] Clothes
274:30 youth] boy
274:38 which] under
276:7 sky-line *Ed.*] skyline

276:21 valley-head *Ed.*] valley head
278:2 beautiful *Ed.*] ⟨half⟩-beautiful
278:14 high-road, *Ed.*] high road,
278:18 high-road *Ed.*] highroad
279:7 lodging-house *Ed.*] lodging house
279:15 half-past *Ed.*] half past
280:14 Bozen *Ed.*] Bozan *see note on* 279:40
281:1 XXIII *Ed.*] XVII
281:3 them.] them any more.
281:20 simple-looking] little
281:25 facciamo *Ed.*] faciamo
282:3 lait *Ed.*] latt
282:21 Trento *Ed.*] Trent *see note on* 281:2
282:32 German–Austrian *Ed.*] German Austrian
282:36 Trento *Ed.*] Trent
284:18 bugle-call *Ed.*] bugle call
284:37 unsavoury *Ed.*] insavoury
285:23 Piazza *Ed.*] piazza
286:1 all] black-coated
286:6 ticket office *Ed.*] ticket-office
286:8 ticket office *Ed.*] ticket-office
287:14 panama *Ed.*] Panama
287:33 amiably *Ed.*] aimiably
289:23 trouser-bottoms *Ed.*] trouser bottoms
289:29 profusion] masses
292:1 womb.] ceiling.
292:5 new creature] bright
292:13 chiffon] black

In this edition the following compound words are hyphenated at the end of a line; these hyphenated forms occur in the base-texts (*TCCI* of part I; and *MS* of part II) and should be retained in quotations:

4:15 ivory-pale
5:4 week-day
9:6 school-teacher
22:6 kiss-curls
26:28 non-commital
30:35 more-than-doubtful
37:18 white-heavy
39:1 ivory-white
39:16 thinking-woman

43:31 mallet-stroke
44:21 Fra-Angelico-faced
45:12 Wire-whiskers
47:30 self-governing
50:25 side-looks
52:21 school-teachers
54:23 wave-lapping
55:39 lobster-voice
57:8 Goddard-women

58:17	arm-chair		180:39	back-ground
64:5	son-in-law		183:3	third-class
67:18	Emmie-gallantry		185:22	promising-looking
67:31	newly-opened		186:10	all-promising
68:14	unheard-of		192:27	non-existent
74:15	re-emergence		196:27	self-conscious
76:4	far-reaching		197:39	third-class
77:14	bank-clerk		199:26	farm-houses
82:18	sea-side		199:28	birch-trees
91:39	Walter-George's		200:3	farm-houses
92:11	t'other-or-which		200:19	heaven-pale
99:15	fools-parsley		200:40	cow-bells
99:36	postage-stamps		201:15	ice-water
103:38	ink-pot		204:22	heaven-array
106:3	fellow-travellers		204:39	*gentle-reader*
108:19	split-wood		205:5	tom-cats
108:22	Vow-Wow		205:26	lovey-doveyness
112:31	bread-and-butter		206:31	god-mother
113:10	dark-brown		207:20	high-road
113:17	tea-table		208:25	water-tubs
114:3	dark-blue		209:6	heavy-muscled
114:15	half-wistful		209:9	gun-carriages
120:8	dressing-gown		209:31	death-struggles
133:10	high-road		211:11	water-ecstasy
144:25	low-stranded		213:35	fire-flies
146:26	mid-heaven		214:28	fir-trees
146:39	lady-in-waiting		214:31	half-marshy
149:1	pale-faced		216:5	ill-bred
151:40	sewer-like		217:25	dawn-rose
152:23	sweet-herb		217:32	half-distracted
153:17	tail-piece		221:37	corn-cockles
154:27	soft-feathered		225:14	semi-conscious
154:38	white-kid-gloved		226:31	man-birth
156:10	blood-flame		234:23	chatter-chatter-chattered
157:11	mid-heaven		241:28	alp-meadows
157:30	trouser-seat		243:20	hay-houses
158:2	ill-tempered		245:7	arm-holes
158:6	prize-fighter		246:3	dun-coloured
158:11	spick-and-spanness		247:27	happy-go-lucky
160:1	ill-bred		248:22	breaking-off
161:14	candle-lighting		250:32	farm-house
161:24	not-very-new-looking		250:35	we're-so-fond-of-one-another
168:6	brass-bound		252:37	aristocratic-looking
170:15	self-possession		254:2	self-sacrifice
170:23	bald-fronted		255:18	mid-stream
175:4	well-kicked		256:12	doe-skin
176:13	march-rhythm		257:17	well-shaped
180:5	upward-tending		257:28	middle-class

260:26 blotting-paper
265:27 iron-bare
266:25 wood-smoke
266:28 snow-stripes
267:13 alp-meadow
267:23 rock-roses
268:12 saw-threads
273:40 water-meadows
282:15 marble-topped

283:25 spell-bound
283:27 forest-leaved
284:18 bugle-call
286:33 heat-fabrications
287:13 weather-battered
287:24 twenty-four
287:34 holiday-feeling
289:15 twenty-five

APPENDIX

Appendix

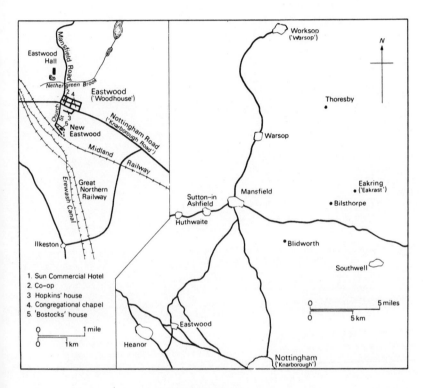

Map 1. Eastwood area, 1912

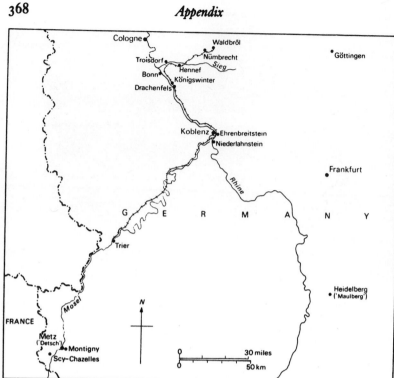

Map 2. Rhineland, 1912

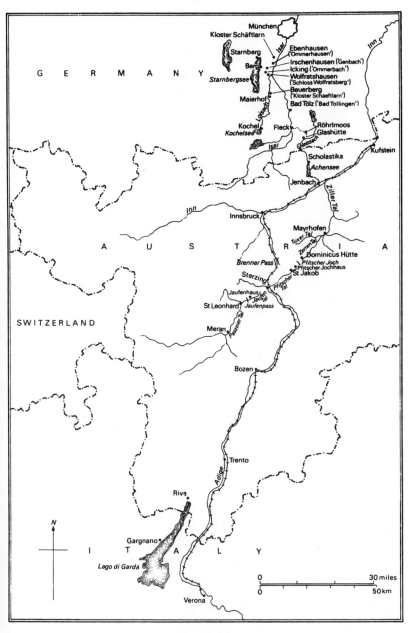

Map 3. Tyrol, 1912

Pounds, shillings and pence

Before decimalisation in 1971, the pound sterling (£) was the equivalent of 20 shillings (20/- or 20s). The shilling was the equivalent of 12 pence (12d).

A price could therefore have three elements: pounds, shillings and pence (£.,s.,d.). (The apparently anomalous d. is an abbreviation of the Latin *denarius;* but the other two terms were also originally Latin; the pound was *Libra;* the shilling *solidus.*) Such a price might be written as £1. 2s. 6d. or £1/2/6; which was spoken as 'one pound two-and-six', or 'twenty-two and six'.

Prices below a pound were written as (for instance) 19s. 6d. or 19/6, and spoken as 'nineteen and six'. Prices up to £5 were sometimes spoken in terms of shillings: so 'ninety-nine and six' was £4/19/6.

The penny was divided into two half-pence and further into four farthings, but the farthing had minimal value and was mainly a tradesman's device for indicating a price fractionally below a shilling or a pound. So 19/11¾ (nineteen and elevenpence three farthings) produced a farthing's change from a pound, this change often given as a tiny item of trade, such as a packet of pins.

The guinea was £1/1/- (one pound, one shilling) and was a professional man's unit for fees. A doctor would charge in guineas (so £5/5/- = 5 gns). Half a guinea was 10s. 6d. or 10/6 (ten and six).

The coins used were originally of silver (later cupro-nickel) and copper, though gold coins for £1 (sovereign) and 10s. (half-sovereign) were still in use in Lawrence's time. The largest silver coin in common use was the half-crown (two shillings and sixpence, or 2/6). A two-shilling piece was called a florin. Shillings, sixpences and (in Lawrence's time) threepences were the smaller sizes. The copper coins were pennies, half-pence (ha'penny) and farthings.

Common slang terms for money were 'quid' for pound, 'half a crown', 'two bob' for a florin, 'bob' for a shilling, 'tanner' for sixpence, 'threepenny-bit', 'copper' for a penny or half-penny.

The pound since 1971 has had 100 pence, distinguished from the old pennies by being abbreviated to p. instead of d.